D0773487

SAVAGE PEACE

◆

SAVAGE PEACE

◆

Americans at War in the 1990s

DANIEL P. BOLGER

★

PRESIDIO

The views expressed herein are those of the author and do not reflect the official positions of the Department of the Army or the Department of Defense.

Copyright © 1995 by Daniel P. Bolger

Published by Presidio Press
505 B San Marin Dr., Suite 300
Novato, CA 94945-1340

Library of Congress Cataloging-in-Publication Data

Bolger, Daniel P., 1957–
    Savage peace : Americans at war in the 1990s / Daniel P. Bolger.
        p.   cm.
    Includes bibliographical references (p.) and index.
    ISBN 0-89141-452-5 (hardcover)
    1. United States—History, Military—20th century. I. Title.
E840.4.B65 1995
355' .032' 097309049—dc20   95-5842
                                                          CIP

Typography and maps by ProImage
Photographs courtesy of the Department of Defense unless otherwise noted.

Printed in the United States of America

For John M. Mitchell, Commander, 1st Battalion (Mechanized), 5th Infantry, Korea, 1990–1991— "Duty is the sublimest word in the English language."

CONTENTS

◆

LIST OF MAPS AND ILLUSTRATIONS

◆

PREFACE

◆

Any author attempting to write about recent events faces the paradox of trying to record instant history. Historians know that the deeper analyses, the finer nuances, and the intriguing details tend to emerge over time, as documents are declassified, participants leave active roles in their organizations and really begin to talk, and the results of various complex activities play out. Often, the patient scribes tell a different, fuller story than that provided by the eyewitnesses, reporters, spokesmen, pundits, and talking heads—the architects of the first cut.

The study that follows is more like a second cut. While not quite history, the result may be judged to be a bit more thoughtful than initial impressions. This book addresses an important contemporary subject, American peace operations, in medias res. With plenty of raw data at hand, some trends become obvious, and the jury is still out.

Recognizing the limits of this kind of effort but convinced of the value of the topic, I have tried to describe and explain the nature of these operations. What are they? Why does America conduct them? How are they carried out? Have American decision makers and practitioners learned anything from previous experiences in these undertakings? How do the electronic news media influence such situations? Where does a resurgent United Nations fit in? These questions, among others, frame today's debate, an exploration proceeding both inside the U.S. armed forces and among the citizenry at large. This book endeavors to contribute to the continuing professional and public dialogue.

In pursuing these matters, it is important to maintain some historical perspective while considering America's role in what, nearly a century ago,

Rudyard Kipling labeled the savage wars of peace. There has been a profusion of U.S. involvements in small confrontations since the Berlin Wall came down in 1989: Cambodia, Haiti, Bolivia, Peru, the western Sahara, Rwanda, post-invasion Panama, south Iraq, and liberated Kuwait, plus many more. While each case merits consideration, this book focuses on the three largest and most important U.S. forays into the ill-defined realm of peace operations. Success in Kurdistan, failure in Somalia, and a decision deferred in the former Yugoslavia furnish useful illustrations of the major aspects of this difficult form of warfare. These three interventions are the parts that serve to illuminate the whole, especially since they have been well covered in the civil and military press.

Along with a historical sense in examining current peace operations, I have necessarily relied upon my own professional experiences as a soldier. That perspective, I trust, lends a thread of realism to this venture. American soldiers cannot afford to relegate the questions of peace operations to mere theorizing, and so, this book is not about the intellectual concepts of international relations or the abstract principles of war making. I have taken my lead from T. R. Fehrenbach rather than Antoine Jomini. This book describes what can happen when you hand an eighteen-year-old American a rifle, send him overseas, and ask him to keep order in lands that know no such thing.

In sending troops on far-flung military operations, defining time and space relationships become important. Time comes first. Americans and allies rely on a twenty-four-hour cycle, where, with apologies to George Orwell, the clock reliably strikes thirteen every day at one P.M. This avoids all that messy A.M. and P.M. stuff, and will be the rule in this book. Unless otherwise indicated, times reflect those in the areas of operations.

Distance can be a more contentious matter, and here I have consciously not used the U.S. Army system. The United States military long ago passed the comfortable era in which soldiers, sailors, airmen, and Marines could ply their separate trades without reference to each other, or to allies. In deference to the Navy and Air Force, not to mention British Commonwealth friends and most of the reading public, I have used English forms of measurements rather than the metric indices more commonly found in U.S. Army and Marine Corps practice. Even soldiers and Marines still measure altitudes in feet, so this should not prove too disconcerting.

Many friends and comrades in arms contributed to the ideas and research that went into this work. They include Jerry Bolzak, Jim Breckenridge, Jim Dubik, Mike Harper, Bruce Jette, Bob Johnson, Terry Juskowiak, Jack

Kammerer, Randy Kolton, Jim Laufenburg, Steve Lofgren, Frank Mac-Kenzie, Angela Manos, Patricia McQuistion, Ralph Peters, Brian Prosser, Eli Rosner, Dan Sullivan, Andy Twomey, and Melissa Wells-Petry. I owe special thanks to Gen. Gordon R. Sullivan, who got me thinking about these issues in the autumn of 1993, and to Col. Walter B. Clark, a veteran infantry commander who has seen his share of wars and rumors of wars. Particular gratitude goes to Dale Wilson of Presidio Press, and I must acknowledge the consistent dedication of my wonderful editor, Joan Griffin. Finally, for my wife, Joy and my children, Philip and Carolyn—none of this would be possible without you.

PROLOGUE
The Dark of the Moon

Butch Cassidy: No. No. Not yet. Not till me and Harvey get the rules straight.

Harvey Logan: Rules—in a knife fight?

Butch Cassidy and the Sundance Kid

Have you ever thought about what it takes to kill a man?

Sergeant Joseph Duffy thought about that very problem early one evening not so long ago. The man he thought about killing was a North Korean soldier trying to pick his way into American-controlled ground. Duffy intended to slay this person with a single shot.

It wouldn't take much—a few ounces or so of rearward pressure from Duffy's right index finger, and Mr. Infiltrator would join his ancestors. Duffy squinted through the black telescopic ten-power sight tube. He saw the enemy soldier as a tan, hatless, dark-haired nodule protruding from a vertical blob the color of wet autumn mud, all framed in a circle of dull green vegetation. The sergeant centered his scope's aiming dot squarely on the North Korean's bobbing, indistinct head.

One slow pull, a lot less force than it would take to open a soft drink can, and the M24 would fire, sending a 168-grain M118 special ball bullet speeding toward the unsuspecting adversary at twenty-six hundred feet per second, almost three times the speed of sound. The slug, about the size of a ballpoint pen cap, would smack into the North Korean's head, drill through his soft matter, and exit in a spray of bone chips, blood, and tissue. It would all take about a second.[1]

Missing the shot didn't even enter Duffy's mind. He was a trained U.S. Army sniper, and if authorized to shoot, he knew how to make his rounds count. The fact that Duffy had never shot anything but cardboard and paper targets really didn't matter. If that guy crossed the line, if the commander approved, Duffy knew what to do.

The line Duffy guarded was a strip nobody could see, but that really didn't much matter either. What you don't see—snipers, North Korean overwatch teams, land mines, things that go bump in the night—can kill you. That's especially true in the most dangerous place in the world, the Korean Demilitarized Zone—the DMZ.

Like most of the truly dangerous things on this earth, you cannot see the line that marks the actual border between Communist North Korea (the Democratic People's Republic of Korea—DPRK) and pro-American South Korea (the Republic of Korea—ROK). This is the invisible military demarcation line, or MDL, one more acronym among the great many associated with Korea, proof positive of pervasive modern martial influence. The MDL meanders some 151 miles, running from the Yellow Sea in the west to the Sea of Japan in the east. If you cross it, you get shot. There have been exceptions over the years, some accidental, some on purpose. But by and large, if you go over this unseen boundary, you stand a good chance of eating a lot of bullets.

It is a bit of an exaggeration, though not by much, to describe the Korean MDL as totally unmarked. The MDL is, indeed, officially designated at irregular intervals (a few hundred feet to almost a mile) by 1,291 two-faced rectangular metal signs, each mounted on concrete posts that jut some five feet out of the red-brown Korean dirt. Originally these signs were yellow— safety yellow, of course, like a highway hazard notice—and bore warnings in English and Hangul (Korean language) on the south plate and Chinese and Hangul on the north side. Each reads, "Military Demarcation Line" and features a unique four-digit number. Now they have faded and become pocked by rust, showing the passage of forty-odd Korean summer monsoons and winter blizzards since they were erected in 1953.[2] Soldiers from both sides are supposed to paint and replace the signs, with each combatant responsible for certain areas.

The Communists never bothered to do anything with theirs. After all, putting North Korean conscript work details that close to a better life might encourage embarrassing defections. Then, just to keep things sporting, the North started sniping at ROK and American sign maintenance teams. It got particularly ugly in the late 1960s. That did it. Nobody wanted to risk lives simply to paint signs.[3] So now the marker plates flake and rust, standing forlornly among tall weeds, a barely noticed string extending from sea to shining sea. You could walk between two of the things—even two of the closer ones—and never even know it. Until you got shot, that is.

For a mile and a quarter (two kilometers, to be precise) north and south of the unseen, almost unmarked MDL stretch buffer zones closely watched by both sides. This area is so little used by men that endangered species have made homes there. Its lush acres shelter huge white Manchurian cranes, ring-necked pheasants, bears, ducks, deer, wildcats, and even a tiger or two. This four-kilometer band, thinly held by a string of fortified, heavily armed outposts and a lattice of aggressive infantry patrols, all armed to the teeth, constitutes the demilitarized zone.[4]

Only George Orwell himself could truly appreciate this sort of incongruous mismatch between what is said and what is done. When he coined the wicked aphorism war is peace in his classic dystopia *1984,* he might well have been thinking about something like the Korean DMZ.[5] In that dangerous no-man's-land, the most militarized demilitarized place on earth, the Korean War has never really ended.

Reading the actual armistice instrument signed in Panmunjom on 27 July 1953 explains only the broader outlines of the actual situation. The temporary truce arrangements, still in effect over four decades later, set up a Military Armistice Commission (MAC) to supervise and resolve truce issues. It formalized the half-mile-wide Panmunjom Joint Security Area (JSA), conveniently straddling the westernmost segment of the MDL, as the site for all meetings. Talks involve North Korea and the Chinese on one side, and on the other the South Koreans, Americans, British, and other allies of 1950–53, speaking for the United Nations Command. In theory, the commission ensures a mutual commitment to preserving the cease-fire. At least that's what the armistice documents say.[6]

Aside from establishing the Panmunjom JSA for conflict resolution, the 1953 armistice agreement also designated the exact course of the MDL and created the DMZ. Here is where the concept went awry, and predictably so. Neither side trusted the MAC or the fruitless 1954 Geneva talks that were supposed to resolve the Korean question. Both sides backed off as required, put out patrols and outposts, and continued hostilities, admittedly at a much reduced level of intensity. Here's the result: anyone who crosses the MDL usually gets shot.

This was not part of the deal. The agreement definitely states: "Neither side shall execute any hostile act within, from, or against the Demilitarized Zone." Only a thousand personnel per side for "civil police and administration" would be permitted in the Zone. The armistice itself prohibited armored vehicles, artillery, crew-served weapons (machine guns, anti-tank guns, mortars), land mines, firing across the MDL, armed overflights anywhere in the DMZ, infiltration across the MDL, and the construction of extensive field fortifications. Both sides comply after a fashion, if you consider ambush patrols, minefields, and fortified hilltops to be compliance. But these are pretty powerful civil police.[7]

All of this armed confrontation has produced side effects that, taken together, lend an air of Kafkaesque unreality to the realm of the DMZ, as if the basic situation was not strange enough. While the war of shells and bullets has subsided, flaring up at odd intervals, the war of words and images continues. The Korean DMZ has evolved into a highly developed theater of psychological conflict, appealing to all of the senses.

Both Koreas have wired powerful outdoor speaker systems into their DMZ guard posts. Day and night, booming Korean-language political speeches, defector testimonies, news reports, and patriotic music echoes back and forth, filling their air with highly charged babble. It is hard to distinguish commentary from music from anything when both sides crank up the volume in an endless contest that gives new meaning to the phrase "battle of the bands."

Though their sector has been greatly reduced since 1971, the Americans have not been wholly neglected by North Korea. Years ago, English-language propaganda programs were more common. Now they are rare. Still, it is not that unusual for Americans to be out waiting in a night ambush position and hear serenades from Joan Baez, Led Zeppelin, Creedence Clearwater Revival, or Jimi Hendrix, interspersed with vicious anti-American diatribes by generic Yankee war resisters, all capped by pleas to defect. Obviously, the Hanoi Communists offered a little technical assistance here.

Visual imagery has not been forgotten. North of the MDL, huge white Hangul letters stand along the slopes north of the MDL, spelling out praise for North Korean "Great Leader" Kim Il-sung and son "Dear Leader" Kim Jong-il, along with condemnations of America, the South, and the U.S./ROK Team Spirit exercises. Both sides distribute safe-passage leaflets, scattered by drifting balloons, to encourage line-crossings. South Korean propaganda handbills often feature scantily clad, or completely undressed, comely women. Whatever effect they have north of the MDL, those mistakenly dumped in the U.S. sector are a favorite of American infantry patrols.

Aside from jangling nerves and offering comic relief, this effort has had its successes, with defections from both sides over the years. Even an American, Pfc. Joey White of the 1st Battalion (Mechanized), 31st Infantry, crossed the line in August of 1982, presumably to seek a better life to the

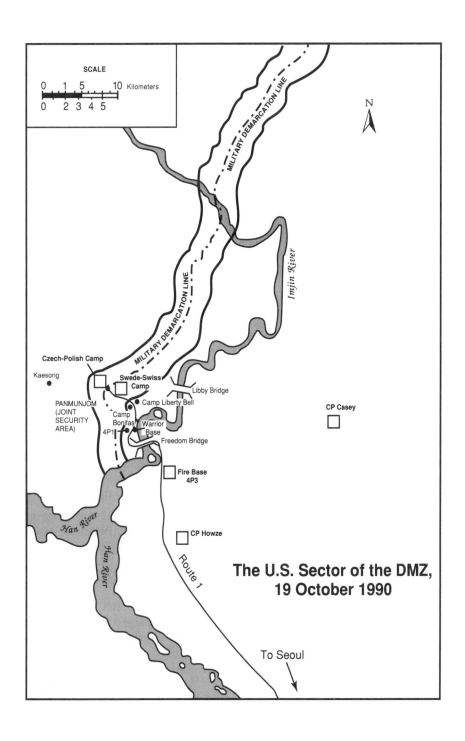

SCALE

0 1 5 10 Kilometers
0 2 3 4 5

N

MILITARY DEMARCATION LINE

MILITARY DEMARCATION LINE

Imjin River

Czech-Polish Camp

Kaesong

Swede-Swiss Camp

Libby Bridge

PANMUNJOM (JOINT SECURITY AREA)

Camp Liberty Bell

CP Casey

Camp Bonifas

4P1

Warrior Base

Freedom Bridge

Fire Base 4P3

Han River

CP Howze

Han River

Route 1

The U.S. Sector of the DMZ, 19 October 1990

To Seoul

North. White brought along some night vision sights and weapons, as North Korean pamphlets promised substantial cash rewards for such items.[8] For some Koreans and at least one American, the psychological bombardment is no joke.

If servicemen can be influenced by the sights and sounds of the DMZ, it was only a matter of time before both Koreas saw the potential in escorting tourists through the Zone to and from the Panmunjom JSA, at least on days when tensions appear to be low and the MAC is not meeting. Incredible as it may seem, the allied half of the JSA hosts some seventy-five thousand guests annually, making Panmunjom one of the most popular tourist spots in the ROK. A few small groups actually get to go beyond the JSA tour and visit the two U.S. sector guard posts. These people have, over the years, included United Services Organizations (USO) entertainers, political leaders (among them Presidents Ronald W. Reagan and William J. Clinton), senior military officers, and a variety of others. Not to be outdone, each year the Pyongyang government brings in about nine thousand visitors of its own.[9]

Hoping to sway opinions, both Koreas subject the tourist flood to the same eyeful and earful that those in uniform receive. In addition, with impressionable civilian guests in mind, each Korea has erected one town in its half of the Zone, model communities handily located within sight of the Panmunjom JSA. The ROKs built Taesong-dong (usually called Freedom Village, but literally "Attaining Success Village"), home to 250 chosen citizens. It is marked by a great steel flag tower, over 100 yards high, flying a vast South Korean flag. North Korea's entry, Kijong-dong ("Model Village"), is a Potemkin village whose residents come and go under cover of darkness. It does boast a tower that reaches more than 150 yards into the sky, complete with a gigantic North Korean flag. The allied soldiers usually call Kijong-dong Propaganda Village, but the name could just as easily be applied to Taesong-dong. Taesong-dong residents, however, really live in their houses, and their rice paddies and ginseng rows cover all the flat spots in the cramped American sector.[10]

Gawking tourists, USO gladhanders, Taesong-dong farmers, weird Joan Baez tapes, king-sized flags, pictures of naked women delivered by lost balloons—these often bizarre aspects sometimes obscure the very real and continuing threat from the Pyongyang regime. By day, the U.S. sector of the DMZ resembles some psywar version of Disney World's "Pirates of the Caribbean," with the interesting parts played by live humans instead of "animatronic" mannequins. But by night, when the tour buses have gone south and the Taesong-dong farmers are locked into their houses, death can come calling on little cat feet.

In the early evening of Friday, 19 October 1990, the North Koreans came. Waiting for them, very much ready, were soldiers wearing the famed Indianhead patch of the "Second to None" division. It was one of the final incidents, if indeed it was even so dignified, in the long and bitter rivalry between riflemen of the 2d Infantry Division and special operators and DMZ Police of the Korean People's Army. It happened on a night when the moon rose black.

If you looked into the right spot on the dark, starry vault over the DMZ that Friday night, you could actually see the little gray-black disk of the new moon. It was hanging just above the horizon, a guarantee of changes to come in future days.

Lots of changes were well under way. There was still a Soviet Union out there, albeit a weakened one already locked into its rattling death spin. Most of the world's attention focused on the sands of Saudi Arabia, where Operation Desert Shield was in full swing, building up strength in men and machines that would eventually liberate Kuwait in a glorious air and armored blitzkrieg in the best traditions of George Patton. But those were the last spasms of yesterday's world and yesterday's ways of war. The new moon, a bad moon indeed, was rising over the Zone.

In a figurative sense, nothing could be more fitting. The DMZ, and the ambiguous shadowboxing in it, had hinted at the post–Cold War world even while most on both sides had planned to refight some 78-speed, world-ending Ragnarok in Germany's Fulda Gap. Though the Korean standoff appeared to be a curious relic of two to six wars earlier, depending on whether you counted the smaller ones, it very much typified what American troops confronted as the twentieth century closed. The DMZ wasn't quite peace, but it wasn't quite war either. A lot of Americans in uniform would soon become well acquainted with that shadow world, the twilight gloom of a savage peace, under the darkest of dark moons.

Most of the American soldiers in the Zone were far too busy for sky gazing. If they noticed the new moon at all, they saw it for what it was and nothing more. And they saw it because the DMZ was pretty much unlit, at least the American part.

Though the North Koreans usually illuminated their half of the DMZ, the U.S. sector stayed blacked out, a tribute to American prowess in unattended sensors, ground radars, thermal imagery devices, and ambient light intensifiers. Sound and seismic sensor chains detected noise and movement. AN/ PPS-5A ground surveillance radars scanned from four sites, two in the American sector and two on hills overlooking the area. A few soldiers looked through thermal viewers, which showed people and animals as white-hot or black-hot, depending upon the type. Some models could switch back and forth at the viewer's discretion. Most Americans looked at the DMZ after nightfall through the greenish glow of night vision goggles and weapons' sights, in which a glowing cigarette lit up like a homing beacon, a flashlight looked like a jet engine, and a full moon would shine as brightly as the midday sun. Familiar with these marvelous toys, the Americans watched and moved confidently in the dark.[11]

The moon's blank black face stared down on infantrymen of the 1st Battalion (Mechanized), 5th Infantry, one of the last "Second to None" line battalions to pull a stint on the Zone. The men followed relatively straightforward orders: "The DMZ Battalion will collect intelligence information, provide early warning, prevent any infiltration/exfiltration, and be prepared to execute contingency plans on order."[12] As in all military undertakings, the DMZ mission came with strings attached, known in the modern era as the rules of engagement (ROE).

In the demilitarized zone, the ROE were pretty direct and clear, a good thing in a place where everyone carries loaded weapons. The rules totaled a mere three and a half typed pages. These ROE reflected a reasonable balance between prudent caution with live bullets and years of bitter experience tangling with unforgiving North Korean bushwhackers.

Leaving aside the fine points, it all came down to two fundamentals. First, if fired upon, U.S. elements enjoyed an absolute right of self-defense. Shooting back if shot at, or otherwise threatened, only made sense. Although such an event would be an interesting interlude for all concerned, the proper response to such circumstances provoked little debate.

The second point could be much trickier. At night, anyone on the U.S. side of the MDL not positively identified as friendly could be engaged, subject to the approval of the battalion commander. Identifying an unidentified person (UIP in army shorthand) at night, then shooting him, was not an option to be lightly exercised. By rights, the Taesong-dong farmers should be home in their model beds, and all U.S. patrols should be plotted. Soldiers using thermal scanners and ground radars supposedly knew the difference between deer, people, and Manchurian cranes.

Predictably, human fallibility sometimes intervened. Over the years, Americans in the DMZ had shot at other Americans, ROK soldiers, and South Korean civilians, not to mention various animals, plants, shadows, and startling noises. Sorting out friend from foe is never easy, and it does not get any easier in pitch blackness under the threat of imminent North Korean gunfire. The commander would make his call with the real chance that the men to the north could join the firefight in strength. Outright combat might well turn against the Americans, or spiral up into something bigger. Nobody wanted to be the man who reignited the smoldering Korean War.

And along with those battle-related anxieties, there was another matter, a reminder that this was no game. Regardless of the foe's reaction and the outcome, the battalion commander knew quite well that clearance to fire would bring down the full scrutiny of the American, ROK, and UN chains of command. He could count on the arrival of a herd of curious staff officers, investigating, interviewing, sampling, spitting paper, and second-guessing. It didn't take Douglas MacArthur to figure out that what made sense one bad night in the DMZ probably would look a lot more careless, ill advised, and stupid when dissected on a clean desk in Seoul.

So if he okayed a shot, the DMZ battalion commander had great incentive to be right. To help him avoid mistakes, the ROE mandated two confirmed sightings before engaging. One might be by radar or thermal imager, but the other had to be by human eyeball, with or without a passive light-amplifying night vision device. In all circumstances, the battalion commander alone could direct engagement against an intruder confirmed to be across the demarcation line—a spot south, in DMZ lingo.

Sensibly, the DMZ rules included an escape clause. "Nothing in these rules of engagement," went the orders, "will prevent a responsible commander or subordinate leader from taking such action as he deems necessary to defend his guard post, patrol, work detail, or vehicle when under attack and a life-threatening situation exists."[13] This left soldiers enough initiative to deal with the wholly unexpected.

These well-tested ROE bound the 1-5th Infantry as it organized to accomplish its multifaceted mission. Its array on the evening of 19 October was similar to what one might find on any other night in the U.S. sector, with a few minor variations.

The 1st Platoon of Company A, reinforced with a two-man sniper team, occupied Guard Post Ouellette, a fortified hilltop bunker complex right on the MDL. The guard post's towers and concrete bunkers bristled with thermal sights of various kinds, and the array included a ground radar system. Barbed wire, cyclone fencing, and wide open fields of fire surrounded the post. A complete circle of deadly M18A1 Claymore mines, designed to shatter into a wicked conical blast of hot, eviscerating ball bearings, ringed the fort, ready to be detonated by remote trigger devices. At night, Guard Post Ouellette's men kept their bunker line manned and ready, their weapons loaded. An armed, well-rehearsed reaction squad dozed on the cool, gray cement in one of the bays carved out of the inside of the hill. If ordered, they could race through the twisting concrete tunnels and passages and sally forth to rescue an endangered patrol, finish off a North Korean probe, or, less dramatic but more likely, take a closer look at something strange.

The 3d Platoon, Company A, held the similar Guard Post Collier, located on an even higher hill to the southwest but back a bit from the MDL. Like Ouellette, Collier featured a radar and numerous thermal systems. It, too, was at the usual level of nighttime vigilance, its bunkers occupied, its reaction squad waiting.

Ouellette and Collier were the fixed pole stars in the little American DMZ universe, upon which the constellations of patrols pivoted. Several elements patrolled or intended to patrol the Zone that night, all with loaded rifles and grenade launchers (machine guns not being allowed by the truce rules). The 1st Platoon of Company B, already out all day reconnoitering, waited in a patrol base in the Zone. Commencing just prior to midnight, they would set three squad-strength ambushes on likely enemy avenues of approach south of Route 1. Three squad-sized patrols added up to the usual nightly effort in the U.S. sector.

This evening, though, 1-5th Infantry had something extra in the DMZ. The day before, two sniper teams had established an area ambush north of Route 1 to deconflict their firing lanes from those of the rifle platoon on the other side of the road. They remained in sector, covering a creek bed known for good reason as "Infiltration Alley." Their particular mission had been well rehearsed, intentionally timed for the night of the new moon.

Finally, later that night as on most nights, a pair of HMMWV (high-mobility military wheeled vehicle—Humvee or Hummer) trucks from Company E would conduct a mounted patrol. This effort went by the acronym MACE, for mobile acquisition and counterinfiltration element. The trucks followed a carefully selected route, stopping at a couple of particularly good observation sites to scan with onboard thermal sighting systems borrowed from TOW (tube-launched, optically-tracked, wire-guided) anti-tank missile launchers.

All in all, the American numbers in the DMZ that evening were typical: about a hundred from 1-5th Infantry, with another hundred or so from the United Nations Command Security Force—Joint Security Area (the JSA Battalion) working in and around Panmunjom. Along with those assigned to these small units, other senior officers and NCOs routinely accompanied patrols and stayed at the guard posts.

Tonight was no exception. The battalion S3 (operations officer, a major) and Company A commander were both at Guard Post Ouellette. The Company B commander was with one of his patrolling rifle squads, and Company E's captain intended to ride with the mounted Humvee element. Unless things went completely awry, these men were with their subordinates simply to be there, to share the experience, and to help and encourage. The senior people would take charge only in a dire emergency. Rifle platoon lieutenants commanded their guard posts. Sergeants led the patrols. That, too, was typical.

On 19 October, as usual, the bulk of the 1-5th Infantry lay outside the DMZ, spread out in various sites on either side of Route 1. But that did not mean they were not involved and interested. Working south along Route 1 to Seoul, which ran through the American DMZ operation like a backbone, one would first encounter Company A's 2d Platoon, defending the short U.S. stretch of the South Barrier Fence, a barrier system running just outside the demilitarized zone. Watching from guard towers and walking the mined barbed-wire and chain-link fence system, the squads tied in with elements of the ROK Army's 15th Infantry Regiment on both flanks. If any North Koreans made it through the web of guard posts and ambushes in the DMZ, the South Barrier Fence acted as a final backstop.[14]

Just beyond the barrier fence lay Camp Bonifas, named after the victim of a 1976 JSA clash and home of the combined American/ROK JSA Battalion, which ran the UN half of Panmunjom. There, on the slope of a wooded hollow filled with picnic tables, an unmarked underground entrance led to the underground Military Armistice Commission Headquarters Area—Tactical Operations Center (MACHA-TOC), the shared command post for the JSA Battalion and 1-5th Infantry.

In a brilliantly lit, soundproofed room about the size of a one-car garage, a dozen soldiers tracked the progress of U.S. operations in their sector of the DMZ and the JSA, under the supervision of a lieutenant from the infantry battalion's staff. Intent junior enlisted men, specialists in intelligence, operations, and fire support, marked maps, kept logs, and spoke to the U.S. elements at work in the Zone. A sergeant and radio operator from the JSA Battalion focused on activities in Panmunjom and ensured smooth coordination between the two battalions. Aside from the usual radio racks, ringing telephones, and neatly marked maps and charts, banks of television monitors offered a selection of views throughout Panmunjom, as well as thermal imagery from Guard Posts Ouellette and Collier and some other spots outside the U.S. sector proper.

The MACHA-TOC reported to the permanently manned TOC of the 3d Brigade, 2d Infantry Division, several miles south at Camp Howze. During an average day, the Camp Bonifas center passed some twenty routine reports to 3d Brigade. This was supplemented by up to a hundred additional discrete items of intelligence information and tactical detail on ongoing missions. Aside from this channel, the JSA Battalion also notified the UN Command (UNC) of certain JSA activities using routine reports and situational updates, as well as by answering questions. Those in the MACHA-TOC worked diligently to keep both 3d Brigade and UNC informed of all developments.[15] If odd events began to transpire, the circuits to Camp Howze and Seoul would get quite a workout. Invariably, in a crisis, both higher headquarters quite understandably wanted to know everything about everything, which could make life in the MACHA-TOC somewhat stressful.

With a raised watch officer post and the screens, radios, telephones, and other electronics going, the MACHA-TOC could be reminiscent of the bridge of the starship *Enterprise.* When something strange happened, the room and its small adjacent conference room would also host either or both of the concerned battalion commanders, their executive officers (XOs), their S3s, and other staff officers. Now and then, even more senior U.S. and ROK officers would arrive to watch a certain event unfold. But such high-level manning was the exception, not the rule. Day and night, the fate of two hundred soldiers in the DMZ, and perhaps the fate of nations, rested on the initiative of a reliable lieutenant and the judgment of these dozen young men, none more than thirty years old and most barely twenty.

Across Route 1 from Camp Bonifas and its MACHA-TOC stood Camp Liberty Bell. There, 1-5th Infantry's mortar platoon waited in massive revetments, ready to fire illumination, high-explosive, or white phosphorus rounds on order in support of U.S. forces in the DMZ. In the same way, a 2d Infantry Division 155-mm battery waited miles to the south, long howitzer barrels protruding from the massive, slab-sided concrete firing bunkers at Firebase 4P3. Like the mortars, the battery kept its tubes manned and its ammunition ready to load. Forward observers with the DMZ units stayed in constant radio communication with the mortar and artillery fire direction centers, activating and adjusting prearranged target locations as the U.S. elements moved or the North Koreans did things. If things went totally to hell, the units in the Zone could work through the mortar and artillery fire direction centers to mass the weight of more than eighty U.S. and ROK Army cannons on a single target. Within minutes, high-explosive shells could be raining into the DMZ, smashing whatever tormented the Americans.[16]

A mile and a quarter south of Camps Bonifas and Liberty Bell, the rest of the battalion waited in two compounds, 4P1 to the west and Warrior Base to the east. The 4P1 area, formerly an artillery fire base, hosted the battalion's administrative headquarters offices, a briefing area for visitors, a small-arms range, and Company E, the antiarmor unit that ran all the mounted MACE patrols.[17]

Most of 1-5th Infantry, including its fleet of M113A3 armored personnel carriers, rested quietly at Warrior Base. But even on a Friday night like 19 October, a few mechanics would be changing an engine in the motorpark. The lights continued to burn in the supply and administrative huts, where the struggle against the army's insatiable paper monster went on. Many in the battalion had settled down to eat dinner at the bright, noisy mess hall. After, they might go for run, shoot some baskets, or watch a video. By midnight, most would sack out on their nylon and aluminum cots, lined up in the typical military way inside the rows of wooden-framed platoon tents.

Yet even here, as "rear" as one got near the DMZ, the Zone exerted its hold. One company, Company D, waited to respond to any problem in the DMZ or JSA. Its sandbagged trucks were fully loaded for immediate movement into combat. This quick reaction force (QRF) company slept in its clothes, ready to go within minutes.[18]

The rest of the patrolling company had responsibilities, too. Its headquarters supported and monitored the platoon in the Zone. Every night, the company recovered one platoon and inserted another, using the concealment of darkness, as the North lacked most night surveillance technology. Two platoons of Company B, plus the battalion's Scout Platoon, were working through the three-day prepatrol training cycle, which included live-firing weapons, day and night drills, and an exhaustive inspection and rehearsal directly supervised by the battalion commander or his S3.

The remaining line company, Company C, had just come off successive periods as QRF and on the guard posts. Now it was out training with its tracked vehicles, working on squad live-fire exercises. It would be next in line for patrolling.

The rifle companies—A, B, C, and D—spent about three weeks each in the various roles: guard post/barrier fence, patrolling, QRF, or training. Company E always had the MACE, but that only took one platoon. Running guard post thermal sights consumed one more platoon of TOW crews, leaving the third free to train. So Company E ran an internal rotation. This system reduced monotony, increased vigilance, and gave each unit a chance to do each part of the DMZ mission.

Headquarters Company enjoyed no such variation. Its specialized supply, mess, maintenance, medical, and communications platoons, plus all staff sections, worked twenty-four hours a day to support DMZ operations.[19] A tendency exists among riflemen to disparage Headquarters Company as sham-artists, pukes, pogues, and REMFs (rear-echelon mother——). A few fit this description. But most of the headquarters troops worked longer hours, on the average, than anyone else in the battalion. They made up in drudgery what they missed in danger.

There really were no days off for 1-5th Infantry. That was the nature of the DMZ mission. The daily ballet of routine and sameness could not help but create patterns, and, like most opponents, the North Koreans liked patterns. In the past, American battalions sometimes fell into the most dangerous trap of all—complacency. Soldiers developed comforting rituals and shortcuts that eased their tasks.

The litany of actions and inactions seems innocuous enough. Some forces, under the guise of "taking care of the troops," did not like to leave men in the DMZ between their day reconnaissance and night ambush missions. Rather than have the squads form into and defend a platoon patrol base, as they might under conditions of open conflict, it seemed more civilized to truck squads in for day patrols, pick them up for a hot meal and rest back at Warrior Base, then truck them back into the sector for night patrols. All of this trucking back and forth along Route 1 happened in full view of North Korean guard posts. A reasonably attentive soul could watch each patrol dismount, then calculate likely patrol areas. And the northerners were definitely attentive types.

Along the same lines, it was not unknown for battalions, eager to release some forces from the grinding patrol rotation, to solicit "guest squads" from other units to conduct patrols. Tank battalion scouts, cavalrymen, intelligence sections, engineers, and air defenders eagerly volunteered, even though such outfits rarely work on dismounted infantry skills. The DMZ amounted to "adventure training" when seen in this light.

If one viewed the DMZ as an onerous work detail, an imposition like mowing the lawn or picking up trash, it only made sense to get out of it as much as possible and thus limit the damage to the battalion's ongoing training. To preserve forces, especially busy commanders and staffers, for conventional training, a few battalions ceded control of the entire DMZ effort to the battalion S2. Under this setup, the S2 took actual authority over each individual squad and guard post, cutting the company commanders and platoon leaders out of the chain to free them for normal training. Other outfits created ad hoc MACHA-TOC teams from injured or new personnel, or from soldiers tasked from the rifle companies, thus leaving the regular S2 and S3 soldiers available for their daily duties and training.

Uniforms developed unusual variations. Now and then, units did not wear the heavy Kevlar helmet during the day; after all, the DMZ was "safe" by day. Others chose not to carry bulky, uncomfortable chemical protective masks, guessing that the North would not "slime" them in the DMZ. Constrictive, awkward flak jackets were rarely worn, despite their proven record as lifesavers against small-arms bullets and grenade fragments.

Certain elements did not camouflage or patrol by concealed routes, believing that their duties involved showing a U.S. presence, though Guard Posts Collier and Ouellette fulfilled that implied task. More strangely, units would camouflage their men, then insist that they wear armbands with "DMZ MP" in bold white letters as they stalked through the darkness. While the armistice and its implementing instructions vaguely discussed identifying symbols, no specifics were given, and no written or oral directives forbade camouflaging these markings when on nightime ambush patrols. But only a few folks bothered to read those documents.

Some battalions, harried by the inevitable accident investigations, tried to curb unintended weapons firings by not allowing troops to load their weapons in the Zone or refusing to let ambushes arm Claymore mines. Others imposed additional ROE, such as requiring a spot south to be a hundred yards across the MDL before contemplating engagement.[20] Playing with the ROE was playing with dynamite—it could limit embarrassing investigations, but it might also endanger soldiers, as the North Korean ROE apparently never varied all that much.

No written directives mandated or condoned these actions. Given the air of unreality about the DMZ, lack of palpable danger in the air, and the practical concerns with avoiding foul-ups that could hurt people, all appeared to be reasonable. Only in the aggregate could they become dangerous, and few units resorted to all of them.

Much of this was simply accepted as "the way we've always done it." In Korea, where American soldiers serve a one-year tour of duty in a unique theater of operations, a year full of exciting and difficult events, it can be tempting to look for the easy solution. So the oral tradition has hypnotic power. Nobody likes to reinvent the wheel, but sometimes you must reexamine your assumptions, especially given the very real history of North Korean DMZ operations.

Lieutenant Colonel John Mitchell, who commanded 1-5th Infantry that October night in 1990, brought no preconceptions to the DMZ. Having jumped into combat as a Ranger company commander in Grenada in 1983 and as a Ranger battalion XO in Panama in 1989, he had learned better. He sized up the odd practices in vogue on the Zone and focused the battalion on the DMZ mission with six simple guidelines:

1. Don't take anything for granted.
2. Go to the source.
3. Use doctrinal language and army systems.
4. How does it relate to the mission?
5. How would we do it in combat?
6. Does it make sense?[21]

In short, John Mitchell's battalion treated the DMZ mission as a combat situation and applied the battalion's training and experience accordingly. For 1-5th Infantry, the DMZ was the primary mission, not another irksome make-work detail. The chain of command ran its own missions, and the command post staff, not some pickup team, manned the MACHA-TOC. Prodded by their battalion commander, leaders became experts on the literature and details of their portions of the DMZ mission.

Training for the DMZ was extensive, realistic, and challenging for soldiers, leaders, and units. Everyone, from snipers and platoon sergeants to clerks and drivers, learned the ROE, the area, and enemy patterns. Mitchell's platoons learned to enter the DMZ under cover of darkness, form patrol bases on the reverse slope of hills out of enemy view, reconnoiter by day, ambush by night, and then exit the Zone the next night. Many times, the men would enter or leave on foot. There were no daylight patrol truck escapades.

A full-scale field exercise north of Camp Howze replicated the U.S. sector on similar terrain, to include guard posts, MACE patrols, the barrier fence, and even North Korean role players. Every company put its squads and platoons through this training. They supplemented it with squad live-fire ambushes on nearby firing ranges. In these dress rehearsals, the battalion followed the same standing operating procedures (SOPs) that it always did with regard to uniforms, communications, and tactics. It did business the same way in the Zone.[22] "Train as you fight" typifies the American army of the 1990s, and 1-5th Infantry was a typical unit if there ever was one.

There was nothing special about the 1st of the 5th. Nobody jumped out of airplanes, rode assault helicopters to battle, or employed state-of-the-art Bradley infantry fighting vehicles. This battalion represented basic, garden-variety line infantry, the successors to a long line that stretched back through the grunts of Nam, Willie and Joe of World War II, the doughboys of the Great War, the walk-a-heaps who chased down the Sioux and Cheyenne, the boys who wore blue and butternut/gray, back all the way to the ragtag militia on the green at Lexington. The battalion's soldiers rode to most fights in boxy, aluminum M113A3s, a Vietnam-era model being replaced by the sophisticated Bradleys. Often, though, especially in hilly, rocky Korea, the men walked and marched and slogged. And regardless of how they got there, the riflemen always trained to fight on the ground.

Fighting on the ground, with nothing but a cloth shirt and trousers to protect most of you, remains one of the toughest jobs in any army. It takes brains, guts, physical strength, and a lot of training. Machines cannot do it; it takes good men. In 1990, the U.S. Army had very good men, and 1-5th Infantry had its share.

John Mitchell knew he had good men, and he trained them to do things to standard in the DMZ. He reasoned this way: Perhaps you could get away with cutting a few corners, and sometimes the path of least resistance looked good and briefed well to superiors and visitors. But soldiers who learned not to take the mission seriously might just forget that there were bad guys, small intense men burning to kill them, lurking out there in the Zone.

The hostiles were there, all right. Forces opposite 1-5th Infantry came from two types of North Korean units: II Corps DMZ Police and VIII Special Purpose Corps infiltrators. Both could be deadly.

The DMZ Police battalions, one per division, actually secured the Zone north of the MDL. They ran the guard towers and repaired the fences and lights. Each frontline division had a DMZ Police battalion, and the II Corps forces opposite the Americans employed about a company along the northern and western faces of the Zone. DMZ Police conducted surveillance, reacted to American and ROK intrusions across the MDL, and guided infiltrating elements to the demarcation line. If a special warfare crossing turned sour, the DMZ units would provide covering fire. Organized as infantry, they kept ample stocks of machine guns, mortars, and recoilless antitank weapons for just such emergencies, conveniently concealed in their guard posts to avoid being charged with overt armistice violations. Not that it mattered; DMZ Police units often brought the things out in broad daylight, as if to thumb their noses at the ROK and U.S. soldiers. If it came up at a MAC meeting, the Communists would merely put on their best stone faces. Politically reliable, highly trained, and assigned for the duration of their years of conscript duty, North Korean People's Army DMZ Police were formidable adversaries.

North Korean special forces, like their counterparts worldwide, are a true elite, a few notches above the DMZ Police. The trained infiltrators along the DMZ could draw upon years of experience in such operations. Armed with small personal weapons, such as Czech Skorpion or Russian AKR automatic carbines, and usually carrying a grenade or two, the infiltrators worked in pairs. Well aware of U.S. thermal devices, they often stayed in the streambeds and wore dark wet suits, which both kept them warm and greatly reduced their heat signatures. They preferred to come on rainy or foggy nights, when thermal systems and light-intensifying starlight scopes did not see all that well. The infiltrators normally gave a wide berth to patrols and guard posts and would fight only if cornered.

There were exceptions, though. One could never be certain of North Korean motivations, but at least a few missions appear to have been hit-and-run raids, designed to shoot an unsuspecting American or South Korean soldier.[23] It had really gotten out of hand in the late 1960s, when America had its attention on Vietnam, though it seemed to have settled down since then. With the North, you could not tell, especially with American eyes glued on Saudi Arabia in the autumn of 1990. The enemy had the capability, and they had the track record. Those were facts.

When 1-5th Infantry assumed the DMZ mission on 25 August 1990, the North Koreans had demonstrated a recent willingness to test American units. In March 1990, during the night of the new moon, 2-503d Infantry experienced what was later determined to be an intrusion in the diked rice paddies east of Guard Post Ouellette, aptly nicknamed Infiltration Alley. Several radar, thermal, and seismic sensor devices registered the activity. Unfortunately, the battalion had no patrols in the area to react. The incident was over before 2-503d Infantry guessed what had happened.[24] The enemy left behind distinctive North Korean footprints and a lot of crushed vegetation to mark their passage. Why did the foe cross? No one knew.

In June of 1990, during a driving monsoon rain, 5-20th Infantry spent several hours tracking a pair of wet-suited infiltrators in the Infiltration Alley creek bed. Again the North crossed under the minimal illumination of a new moon. The 5th of the 20th videotaped the encounter, using one of the thermal imaging systems at Guard Post Ouellette. Lieutenant Colonel John Lewis, commanding 5-20th Infantry, finally flushed the enemy pair by alerting and deploying a MACE patrol into the Zone. Once the men dismounted, they sighted the hostiles and received Lewis's authority to engage. The 3d Brigade commander, Col. Michael Sherfield, was in his TOC, following the action. He approved the battalion commander's decision.

It never came to shooting. As the MACE closed, the enemy duo fled north. In the videotaped record, one could clearly see two dim gray human figures huddling near the base of an electrical power pole in Infiltration Alley.[25] What were they doing? Nobody really could say. Some senior officers in Seoul, who had not seen the video record, discounted the whole affair: units in the DMZ were always seeing things.

John Mitchell disagreed with the Seoul officers. He had seen the tape and talked to John Lewis. During their intensive pre-DMZ training, Mitchell's S2, S3, and company commanders all watched the videotape. They talked to their comrades in 5-20th about that night. Coupled with the 2-503d report, the June intrusion demonstrated that the enemy was not afraid to test the Americans.

It appeared that the North Koreans favored the dark of the moon and the rice paddy dikes and creek washouts of Infiltration Alley. Perhaps the two recent crossings were paving the way for a more dangerous foray, one aimed at making a point by tagging a U.S. patrol or guard post. As the North could select the exact time and place of the crossing and evidently get out before the U.S. troops could react, they held the initiative. The United States did not make countercrossings in pursuit, and dumping MACE patrols from the lit, heated 4P1 garage into a previously unreconnoitered part of the coal black, damp, cold DMZ seemed like a recipe for trouble. Passively sitting there wouldn't stop them, and even Mitchell's well-trained soldiers could not guard everything all the time.

So the 1st of the 5th had to gain control of the when and where variables and do so without sparking the Battle of Infiltration Alley. With most of the battalion's preferred offensive claws pulled, it would not be an easy task. But there were ways.

The battalion worked hard to be innovative. The rifle platoons religiously employed concealed patrol bases; when they entered the DMZ, they stayed until their tasks were completed. Radar and thermal teams received permission to set up at nearby ROK guard posts overlooking the U.S. sector. The MACE selected eight observation post locations and rehearsed getting there from 4P1, recording the timings in the event they had to go in unexpectedly. MACE sections coordinated to patrol in the flanking ROK sectors to examine little-used trails leading into the American part of the Zone. Sniper teams often accompanied both ground and MACE patrols, often breaking off or staying behind, and Guard Post Ouellette always hosted a pair of snipers. Reaction forces at the guard posts and South Barrier Fence and the QRF company at Warrior Base rehearsed and rehearsed, learning the terrain of the Zone.

American technology also assisted the battalion. The guard posts experimented with placing additional thermal sights detached from otherwise unused Dragon antitank missile launchers. The S2 sought and issued a wide array of test items and experimental gadgetry: handheld thermal viewers, filmless cameras that stored pictures on computer disks, palmcorder video systems, directional microphones, crystal clear monocular Litton night scopes the size of toilet paper tubes, and infrared chemical light tubes invisible without American-style night sights. All of these ideas, approaches, and implements offered ways to gain ascendency over the North Koreans, to limit their initiative in space and time.[26]

Curiously, one of the better ways came from a Chinese commander who had died more than twenty-three hundred years before John Mitchell first put on an American uniform. In his book *Art of War,* Sun Tzu wrote that "all warfare is based on deception."[27] Well, Mitchell had told his soldiers to ask themselves "How would we do it in combat?" Sun Tzu offered one answer.

The 2d Infantry Division Demilitarized Zone Standing Operating Procedures (DMZ SOP), 22 January 1990 edition, said this about patrol planning: "The variety of patrols that can be run in the DMZ is limited only by the imagination of the battalion S2/S3 and the restrictions of the DMZ SOP."[28] The 1-5th Infantry's S2, Lt. Roman Fontes, and S3, Maj. Daniel Bolger, evidently had enough imagination. They had read their Sun Tzu, and they understood Lieutenant Colonel Mitchell's intent. Together, they devised a scheme.

Having studied the North Korean DMZ Police and special operators, Bolger and Fontes formed some planning assumptions. In the intelligence arena, Fontes correctly noted that the enemy would likely try to penetrate the MDL during times of minimal illumination. He also identified four likely enemy avenues of approach into the U.S. sector, with Infiltration Alley being the favorite. He could not say whether the bad guys would come to look, shoot, or both, but he reminded Mitchell, Bolger, and the rest that if you let them in where and when they chose, the northerners enjoyed all the options.

Bolger took what Fontes gave him and added some considerations on U.S. methods. Previous DMZ encounters had featured slow or confused American reactions as commanders frantically moved rifle squads or mounted MACE units toward the suspected intruders. Bolger doubted the wisdom such unprogrammed movement in the face of a North Korean element that had gone to ground. At night, the stationary force has the advantage, as movement creates noise and shadows that attract attention. In addition, the last thing anyone wanted was U.S. units blundering into each other in the dark—friendly fire, blue on blue, fratricide. To prevent infiltration, the Americans had to be the sitters, and the bad guys had to be the movers.

Making the North Koreans dance to 1-5th Infantry's tune brought Sun Tzu into play. Could the Americans create a deceptive event that would focus the North Koreans where 1-5th wanted them? Bolger and Fontes thought so. An area ambush focused around the deception area, a baited ambush in Fort Benning terminology, might well do the trick.[29] The northern forces were reputed to think the Americans ill disciplined and sloppy about security. What if the battalion played to those perceptions and made the enemy an offer he could not refuse?

There was one thing in the 1-5th Infantry inventory that the North Koreans wanted: a SINCGARS (single channel ground and airborne radio system) frequency-hopping radio. This model of radio offered a technological cure to American soldiers' notoriously poor communications security. Americans had a bad tendency to use radios like their home telephones, gabbing away in clear text. The North Koreans loved that, as had the Vietnamese Communists in their day. But now those good old days were over. With SINCGARS, the Americans could talk all they wished without being intercepted, because the radio skipped about 150 times a second, in addition to using other encryption systems.[30] If Pyongyang could get hold of a SINCGARS, they could again listen to the ever-talkative Americans or perhaps even reverse-engineer the device for their own uses.

Neither Bolger nor Fontes knew for sure that the North Koreans wanted a SINCGARS. Maybe the enemy already had one. But as any John le Carré reader could tell you, coded communications are hot items. Offering one looked like a good bet.

Risking the real thing would be dumb. Bolger recommended creating a decoy SINCGARS radio. This could be easily done since radiomen usually carried it inside a green nylon rucksack, with only a black plastic handset dangling on a spiral cord and a thin whip antenna sticking out the top. With a suitable dummy inside, the rucksack might be convincingly lost in Infiltration Alley. The chosen site would be within radar and thermal coverage of Guard Post Collier and Radar Site 1 (outside the U.S. sector), but in dead ground relative to Ouellette, so as not to be too obvious. The bag would be placed at the apex of a well-concealed area ambush.[31]

The battalion incorporated a sniper section well trained to establish this sort of area ambush. Expert shots by day and night, the twelve snipers also lived up to their radio callsign of Shadow. They knew how to conceal themselves, and they displayed boundless patience and thoroughness as they lay hour after hour in the DMZ, watching and waiting, covering their assigned ambush kill zones. By 19 October, the snipers had almost two months of DMZ experience. When they weren't in the Zone, they were spending hours on end at the range, with and without nightsights, shooting round after round to keep their edge.[32] Two of the snipers had seen action in Panama with the 75th Ranger Regiment. They knew their business.

Once the snipers and rucksack were emplaced, all patrols would stay south of Route 1. A reaction squad at Ouellette, under Lt. John Maffey, would be told to choose and rehearse routes to both sniper positions in the week before the mission. But the riflemen were not expected to go anywhere unless things went haywire. The only movers out there would be bad guys.

Under this plan, if the North Koreans came, Mitchell now held all the cards. He would know right where they were going. He would have eyes and rifles covering them. His radars and thermals could confirm the sightings. Chances for fratricide had been minimized. The variables that used to favor the northerners could be adjusted to work against them.

Shooting the North Koreans represented one option. There were others. Mitchell could illuminate them. He might choose to watch the event and record it for use at a MAC meeting—stealing U.S. equipment was definitely bad form. Even if enemy ninjas crept in and managed to lift the bag unseen—an unlikely scenario given the battalion's focus—the foe would get only a rucksack, a handset, an antenna, and some ballast.

Mitchell approved the scheme, agreeing to try it on the night of the new moon in Infiltration Alley. Bolger and Company A commander Jim Klingaman would be forward at Ouellette. Fontes and Mitchell expected to be in the MACHA-TOC. The requisite patrol plans went to 3d Brigade, where Colonel Sherfield approved them. The snipers, Maffey's 1st Platoon, the Collier platoon, a MACE section, the MACHA-TOC crew, and a few others received a full briefing and began detailed, repeated rehearsals. The rest of the battalion was told enough to keep them from interfering through good intentions.

Frankly, nobody thought the idea would work. It was just another ploy, just another effort to keep the bad guys guessing. This time, though, the fish bit.

Roman Fontes himself inserted the bag at 1300 on the brilliantly sunny afternoon of 19 October. The demilitarized zone displayed all its natural autumn splendor, highlighting red, yellow, and orange treetops in a spectacle that would rival New York's Hudson River Valley. It was one of the most pleasant times of year in otherwise hot, wet, or cold Korea. Taesong-dong farmers puttered about on small tractors, bringing in the last of this year's rice crop, leaving the paddies dry and dusty brown. The crisp, clear air allowed fine viewing from all guard posts overlooking Infiltration Alley: Collier and Ouellette to the south, and North Korean posts 219, 220, and 221 to the north.

Onto this stage rolled Fontes. The battalion S2, who had created the decoy SINCGARS rucksack a few nights before, played the radioman for a Humvee patrol from Company B, 102d Military Intelligence (MI) Battalion. The MI soldiers made a weekly daylight run into the Zone to change the batteries on the finicky ground sensor strings. They were rather lax, treating the whole effort as a chore, and the North Koreans knew it. Fontes told them not to change a thing.

The Humvee team motored slowly around the benign, sunlit Zone, stopping three times to service the camouflaged strips of seismic detectors. At each halt, the driver kept his seat with the motor idling. The sergeant riding up front climbed out, slung his rifle, and began changing the batteries. While all this went on, two other soldiers dismounted from the rear of the small, flat truck to take a knee and provide security, rifles level. It wasn't quite to 1-5th Infantry standards, but that was just as well today. Fontes was one of them.

At the fourth string, not far from a lone tree and a MDL marking sign that identified the center of Infiltration Alley, Fontes moved a bit farther off, found a nice hard dike, and sat down, M16A2 rifle across his lap. He made a show of facing north and pushing back his coal-scuttle Kevlar helmet. The S2 could see the small, bottle-green figures of two North Korean DMZ Police in the tower at Post 219. They were watching him.

Fontes gazed around, watching the sergeant replace a battery. He slowly eased out of his rucksack, stood up, and stretched. He had practiced every move as if he were Al Pacino, but he hoped it all looked natural. The folks in 219 were still there, still looking. Fontes barely glanced their way as he ambled toward the sergeant, as if to tell him something. The rucksack with its "radio" was left behind for the moment, a weight off a tired soldier's shoulders.

Suddenly, the Humvee gunned its engine and the driver blasted his horn twice. The sergeant dropped what he was doing, unslung his weapon, and began motioning wildly, shouting to his troops to remount. Fontes and the other security man, electrified by the horn, sprinted to the truck and clambered aboard. The truck bucked and started rolling even before the security team sat down. It headed south, toward Route 1. A few Taesong-dong farmers looked up. Near the JSA in Panmunjom, an alert whistle started to wail. What was going on?

In this confusion, the radio rucksack stayed behind, right on the dike top, but far enough from the trails that it could not be easily seen. Except, that is, by those supposed to see in North Korean Guard Posts 219, 220, and 221.

Two sniper teams also watched the whole scene, and a third at Ouellette heard about it, as it was not visible from there. To the west, with a line of sight parallel to the MDL, Sgt. Joseph Duffy and Spec. Don Alcantara, callsign Shadow 1, waited in the underbrush about 150 yards away from the rucksack. Staff Sergeant Dennis Perkins and Spec. Tony McKinney, callsign Shadow 2, were about three hundred yards to the south at a ninety-degree angle to Shadow 1, folded into the hummocks rimming a bare rice paddy. Both teams had taken up their hides the day before the bag drop, staying behind after tagging along with rifle platoon ambush patrols. Now they had something to watch.

The North Koreans were definitely interested, and the MI truck was barely out of sight before extra sentinels began to crowd the enemy guard towers. Some had cameras; others seemed to be sketching things. Did they believe Fontes's one-act play? Maybe.

By sheer happenstance, reflecting the chance that Carl von Clausewitz rightly said plays such a big part in armed conflict, the S2's concluding performance coincided almost to the minute with two other DMZ events. Fontes and 1-5th Infantry had nothing to do with either of them. Indeed, the busy intelligence officer learned about both much later.

First, a South Korean delegation that had visited Pyongyang returned through Panmunjom that same afternoon. This naturally kept the JSA on pins and needles all day. No tour buses visited. Suspicious North Koreans probably expected something out of the ordinary. All enemy posts were at full manning and then some.

Second, a North Korean patrol approached unusually close to the MDL on the western face of the U.S. sector, near the village of Taesong-dong. The JSA Battalion alerted its internal QRF, sounding the Klaxon. In the north, where the DMZ Police surely recognized the signal for what it meant, this activity may have lent credence to the Humvee's hasty departure. Perhaps Fontes and friends had been responding to a general American alert. It probably looked that way from the north side.

A half hour before sunset, Fontes came back, this time aboard SSgt. Louis Olvitt's MACE patrol truck, with the second MACE vehicle in trail. The S2 and several decidedly more professional security men dismounted within a few hundred yards of the rucksack to search for it. They made it look good and made sure not to find it. It made sense and painted a few more strokes on the picture for the North Koreans.

Just before he reboarded in mock frustration, with night coming on, Fontes heard something chilling: multiple voices talking in low Hangul tones. Those had to be enemy soldiers. The sounds came from a dense golden-orange thicket, barely across the imaginary MDL. So they were already near.

Careful not to disclose what he had heard until out of earshot—some northerners spoke excellent English—Fontes left in accord with the script. He reported the voices when the MACE trucks were safely back on Route 1 and headed south. Shadow 1 confirmed Fontes's radio message.

This report found the whole U.S. sector at full alert, normal procedure just before dark. Aware that the decoy had begun to affect things, the duty officer in the MACHA-TOC called Lieutenant Colonel Mitchell and JSA Battalion commander Lt. Col. Tom Turner from their dinners.

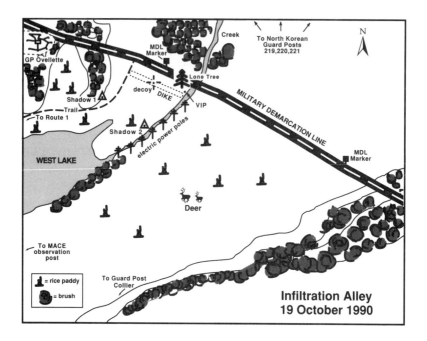

Bolger, Klingaman, Maffey, and the entire platoon at Ouellette heard Fontes's radio report too. The major and the captain raced from Ouellette's underground TOC, passing sergeants and privates hurrying to their concrete bunkers in the gathering evening gloom. The two officers pulled themselves up the long ladder that led through Ouellette's centerpiece, a massive lattice lookout tower with an enclosed viewing platform on top. They climbed through the trap door, breathless. Below them, Maffey was circulating around the bunker line, checking his men, talking to them, going over things.

From the tower, Bolger, Klingaman, and thermal sight operator Sgt. Bob Jackson strained to see to the east. Specialist William Ferguson, a sniper, had gone through another trapdoor to the tower roof to see if a few more feet of elevation made a difference. They could hear him rustling around up there, assuming a prone position on the flat, shingled roof, no doubt settling his M21 sniper rifle into the hollow of his right shoulder. If a shot from Ouellette had to be taken, Ferguson would pull the trigger.

The men in the tower longed to see through the trees and over the folded dirt, into the dead ground that held the decoy and the Shadow 1 soldiers. The brilliant hues of the fall afternoon were swiftly dulling to grays and blacks when Klingaman pointed east, wordlessly. Two groups of birds rose suddenly from the thicket on the enemy side of the MDL. Jackson, his eye glued to the thermal scanner, said quietly that two deer had just run across the MDL, heading south into Infiltration Alley. Watches throughout the battalion showed 1905, just after the last light faded.

The tower radio speaker crackled: "MACHA-TOC, this is Shadow 1. I have one person moving near the lone tree, over."

"This is MACHA-TOC, roger."

A new voice cut in. "MACHA-TOC, this is Collier TOC. Radar reports one Uniform India Papa [a UIP, an unidentified person, a bogey] across the MDL at grid BT 97870244. Definitely human, over."

The MACHA-TOC acknowledged, as did both Shadows, whispering now. You could almost hear men all over the DMZ suck in their collective breaths. The bad guys were here, one coming for the bag, the rest covering him. One American in each sniper team had long since locked and loaded. Fingers pressed lightly on triggers, waiting. A few more steps and the enemy would be in the kill zone.

It was going exactly like the rehearsals. The 1-5th had set the snare, and the enemy was walking right in. In the darkened cement-lined trenches and tunnels of Ouellette, Lt. John Maffey's reaction squad waited, eyes wide, quiet, listening to the radio traffic from the nearby guard post TOC. A few of the men who had time to think, like the S3 in the Ouellette tower, wondered to themselves: Are we really about to kill an infiltrator?

In war novels and movies, soldiers would get all worked up about that. But these people did not have time for that now. Training took over, the result of months and years of range firings and mock combat exercises. The snipers in particular were a great deal more concerned with the eight steady-hold factors of marksmanship, plus potential return shots from the north, than any larger implications of man's inhumanity to man.

"Shadow 1, this is Bobcat 6, over." It was Mitchell, now in the MACHA-TOC. Fontes had also arrived. The clock showed 1918. Mitchell's voice was low and calm, just like always. "What have you got? Over."

"Bobcat 6, this is Shadow 1. One Uniform India Papa near the lone tree, over."

In the MACHA-TOC, the young privates and specialists had activated all the right precautionary measures. The MACE at 4P1 was on standby, vehicles loaded, as was the QRF company across the street at Warrior Base. The mortar platoon at Liberty Bell and howitzer battery at distant Firebase 4P3 manned their entire array of tubes, with data set and ammunition lined up. At 3d Brigade, Colonel Sherfield was hurrying to his command post. And at 2d Infantry Division headquarters at Camp Casey, Maj. Gen. C. Glenn Marsh was pulled out of a dinner party and told that something was going on in the U.S. sector. He sent word to his helicopter pilots to stand by for a night flight to the north. John Mitchell would have plenty of help if he needed it.

Right now, the main thing was to keep everyone on an even keel, working as they had been trained. Mitchell knew that clear, cool heads made the best decisions, and he would do his part to keep folks that way. Calmly, almost nonchalantly, the battalion commander asked the question that everyone on the net wanted answered. "Is he moving toward the bag? Over."

Sergeant Duffy's voice rasped, almost inaudible, "Negative. He's stopped. Appears to be squatting down, over."

If he was across the MDL, he was just barely across, at least by the radar sighting, which was usually pretty solid. Roman Fontes's voices indicated that this visitor had help just across the line. He had probably come for the bag, hoping to make a quick grab at dusk and scamper back, a hero of the Democratic People's Republic.

But now it was very dark, the moon had come up black, and finding a drab green bag among the drab, greenish grass mat atop the dike had become impossible. The first telltale wisps of ground fog were rising from the sun-warmed creek bed as the air cooled rapidly. The Shadows could still see the decoy, but they knew where to look. The interloper did not, and he had halted.

Meanwhile, in the underground MACHA-TOC, John Mitchell began to explain things to Sherfield down at Camp Howze, who had arrived in his 3d Brigade TOC. The brigade commander acknowledged and told the 1-5th Infantry commander to let it play out some more. That made sense, and it matched Mitchell's thinking too.

Every scanner in the U.S. sector keyed on Infiltration Alley, trying to determine if the North Korean had moved and, if so, where. Two conflicting reports came in almost simultaneously.

Shadow 1 stated that the hostile was now beyond the base of the lone tree, just north of the MDL, sitting or squatting. Radar at Collier could not confirm this but did announce that it had lost the original fix south of the MDL. That one was melting back into the woodwork. It was 1929.

But Guard Post Ouellette's tower operator, Sergeant Jackson, picked up two UIPs almost two hundred yards south of the MDL, kneeling on a paddy dike. Bolger and Klingaman looked. Radar Site 1 and Collier could not confirm, nor could Shadow 2, though the figures should have been pretty close to their position. Sergeant Duffy and his Shadow 1 mate, Specialist Alcantara, could not see the new UIPs.

By the ROE, Mitchell held the power to shoot the two UIPs without another question, provided someone with a weapon could see to engage them. The MACHA-TOC had already accounted for all Taesong-dong farmers, U.S. patrols, and ROK flank outfits. But Mitchell perceived that something did not smell quite right. He heard his S3, Bolger, ask Shadow 2 again if he had line of sight on the two UIPs.

"Bobcat 3, this is Shadow 2. That is a negative, over."

That didn't sound correct, unless Perkins's team was out of position.

Shadow 2 reminded the MACHA-TOC that the UIP near the lone tree was still there, hunkered down. Duffy also reported that the team's handheld thermal viewer was failing, its batteries giving out. And, to top things off, the fog was thickening into something more than tendrils and patches.

While all this transpired, and 3d Brigade and Seoul asked their inevitable questions, the battalion commander took the precaution of scrambling Staff Sergeant Olvitt's MACE to put some more thermal eyes on the situation. Now the wisdom of rehearsed positions paid off. The trucks took about eight minutes to roll to a good preplanned observation post, scanning north into Infiltration Alley from a turnoff just off Route 1. They remained well south of the Shadows.

Though their vantage should have been good, the MACE scanned without any luck. "MACHA-TOC, this is Eagle MACE 22. Nothing found. Fog is getting pretty bad, over."

Collier radar chimed in. It showed two deer well to the east and none of the UIPs.

Mitchell asked a very good question at that point. "Ouellette TOC, do you have a fix on Shadow 2? Over."

After a few seconds, the answer came back, "Negative, over."

In the Ouellette tower, Bolger, Klingaman, and Jackson looked at each other, faces glowing in the red light of the thermal system's scope. Before any of the three could say anything, Mitchell was on the net again.

"Shadow 2, this is Bobcat 6. Crack an India Romeo [IR, infrared] chemlight, over."

On Jackson's sight, an angry little white star bloomed atop the two UIPs. Sure enough, the other UIPs were Shadow 2. That pretty much ended it, though it took another hour or so to be certain. The fog came in, turning a black night opaque. The bad guy went home without his prize.

In the morning, a MACE patrol, led by the tireless Staff Sergeant Olvitt and Lieutenant Fontes, "found" the lost rucksack. They also discovered and videotaped a myriad of footprints about ten yards past the lone tree and its MDL marker, as well as a trail leading into that golden-orange thicket on the north side of the demarcation line. It all made for a nice after-action report.

The deception had worked and not worked, tricking some hostiles and delivering a night more interesting than most in the Zone. Mitchell's chain of command took little official notice of the affair, believing strongly in the National Basketball Association motto of "No harm, no foul," and hence no investigations. It never came up in any MAC session.[33]

Except for those who went through it, out there in the Great Gulp with loaded weapons, pounding hearts, and a strange wraith gliding toward them, it was as if it had never happened. Yet the North Koreans did not try anything else against 1-5th Infantry, which completed its DMZ stint without any infiltration attempts or friendly casualties. Perhaps the enemy had learned something on 19 October that made them hesitate. Nobody could be certain. In the dangerous half-war of the Korean DMZ, under the dark of the moon, that was probably victory enough.

Notes

The epigraph is from the motion picture *Butch Cassidy and the Sundance Kid* (Hollywood, Calif.: Twentieth Century Fox, 1969). William Goldman wrote the story.

1. "The Soldier Armed: M24 7.62-mm Sniper Weapon System," *Army* (February 1991): 63–64; Ian V. Hogg, ed. *Jane's Infantry Weapons* (Alexandria, Va.: Jane's Information Group, 1992), 226.

2. U.S. Department of the Army, Headquarters, 1st Battalion (Mechanized), 5th Infantry, *Bobcat DMZ Study Guide 1990* (Camp Howze, Republic of Korea: 1-5th Infantry Division, 1 August 1990), 2. The DMZ remains dangerous, as demonstrated in December, 1994, when North Korean gunners downed an errant American helicopter. One soldier died, and the other was held for a brief period.

3. Maj. Daniel P. Bolger, USA, Leavenworth Paper 19, *Scenes from an Unfinished War: Low-Intensity Conflict in Korea, 1966–1969* (Fort Leavenworth, Kans.: Combat Studies Institute, 1991), 100–01. For an account by a participant, see Lt. Col. Walter B. Clark, USA, "A Case Study in Reaction to Communist Aggression" (Carlisle Barracks, Pa.: Army War College, 1970).

4. Maj. Wayne A. Kirkbride, USA, *Panmunjom: Facts About the Korean DMZ* (Elizabeth, N.J.: Hollym International, 1985), 48–49.

5. George Orwell, *1984* (New York: Penguin, 1981), 17.

6. Walter G. Hermes, in "Armistice Agreement of 27 July 1953," *Truce Tent and Fighting Front* (Washington, D.C.: U.S. Government Printing Office, 1966), 516–38.

7. Bolger, *Scenes from an Unfinished War,* 23. In compliance, Americans and South Koreans assigned to DMZ units wore armbands that had the acronyms "DMZ MP" (Demilitarized Zone Military Police) displayed in English and Hangul text.

8. James P. Finley, *The U.S. Military Experience in Korea 1871–1982* (San Francisco: Headquarters, U.S. Forces Korea, 1983), 178–241. In 1988, the army redesignated 1-31st Infantry as 1-5th Infantry.

9. Kirkbride, *Panmunjom,* 4, 28, 79.

10. 1-5th Infantry, *Bobcat DMZ Study Guide 1990,* 34; U.S. Department of the Army, Headquarters, 2d Infantry Division, "VIP Briefing Text," in

Demilitarized Zone Battalion Standing Operating Procedures (Camp Howze, Korea: 2d Infantry Divison, 22 January 1990), G-1-1 to G-1-5 (hereafter cited as *DMZ Battalion SOP*).

11. "Guard Post Collier Briefing" and "Guard Post Ouellette Briefing" in 2d Infantry Division, *DMZ Battalion SOP*, C-4-1 to C-4-2 and C-5-1 to C-5-2.

12. Ibid., 2. The verbiage for this mission would get second looks at most service schools. It specifies who and what, but assumes away when (on assumption) and where (the U.S. sector of the DMZ). Why is not explained, but could be undestood as "to secure the U.S. sector." Note that the battalion was instructed to "be prepared to execute contingency plans on order," a mixture of doctrinal terms. "Be prepared" means "do next." "On order" requires immediate execution when the order arrives. The contingency plans were really "be prepared" tasks.

13. "Rules of Engagement for DMZ Operations," *DMZ Battalion SOP*, F-1 to F-4.

14. Enclosure 2 "U.S. Task Organization" to U.S. Department of the Army, Headquarters, 1st Battalion (Mechanized), 5th Infantry, "Memorandum for Commander, 3rd Brigade, 2nd Infantry Division, Subject: Incident of 19 October 1990," 22 October 1990.

15. "MACHA-TOC Operations and Reporting" to U.S. Department of the Army, Headquarters, 1st Battalion (Mechanized), 5th Infantry, *DMZ Battalion SOP*, 15 July 1990.

16. 2d Infantry Division, "VIP Briefing Text" and "Fire Support" in *DMZ Battalion SOP*, G-1-4 and J-1 to J-6. In October 1990, firing batteries rotated to 4P3 from the 2d Infantry Division's three direct support artillery battalions: 1st Battalion, 4th Field Artillery (155-mm, towed), 1st Battalion, 15th Field Artillery (155-mm, self-propelled), and 8th Battalion, 8th Field Artillery (155-mm, self-propelled).

17. "Patrolling—MACE Operations" in *DMZ Battalion SOP*, D-3-1.

18. "VIP Briefing Text" in ibid., G-1-5.

19. "DMZ Mission Changeover" in *DMZ Battalion SOP*, I-2-1 to I-2-6.

20. U.S. Department of the Army, Headquarters, 1st Battalion (Mechanized), 5th Infantry, "DMZ Tactics," (Camp Howze, Korea: 1-5th Infantry Divison, 15 December 1990) 1–10.

21. Ibid.

22. Ibid.

23. Joseph S. Bermudez Jr., *North Korean Special Forces* (Surrey, England: Jane's Publishing, 1988), 8, 26, 34, 63, 157.

24. Maj. Daniel P. Bolger, USA, "Statement of 4 June 1991" (Camp Casey, Korea: 4 June 1991), 1.

25. Ibid.

26. 1-5th Infantry, "DMZ Tactics," 1–10.

27. Sun Tzu, *The Art of War,* trans. and ed. Brig. Gen. Samuel B. Griffith, USMC (Oxford, England: Oxford University Press, 1963), 66.

28. "Patrolling" in *DMZ Battalion SOP,* D-1-C-1.

29. U.S. Department of the Army, United States Army Infantry School, *SH 21-77: Dismounted Patrolling* (Fort Benning, Ga.: U.S. Army Infantry School, 1985), 4-30 to 4-31.

30. John Williamson, ed., *Jane's Military Communications 1992–93* (Alexandria, Va.: Jane's Information Group, 1993), 119–20; U.S. Department of the Army, *Weapon Systems* (Washington, D.C.: U.S. Government Printing Office, 1 March 1991), 139. The full acronym is SINCGARS-V, single channel ground and airborne radio system, very high frequency. SINCGARS has been in use on the Korean DMZ since December 1987. DMZ units received priority when the radios were initially issued.

31. The account of operations on 19 October 1990 comes from 1-5th Infantry, "Incident of 19 October 1990" and enclosed TOC logs from the MACHA-TOC and the S2 section. For general background on the battalion, see also Headquarters, 1st Battalion (Mechanized), 5th Infantry, *DMZ Mission 1990* (Tongduchon, ROK: Yi Publishing, 1990), an unofficial yearbook-style photographic record of the battalion's DMZ mission.

32. 1-5th Infantry, "DMZ Tactics," 7, discusses the priority placed on well-trained battalion snipers.

33. Bolger, "Statement of 4 June 1991," 1. On 1 October 1991, 1-503d Infantry turned over the U.S. sector to the JSA Battalion, formally ending the 2d Infantry Division's DMZ mission. The JSA Battalion and ROK Army units have since subdivided the former U.S. sector to facilitate JSA work in and around Panmunjom. For a description of America's final days in the DMZ, see SSgt. William H. McMichael, USA, "The DMZ: Still Running Hot and Cold," *Soldiers* (September 1992): 18–20.

PART ONE

◆

"Operations Other Than War"

War is hell, but peacetime is a mother——.

> Heard among American soldiers, post-Vietnam

CHAPTER 1
A World of Hurt

"Peace, peace," they say, but there is no peace.

Jeremiah 6:14, the Bible

The United States Army really didn't know what to call the events that happened to the 1st Battalion (Mechanized), 5th Infantry, on 19 October 1990. You surely could not claim it as war if you limited your definition to replays of the Battle of the Bulge or the siege of Khe Sanh. But what else makes young soldiers go hunting for each other with loaded rifles? Whatever it was, it wasn't peace.

The American military has been wrestling with this problem for a long time. Situations like the DMZ have worn many labels over the years—emergency conditions, small wars, police actions, constabulary missions, stability operations, peacetime contingencies, low-intensity conflict, peacekeeping, peacemaking, peace enforcement—the struggle to name this ambiguous yet lethal phenomenon very much reflects its inherent frustrations. Although the title changes, the song remains the same.

In 1993, the American army, which bears the brunt of this challenge, introduced the latest attempt to identify this brand of conflict. Military writers settled on a phrase that tries to pin it down by saying what it is not. In the aptly numbered chapter 13 of the army's premier doctrinal work, *FM 100-5 Operations,* the service explains "operations other than war" (OOTW) as "minimizing the need for combat operations by defusing crises and nurturing peaceful resolution of contentious issues." The chapter then notes that OOTW "will not always be peaceful actions" and offers as examples counterdrug efforts, peacekeeping, noncombatant evacuations, and rescue raids,[1] all of which can entail a lot of fighting. When it looks like a duck, swims like a duck, and quacks like a duck, why does the army persist in calling this bird by other names?

Because it's a very unpleasant reality, you see. The American defense establishment has shown the foresight to deal with this prickly issue. But the military isn't quite sure what it's got here, even though they have been at it since the first European settlers began their tragic love-hate embrace with the American Indian peoples. Today's OOTW concept may sound inadequate, vague, or even a little silly, but it deserves a lot of respect. For the first time, the U.S. Army, and the U.S. armed forces in general, have publically acknowledged that combat smaller in scale than a World War II or Gulf War crusade deserves significant official attention. OOTW may not be the best term or set of ideas, but it's a start, however tentative.

Soldiers involved in OOTW know better. They soon revert to a less ambiguous view than those who compose field manuals. When you carry a loaded rifle, get shot at, lose buddies, and live under the threats and stresses that go with those developments, it's war, plain and simple. Fighting men learned long ago that the only bright line is the same as always: the frontier, the American border. Out past there lie the badlands, Indian country. Out there, you are automatically at war in what the drill sergeants call "a world of hurt." That is the world of today's U.S. armed forces.

That world has always been there, of course. Americans found it easy to ignore, eclipsed as it was by the looming, gargantuan bulk of the Soviet Communist menace. Busily watching and parrying the opportunistic Soviets, who stirred up plenty of mischief and pain outside their fortress empire, Americans sometimes mistook causes for effects. They thought Moscow was stirring the pot, when in fact the pot was pretty much stirring itself. And when the Russians went under, the lid blew off.

It wasn't supposed to turn out this way. When the Berlin Wall came down on a magical night in November 1989, some wise men figured that the world had changed forever, that universal peace had arrived. Intellectual Francis Fukuyama coined the phrase "the end of history,"[2] and he was not alone in that thought. Once the Union of Soviet Socialist Republics passed out of existence on Christmas day of 1991, the dawn of global concord seemed to be glowing at the eastern horizon. What we were seeing instead was the glare of fires down below.

Fueled by entrenched economic disparities, long-suppressed hatreds and old feuds burst up to the surface. The tense but definite borders of the Cold War gave way to waves of seemingly unlicensed violence. Much as we condemned the Iron and Bamboo Curtains, they and their heavy-handed masters kept many awful trends in check. Now most of the walls are down, and America is discovering that often, when you're the only builder left, floods are worse than dams.

The same American-led tide that swept away the USSR also just about finished off Karl Marx, father of scientific socialism. Except for Pyongyang, Beijing, and Havana, Marx has been relegated to the graduate school philosophy seminars where he probably always belonged. By all accounts a loathsome, lazy individual as well as a bad political theorist and economist, this ludicrous nineteenth-century curiosity deserved oblivion. Marx borrowed his concept of the dialectic (thesis against antithesis produce synthesis) from G. W. F. Hegel, a bona fide intellectual giant. He lifted his ideas on materialism from Franz Feuerbach. He begged his own material means from Friedrich Engels. A hypochondriac who never held a job in his life, he championed "the proletariat" but could not bear to rub elbows with his beloved masses.[3] He was, in most respects, a fraud.

So why were his ideas so popular? In short, Marxist thought has always been seductive because it revolves around one very real aspect of the human condition: the uneven distribution of material prosperity. That's an undeniable fact of life.

Marx argued that the class in power would always oppress and impoverish the masses on the bottom. But he did open the door to salvation, if only in a material sense, which was all that mattered to him anyway. Marxist scientific socialism offered comfort to the have-nots. Not only was poverty the result of evil exploitation by greedy overlords, it would, indeed must, pass away as a result of class struggle. The victims would ultimately triumph and so could take any steps, fair or foul, to encourage that final victory. "The philosophers," wrote Marx, "have only interpreted the world in various ways; the point, however, is to change it."[4]

Marx proved more of a thinker than a doer, but he got the ball rolling. A Russian attorney and minor nobleman's son named Vladimir Ilyich Ulyanov took the name Lenin, created a disciplined revolutionary party, grabbed the controls of the drifting hulk of Imperial Russia, and invented Soviet Russia. A Chinese schoolteacher named Mao Tse-tung organized a mass, peasant-based uprising that reunited and communized the once-great Middle Kingdom. Ho Chi Minh, Kim Il-sung, Fidel Castro, Maurice Bishop, Daniel

Ortega—in case after case, the men of action read their Marx and acted. Power to the people, they cried. Well, the people got their power, all right, usually in the form of jackboots smack in their amazed, slack-jawed faces.

Inspired and conquered by ruthless, determined revolutionaries, a good many people fell under the sway of various interpretations of Marx. Whole societies tried what passed for the bitter philosopher's somewhat nebulous methods. Dictatorial zealots slaughtered millions to hammer reality into conformity with some rather half-baked theories. Most of these grim social-ist experiments have imploded in recent years, though a few hang on, as if to remind us of the bad old days.

Americans must be wise enough not to celebrate too much when regard-ing the collapse of Marxism. The utter bankruptcy of scientific socialism only invalidates Marx's prescriptions, not his definition of the problem. Wealth remains concentrated in the hands of the few, about one billion out of the earth's five. Many suffer around this troubled planet. With or without the doctrinaire Soviet belief system, that reality creates problems for every country, but especially the current kingpin, the United States of America. As Marx warned, the underclass reflexively reviles those in power. He sure had that right.

Like the Roman Empire, the mighty Islamic Empire of the Umayyids, the Mongols under the Great Khans, or the British Empire under Queen Victoria, America today stands supreme over the known world. Ten centu-ries from now, historians studying our era will invariably color most of the globe blue (our map color) to depict the spread of American influence and power, as surely as red once marked the British tide and the Soviet sphere.

America dominates the Western Hemisphere (minus defiant, pathetic Cuba), the Pacific reaches, Australasia, and the littoral regions of Asia marked by Japan, South Korea, Taiwan, Singapore, and Thailand. The United States holds sway over Europe to the border of the former Soviet Union, as well as most of the Mediterranean. The richer, more important Middle Eastern countries defer to America, to include Saudi Arabia, Egypt, Israel, and Pakistan. Only China, India, Russia, the bulk of the Soviet suc-cessor states, rogues like Iraq and Iran, Libya, perhaps Syria, and most of restive Africa fall outside the U.S. orbit. Even so, Washington enjoys influ-ence in all of these areas.

Most Americans, not to mention most of the world, would object to this characterization. Many might charge that the United States is no empire, at least not in the classical sense. Beyond that, the majority of Americans do not acknowledge their preponderance of strength in this world. But, objections and details aside, America is a global empire and by far the most powerful state.

The objection that America is no empire represents a problem in perspective. Hardly any imperial power admits to what it has done; for the truth, ask those subjugated. Whether or not Americans intended this outcome, it exists, a consequence of the overwhelming power of the United States. Former Canadian Prime Minister Pierre Eliot Trudeau once remarked, "Living next to you is in some ways like sleeping with an elephant; no matter how friendly and even-tempered the beast, one is affected by every twitch and grunt."[5]

Other empires have also found themselves in this situation. The Romans marked their *limes,* their boundaries, with fortified walls in Great Britain and on the Danube, then tied it all together with their renowned roads—all in the name of the Senate and people of Rome. The emperors came later. At the height of imperial rule, however, only a few provinces were administered directly by Rome. Most areas were, in fact, ruled by locals in league with Rome, with Cleopatra of Egypt and Herod of Palestine coming immediately to mind. The Romans claimed they governed a republic with some associates and military holdings—this legal fiction persisted to the very end of the imperial period, with legions marching under standards marked "SPQR," *Senatus Populusque Romanum* (the Senate and people of Rome).[6] Yet the known Western world learned Latin, wore Roman dress, aped Roman styles, and even absorbed Roman perversions. It appears that most common people knew they formed an empire, whatever it called itself.

The British, although bombastically imperial by the last days of the nineteenth century, disdained a heavy hand. They also preferred indirect rule. The bloody nose they received in the American colonies convinced the British to work the local angles. Hence, those lands shaded red on the vast maps of the Kipling era were often officially dominions, allies, affiliates, associates, clients, or just unofficially affixed to the British orbit. The British seldom took direct charge. Instead, they planted garrisons and coaling stations, weaving a thin web of civil servants, railways, telegraphs, and sea-lanes that girdled the globe.[7] But in 1890, who except perhaps the testy powers of mainland Europe could doubt that London made the rules, spoke the language, and set the trends for much of the world?

America has done better than the Romans or British, and at far less cost to the homeland. Americans do have their overseas garrisons, far-flung fleets, and foreign aid, but, frankly, these are all secondary. Centurions and roads staked out the Roman world. Tommy Atkins and steamships built the British realm on which the sun never set. America won and keeps her predominance with regiments in smartly pressed blue suits and tasteful "power ties," peddling IBM computers, Big Macs, and MTV. And do not be fooled: the power generated is every bit as real.

American citizens who do not believe their own strength make the mistake of looking inward too much. There are plenty of problems at home, and these should not be discounted. Some challenges, such as race relations, social violence, educational shortcomings, and the breakdown of the traditional family, deserve significant attention. But reports of America's demise have been greatly exaggerated.

Looking outward, in comparison to the rest of the world, America stands as Gulliver among the Lilliputians. The United States boasts a gross domestic product in excess of $5 trillion, plus perhaps as much again hidden in overseas properties, multinational corporations, cooperative ventures, and other productive means. America's actual cumulative wealth, not just the yearly output, exceeds $17 trillion. This vast hoard, expanding daily, amounts to at least a quarter of the world's economic largess. America's 250 million people, though, represent only 5 percent of the planet's 5 billion.[8] Truly, Americans are blessed.

Comparative Statistics—Selected Countries
1992–93 Data

State	Area	Pop.	Lit.	Life	GDP	Govt.	Per cap.
Bangladesh	56	122	29%	55	20	15%	180
Brazil	3,286	156	76%	63	462	36%	3,090
Britain	94	58	99%	76	903	35%	15,535
Canada	3,849	27	99%	76	500	26%	19,020
China	3,696	1,100	75%	68	603	82%	547
Cuba	44	11	98%	73	29	95%	2,644
Egypt	387	55	45%	62	38	40%	700
El Salvador	8	6	65%	67	5	10%	940
Fiji	7	.7	80%	70	1	34%	1,540
France	220	58	99%	78	984	43%	17,830
Germany	138	82	99%	76	1,100	30%	18,000
Greece	51	10	96%	77	55	46%	5,840
Haiti	11	.7	23%	46	3	20%	440
Honduras	43	5	56%	67	5	16%	960

Comparative Statistics—Selected Countries
1992–93 Data
(Continued)

State	Area	Pop.	Lit.	Life	GDP	Govt.	Per cap.
India	1,266	903	36%	58	267	18%	321
Indonesia	735	197	62%	60	89	21%	479
Iraq	168	18	70%	66	35	50%	1,940
Israel	8	5	88%	74	52	44%	11,296
Japan	46	125	99%	79	2,100	17%	19,400
Kuwait	7	1	71%	74	21	31%	10,500
Mexico	762	90	88%	73	186	20%	2,170
New Zealand	104	3	99%	76	45	47%	13,100
Nigeria	357	95	43%	55	28	15%	239
North Korea	47	22	95%	70	30	89%	1,427
Pakistan	310	125	26%	57	37	24%	293
Philippines	116	67	88%	65	38	27%	667
Russia	6,478	149	99%	69	665	70%	4,463
Rwanda	10	8	50%	51	2	15%	310
Saudi Arabia	840	16	52%	65	73	30%	4,720
Somalia	246	7	12%	33	2	none	210
South Korea	38	44	95%	70	210	16%	4,920
Spain	195	39	97%	77	144	34%	11,400
United States	3,619	255	99%	76	5,300	24%	21,300

State   = name of state
Area   = in thousands of square miles
Pop.   = population in millions
Lit.   = percent of literate adults
Life   = life expectancy in years
GDP   = gross domestic product
Govt.   = government spending percentage of GDP
Per cap. = GDP per capita

Sources: U.S. Department of Commerce, *Statistical Abstract of the United States* (Washington, D.C.: U.S. Government Printing Office, 1993), 840–54. Numbers verified against The World Bank, *World Development Report 1992* (New York: Oxford University Press, 1992); *International Institute of Strategic Studies Military Balance 1992–93* (London: Brassey's, 1992); and John W. Wright, ed., *Universal Almanac 93* (Kansas City, Mo.: Andrews and McMeel, 1993). Statistics for lesser-developed countries are as reported by those governments.

Why is America so rich? It is worth a look, if only to explain why it will be so hard for likely competitors to match it. Things did not happen by accident. Although an envious Otto von Bismarck supposedly grumbled that "God protects fools, drunkards, and the United States of America,"[9] one could counter with the Protestant aphorism that the Deity helps those who help themselves. America's rise to greatness has been neither easy nor quick.

The United States's predominance results from many factors. The most important certainly include a sound political constitution, an unabashedly capitalist economy, and a vibrant, open society, all built on a continental scale. You cannot build a superpower in a clothes closet, and though America is not truly self-sufficient, its continental expanse, fourth largest in the world, offers resources that give it much more than most lands.

America possesses an impressive mix of agrarian productivity; mineral and biological wealth; the right mix of rivers, harbors, plains, and uplands to allow commerce; and a climate temperate enough to make production both possible and profitable. This treasure house, won by years of back-breaking labor and violent conflict, supports a fairly diverse populace, third largest among the world's states. Americans are numerous enough to stand tall on the world stage yet not so teeming as to overwhelm the physical resources of North America.

It took blood, sweat, and tears to create modern America, and anyone looking for a shortcut must be willing to go through the gut-wrenching changes represented by civil strife, social tensions, industrialization, urbanization, and conflicts at home and abroad, all spread across many uncertain decades. While working through this turmoil, the United States expanded to its continental limits, exploited its vast natural and human resources, and, in a crucial development, institutionalized means to resolve internal disputes.

That last point has allowed America to become, in Ben Wattenberg's memorable words, the "first universal nation."[10] Free speech, active courts, and an open political process give voice to most social concerns without need for violent revolt. Aside from the Revolutionary War, the Civil War represents the only massive internecine bloodbath. By comparison with most country's experiences, the tragic Indian wars or rioting in the late 1960s amount to footnotes. America, for the most part, welcomes the expansion of the talent pool represented by its diversity.

The emphasis on private property and advancement by merit has made the American businessman the standard-bearer of Yankee power worldwide.

Rather than trade following the flag, it has usually been vice versa. Today, the United States of America stations just under a half million military, foreign service, and aid agency people overseas. Compare that to almost eleven million Americans traveling overseas every year, two-thirds of them on business. Another two million or so American private citizens live permanently in foreign countries.[11] All of them buy, and many of them sell. These folks, not the Peace Corps volunteer or the U.S. Marine, become the faces of America to most of the global community.

By the standards of Cleveland or Atlanta, that should not be a problem. Most things in America are for sale, and the only criteria for business has often been legal tender. United States citizens often assume that their foreign counterparts understand and subscribe to American cultural norms, such as free speech, hard work, fair play, honest government, and the value of education. Such mistaken impressions come honestly to people who scoff at learning geography and assume that anyone can understand English spoken loudly and slowly enough. They are the conceits of an empire. We would have heard their like in the Roman Forum of A.D. 30 or in a London gentleman's club in 1885.

Free to bargain, buy, and sell, Americans suppose the same things about labor, goods, and services overseas, and they bring the dollars and know-how to get what they want. When industrial goods were the main needs, Ford Motor and U.S. Steel stepped up to the plate, selling and buying. Today, when information and entertainment appear to be in more demand, Silicon Valley and the Disney conglomerate have joined the lineup. Mickey Mouse, Coca-Cola, and Microsoft straddle the oceans, from New England to New Guinea. Consequences follow.

Military matters certainly bend to these developments. America's armed forces have become, in effect, security guards for America, Inc. When some of the millions of Americans living or traveling overseas get in trouble, the U.S. armed forces protect them or at least give it a try. They keep instability under control, to keep the airways open, the sea-lanes free, and the cash flow flowing. They guarantee relationships with key friends, clients, and allies. Finally, just to prove that Marx did not have everything right, they also put it on the line for American political ideals. It isn't all for dollars, which adds just enough unpredictability to Yankee behavior to drive adversaries to distraction.

Those foes just aren't what they used to be. Russia is a basket case, working hard simply to keep itself in one piece. The Russian nuclear threat

Americans Abroad

Residents	2,367,000
Business travelers	6,852,600
Tourists	3,805,000
Total private citizens	13,024,600
Armed forces	344,000
Other U.S. agencies	143,910
Total official U.S.	487,910

Sources: U.S. Department of Commerce, *Statistical Abstract of the United States* (Washington, D.C.: U.S. Government Printing Office, 1993), 357, 839; Don Mace and Eric Yoder, eds., *Federal Employees Almanac 1993* (Reston, Va.: Federal Employee News Service, 1993), 332; verified against United Nations, *1989 Demographic Yearbook* (New York: United Nations Press, 1991), 521.

now relates more to accidents or terrorism. Maintenance and reliability did not characterize most Soviet engineering, so much of the rocketry may well be impotent, and most of the nukes may be inert. Still, the danger cannot be wholly discounted.[12] If, however, thirty thousand warheads suddenly arced over the North Pole, what could America do anyway except pray and then radiate? Save for retaining a residual capacity to end the world, the Russians have essentially dropped off the screen.

The great bogeymen, Japan and Germany, barely come up to America's belt. Both amount to offshore subsidiaries of America, Inc., created to make and sell things in the USA. The former Axis powers have been hobbled by their moderately sized populations, medium-strength military forces, and lack of assured access to natural resources, not to mention the baggage of aggressive, nationalistic excesses during World War II. None of those aspects appears likely to change in the foreseeable future.

Britain and France rank just behind the Japanese and Germans. These medium powers have more military strength and more will to use it than Germany or Japan, but they share the same population and resource limits. They cannot be discounted, but, frankly, they have had their day.

All four countries will stay where they are in the power rankings because they are coloring inside some pretty narrow lines, at least by U.S. standards. Careers there are not always open to talents, and prejudices exist by law. Thus, all have stable or declining populations, and none welcome the new blood and ideas of immigrants. Few would envy the third-class citizen status of a Turk in Bonn, an Algerian in Paris, a Pakistani in London, or any foreigner in xenophobic Tokyo.[13] Repulsive though such attitudes might be in Vermont or Ohio, such policies and beliefs suit those countries' traditions and cultures.

Once below Russia, Japan, Germany, Britain, and France, the field opens considerably. China certainly has the potential to turn into something, as do India and, to a greater extent, Brazil. Perhaps one of them will be America's successor as leader of the world. But it won't happen soon. China's Communist legacy and huge populace, India's ethnic strife and population pressures, and Brazil's relative poverty and illiteracy all prove formidable obstacles to progress.

The other developed powers seem content to continue drafting in the wake of the American leviathan. Many of them, such as Canada, Italy, the Scandinavian countries, and the Republic of Korea, have played important roles on the world stage. But in the greater scheme, they serve as utility infielders to the American sultan of swat.

Farther down the food chain, it gets really ugly. In the old days, one referred to America and its allies as the First World, the Communist bloc as the Second World, and the rest, including the unhappy castoffs of European empires, as the Third World. Some call them the South (they tend to be located on or south of the equator), less-developed countries, underdeveloped countries, nonaligned countries, or simply minor states. It doesn't matter what you call them. Indeed, for most of these hapless polities, the best thing to call would be 911.

Two examples will suffice. Somalia, which became a thorn in the sides of two American presidents, offers a particularly bad case. The average Somalian gets by on $210.00 a year. Only 12 percent can read or write. Their country has been at war for nearly twenty years. Is it any wonder they turn to the grenade and rifle?

Look at El Salvador, for years a U.S. ally. Again, the pattern applies. The usual salary totals $940.00 annually. Nearly 35 percent cannot read or write. And the country has been wracked by guerrilla warfare and government repression for fifteen years. The prospects for Jeffersonian democratic capitalism look dim indeed.

By way of comparison, let's equate some of the larger American multinational concerns with countries: Haiti made $3 billion in 1992; Hershey Corporation made almost three on chocolate bars and the like. Rwanda made $2 billion; Land o' Lakes made more.[14] It's a depressing litany.

1992 Sales for Selected Fortune 500 Corporations

Company	Sales
American Standard	3.5
Apple Computer	6.3
Avon Products	3.6
Campbell Soup	6.2
Coca-Cola	12.0
General Electric	60.0
General Motors	124.0
Gillette	5.0
Hershey	2.9
IBM	64.0
J. E. Seagram	3.6
Land o' Lakes	2.4
Liz Claiborne	2.0
Maytag	3.0
Pepsico	19.7
Proctor and Gamble	27.0
Quaker Oats	6.1
Reader's Digest	2.3
Sara Lee	12.0
Xerox	17.0

Sales are recorded in billions of dollars.

Source: John W. Wright, ed., *Universal Almanac 93* (Kansas City, Mo.: Andrews and McMeel, 1993), 262–63.

Even the American poor, by no means living well in contemporary society, would be among the gentry by the standards of most countries. Of America's poor, 40 percent own their own homes, with an average house worth $46,600. Some 60 percent own at least one automobile, enjoy air-conditioning, and cook in microwave ovens. According to U.S. government data, the poverty line starts at $7,143 for a single person, or $14,335 for a family of four. Americans at the poverty line outpace the average earnings of the typical citizen in Greece and South Korea, which are not Third World countries.[15]

You get the picture. One hesitates to look at more than a hundred unique disasters and then blithely generalize, but the similarities among these sad situations demand comment. Many of these places would not even be countries except for certain European colonial agreements late in the last century. Cursed with borders set by others, burdened by crushing poverty, ill health, medieval religions, ethnic and tribal blood feuds, and unrelieved ignorance, it is no wonder that many such states lurch desperately from dictator to junta to revolution, with damn little relief for the poor people at the bottom.

And then into this comes the Yankee trader, Brooks Brothers coat over his shoulders, Apple Macintosh Power Book in his fine leather briefcase, Daytimer scheduler open, shining Cross pen poised. He peddles jobs, services, loans, and opportunities in local ventures, often at wages far better than those offered by a Third World state's own businesses, though the salaries range well below U.S. levels. His advertising, music, sports, television, and movies depict a universe of glamor and violence, awash with material plentitude. The aggressive business traveler offers the locals McDonald's Big Macs, MTV and Michael Jackson, Chevrolet Cavaliers, Trane air conditioners, and the like. The prices are just about the same, of course, from Waterloo, Iowa, to Bombay, India. When you earn $30,000 a year, a Big Mac is lunch. When you earn $30, it's an investment. But that doesn't mean you don't want it.

As the owner of the emporium, the United States collects its fees and quitrents as it can, overseas tax shelters being what they are. Because all American individuals enjoy civil rights, and under legal interpretations corporations have been designated individuals, the U.S. government makes few attempts to regulate overseas business activities, no more than it would tell tourists which towns to visit. To elected leaders in Washington, D.C., smaller countries' complaints about American business excesses amount to personal problems.

America often says it wants stability in the world community. Out in the badlands, stability equates to a lopsided status quo: one billion Americans and their Western retainers rich, four billion poor. The last thing those four billion want is more stability, nor do many wish to go through the decades of dislocation pioneered in Europe, Japan, and North America while the rich get richer off in the distance. Most people on the globe demand change, and they want it now.

Supreme atop this world of hurt, the United States enjoys most of the benefits of empire and few of the responsibilities. It's extremely remunerative for the 250 million lucky enough to live in the United States. In many quarters, though, Americans are perceived as global slumlords, taking in the rent and giving back—well, not much, and all of it with a price tag attached. Is it any wonder that at Uncle Sam's global shopping mall, the customers are seldom pleased and the security guards are always busy?

Incredible and largely intractable economic disparity typifies the suspicious states of today's world, but this is hardly the only problem. The others feed on material distress and increase material deprivation.

Population stresses certainly overburden underdeveloped countries. The American empire has given them vaccines and the Green Revolution in farming to keep them alive, but their poor states cannot absorb the millions that need to be sustained. Nigeria, Indonesia, India, and Bangladesh exemplify many countries groaning under the crush of their own teeming populace.[16]

It is easy to sit in a television studio in Washington and pontificate about the importance of birth control, but that doesn't play well in small villages in Chad or Honduras, where children often offer one of the few joys in a hard life, not to mention much-appreciated additional labor. So the babies keep coming, and, thanks to the World Health Organization and better crops, they survive in greater numbers than at any time in history. Most can look forward to a grim hand-to-mouth existence, underemployed in decrepit, semisocialist economies or scratching out a living by handiwork and agriculture techniques akin to those of Medieval Europe. Encouraged by ubiquitous advertising, they long for a better life. Not surprisingly, desperation breeds violence. The AK-47 becomes very attractive.

Ethnic and religious disputes follow, and these represent Third World growth industries. Nationalism, the belief that each ethnic group deserves its own state, has become especially virulent. It may appear strange that wretchedly poor peoples would waste their few treasures and already tenuous lives battling to carve unviable microstates out of the hide of all too shaky countries. But to participants, this sort of thing promises relief from their miseries. If they succeed, they think that their new polity will make up in homogeneity what it lacks in resources. The intermixing of diverse minority peoples in most regions dooms these efforts to conflict and frustration. Even Stalin, Hitler, and Pol Pot couldn't kill everyone, nor will ethnic cleansers. That's not to say they won't try.

Religious confessional splits parallel ethnic violence. Sophisticated Manhattanites may find the distinctions between Sunni and Shiite Muslims quaint, or consider Orthodox and Catholic Christians pretty much the same ilk. A few more subscriptions to the *New York Times,* a couple of wine and cheese mixers, and this could all be cleaned up. So some think.

Out in the wider world, these are not trivial issues but life and death itself. The best example of this, and the starkest, stems from Islam. A proselytizing religion since the seventh century, Islam offers a simple and uncompromising road to salvation. For the downtrodden and bitter, Islam confronts MTV and *Rambo* with traditional belief and offers an alternative for those frightened and confused by the overwhelming nature of American socioeconomic influences. If you believe, say Muslims, all will come out right. Science, money, and firepower do not count.

While this may be true for personal salvation, Islam's determined adherence to tradition does not square with the political and economic license necessary for modernity. Islam requires certainty and constancy, not the accommodation of change and questioning endemic to the scientific dictates of industrialized culture. Islam includes a billion people worldwide, and it is fundamentally opposed to many core American beliefs.[17] Saudi sheiks and Egyptian presidents may cut deals with Washington, but they dare not embrace America too much. Anwar Sadat, killed by Islamic radicals for cozying up too much to Uncle Sam, could attest to that.[18]

While it's tempting, one should not view the Muslim movement as some sort of desert-born successor to Communism, or as the ultimate threat to life on earth.[19] Indeed, the Muslims are just the most obvious of a variety of folks with similar problems. Any critiques of Islam as hostile to modernity apply in spades to those ensnared in traditional Christianity (in all its warring sects), Hinduism, Confucian philosophies of social order, and various other beliefs. The popularity of these traditional faiths and philosophies reflects the outright rejection of American culture. The more the lesser-developed countries see of Hollywood and Wall Street, the less they like it. It's not rational, it just is.

American ideals of ethnic and religious tolerance, barely honored in most of the industrialized countries, fall on deaf ears among the wretched of the earth. As the Bible said, for those with little, what little they have will be taken from them. Worse, they will shoot it downrange or blow it up in the name of tribal loyalties and jealous gods.

Thanks to modern technology, the world's troublemakers do not lack for means to kill each other. During the Cold War, the Soviets and, to a lesser extent, the Americans flooded the Third World with weapons and ammunition. Both armed allies, surrogates, and proxies to the teeth. A lot of those armaments remain in use, often under new ownership and sometimes targeted at the original supplier.

The two giants first unloaded their remaining World War II arsenals, then more modern equipment as the Cold War dragged on. The pattern for most weapons saw them migrate from frontline service to reserve components and finally to allies, friends, and paying customers. Certain special items, such as the American F-5 Freedom Fighter and the Soviet T-72 "monkey model" tank, were custom-built for export.[20] Other new equipment, such as the American F-4 Phantom or Soviet MiG-29, was offered almost immediately to selected allies. Warships, jet fighters, machine guns, radios, radars— all but the hottest items were made available for cash or for free, depending upon how much the superpower valued the client.

When allies clash or today's friends become tomorrow's enemies, all of the arms dealings can create very strange situations. America sold the light cruiser USS *Phoenix* to Argentina, which renamed it the *General Belgrano* and employed it in 1982 against America's British allies as they retook the Falkland Islands. Both fundamentalist Islamic Iran and the Socialist Republic of Vietnam, implacable foes of Uncle Sam, use American tanks, aircraft, and artillery inherited from the doomed shah and the liquidated Saigon government. In fact, the USS *Vincennes,* working with a battle group that included U.S. Navy F-14 Tomcats, engaged an Iranian civil airliner that it mistook for an attacking Iranian F-14 Tomcat. Given that America shipped out 1,947 armored vehicles and 171 combat aircraft in 1992 alone, some to states of dubious leanings and solidity, there will only be more of this.[21]

Not that the Soviets helped matters. Along with the wicked Kalashnikov automatic rifles that serve as the symbol for revolution worldwide, during the Cold War years the Russians sold or gave away some thirty-one thousand tanks.[22] Though numbers of these are now busily tearing off strips of the old Leninist state, a good many can be found on duty with the minor countries of the world. Libya disposes more than 4,700 armored fighting vehicles, Syria maintains 7,800, Ethiopia has 1,750, North Korea keeps 7,500, and Iraq had built a park of 11,750 tracked combat vehicles prior to Desert Storm.[23] The tanks represent the tip of the steel iceberg of weapons sent out from Soviet factories and now at work across the restive continents.

These massive conventional arsenals are bad enough, but the Soviets proved liberal with even more horrifying stuff. Moscow gave out a good bit of her ballistic missile and toxic chemical technologies. This is why

Arms Sales—Sellers
1992

State	Amount
United States	9.7
Russia	6.8
Britain	2.6
France	2.0
China	1.3
Germany	.3

Arms Sales—Buyers
1992

State	Amount
Taiwan	10.7
Saudi Arabia	4.5
Iran	3.7
Egypt	1.9
India	1.9
Israel	1.5
Indonesia	1.4
Kuwait	1.4
Iraq	1.4
Cuba	1.3
China	1.1
Malaysia	1.0
Myanmar	.9
UAE	.9
Singapore	.6
Syria	.5
Thailand	.5

All figures in billions of dollars.

Sources: Richard F. Grimmitt, "Arms Trade with the Third World," *International Defense Review: Defense '92* (Surrey, England: Jane's Information Group, 1991), 57–59; "International Arms Sales: Race to Disaster," *The Defense Monitor* (September 1993): 1–7.

America now confronts the prospect of a North Korean atomic bomb or Baghdad launching chemically armed rockets. These people may have also discovered the joys of cooking up gruesome biological weapons: anthrax, Q fever, botulinum, ebola fever, Red Tide poison, and tularemia, plus old favorites like cholera, smallpox, and the Black Plague.[24] One can hardly wait to see some annoyed dictator unleash these gremlins.

Proliferation of such nightmares and most conventional arms continues, heedless of America's best efforts. The Communist cave-in made only a little difference. Russians and Chinese need cash, and they don't make Big Macs.

Throwing all of these shooting irons into the global witches' brew of crushing poverty, exploding populations, and long-standing ethnic and religious feuds makes for real trouble. International agencies squabble about the exact count, but the authoritative *Journal of Peace Research* counted fifty-one wars raging in 1992.[25] Those who would enforce Pax Americana have their work cut out.

Americans have taken on that burden, however reluctantly. If the U.S. citizenry and their industrialized associates were truly the heartless, decadent moguls envisioned by the likes of Franz Fanon, they would simply rape the labor and resources of the weaker states and laugh all the way to the bank. The Communists always made that argument.

In slavishly adhering to Marxist dogma, they missed something important. The same political and economic freedoms that brought America to planetary prominence urge Americans to do something to help the rest of the world. Unfortunately, there is no easy solution to economic disparity.

Even if America and its fellow modern countries could somehow distribute all of their largess to the other four billion people on the globe, the net increase per individual would be one four-thousand-dollar payment a year—hardly a king's ransom. Depleting the Western countries seems logical only in a zero-sum world economy, which obviously is not the case. Wealth does grow over time. A thousand years ago, the concept that 20 percent of the planet, totaling a billion people, might live like nobles would have seemed utterly unthinkable. Ten centuries from now, most of the world may enjoy the equivalent of an American middle-class lifestyle. It's small comfort to today's serfs and villeins, of course.

Until then, Americans do what they can. Like the Romans with roads and aqueducts and the British with literacy and railroads, Americans are creating a legacy to their far-flung empire. United States government policies and private citizen and corporate initiatives have already created a better life for billions worldwide, with everything from medicines to hybrid seeds to computers. Direct U.S. government foreign aid in 1993 alone totaled $16 billion, no mean sum. America has bequeathed nearly $390 billion since 1945.[26] The American track record, both government and private, has been extraordinarily generous. But in light of the extreme economic gulf between the rich and the poor in the world, these undertakings receive little credit. They aren't ever refused, though.

Capitalist economic power, the product of a multiplicity of discrete individual activities, does not easily assist other states. Military power does. Since rising to world dominance, Americans have often thought of others first, many times to the detriment of their own best long-term interests (consider Vietnam). In this century, Americans have done most of their bleeding and dying for others.

The Soviet collapse ended the last major threat to American survival, just as the fall of Carthage and the end of Napoleonic France removed the primary menaces to Republican Rome and nineteenth-century Britain respectively. Like these mighty empires, the United States employs its armed forces for three purposes: to protect American lives, to protect American property, and to advance American principles. The Romans and British followed the same triad, but they stressed the first two. Those preoccupy Americans too—but that third one has a powerful hold, a reflection, perhaps, of the country's original revolutionary heritage.

Over time, as its power has burgeoned, the United States has become far more willing to send its ships, planes, and battalions into action for abstract ideals like freedom and democracy. Even in the world wars, the American response far exceeded any real threat to the country. Americans liberate countries without very many strings attached. They rebuild former enemies—witness Japan and Germany. Marxists see dark economic conspiracies at work, but that is often quite a stretch. It applied in Kuwait in 1990, but certainly not in Korea in 1950, the Dominican Republic in 1965, or Somalia in 1992. Often, Americans go in merely because they are asked.

The minor countries perceive this. That explains why the same governments that routinely decry American "neocolonialism" and "economic imperialism" look to Washington for leadership in crises. Common folk scan the sky for American aircraft or look out to sea for U.S. ships when natural or man-made trouble strikes. Along with Islam, Confucian tradition,

World Conflicts 1992

Location	UN Involved	U.S. Involved	Non-UN Peacekeepers
Afghanistan	No	No	No
Algeria	No	Yes	No
Angola	Yes	No	No
Azerbaijan	No	No	Proposed (Russia)
Bangladesh	No	Yes	No
Burundi	No	No	No
Cambodia	Yes	Yes	No
Chad	No	Yes	No
Colombia	No	Yes	No
Cyprus	Yes	Yes	No
Djibouti	No	Yes	Yes (France)
El Salvador	Yes	Yes	No
Egypt	No	Yes	Yes (MFO)
Ethiopia	No	No	No
Georgia	Yes	Yes	No
Guatemala	No	Yes	No
Haiti	Yes	Yes	No
India (internal)	No	Yes	No
India-Pakistan	Yes	No	No
Indonesia	No	Yes	No
Iran	No	No	No
Iraq	Yes	Yes	No
Iraq-Kuwait	Yes	Yes	No
Israel-Palestine	Yes	Yes	Yes
North-South Korea	Yes	Yes	No
Laos	No	No	No
Lebanon	Yes	Yes	No
Liberia	Proposed	Yes	Yes (ECOMOG)
Moldova	No	No	Yes (Russia)
Morocco	Yes	Yes	No
Mozambique	Yes	No	No
Myanmar	No	No	No
Niger	No	Yes	No
Northern Ireland	No	No	No
Papua New Guinea	Proposed	Yes	No
Peru	No	Yes	No
Philippines	No	Yes	No

World Conflicts 1992
(Continued)

Location	UN Involved	U.S. Involved	Non-UN Peacekeepers
Rwanda	Yes	Yes	Yes (OAU)
Senegal	No	Yes	No
Sierra Leone	No	Yes	No
Somalia	Yes	Yes	No
South Africa	Proposed	Possible	No
Spain	No	No	No
Sri Lanka	Proposed	Yes	No
Sudan	Proposed	Possible	No
Tadzhikistan	No	No	Proposed (Russia)
Togo	Proposed	Yes	No
Turkey	No	Yes	No
Venezuela	No	Yes	No
Former Yugoslavia	Yes	Yes	No
Zaire	Proposed	Yes	No

MFO = Multinational Force and Observers
ECOMOG = Economic Community of West African States Cease-fire Monitoring Group
OAU = Organization of African Unity

Sources: Peter Wallenstein and Karin Axell, "Armed Conflict at the End of the Cold War," *Journal of Peace Research* (August 1993): 336–45; U.S. Central Intelligence Agency, *Worldwide Peacekeeping Operations, 1993* (Springfield, Va.: National Technical Information Service, 1993).

and virulent nationalism, this more rational version of the South Seas cargo cult thrives in many countries—and well it should.

Giving away CARE packages and money only goes so far, and the United States does not put its faith in these kinds of international welfare programs. Because the American republican government is a limited entity, it cannot do much to direct its muscular, disparate, privately owned and administered economic strength. So how does Washington work its will on a planet of unruly, suspicious, and unhappy smaller states?

Not surprisingly, the United States has long promoted "collective secu-rity," the idea that strong ties between countries can permit the same sort of legal, procedural conflict resolution that keeps social order in America.[27] This favored solution, in line with American political ideals, proposes that all governments are equal under the international regime: one state, one vote, if you will. Another way to look at it, according to American business practices, might be to consider collective security as a stock offering. All of the shareholders will make an investment, have a voice, and reap dividends, but the majority holders in America will invest the most, speak the loudest, and garner the greatest benefits.

Collective security worked fairly well in both world wars, when America joined formal alliances already at war against obvious threats. It also made sense in the Cold War, as epitomized by NATO (North Atlantic Treaty Or-ganization), and less successful imitators like the late, unlamented SEATO (Southeast Asia Treaty Organization) and CENTO (Central Treaty Organi-zation). America has supplemented many of these long-term bonds with bilateral ties to strong allies like Japan, Israel, the Republic of Korea, and, in a renowned "special relationship" with the estranged mother country, Great Britain.

The United States has also built successful ad hoc coalitions to meet specific challenges.[28] America assembled and led triumphant international teams in the Dominican Republic in 1965, the Sinai Multinational Force peacekeeping effort in 1981, Grenada in 1983, and the war to free Kuwait in 1990. One might mention as well the ones that failed: the free world ef-fort in Vietnam or the abortive Lebanon multinational effort of 1982–84, for example. For a people warned by George Washington to beware "entangling alliances," Americans have certainly come a long way.

But what about collective security absent a defined enemy? Between the world wars, and today after the Cold War, collective security becomes a more ambiguous proposition. NATO supposedly proves that collective se-curity encourages stability, and stability permits economic growth. Ameri-cans like that, and so do the other developed countries. The other four-fifths of the earth's people tend to think otherwise. After all, NATO unified the efforts of the haves, countries with a substantial common political, eco-nomic, and cultural heritage. Whatever its virtues as a military alliance— and they are debatable—NATO has forged strong economic ties between its European members, Canada, and America. That appears to be the great side benefit of collective security.

Whatever terrific things it has done for its members' economies, NATO's strength and vitality as a political and military system has been greatly exaggerated. Discord has been significant, with each member throwing its weight around on occasion. Greece and Turkey went to war and are still bitter foes. The French have always cut their own course. Countries refuse basing and overflight rights for unapproved missions: the Netherlands and Belgium denied landing rights for American cargo aircraft bound for Israel in 1973, and France made U.S. aircraft go around its airspace to attack Libya in 1986.

Most of the NATO powers have proven enthusiastic only about defending themselves. Out-of-area operations have been restricted to exercises and token deployments or efforts not under the NATO banner. Korea, Vietnam, the Falklands, and the Gulf War involved NATO members, but the alliance stayed home.

NATO's ability to defend Europe can also be doubted. Its armed forces have always featured a bizarre pastiche of mixed doctrine, weaponry, and skill, speaking a dozen distinct tongues. Only Soviet qualms about nuclear Armageddon prevented the beating this heterogeneous outfit really deserved.[29] Without American nuclear weapons, the whole house of cards would have blown away decades ago. Europe's defense began in concrete missile silos in places like Minot, North Dakota, not on the north German plain or in the Fulda Gap.

In sum, NATO was always willing to fight to the last American, and that remains so. If America will not join in a big way, NATO does not act. The bleeding wound of Bosnia demonstrates that. We should not be surprised when NATO's squabbling, poverty-stricken analogs in Asia, South America, the Middle East, and Africa also fumble most of the balls tossed their way. To the lesser-developed countries, NATO merely gathers the usual suspects, and the alliance's unwillingness to bring in new Eastern European states or resolve the mess in Yugoslavia indicates that such treaty organizations might not be worth the pain.

America works hard to convert these skeptical pauper states to the virtues of collective security. The United States treats her moderate to puny fellow countries with far more deference and decency than most deserve. Given its massive strength, Washington could bulldoze its allies and associates into acquiescence. Instead, it negotiates with these countries as equals, which they most certainly are not. But that political equality goes some way toward soothing the envy generated by vast economic disparities.

This sort of thing reaches its logical conclusion in the United Nations, a monument to America's passion for collective security. The UN General Assembly represents one state, one vote run riot, with those four billion have-nots only too willing to try to direct America to do all sorts of things.

Yet the UN lacks teeth, even in its vaunted Security Council centered on America, Russia, China, Britain, and France. The UN can only enforce what its constituent states allow it to enforce. It has no troops or money of its own, except as donated by the membership. The General Assembly resembles the local high school's student council—plenty of blather and great fun but hardly to be taken seriously. These days, the UN gets serious only when America gets serious about UN matters.

Americans regarded the UN as a bad joke during most of its history. After some initial enthusiasm, peaking in the UN Korean intervention of 1950, the United States pretty much turned its back on the world body during most of the Cold War. The Soviet Union, singing from the Karl Marx hymnal, enlisted the swelling Third World choir in battering Uncle Sam for the crime of being exceedingly wealthy.

But now Red Russia has disintegrated, and America has developed a renewed interest in the idealistic appeal of UN-led collective security, or "collective engagement" and "enlargement," as Presidents George Bush and Bill Clinton call it.[30] If the UN and world government ever work, Americans will have made it so at the cost of their own sovereignty. No wonder UN headquarters is in New York City.

American collective security after the Cold War focuses on the United Nations, in a way trying to "NATOize" the globe. But the other 80 percent of the world endures many more problems than NATO. Simply keeping order will be quite an undertaking.

The UN has done some minor, unimpressive peacekeeping work over the decades. After getting badly burned in the American-engineered United Nations' decision to enter the Korean War, the old Soviet Union inculcated the belief that superpowers should not intervene to keep the peace among battling states. The United Nations blue berets hailed primarily from smaller countries and neutrals, with the Canadians, Scandinavians, Irish, Pakistanis, and Fijians as typical contributors. These observer missions came in only with the consent of the warring parties, in accord with Chapter 6 of the UN Charter. Their good intentions merited the 1988 Nobel Peace Prize, but UN peacekeeping always promised more than it delivered. In cases like Cyprus and the Congo, the UN merely created more versions of the Korean DMZ. Often, as in Lebanon, the peacekeepers failed outright.[31]

The collapse of the USSR and the coincident success of the UN-sanctioned war to liberate Kuwait made the United States anxious to buttress and expand United Nations operations. President Clinton, described by his National Security Adviser Anthony Lake as a pragmatic neo-Wilsonian, encouraged this sort of thing, at least up to a point. The goal involves creating enough stability in war-torn areas to permit countries to develop politically and economically.[32] Woodrow Wilson and Franklin D. Roosevelt would have been proud.

Led by the activist Secretary General Boutros Boutros-Ghali of Egypt, the UN acted on the Bush-Clinton initiative. The organization rapidly expanded its peace enforcement operations.[33] America joined these efforts, and for the first time since the Korean War, substantial U.S. forces served under the baby blue and white United Nations ensign. Thanks to American backing, the UN has never been more powerful.

Energized by the potential of American power, the world body started carrying out operations under Chapter 7 of its charter, which are actual peacemaking interventions to restore order inside a country, with or without local consent. Finnish General T. Hagglund, former commander of the moribund United Nations Interim Force in Lebanon (UNIFIL), noted that "an intention to deter or frighten requires forces which are as frightening as possible. For this kind of mission, great-power battalions, professional soldiers and all the means at their disposal, are preferable."[34]

Even though Bush and Clinton encouraged the UN to commence operations along this line, America proved unwilling to plunge full-bore into these dicey situations. UN attempts without America in the lead, such as Bosnia, Somalia, and initially in Haiti, have been uniformly disappointing. Like America's NATO allies, Boutros-Ghali and the others in his Turtle Bay headquarters try to lean on the United States to do the really tough jobs.

If it hopes to succeed in the newly assertive role, the UN will need a massive American commitment. Right now, the UN lacks the structure to plan and direct simultaneous far-flung combat operations designed to restore order in the places wracked by the globe's fifty-odd conflicts. Only America, and to a lesser extent Britain and France, really have much current expertise in these operations.[35]

That, in essence, underlies the American public's disquiet about placing U.S. troops "under UN command." Of course, America fought the Korean

Peacekeeping Operations
1993

Location	Operation	Established	Size	U.S. Role
Angola	UNAVEM II	1992	105	funding
Cambodia	UNTAC	1992	21,100	observers
Cyprus	UNFICYP	1964	1,529	funding*
El Salvador	UNOSAL	1991	397	funding*
Georgia	UNOMIG	1993	88	funding*
Haiti	UNMIH	1993	1,637	observers*
India-Pakistan	UNMOGIP	1948	38	funding*
Israel	UNTSO	1947	244	observers*
North-South Korea	UNC	1950	855,000	forces*
Kuwait	UNIKOM	1991	333	observers*
Lebanon	UNIFIL	1978	5,242	funding*
Liberia	UNOMIL	1993	300	funding*
Moldova	Russian	1992	1,500	none
Mozambique	UNOMOZ	1992	6,498	funding
Rwanda	UNOMUR	1993	30	funding*
Egypt (Sinai)	MFO	1982	2,100	forces*
Somalia	UNOSOM II	1993	28,000	forces
Syria	UNDOF	1974	1,121	funding
Western Sahara	MINURSO	1990	330	observers*
Ex-Yugoslavia	UNPROFOR	1992	24,882	forces*

United Nations Command (UNC) in Korea is a belligerent, and thus not formally considered to be conducting peacekeeping operations. U.S. forces entered Haiti and Rwanda in 1994.

U.S. roles:
  Funding—the U.S. provides 31.7 percent of the funding for each UN-sponsored operation.
  Observers—individuals assigned to peacekeeping missions.
  Forces—sions.

*U.S. military assistance agreements with one or more parties to the conflict (sales, grants, stationing, training, and/or exercises).

Sources: U.S. Central Intelligence Agency, *Worldwide Peacekeeping Operations, 1993* (Springfield, Va.: National Technical Information Service, 1993).

War under UN authority, and John Mitchell and his men still flew the UN flag at Guard Posts Ouellette and Collier. Indeed, U.S. forces have served under foreigners since Yorktown in 1781, to include both world wars. Germans, British, and South Koreans, among others, commanded Americans during the Cold War period. But there are foreigners and there are foreigners.

To date, Americans have been led only by those foreign leaders who represented allied states at a similar level of development. The Congress and people can accept that. What scares them is the idea that some befuddled Third World soldier, used to parading his thousand-man palace guard of an army, might end up trying to direct U.S. Marine landings or a naval carrier battle group's evolutions. In the UN, that sort of blunt thinking represents Yankee imperialism, racism, and ethnocentrism (as if America was a single ethnicity or race). If America truly signs on for one state, one vote, it should accept a task force commander from sub-Saharan Africa or Latin America. But that will rarely happen, and only when it doesn't matter.

More likely, America will continue its pattern from the Cold War, using its collective security arrangements when those work, building unique new ones if possible, going it alone when that makes sense. As President Clinton said during his 1992 campaign, "Our motto in this era must be 'together where we can, but on our own where we must.'"[36] Either way, and in all the gray shades in between, America's armed forces remain fully engaged beyond the frontier, reluctant legions for a reluctant empire.

Notes

1. U.S. Department of the Army, *FM 100-5 Operations* (Washington, D.C.: U.S. Government Printing Office, 1993), 13-2 to 13-3.

2. Francis Fukuyama, *The End of History and the Last Man* (New York: Free Press, 1992).

3. Edmund Wilson, *To the Finland Station* (New York: Harcourt, Brace, 1940), 112–345. Among writers on Marx, only the hard-core leftist hagiographers ignore his unsavory characteristics and behavior.

4. Karl Marx, "Theses on Feuerbach" in David McLellan, ed., *Karl Marx: Selected Writings* (Oxford, England: Oxford University Press, 1977), 158.

5. Lawrence Martin, *The Presidents and the Prime Ministers* (Toronto, Ontario: Doubleday Canada, 1982), 241. Trudeau said this on 25 March 1969 at a press conference held in Washington, D.C., during meetings with President Richard M. Nixon.

6. Albert A. Nofi, "The Fall of Rome," *Strategy and Tactics* (July–August 1973): 4–21.

7. Byron Farwell, *Mr. Kipling's Army* (New York: W. W. Norton, 1981), 11–22.

8. U.S. Department of Commerce, *Statistical Abstract of the United States* (Washington, D.C.: U.S. Government Printing Office, 1993), 555, 840–54. This official government source records American-owned multinational corporate sales as $3.2 trillion in 1990. Interestingly, foreign investment in American corporations totaled $1.4 trillion in that same year.

9. This quote may be apocryphal, although it is in line with several other sarcastic anti-American comments made by German Chancellor Otto von Bismarck throughout his lifetime.

10. Ben J. Wattenberg, *The First Universal Nation* (New York: Free Press, 1991); Samuel Huntington, "The Clash of Civilizations," *Foreign Affairs* (Summer 1993): 40. Indian-born intellectual V. S. Naipaul refers to the American-led West as a "universal civilization" that "fits all men."

11. Department of Commerce, *Statistical Abstract,* 357, 839; Don Mace and Eric Yoder, *Federal Employees Almanac 1993* (Reston, Va.: Federal

Employee News Service, 1993), 332; United Nations, *1989 Demographic Yearbook* (New York: United Nations Press, 1991), 521.

12. International Institute for Strategic Studies, *Military Balance 1982–93* (London: Brassey's, 1992), 92–93; "Ukraine Warned Its Missiles Need Care," *Washington Times,* 6 November 1993.

13. For a fuller development of these ideas, see Wattenberg, *First Universal Nation.*

14. John W. Wright, ed., *Universal Almanac 93* (Kansas City, Mo.: Andrews and McMeel, 1993), 262–63.

15. Ken Adelman, "Poor Data Yields Misleading Report on Poor," *Washington Times,* 8 October 1993.

16. Department of Commerce, *Statistical Abstract,* 840–54. Bangladesh hosts 2,178 persons per square mile, India has 713. By comparison, the United States has 70 persons per square mile.

17. Ibid., 69. The world's largest religious strain, Christianity, includes 1.8 billion. Islam totals 971 million.

18. R. Ernest Dupuy and Trevor N. Dupuy, *The Encyclopedia of Military History* (New York: Harper and Row, 1984), 1,364. See also Maj. Ralph Peters, USA, "The Rejection of the West" (Washington, D.C.: Army Staff, May 1994), for more on Islamic rage.

19. Huntington, "The Clash of Civilizations," 48. Huntington argues directly: "a central focus of conflict for the immediate future will be between the West and several Islamic-Confucian states."

20. Ray Bonds, ed., *The U.S. War Machine* (London: Salamander Books, 1983), 200–201; Viktor Suvorov [pseudo.] *Inside the Soviet Army* (New York: Macmillan, 1982), 184–85. See also David C. Isby, *Weapons and Tactics of the Soviet Army* (London: Jane's Publishing, 1988), 114–15.

21. Bryan Perrett, *Weapons of the Falklands Conflict* (Poole, England: Blandford Press, 1982), 36, 43; Anthony H. Cordesman and Abraham R. Wagner, *The Lessons of Modern War,* vol. 2, *The Iran-Iraq War* (Boulder, Colo.: Westview Press, 1990), 390–94; "International Arms Sales: Race to Disaster," *The Defense Monitor* (September 1993): 1–7.

22. Isby, *Weapons and Tactics of the Soviet Army,* 154–55.

23. Richard Jupa and Jim Dingeman, *Gulf Wars* (Cambria, Calif.: 3W Publications, 1991), 24–25; James F. Dunnigan, *How to Make War* (New York: William Morrow, 1988), 579–84.

24. Rick Atkinson, *Crusade* (Boston: Houghton Mifflin, 1993), 87–88, notes that the Iraqis possessed both anthrax and botulinum capabilities dur-

ing the 1990–91 Gulf War. In Isby, *Weapons and Tactics of the Soviet Army*, 294–301, along with a review of ballistic missile, nuclear, chemical, and biological means and exports, the author mentions Soviet experiments in engineering genetic material for biological warfare purposes.

25. Peter Wallenstein and Karin Axell, "Armed Conflict at the End of the Cold War," *Journal of Peace Research* (August 1993): 336–45.

26. Department of Commerce, *Statistical Abstract*, 806.

27. President George H. Bush, *National Security Strategy of the United States* (Washington, D.C.: U.S. Government Printing Office, 1993), i–ii, 1–6. These goals have been followed, though with some changes in emphasis, by the Clinton administration.

28. Gen. Colin L. Powell, USA, *National Military Strategy of the United States* (Washington, D.C.: U.S. Government Printing Office, 1992), 5.

29. Jeffrey Simon, ed., *NATO—Warsaw Pact Force Mobilization* (Fort McNair, D.C.: National Defense University Press, 1988), 1–27, 543–51.

30. Bush, *National Security Strategy*, i–ii; Thomas L. Friedman, "Clinton's Foreign Policy: Top Adviser Speaks Up," *New York Times*, 31 October 1993.

31. William H. Lewis, ed., McNair Paper 17, *Military Implications of United Nations Peacekeeping Operations* (Fort McNair, D.C.: National Defense University Press, 1993), 12–15; U.S. Central Intelligence Agency, *Worldwide Peacekeeping Operations, 1993* (Springfield, Va.: National Technical Information Service, 1993), lists the following demilitarized zones: Cyprus (1964), Sinai (1982), Kuwait (1991), and Rwanda (1992). These are in addition to Korea (1953) and the defunct DMZ in Vietnam (1954–75).

32. Friedman, "Clinton's Foreign Policy"; President Bill Clinton, "Address to the General Assembly of the United Nations, 27 September 1993" (Washington, D.C.: Federal News Service, 1993), features references to Franklin D. Roosevelt, conflict resolution, and sustainable economic development under the rubric of collective security.

33. CIA, *World Peacekeeping Operations, 1993;* Jeffrey Gedmim, "The Secretary-Generalissimo," *The American Spectator* (November 1993): 30–36.

34. Lewis, *Military Implications of UN Peacekeeping Operations*, 13.

35. Lucia Mouat, "Can the UN Be the World's Cop?" *Christian Science Monitor*, 6 October 1993.

36. Peter Rodman, "Bill's World," *National Review* (15 November 1993): 34. Clinton made the statement at an April 1992 appearance in New York City.

CHAPTER 2
The Hand of Iron

You may fly over a land forever; you may bomb it, atomize it, pulverize it and wipe it clean of life—but if you desire to defend it, protect it, and keep it for civilization, you must do this on the ground, the way the Roman legions did, by putting your young men into the mud. The object of warfare is to dominate a portion of the earth, with its peoples, for causes either just or unjust. It is not to destroy the land and people, unless you have gone wholly mad.

T. R. Fehrenbach
This Kind of War

It isn't surprising that most Americans seem damned confused by what their soldiers, sailors, airmen, and Marines have been doing lately. Men have been coming home in body bags, but the country is not at war. Something new and ugly is happening. Or is it? The people in the armed forces aren't always sure either.

The Clinton administration has absorbed most of the criticism, being accused, as has nearly every American presidency since that of George Washington, of having no plan for the country's foreign policy. All this peacekeeping stuff, or whatever you call it, just typifies the supposedly fuzzy thinking inside the District of Columbia beltway. So goes the line out in Peoria, Birmingham, or Reno.

Words mean things, and sometimes the inability to name a phenomenon tells you that, at the very least, the name givers are not quite sure what they are labeling. Peacekeeping, stability operations, peacetime engagement, peace enforcement, operations other than war (the army's "all others" category of OOTW)—there have been all sorts of titles. Much ink has spilled narrowly delineating the nuances that separate peacemaking from peacekeeping from peace enforcement.

One 1993 session at a prestigious National Defense University conference proposed definitions that split the whole thing into three levels and nine sublevels, ranging from "observing" through "protection of humanitarian relief operations" to "high-intensity operations." Drawing upon the United Nations Charter, other participants choose to identify these efforts as Chapter 6 actions (with consent of all parties) and Chapter 7 operations (imposition of a solution on one or more unwilling parties)—a fairly clear distinction. Unfortunately, the same commentators then go on to admit that most situations end up as a murky "Chapter 6 1/2," in which an initially agreeable belligerent elects to resume hostilities, or the separated groups choose to pool their nasty talents against the UN forces in their midst, or both, intermixed with pious stretches of compliance.[1]

This brand of enthralling intellectual debate may interest United Nations attorneys, busy academics, armchair strategists, and military doctrine writing committees. Unfortunately, all of their neat, often contradictory, taxonomies break down and blur in ugly little places like the Korean DMZ's Infiltration Alley or on the streets outside Mogadishu's Olympic Hotel. Like the Supreme Court considering the issue of pornography, soldiers out there in the Great Gulp can't define what's happening, but they know it when they see it.

A significant number of American defense experts, in and out of uniform, doggedly insist that this name defying, ubiquitous, ongoing struggle is not under any circumstances to be considered war—hence the whole OOTW drill. The U.S. Army, which tends to try for precision in such concerns, defines war as "open and declared armed hostile conflict between political units such as states or nations." This requires "the use of force in combat operations against an armed enemy [the means] to secure strategic objectives [the ends]."[2] Carl von Clausewitz probably could sign up for that (though interestingly enough, the 1-5th Infantry's friend Sun Tzu might not).

The reason General von Clausewitz and Master Sun would part ways on this definition involves the means to reach political ends. The favored American way of war flourishes in narrow confines: open and declared conflict against a conventionally organized foe. Some would claim that this preference goes all the way back to George Washington's rejection of partisan warfare as a campaign method—even though, of course, much of the American Revolution featured citizen militiamen and partisan rangers.[3]

Despite these practical diversions, the official line has been fairly steady from the green at Lexington to the shadow of the hydrogen bomb. Americans define war as being waged against a uniformed, disciplined opposing state's armed forces, the sort who will fight fairly, the way the Americans do. Today, these types of opponents bring tanks, jet planes, and warships. They duke it out like men, toe to toe, in the tradition of Patton and Rommel. Since 1945, American men at arms have ruthlessly crushed the foes dumb enough to share these limited beliefs. For some Americans, OOTW could just as easily be called TWWRND—things we would rather not do. Desert Storm, a magnificent accomplishment, was a thing we would rather do: war by the American definition. Somalia definitely falls under OOTW.

Sun Tzu, Mao Tse-tung, Ho Chi Minh, Muhammed Aidid (and certainly Francis Marion, John Mosby, and "Wild Bill" Donovan) obviously considered this OOTW category as war. For them, the means do not matter—they are chosen to achieve the ends, not to match some preconceived view of combat. Military power can be applied in many ways besides battle. The key is to get the political outcome you desire. As Sun Tzu said, "To subdue the enemy without fighting is the acme of skill."[4] That thought is crucial for the pygmy states and movements confronting Uncle Sam. As Saddam Hussein proved, and the North Koreans and Chinese could have warned him, it does not pay to fight inside the small box the Americans like to call war.

If Uncle Sam's enemies hope to succeed, they expand their means of war. A hostile element can use engagements and stage events to beat the Americans in their own living rooms, via the good offices of the Cable News Network and its fellows. The North Vietnamese stumbled upon this during the 1968 Tet Offensive and then played it hard thereafter. The Iranians in Tehran in 1980 and Muhammed Aidid in Mogadishu in 1993 also worked this angle.[5]

The American military's artificially narrow definition of war has never matched the real world or its own heritage of small, ambiguous wars. Indeed, even by contemporary U.S. Army parlance, America has largely conducted "limited wars" and that ugly OOTW stuff. Since the book tells us that "general war" entails "the total resources" of the country and "survival is at stake," only the Revolutionary War and the Civil War meet this strict formula—and these were massive internal struggles, and hence not real wars either.[6]

This sort of incongruity between book doctrine and events has become obvious as this century draws to a close. All of the various models, rules of thumb, and exceptions to the models and rules of thumb that have arisen to justify the American armed forces' small view of war serve to point out its obsolescence. The fact that the U.S. Army has enjoyed about a hundred hours of what it would call war (albeit limited war) since 1945 should be cause for alarm. This is especially true given that the country has paid a blood debt of nearly a hundred thousand dead doing that hard-to-label something else in Korea, Lebanon, the Dominican Republic, Vietnam, northern Iraq, Somalia, and other distant lands.[7]

The OOTW issue is surprising only in that these activities have been officially recognized at all. New ideas rarely achieve even partial acceptance, especially when the older concepts have been institutionalized by powerful, successful, bureaucracies.[8] Generals are always accused of preparing for the last war, and Americans have sometimes wandered down that trail. New views are hard to sell.

With regard to accommodating change, the United States defense establishment is doing quite well. A more typical case, perhaps the all-time classic, arose in Europe when late Renaissance churchmen attempted to sustain belief in Claudius Ptolemy's earth-centered universe, a long-held model under attack by energetic new scientists. Smart people spent decades desperately inventing crystalline spheres and angelic anomalies, with all the supporting mathematics calculated out in painstaking detail, to account for the realities of the heavens. The more Nicholaus Copernicus, Galileo Galilei, and Johannes Kepler observed and analyzed, the less the classical earth-centered universe made sense. But highly educated people clung to it with a violent faith. Martin Luther, certainly no friend of the papacy, called Copernicus "an upstart astrologer" and a "fool" who wanted "to reverse the entire science of astronomy." Copernicus did not live to suffer this critique; he wisely had his book published after his death. Galileo landed in prison. Kepler's mother was jailed because the authorities could not get their hands on him.[9] But the astronomers were right, and truth had its own weight. Today, we wonder how the church could have been so shortsighted.

A century from now, military historians will likely take a more charitable view of today's U.S. armed forces' wrestling match with the post–Cold War world. To extend the astronomer analogy, it is as if the pope and his chief cardinals had bequeathed a research grant on Galileo, not quite sure if he was right, but dead certain that he was on to something. All four services, and the defense community as a whole, have recognized the challenges posed by what the army calls OOTW.[10] That's pretty good for a bureaucracy.

It is noteworthy that the U.S. Army, long maligned as the most staid and conservative of the four services, has led the way in confronting this important issue. True, the tendency of some traditionalists to try to split real war from OOTW has not helped. But in the greater scheme, the very inclusion of OOTW in army doctrine represents a remarkable leap forward toward a wider definition of war, more in consonance with the troubled world America dominates.

In typical American fashion, practice is leading theory anyway. Out there past the palisades, Americans in uniform are solving the problems without reference to books or academic conferences. To understand what has arisen in practice and has at last spurred the doctrinal engine to act, you have to know the answers to three questions. What is the nature of military force? What types of military force are most effective? And, finally, how does America use its powerful armed forces?

The nature of military force has not changed all that much from the Cro-Magnon era. Force is a club, a blunt object good for beating in heads or threatening to do so. The clubs have evolved to become so powerful that we dare not use some of them. But their purpose remains pretty much the same.

Military force is employed to secure a political aim. By themselves, armed forces cannot achieve political ends, unless the end has become the utter annihilation of the foe, as in Rome's final assault on Carthage. In almost all cases, the military acts against some intermediate objective: the army of Northern Virginia, the ball bearing plants in Schweinfurt, the Ho Chi Minh Trail, or Saddam Hussein's Republican Guard. The incapacitation of that objective, whether by destruction (total or, more typically, partial) or seizure, compels the enemy to bend to the friendly political will. You can belt them with the club, just tap them, or merely brandish it, but in every situation, the club plays its part.

All that is fairly evident, right out of the Dick and Jane school of strategy. But although the idea of relating military means to political ends remains deceptively simple, it is not easy. This is true in a big way for the world's only superpower.

Given America's strength, its citizens' proclivities, and its sometimes tempestuous relationship to the unhappy wider world, American political ends, our sanctified and often-invoked national interests, can be thought of as existing in four concentric circles.[11] The most important things can be found at the heart. At that vital core lies America's preeminent interest, its very survival as a state. Currently, no power actively threatens that central pillar. That's a big difference from the Cold War.

Next out from the now secure core, one finds a concern for the safety of American citizens, a standard casus belli. With millions abroad in an unsafe world, this political aim gets a workout.

Safeguarding American economic interests and property comes next. Many American alliances reflect shared trade and business ties, and these bonds often transcend political links. Saudi Arabia, South Korea, and Pakistan are not Jeffersonian democracies, but they are active U.S. trading partners and allies. Access to resources and safety of allies have often required U.S. armed forces to act.

Finally, Americans do intervene in world affairs for moral reasons. Americans retain their traditional desire to promote democratic capitalism and human welfare. This fourth ring of interests, the least vital in any sense of realpolitik, marks America as a true superpower, with energy to spare on efforts of conscience. In many ways, such undertakings represent preventive measures, designed to address problems before they threaten American economic concerns or lives. But that suggests a logic better generated in hindsight. Sometimes, American use of force just is not rational. Americans act because they can, cognizant that with great power comes great responsibility.

All four American interests blur and interact, especially in the three outer circles. For example, deploying a Marine battalion to restore order in a restive foreign seaport automatically places American lives in danger, may affect business matters, and reflects American values. Sending in C-141B Starlifters full of grain may end a famine, but it puts lives in danger if local armed insurgents object to "Yankee imperialism." It's hard to say which interest or interests are at play and probably not important to draw the line anyway.

There are also second-order and third-order effects, as sympathetic states and movements might choose to beard Uncle Sam by acting against other American citizens or businesses. In 1979, mobs in Pakistan and Libya attacked American facilities to express outrage over U.S. reactions to the seizure of the embassy in Tehran, Iran.[12] Sharp distinctions between American interests get very confused once force has been committed.

This suggests why textbook approaches to peacekeeping and peacemaking so little reflect reality. America uses force in an open-ended system, an experiment that mutates every time another ingredient gets tossed in. American forces automatically change the chemistry of any environment they

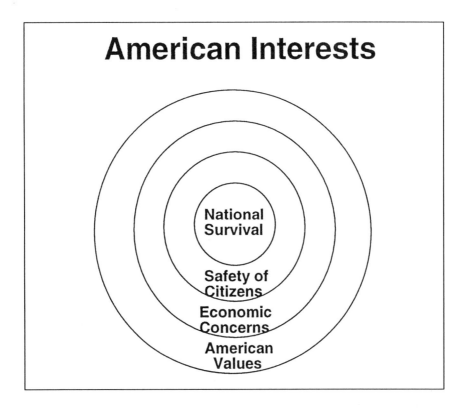

enter. Somebody out there will not accept the dominant superpower as an impartial arbiter. And then the fun starts.

Americans hope for a world of stability and predictability, a world of order. Citizens abroad and American corporations function best in an environment of peace and prosperity. Stability, then, has become the overall goal for American foreign policy.[13] This is quite a task on a planet seething with discontent among 80 percent of its inhabitants, disgruntled folks who want their piece of the pie now. The use of force, often cloaked by the banner of collective security, has become an important means to that end.

For this, the United States sends forth its legions, to keep order in a disorderly world. That imposition of American will is perceived as war by many of its unwilling recipients, whatever those in Washington may call it. When armed Americans cross over the bar, and go out into those

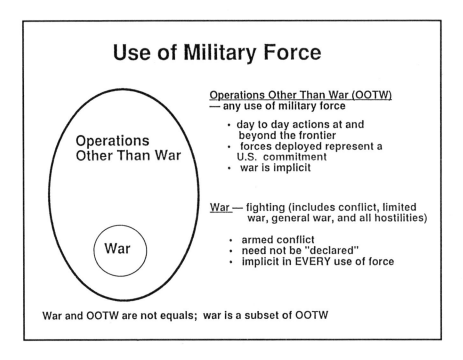

Use of Military Force

Operations Other Than War (OOTW)
— any use of military force

- day to day actions at and beyond the frontier
- forces deployed represent a U.S. commitment
- war is implicit

War — fighting (includes conflict, limited war, general war, and all hostilities)

- armed conflict
- need not be "declared"
- implicit in EVERY use of force

Operations Other Than War

War

War and OOTW are not equals; war is a subset of OOTW

badlands, into Indian country, America is at war. That said, it should be acknowledged that we are at war now and have been at war almost continuously since 1775.

What the army has named operations other than war has become the way American armed forces routinely relate to much of the globe, much as the idea could have once defined relationships to Indian tribes along the frontier. For Americans in uniform, that type of war is what passes for peace. And though we may not like the current terminology— our present army definition of war is far too narrow, and OOTW too confusing—it is evident that forces conducting OOTW do so most effectively when they acknowledge its true nature. OOTW is not some pale twin of real war, but its parent, forever pregnant with the violence of outright combat. To deny that awful fetus is to deny the true nature of OOTW: war by other means, to impose America's will, stabilizing an unstable world.

That brings us back to military force, to that huge, knotted billy club. America relates to the world with its club unslung and ready, like an early-

1900's policeman walking his beat. The club represents destructive power, but its appearance in the hands of a trained user can control the streets without ever requiring its use. Millions of Americans travel, do business, and serve in uniform among alien populations who have every reason to want to do them harm. Except, of course, there is that club.

Armed power, that club, displays an important duality, a yin-yang dynamic tension of destruction and control. Successful use of force requires both; John Mitchell controlled the DMZ because he was ready to shoot the first North Korean who tested him, and they knew it. It is possible to try to break this relationship, but that is a perilous action. Using force well requires both hammers and tongs.

Destruction typifies the public view of what the armed forces do. Directed against the uniformed enemy, his military-related economy, and his ruling clique, destruction kills people, breaks things, and disrupts the coherence of the hostile war effort. All of our armed services carry out destruction tasks, ranging from quick missile strikes to massive, sustained joint campaigns. Recent experience in the war against Iraq indicates that Americans do this very well indeed. We can apply as much or as little destructive power as we need to accomplish our purposes.

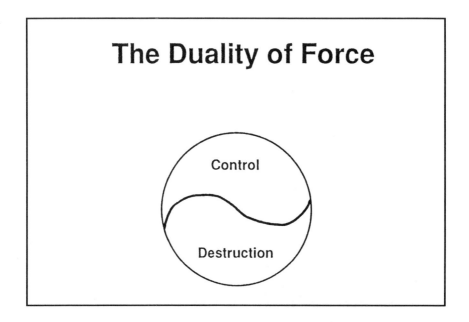

The Duality of Force

Control

Destruction

Military Force: Destruction and Control

DESTRUCTION—killing, breaking, disrupting armed forces

Methods: bombardments, raids, strikes, airland operations, amphibious assaults, air superiority, sea control, interdiction (air, land, and sea)

Examples (since 1975): shootdown of Libyan aircraft (1981), destruction of Grenadan army (1983), bombardment of Lebanon (1983–84), raid on Libya (1986), shootdown of Libyan aircraft (1989), destruction of Panama Defense Force (1989), air campaign against Iraq (1991), ground campaign against Iraq (February 1991), attack on Somali warlords (1993), cruise missile strikes on Iraq (1993)

CONTROL—taking, holding, and controlling people, land, and resources

Methods: airland operations, shows of force, peacekeeping, peace enforcement, nation-building, sea control, counternarcotics operations, proinsurgency, counterinsurgency, disaster relief, aid to civil authorities, rescues, noncombatant evacuations, airspace control

Examples (since 1975): Korean DMZ (1953–), SS *Mayaguez* incident (1975), Kolwezi evacuation (1978), El Salvador counterinsurgency (1979–91), Iran hostage rescue attempt (1980), Nicaragua proinsurgency (1981–90), Sinai peacekeeping (1982–), Lebanon (1982–84), Grenada intervention (1983), SS *Achille Lauro* incident (1985), Gulf of Sidra operations (1986), Bolivia counternarcotics (1986), Persian Gulf convoys (1987–88), Honduras show of force (1988), Panama intervention (1989–90), Liberia evacuation (1990), Somalia evacuation (1991), liberation of Kuwait (1991), Kurdish relief (1991–) Bangladesh typhoon relief (1991), Somalia peace enforcement (1992–94), Macedonia peacekeeping (1993–)

Control may be a little less obvious than slaying and smashing, but it has been a fundamental role of the military since primitive peoples first resorted to arms. Control involves taking, holding, and controlling people, land, and resources. It implies preservation and prevention of mayhem. There must be someone and something left to control.

Because people make their homes on the ground, not in the air or in the water, control very much relates to dominating terrain. Actions in the air and on the sea often affect matters, sometimes significantly, but control occurs in the dirt. It has always been this way, even for sea powers like Athens or Britain. Sooner or later, if control is what you want, the foot soldiers must go in.

Control is the military means of achieving political stability. It is not an end in itself, as it can at best police the malefactors and sit on them. And it depends upon actual and threatened destruction to work. You cannot have control without the capacity to destroy.[14]

There is a temptation to equate war with destruction and OOTW with control, and that can be a beguiling oversimplification. All war, whether OOTW or that waged in the American style, incorporates destruction and control. Destruction without control is pointless; control without destruction is toothless. You need to bring both, then adjust the actual proportion employed based upon the local situation.

Out past the frontier, Americans must be ready for both aspects of their profession. Humanitarian missions in underdeveloped countries can quickly degenerate into battle, and woe to those in uniform who place inordinate faith in agreements, handshakes, smiles, and UN rhetoric. When things go to hell, there is no substitute for a clean, loaded M16A2 rifle.

Building effective, global military forces, those capable of accommodating OOTW and its terrible offspring, those suited to destroy and control, has been America's principal challenge in recent years. As in the larger strategic questions, practice has led theory.

In the past, armies and navies could force decisions through independent operations, with cooperation the exception rather than the rule. This division of effort was enshrined in the venerable United States War and Navy Departments, coequal and jealous of prerogative. The formal split lasted through World War II. The rise of airpower and the communications network that went with it, fused the long distinct aspects of landpower and airpower into a new form of warfare, sometimes called triservice, triphibious, or, in the doctrinal parlance, joint. Significantly, it was the chief of the soon to be separate American air forces, Gen. Henry H. "Hap" Arnold, who summarized the development: "The greatest lesson of this war has been the extent to which air, land, and sea operations can and must be coordinated by joint planning and unified command."[15]

The U.S. Army, which owned no shipping or transport planes by 1947, knew that it would be campaigning overseas and, lacking another mass mobilization, would be fighting with ten divisions at best. It needed to hitch a ride, and it needed the destructive firepower of fleets and modern aircraft to even numerical odds. Yet soldiers, then and now, could not walk on water (except perhaps Douglas MacArthur on his better days), and despite some flirtation with missilery, they don't have an excess of firepower. The army's tanks, howitzers, and armed helicopters remain rather puny implements compared to jet bombers and missile cruisers. Accordingly, army officers, trained to think of combined-arms cooperation on the battlefield, looked back at World War II experiences and attempted to institutionalize the joint warfare techniques developed in combat. From General of the Army Omar N. Bradley to Gen. Colin L. Powell, soldiers, abetted by some sailors, airmen, and Marines, have pushed very hard to realize Arnold's greatest lesson.[16]

The army, of course, embodies the ultimate horrors of war: mud, sweat, rain, heat, cold, exhaustion, despair, trenches, barbed wire, gut shots, sucking chest wounds, throats slit at night, men slaughtered like cattle. Americans do not like to think about that sort of ugliness, let alone participate in it. New technologies available at the outset of the atomic age seemed to promise better than that. A gleaming jet fighter, a sleek destroyer, a humming computer—these items appeared to herald an age of push-button warfare, war as a Nintendo game, war from a distance, war without mud and blood.

So as America reorganized to contend with the Cold War, other voices rose in chorus. They vowed to take all that slime and gore out of the military equation and at the same time streamline the command structure—one-stop shopping for warfare, if you will. The air force, the sea services (navy, Marines, Coast Guard, merchant marine), and a clutch of civilian intellectuals in the newly formed Department of Defense offered, and some circles still advocate, seductive alternatives: airpower, seapower, and systems analysis. Because these approaches focus mostly upon destruction and largely exclude control, they are at best partial solutions and at worst outright bullshit.

Classic airpower theory advocates direct, brutal attack to destroy the enemy economy and populace. Italian air enthusiast and officer Giulio Douhet, in his visionary *The Command of the Air,* argues that a campaign of destructive aerial bombardment can decide a war without need for armies or fleets. Douhet described a flying armada, raining down high explosives, incendiary devices, and toxic chemical munitions. Such an independent air arm, launched from the home country, could supposedly end the fighting in one great blow against the foe's "vital centers" of war making. Some sort of constabulary would then occupy the blasted landscape and round up the cowed, bomb-shocked survivors of the beaten opponent.[17]

The good news about this purely destructive strategy involves friendly casualties—very minimal, a few aircrew specialists rather than the millions killed on the 1914–18 Western Front. The bad news, unless working for a thug like Hitler or Saddam Hussein, relates to the horrendous butcher's bill among helpless enemy civilians living in those Douhet-designated vital centers of politics, transportation, and industry. In sum, raw airpower theory substitutes their corpses for those of our ground battalions and asks us to call that success.

In the American military tradition, no battle, campaign, or war may truly be counted as a victory if it exacts too high a cost in human lives. Our heritage encourages us not only to be careful about our own people, but also to employ extraordinary measures to safeguard innocent civilians, to include enemy nationals. We will accept a short, sharp clash that ravages the adversary's armed contingents. Americans will not countenance a bloodbath in any form.

Despite the claims of some, we never have. Even our lapses—Dresden, Tokyo, Hiroshima, Nagasaki—can be numbered on a single hand with a finger to spare. Brave Eighth Air Force bomber crews suffered horrific casualties in World War II, trying to carry out daylight pinpoint bombing in Europe. The army air forces rightly paid that price to hit specific military targets rather than simply dump hell on Germany. In Korea, Vietnam, and Iraq, we lost precious pilots in our determination to prevent civilian casualties. That is the way we do it.[18] Americans refuse to consider absolute devastation as a legitimate war tactic.

Accordingly, contemporary American military practice tends to stress the minimum application of force necessary to subdue the opposition and maximum efforts to preserve American lives. This nicely matches our national political aim of stability and a climate for steady economic growth. We tend to rebuild former foes and thus make them into friends, as in Germany and Japan.

Outright, naked destruction—the really big hammer—remains in our bag of tools. But we do not like to use it. When we do, it is only as the last resort. Killing people and breaking things, taken to the extreme, leaves very little to rebuild or befriend. This is why military force must include consideration of elements capable of seizing and controlling populations, not simply slaughtering them. As much as the fear of cataclysmic retaliation, that concern also explains why Americans have not used nuclear weaponry since bombing Nagasaki, and why we could never quite bring ourselves to bomb North Korea, North Vietnam, or Iraq into the Stone Age.

Airpower alone has won a few minor conflicts: reprisals against Libya and Iraq, unopposed airlift missions, and some aerial exclusion patrols. But air cordons, airlifts, and bombardments cannot free threatened American citizens, end an insurgency, or control a demilitarized zone. Even in Desert Storm, bombing alone did not evict the Iraqis from Kuwait—it was close, but no cigar.[19] Except for a Doctor Strangelove, willing to devastate the planet to possess the radioactive cobalt-salted embers, victory through airpower remains a chimerical proposition. In the contemporary world, airpower by itself does not work.

Seapower tries to do what airpower cannot. Traditional seapower, as expressed in RAdm. Alfred Thayer Mahan's *The Influence of Sea Power upon History,* proposes that wars can be won at sea without resort to costly land campaigns.[20] In this view, the theory of victory would be to eliminate the opposing fleet and then clamp down a blockade so tight that the adversary collapses due to economic privation.

Mahan and his adherents did not consider the potential versatility that might be added by some forces capable of taking and holding terrain. He ignored armies, except as a foil to demonstrate the bloody alternatives to his preferred brand of navalism. He even gave short shrift to littoral operations.[21] For Mahan, everything revolved around command of the sea, to be determined by a clash of mighty fleets. Mahan preached almost pure destruction, first by a massive spasm of fleet combat on the open ocean, then by slow, steady economic constriction. It resembled siege warfare on a continental scale.

This may work, but even when it does, it takes a great deal of time. In the Napoleonic wars, the great British sea supremacy won at Trafalgar in 1805 did not prompt French collapse for almost a decade. Union warships and expeditions tried to close Confederate harbors and eliminate blockade-runners for more than four years during the American Civil War; they finally took the last major port city a few months prior to the fall of Richmond. The British Royal Navy blockade of 1914 helped strangle Imperial Germany, but it was hardly the sole factor, and the Germans held out, full of fight, for more than four years. Naval blockades take time.

Today, nobody wants to mark time for years, least of all the restive American citizenry. President George Bush surely understood this. He elected not to wait to see how long it would take for an economic embargo to force Saddam Hussein's Iraq to back down. Instead, he chose to unleash Operation Desert Storm.

Along with being slow, a naval blockade may not work at all against most enemies. The Royal Navy barely affected Adolf Hitler's Nazi German war machine during World War II. The old Soviet Union, which enjoyed a substantially self-contained military economy, could have outlasted a Mahan-style naval cordon. Finally, one might find it hard to cut off supplies and sustenance to today's multiplicity of subnational warlords, terrorists, and other bargain-basement troublemakers. By design, command of the sea works best in conventional wars waged against industrialized foes—the last thing America can expect.

Seapower did decide the Pacific phase of World War II, and it has been the crucial factor in many small incidents, to include shows of force, evacuations of citizens, and reprisal raids. To be fair, most of these included some air and land elements, in the form of carrier-based jets and embarked Marines. The problem is that, though America has by far the largest and most potent war fleets on earth, the cutting edge remains rather fine: a few hundred cruise missiles, a few hundred planes, and a few thousand Marines.[22]

Sometimes, that is enough. But often, as in Vietnam, the Dominican Republic, Grenada, Lebanon (twice), Panama, Northern Iraq, and Somalia, a quick sea-launched expedition is not enough. Though it sometimes works, you cannot sail around a lot of problems—you have to go ashore and stay. In those cases, and in most cases, seapower alone cannot do the job.

At least airpower and seapower adherents have theories to build upon, inadequate though they may be, and Mahan and Douhet remain giants in the study of military affairs. The final group of naysayers to joint warfare do not even enjoy the dignity of a well-articulated theory. If Douhet and Mahan place their faith in planes and ships manned by stout-hearted men, systems analysts have chosen to place their faith in numbers, and people be damned. For these accountants of war, there are no uncertainties or frictions, no human factors, and no surprises, just unconsidered variables.

Systems analysts apply the techniques of modern economics, mathematical modeling, and business forecasting to war. They seek to quantify everything, thus allowing them to answer the famous question posed by defense intellectuals Alain C. Enthoven and K. Wayne Smith: "How much is enough?" Human nature, with its infinite variations and unpredictability, is normally left out of the calculation—it's too messy. A systems analyst can tell you exactly how much it takes to win: what to use, when to use it, and where. He can destroy things pretty well, selecting the best bomb, the right target array, and even the proper fusing.[23] So goes the argument, and it might pan out if the analyst can get the numbers and the equations exactly right. Otherwise, it's garbage in, garbage out.

That's the usual result when the situation must allow for humanity's influence. Nobody, not even the most sophisticated of social scientists or the most insightful of psychologists, has ever figured out how to assign a concrete numerical value to human nature, personality, and culture. Those things play heavily in that most human of endeavors, warfare.

The original batch of systems analysts were undaunted by that objection. Led and encouraged by Secretary of Defense Robert Strange McNamara, whiz kid analysts raised number crunching to a high art in the 1960s. Armed with computers and an unshaken faith in their process, the whiz kids took the Pentagon by storm, revolutionizing budgeting and arms procurement.

Then, satisfied that they had the ultimate system well in hand, they tried their nostrums in the jungles of Southeast Asia. Not surprisingly, the business accountants kept a fair to middling handle on using air bombardment to tear gouges out of the primitive North Vietnamese economy. They forgot, however, to allow for those "x-factors" like enemy willpower, the efficacy of bicycle transport, or a home industry in small arms.

Bad as they did up North, the boys had barely a clue as to how to judge the attempts to secure the southern countryside by the Americans and their hapless South Vietnamese allies. Not that they didn't try; the voluminous outpourings of their computerized Hamlet Evaluation System, if dropped from bomb racks, could well have choked Haiphong Harbor in fanfold paper. The very statistical categories chosen to measure progress in controlling the South seem laughable in hindsight: miles of roads open, amount of rice harvested, numbers of Communist defectors, numbers of incidents of various types, among others. Somehow, somewhere, some way, it would all add up. It never did and still doesn't.

Despite the gruesome debacle in Southeast Asia, systems analysis still has many advocates, not the least former Secretary of Defense Les Aspin, who learned and practiced it as an army captain in the Pentagon. The discipline's most damning eulogy, though, was written during the Vietnam War by distinguished journalist David Halberstam. Even today, his words burn like fire, exposing the absurdity of those who dare to reduce war to a formula:

And there was that confidence which bordered on arrogance, a belief that he could handle it. Perhaps, after all, the military weren't all that good; still they could produce the raw data, and McNamara, who knew data, would go over it and extricate truth from the morass. The portrait of McNamara in those years at his desk, on planes, in Saigon, poring over page after page of data, each platoon, each squad, studying all those statistics. All lies. Talking with reporters and telling them all the indices were good. He could not have been more wrong; he simply had all the wrong indices, looking for American production indices in an Asian revolution.[24]

Systems analysis is not a bad way to balance the family checkbook, or even that of the Department of Defense. But it's no way to run a war, an operation other than war, or anything else involving people, shooting, and fear.

Today, after fifty years of occasionally bitter experience, America has learned that most crises, conflicts, wars, OOTWs, and other unpleasant interludes demand all three aspects of military power: air, sea, and land. In an exhaustive study of forty-four uses of force since 1975, one careful analyst discerned that airpower alone resolved 18 percent, seapower alone dealt with 27 percent, and a joint force served to meet 50 percent.[25] Those numbers tell us something about what works in today's dangerous world.

Based upon this hard-won knowledge, the U.S. defense establishment has progressed beyond the pat answers of airpower, seapower, and systems analysis, though each still contributes its share to the defense of America. Systems analysis forms the centerpiece of most peacetime resource decisions, and it has served well. Thankfully, it no longer occupies a place as a bastard form of strategy.

Airpower and seapower have also been subordinated. Alluring though they can be, these technological silver bullet concepts are no longer sufficient, if they ever were, to meet America's military requirements. The 1986 Department of Defense Reorganization Act (often called the Goldwater-Nichols Act) merely formalized what Americans in uniform had known, and largely carried out, since 1941. Over the last five-plus decades, joint operations have evolved into the standard American approach.

This joint effort has yet to receive the appropriate bumper sticker name that will immortalize it along with the traditional disciplines of airpower, seapower, and landpower. "Joint" is an adjective that reminds most listeners of their knee (or, for a few, illicit substances). "Joint" doesn't sing. As with OOTW, it's that labeling problem again, typical during times of institutional transition. Perhaps "warpower" is as good a name as any.

Warpower is the cohesive, unified effort of air, land, and sea forces directed against those objectives most likely to compel foes to bend to America's will. The scale of the effort varies based upon the degree of American interest. But whichever interests have been engaged, the nature of the enterprise remains the same. It is war, even if today we find it expedient to call it OOTW.

Warpower originates from the unified effort of landpower, seapower, and airpower. They may be considered to form an iron triangle, whose structural strength comes from the integrity of all three parts. Without one side, or with one portion inordinately weakened, it is incomplete. Whatever would be left, it would not be warpower. In its proper form, the warpower triangle generates forces far more capable than the mere sum of their parts.

Airpower dominates the aerospace dimension. It contributes a strong destructive component. Aside from maintaining a nuclear capability, airpower can deliver rapid precision and mass strikes launched from distant bases, sometimes from America itself. In support of its own strong compos-

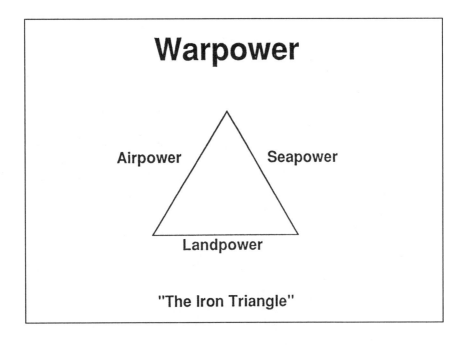

ite wings or other services, airlifters can swiftly bring in supplies and forces. In the atmosphere and in space, airpower provides surveillance and communications for all American forces. Americans will enjoy air superiority in almost all conceivable contingencies. Thanks to airpower, Americans generally expect, as they were told at Utah and Omaha Beaches in 1944, "when you see aircraft overhead, they will be ours."[26]

Seapower dominates the oceans, to include its depths and the air above it, and it influences the coastal regions. It serves as a versatile portion of the triangle, not as fast to the scene as airpower but fast enough, not as destructive as airpower but destructive enough, and even enjoying a fair ability to control terrain thanks to embarked Marines. Seapower incorporates some airpower and landpower, making it a triangle within a triangle. It includes expeditionary forces that can be present forward, react to crises, and project power ashore, to include air and missile strikes, gunfire, and Marine assault forces. Seapower also moves supplies and forces over the oceans, to include escorting convoys and clearing mines from beaches and harbors. Americans can expect that their navy will rule the waves.[27]

Landpower, the weakest but in some ways the most important leg, builds around soldiers and Marines. It can destroy in its own right, but exists to control lands and peoples. Landpower alone can hold ground. As was once said of the British army, American land forces are projectiles fired ashore by the air force and navy. But these projectiles come ready to stay.[28]

Compared to the other struts, landpower is relatively weaker for two reasons. First, Americans have always distrusted and shunned large armies. The Constitution empowered Congress to "provide and maintain" the navy but to "raise and support" armies, implying that the former is permanent and the latter children of crisis.[29] Large though the U.S. Army may appear to be, it is small measured against its tasks, and against the size of the traditionally unmilitary American populace.

As Washington discovered with his recalcitrant militia, nobody wants to be in the infantry. "Minuteman" speaks to readiness, but says even more about staying power. If anything, the tragic stresses of modern war have only made this worse. When Dustin Hoffman searched for postcollege employment in *The Graduate,* the word whispered his way was "plastics," not "grunt." Getting killed or maimed can ruin your upward mobility. Modern technology may be expensive, but to a degree, it does allow Americans to pay for mechanical substitutes for their precious flesh and bones—hence our big navy and large air force. Send a bullet, not a man, goes the U.S. military maxim. When we can, we do.

Second, aside from the political and cultural inhibitors, American landpower is less strong because it fights at the end of a long tether. Projecting landpower is no mean feat, and even America cannot simultaneously and immediately move its dozen or so available divisions of active duty Marines and soldiers. Only light forces can move in strength by air. About one light or airborne division can move in almost two weeks, a bit faster once the new C-17 Globemaster III comes fully into the air force inventory.

Sealift is substantially slower, but it can bring in heavy equipment and needed bulk supplies of fuel and ammunition. Only two Marine expeditionary units (each with a battalion landing team, an air squadron, and a service support element) are afloat forward on an average day, one in the Pacific and one in the Mediterranean or Atlantic. They can land as soon as they reach the right place, sea conditions and tactical situation permitting. Like the army airborne and light infantry, these Marines represent the vanguard of much larger and more powerful follow-on forces.

After a few weeks, another three full brigades of Marines can move on dedicated assault shipping, ready for a beach incursion. Three more Marine brigades can marry up with preloaded floating stocks, as can an army armored brigade, although these forces require secure port facilities to disembark. Another eight army mechanized and armored brigades can fly in troops to marry up with prepositioned equipment at secure compounds: five in Europe, one in Korea, and two in the Middle East. The fixed sets are only useful if the fighting occurs nearby, and if some miscreants don't get to them first.

Landpower Projection

Time	Force	Transportation Means
2 days (or less)	USA battalion (airborne, air assault, or light infantry)	air
4 days	USA brigade (airborne, air assault, or light infantry)	air
	USMC expeditionary unit (battalion landing team)	sea (amphibious)
12 days	USA division (airborne, air assault, or light infantry)	air

Landpower Projection

Time	Force	Transportation Means
15 days	USA brigade	prepositioned afloat
	Two to four USA brigades - four in north-central Europe - one in southern Europe - two in southwest Asia - one in Korea	prepositioned in theater
	USMC expeditionary brigade (regimental landing team)	prepositioned afloat
30 days	Two USA divisions (armored, mechanized, or air assault)	sea
	USMC expeditionary unit (battalion landing team)	sea (amphibious)
	Two USMC expeditionary brigades (regimental landing team)	prepositioned afloat
45 days	Marine expeditionary force (Marine division)	sea (amphibious)
75 days	Two USA divisions (armored or mechanized)	sea
180 days	Five USA divisions (includes Army National Guard brigades)	sea

Notes:
1. This depicts major ground combat forces only; army and Marine units come with substantial organic and attached artillery, aviation (Marines include attack jets), combat support (engineers, signal), and logistics capabilities. Force sizes are battalion (500 to 1,000 troops), brigade/regiment (2,500 to 3,500), and division (10,000 to 20,000).
2. Personnel arrive by air to link up with prepositioned unit sets, either at ports of debarkation or at fixed sites.

Sources: Gen. John W. Foss, USA (Ret.), "Association of the U.S. Army Background Brief: Power Projection" (March 1993), 1, 4; James F. Dunnigan, *How to Make War* (New York: William Morrow, 1988), 274, 280, 283. Dunnigan lists the total U.S. lift capacity at 48,840 Marines, about one and a third Marine expeditionary force equivalents. He also notes that 50 percent of all the Marines in the world belong to the USMC; America believes in a strong, capable Marine Corps.

For action elsewhere, the navy-run Military Sealift Command is presently working to create a fleet capable of delivering army divisions and supplies for all services. America's fifty-three roll-on/roll-off ships can bring in two army divisions, both armored, in 30 days, and five divisions, two of them armored, to any port in the world 75 days after notification. This fleet could unload, turn around, and deliver another five army divisions (including the first National Guard brigades) within 180 days.

Only America can project that kind of power across oceans. Most OOTWs require five brigades or less, and the first few battalions, even a few tanks, can be on the ground about a day or so after notification. Larger wars, at least since 1945, average about ten divisions. Even in a time of declining resources, airlift and sealift have gotten their due.[30] These investments stand as proof positive that the iron triangle will include its landpower leg.

It's expensive and takes a lot of hard, costly training, but bringing the full team pays off in battle. Warpower, states *Joint Publication 1: Joint Warfare of the U.S. Armed Forces,* "can disorient an enemy who is weak in one or more of the dimensions of warfare, helping to create a mismatch between what the foe anticipates and what occurs."[31] As the planet's sole superpower, when the United States brings its joint array to bear, even when not in preponderant strength, Americans will more than likely find a vulnerability in less fully endowed opponents. Unified warfare brings many types of tools, not just raw quantity. That is why America relies upon warpower.

Perhaps, to gain full recognition as a strategic means, warpower must find its own theorist, its Giulio Douhet, Alfred Thayer Mahan, or Carl von Clausewitz. But Americans are impatient with theorizing and book learning, and our military's actions have already given us practical warpower. The thinking will catch up.

With the ascendancy of warpower, it is no longer proper to talk of army, navy, Marine Corps, and air force strategies. These services do not fight wars, but organize, train, sustain, and provide forces to those who do: the National Command Authorities and the unified commanders in chief (CINCs).

The National Command Authorities normally consist of the civilian portion of the chain of command: the president and the secretary of defense. The term National Command Authorities is a Cold War euphemism for "whoever is left to be in charge" had Moscow ever unleashed its thermonuclear brood. As the president and secretary could have been atomized on the first volley, some civilian in the chain of succession, perhaps the vice president, the Speaker of the House, or even the education secretary, would have to give the fateful orders and bring down the temple of civilization. During the Soviet-American standoff, communications networks grew and improved to include hardened underground facilities, flying command posts (code-named Looking Glass), and even ways to contact submerged nuclear submarines. Always, the goal was to permit positive command by a designated civil figure.

It never came to that, but the system is in place anyway, admittedly at a much-relaxed degree of readiness. These measures, and especially the thinking behind them, still serve a useful purpose. It is not inconceivable that some determined terrorist group could strike at the president and secretary of defense during a crisis. Health problems, transportation accidents, and other unforeseen communications lapses have happened before and will occur in the future, and both Murphy and Clausewitz agree that these troubles will likely arise at the precise moment of crisis. If so, and if the president became incapacitated, one of the other authorities, in due constitutional order of succession, would make the call.[32] As Harry S Truman discovered in 1945, this is no joke.

Normally, the principals fill their elected and appointed roles. The president, in his roles as commander in chief of the armed forces and chief executive, directs foreign policy. He is assisted by the vice president and his cabinet secretaries: state, defense, treasury, justice, commerce, and others as needed. The director of central intelligence, who coordinates all intelligence organizations and heads the Central Intelligence Agency (CIA), joins in the process. The chairman of the Joint Chiefs of Staff (JCS) represents the uniformed military, occasionally accompanied by one or more of the service chiefs if something requires special expertise or if the service chief has exercised his privilege of access.

The president, vice president, secretary of defense, and secretary of state form the statutory core of the National Security Council (NSC), America's premier foreign policy deliberative body. They receive advice from the director of central intelligence and the chairman of the JCS, and others as the president so designates. And he always so designates. The elite NSC staff includes a mixture of civilian appointees, State Department foreign service officers, military officers, personnel from the CIA and other intelligence organizations, and representatives from other cabinet departments, bureaus, and agencies.

This impressive, diverse talent farm must be organized to produce something useful. During the Cold War, presidents have found it useful to appoint a special assistant for national security affairs, commonly called the National Security Adviser. Some of the more famous men to hold this title include Maxwell Taylor, Henry Kissinger, Zbigniew Brzezinski, and Colin Powell. The National Security Adviser, more than any other individual, works to bring order out of the typically loose, contentious NSC principals and their staffs. Nothing is neat or especially well ordered, but it works and usually stays within the bounds of the Constitution and American traditions. We would do well not to expect or criticize too much.

Ideally, the president, his advisers, and his cabinet secretaries work in the realm of strategy, assigning means to gain ends, then leaving it to the military CINCs to carry out operations. Strategy is defined as "the art and science of developing and using political, economic, psychological, and military forces as necessary during peace and war."[33] While all of the NSC cooks, not to mention Congress, the public, and the news media, can and do contribute to the stew, final responsibility rests with the president. Truman said it best: the buck stops here.

Note that strategy does not belong to people in uniform. The JCS chairman usually has his say, but that is not a necessity. By courtesy and long practice, the secretary of defense transmits all orders through the chairman and his Joint Staff in the Pentagon's National Military Command Center (NMCC). There is no requirement to do this; the president and the secretary, or others the president empowers, can speak directly to field commanders, bypassing the chairman. The chairman does not command anything except his Joint Staff personnel. He is an adviser.[34]

The real commanders are the CINCs, the theater commanders, the four-star generals and admirals most responsible for translating the president's strategy and secretary's orders into military success. The CINCs create warpower out of the forces allocated by the president and secretary.

The CINCs practice "operational art," described as "the employment of military forces to attain strategic goals through the design, organization, integration, and execution of battles and engagements into campaigns and major operations."[35] Theater CINCs are American proconsuls, Yankee viceroys, bringing together diverse joint forces to accomplish sometimes murky missions.

The language of American defense bristles with the importance of the CINCs' role. Intentionally, projects like Just Cause, Desert Storm, Provide

Comfort, and Restore Hope are called operations. Typically, CINCs delegate operational control (OPCON) over apportioned forces, which allows the unified commander to form task forces and issue mission orders, yet saddles their parent services with all the logistical and administrative requirements, all to give the greatest possible freedom of action to the practitioner of operations.[36] Everything emphasizes the primacy of operations—not coincidentally, the army's most important field manual bears this same name. The operational art represents the pinnacle of military command in this age of warpower and operations other than war.

The operational art, named by the Germans, beaten to theoretical pablum in Soviet doctrinal literature, and practiced best by joint American forces, is a product of the complexity of modern combat. Prior to the mid-nineteenth century, monarchs and republics issued orders to their field commanders, who then fought it out. The governments practiced strategy; the generals and admirals, tactics—the art of winning battles. In some cases, the monarch himself (Frederick the Great or Napoleon, for example) combined both functions in the tradition of Alexander the Great or Genghis Khan. In other situations, a designated lieutenant (the Duke of Marlborough or Maurice de Saxe) carried out strategic and tactical functions for the crown. In this second variation, we see the first glimmerings of the operational level of warfare.

A reasonable approximation of operational art emerged almost simultaneously in America and Prussia in the middle decades of the nineteenth century. It followed naturally that the two countries most closely identified with the greatest economic triumphs of the industrial age found cause to apply certain managerial ideas and schemes of specialization to the demands of warfare. Of course, each country did things in its own unique way.

In America, President Abraham Lincoln and Gen. Ulysses S. Grant worked out the idea of coordinating land and sea campaigns as they struggled to defeat the southern Confederacy. In synchronizing massive riverine, land, coastal, and oceanic activities, they were much closer to warpower by 1864 than anyone else got until World War II. But being Americans, and hence not given to a lot of categorical abstract thought, neither they nor their subordinates institutionalized their efforts. They assumed that the Civil War had been unique, and that was that. The next war would have its own solutions. America's Civil War leadership underestimated their own significant and farsighted contributions, and so, unfortunately, everything had to be relearned over the next century.

In Prussia, the spiked-helmet crowd captured the lessons of modern industrial management and task specialization only too well, creating the storied General Staff and a united Imperial Germany. The brilliant 1864 Danish War, 1866 campaign in Austria, and 1870–71 victory over France were the most rapid, decisive conquests of the railroad and telegraph period. The General Staff, epitomized by Gen. Helmuth von Moltke, existed to plan and carry out such campaigns, to perform operational art on a continental canvas. Over the next eighty years, Moltke's successors tried and failed to match his excellence. The Germans captured the process well, but given all sorts of troubles (many self-inflicted), they never were able to generate true warpower. And though the army and later the other services proved able, they lost touch with their political leaders, who in turn lost touch with reality. Instead of profiting from Germany's operational prowess, Europe suffered through the intransigent aggression of the kaisers and the diabolical mayhem of Adolf Hitler. It was enough to give the operational art a bad name. The Soviets, who had been at the business end of German operational skill during World War II, adopted the concept whole hog. They then proceeded to make many of the same mistakes.

The Americans used operational art without calling it that. Theater command structures and campaign planning originated in World War II and have existed, with variations, ever since. In the 1980s, during digestion of the hard lessons of Vietnam, the services swallowed their distaste for borrowing from Nazis and Russian Communists and adopted their concept of an intermediate level of war, between the strategy from Washington and the tactics of the battlefields. Operational art received its formal designation in the 1982 version of the army's *Field Manual 100-5,* with the other services closely following. The present flowering of joint doctrine, still in progress, has been marked in Congress by the passage of the Goldwater-Nichols Act in 1986. At last, the United States has begun to place in print ideas and techniques in ferment since the time of Lincoln and Grant.[37]

Thus, beneficiaries of more than a hundred years of experimentation and effort, today's nine CINCs stand ready to carry out the strategic bidding of their president. Each directs a joint staff drawn from all the services, and each directs forces apportioned according to missions in progress. In the broadest sense, the unified commands split into two groups: five organized by geographic region, and four by function.

A CINC normally supervises operations in his theater through five component commands: army forces (ARFOR), navy forces (NAVFOR), air forces (AFFOR), Marine forces (MARFOR), and a special operations command (SOC). There are variations, especially in the four functional unified commands. The army and Marine Corps, for example, have minimal roles in nuclear deterrence under U.S. Strategic Command. In a similar vein, the Marines do not contribute dedicated forces to the U.S. Special Operations Command, U.S. Transportation Command, or U.S. Space Command, although Marines receive support from those commands. These minor commonsense exceptions aside, CINCs are responsible for integrating all of the service components into warpower.

Coalescing warpower does not just happen. Under the unified commands, service components direct day-to-day missions and, in rare cases, specific operations. General H. Norman Schwarzkopf, for example, decided to conduct the Gulf War through his habitually assigned major component commanders. This can be difficult, because America's unified commands

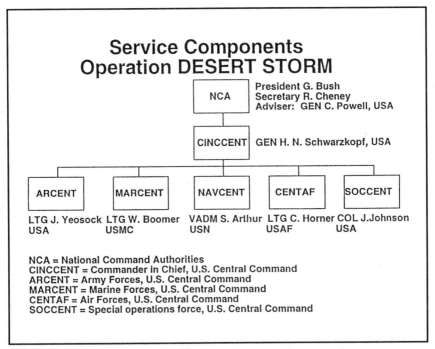

Source: U.S. Department of Defense, *The Conduct of the Persian Gulf War* (Washington, D.C.: U.S. Government Printing Office, 1992), K-21 to K-22.

often have several irons in the fire simultaneously, which requires the CINC to coordinate multiple operations rather than focus on one. That happened to Schwarzkopf in January 1991, when circumstances demanded a noncombatant evacuation operation in Somalia just as Desert Storm began.[38]

Usually, then, CINCs meet each new challenge by creating a Joint Task Force (JTF), often in accord with a contingency plan already on file. A JTF includes a selection of the right elements organized by service components like the unified command or by mission, whichever makes more sense. JTF South, created for Operation Just Cause in Panama, typifies a mission arrangement.

During campaign planning, the CINC and his JTF commanders ensure full integration of warpower by identifying clear chains of command for airpower, seapower, and landpower. Everyone agrees that the navy should handle seapower, which often entails working with the Coast Guard and merchant marine. The other two disciplines, airpower and landpower, can be more contentious.

The officer in charge must designate his airpower commander (the Joint Force Air Component Commander—JFACC), who plans, directs, coordinates, and deconflicts all air operations—not a simple job when every service has its own substantial aviation arms. The airpower commander can

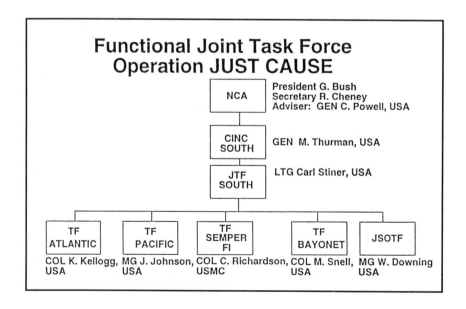

apportion and assign missions to all subordinate air elements, to include those integral to army and Marine units and navy surface ships (and that concession was not won easily). Normally, the JFACC allocates such organic airpower back to the service units that use it, but there are exceptions, and the JFACC has the authority to take charge of every piece that flies, either in bulk or as selected entities. Typically, the JFACC will be an air force or navy officer, whichever brings the preponderance of air strength to the battle.

Task Force Missions
JTF South organized based upon assigned objectives.

TF Atlantic: isolate Colon city; secure central area and northern area of the Panama Canal.
   * 3d Brigade, 7th Infantry Division (Light) (+)

TF Pacific: conduct follow-on parachute assault into Torrijos-Tocumen Airport; secure areas south and east of Panama Canal.
   * 1st Brigade, 82d Airborne Division (+)

TF Semper Fi: secure Bridge of the Americas and areas west of the Panama Canal.
   * 6th Marine Expeditionary Brigade (-) (Forward)
   * 2d Battalion, 27th Infantry (+)

TF Bayonet: secure objectives in Panama City.
   * TF Gator (4th Battalion (Mechanized), 6th Infantry (+))
   * TF Red Devil (1st Battalion (Airborne), 508th Infantry)
   * TF Wildcat (5th Battalion, 87th Infantry)

Joint Special Operations Task Force: seize Torrijos-Tocumen by parachute assault; seize Rio Hato by parachute assault; execute special operations missions.
   * TF Red-T (1/75th Ranger Regiment (+))
   * TF Red-R (75th Ranger Regiment (-))
   * TF Black (3/7th Special Forces (+))
   * TF White (SEAL Teams 2 and 4)
   * TF Blue (SEAL Team 6)
   * TF Green (1st Special Forces Operational Detachment—Delta)

Sources: Thomas Donnelly, Margaret Roth, and Caleb Baker, *Operation Just Cause* (New York: Lexington, 1991), 81–83; Lt. Gen. Edward M. Flanagan Jr., USA (Ret.), Battle for Panama (McLean, Va.: Brassey's, 1993), 32–45.

While there is always a JFACC, there may or may not be a Joint Force Land Force Commander (a generic COMLANFOR). It depends upon the Marine role. If the Marines are already ashore and fighting, either the army or the Marine commander can be designated to take over a LANFOR post. Should further Marine landings be contemplated, as during the Gulf War, it is logical to have the Marines and army report separately to the joint commander. This was the pattern during Desert Storm. In Somalia, the Marines informally assumed the LANFOR role, directing soldiers from the 10th Mountain Division (Light Infantry) and other army units. But with due regard for army sensitivities and variances in the nature of army and Marine methods, the Marine headquarters did not assume the LANFOR mantle. To date, unlike the routine designation of a JFACC, the LANFOR expedient has not officially been tried on a major operation.[39]

The habitual principles used to organize warpower for specific missions cannot be carved in stone. Operational art requires lateral cooperation between the CINCs and their subordinates as well as between different members of the armed forces. Hostile states and movements have a bad habit of appearing on the fault lines between unified commands—fighting Iraq involved both U.S. Central Command and U.S. European Command.[40]

To sort all of this out, the president and secretary of defense issue a Unified Command Plan, updated and adjusted regularly. This scheme defines the areas of responsibility for each command. Specific operation plans and orders further define the supported (primary) CINC and supporting commanders (all others) for each ongoing mission and possible contingency. Every land mass, every ocean depth, even airless space, fall under the interest of one of the unified commanders in chief.

America's unified commands cooperate to maintain stability in the world through prudent application of warpower. Thanks to modern communications wizardry, they have plenty of assistance, both welcome and not.

The awesome information transfer capacities of the U.S. Space Command make possible modern American joint warfare. Communications and navigation means once honed to ensure absolute control of nuclear weapons now serve to tie together all U.S. forces. Individual rifle squads and aircrews find their way by checking their position through a constellation of satellites. Right now, all American components can talk to each other on common radio systems. In the near future, they will be able to share data, facsimile documents, and imagery too. Much of the force can already do that.

Frontline U.S. commanders and their people have access to massive amounts of information, and they can share a lot of it with their chain of command as it comes in, in real time, as the military says. Higher headquarters can also provide instantaneous feedback and useful information, request updates, or issue orders. While it would have been difficult (though not impossible) for President Bush to have talked to Sgt. Joseph Duffy in the Korean DMZ on 19 October 1990, the White House could easily have spoken directly to Lt. Col. John Mitchell, or any and all echelons in between. Those links exist and are tested every day.[41]

With this blessing comes a curse, the desire to know too much, to gain certainty by knowing as much as possible. It is the systems analysis problem again—garbage in, garbage out. But now it happens at the speed of light.

In a perfect world, senior leaders would not interfere with operations. But this is not a perfect world. There is a strong temptation to use modern communications to micromanage ongoing military events. A naval officer who worked in the Pentagon in the early 1960s observed the beginnings of this tendency: "Modern communications also affected the civilians. There was a fascination with this. They had an attitude of 'I'm in charge' and had the tools to be in charge."[42] And we must be clear about this—the urge to "help" also extends into the uniformed ranks.

The Cable News Network and its competitors contribute to this, providing raw footage of operations as they happen. The American military expects such coverage and finds it useful as a check against official reporting through the chain of command. Still, although CNN, Reuters, and the Associated Press almost invariably get it on, they do not always get it right.

This seems obvious, as the news media have their own audiences to satisfy. Department of Defense orders state that "open and independent reporting will be the principal means of coverage," and independent is the key word. While the armed forces do issue credentials, control certain information to protect forces, and escort news people, the media does not always play by these rules.[43] CNN and friends show and tell as they see fit, almost always aided by flocks of expert witnesses only too willing to second-guess every move. Urgent reports and studio talking-head expertise collide with the information cascading from the official sources, like overlapping waves in a pond full of thrown pebbles. The CNN feed often appears to outpace the formal reporting process—ship captains, pilots, and riflemen often find it difficult to keep up the travelogue while they work through a hail of gunfire.

In the center of these maelstroms of images and data one finds American decision makers, both civilian and military. For the chain of command, with CNN blaring, radios humming, faxes churning, and instant analysts begging for attention, there is a strong sense of being right there, of really knowing what's going on. But these impressions can be highly deceptive. Whatever a camera lens, a telephone speaker, or a satellite photograph tells you can be at best only part of the picture. It is a truth, but seldom the whole truth.

To act and issue orders based on such incomplete views is foolhardy. The chain of command must trust its field leadership. Second-guessing from an air-conditioned office is as easy as quarterbacking a football team from a lounge chair and about as effective. CNN, satellite shots, and instant communications aside, the person on the scene still knows best. General George Patton, well aware of his own surging impatience, cautioned himself as much as others: "In war nothing is ever as bad, or as good, as it is reported to higher headquarters."[44] Everybody from the president on down acknowledges that, but it's hard to resist plunging in.

Modern information exchange systems, catalyzed by the immediacy of the American political and social climate, have the effect of telescoping the normally distinct layers of strategy, operations, and tactics, often from the bottom up. A firefight, an accidental killing of a civilian, or a misdirected shot can mushroom into major political flaps, sometimes sparking shifts in U.S. foreign policy. If he's not careful, some guy at the level of Lt. Col. John Mitchell in Korea may end up altering not just the local tactical situation, but operational plans and even strategic policy.

Somehow, the unified command CINCs have to allow for all of these possibilities, walking the fine line between enough supervision to help and not so much as to stifle subordinate initiative. The CINCs also must confront and calm the concerns of the president, the secretary of defense, and the Joint Chiefs of Staff, with a sidelong glance at the CBS *Evening News* in the process. That's the nature of the beast, and another brick in the rucksack for America's unified commanders in chief. It is one reason they call it operational "art."

This, then, is the structure that underpins America's use of military force in a dangerous, distrustful world. America is already at war with much of the globe, albeit in the guise of OOTW rather than in the style of Anzio. Arguing about whether an operation constitutes low-, mid-, or high-intensity combat, or if it occurs in peacetime competition, conflict, limited war, or general war really doesn't matter.[45] Once Americans enter the underdeveloped world, they are at war. It only remains to be seen who will draw and fire first.

The United States wants to impose stability on a world that doesn't always want to cooperate, and yet America's well-being and economic power depend on doing business with these distrusting, disrespectful folks. So America's use of force weighs heavily in favor of control, and hence landpower, intimately backed by destructive power. This eats at the sincere American wish to substitute some kind of technology for young men in fatigue shirts. But that's not in the cards. In the words of the Duke of Wellington, who knew much of wars both great and small, to keep order "there is but one way—to do as I did—to have a hand of iron."[46] Warpower is America's iron hand.

Notes

The epigraph is from T. R. Fehrenbach, *This Kind of War* (New York: Macmillan, 1966), 427.

1. William H. Lewis, ed., *Military Implications of United Nations Peacekeeping Operations,* McNair Paper, 17 (Fort McNair, D.C.: National University Press, 1993), 12–13, 32–38.

2. U.S. Department of the Army, *FM 100-5 Operations* (Washington, D.C.: U.S. Government Printing Office, 1993), 2-1, glossary-18.

3. Russell F. Weigley, *The American Way of War* (Bloomington: Indiana University Press, 1977), 13.

4. Sun Tzu, *The Art of War,* trans. and ed. Brig. Gen. Samuel B. Griffith, USMC (Ret.) (Oxford, England: Oxford University Press, 1963), 77.

5. Lt. Gen. Phillip B. Davidson, USA (Ret.), *Vietnam at War: The History, 1946–1975* (Novato, Calif.: Presidio Press, 1988), 339, 434–42, 727–29. For the Iran case, see Capt. Paul B. Ryan, USN (Ret.), *The Iranian Hostage Rescue Mission: Why It Failed* (Annapolis, Md.: U.S. Naval Institute Press, 1985), 6–13.

6. Department of the Army, *FM 100-5,* 2-3.

7. "Service and Casualties in Major Wars and Conflicts," *Defense 91* (September/October 1991): 47.

8. Thomas Kuhn, *The Structure of Scientific Revolutions* (Chicago: University of Chicago Press, 1970), 66–91.

9. Carl Sagan, *Cosmos* (New York: Random House, 1980), 50–67.

10. U.S. Department of Defense, *Joint Publication 1: Joint Warfare of the U.S. Armed Forces* (Washington, D.C.: National Defense University Press, 11 November 1991), 2–3. This doctrinal overview was distributed to every active and reserve field grade officer, senior NCO, and senior civilian in the armed forces and defense establishment. See also U.S. Department of the Navy, *From the Sea* (Washington, D.C.: Department of the Navy, 1992), 2; and U.S. Department of the Air Force, *Global Reach—Global Power* (Washington, D.C.: Department of the Air Force, 1992), 9.

11. President George H. Bush, *National Security Strategy of the United States* (Washington, D.C.: U.S. Government Printing Office, 1993), 3.

12. Ryan, *The Iranian Hostage Rescue Mission,* 9; Daniel P. Bolger, *Americans at War: An Era of Violent Peace, 1975–1986* (Novato, Calif.: Presidio Press, 1988), 171.

13. Bush, *National Security Strategy,* 3.

14. RAdm. J. C. Wylie, USN (Ret.), *Military Strategy: A General Theory of Power Control* (Annapolis, Md.: U.S. Naval Institute Press, 1989). The idea of control, and the deficiencies of classical airpower and seapower ideas, is superbly analyzed here. See also Col. Kenneth Allard, USAF, *Command, Control, and the Common Defense* (New Haven, Conn.: Yale University Press, 1991), 254–64; Gen. Harold K. Johnson, USA, "A Perspective on Firepower: Remarks to Association of the United States Army Firepower Symposium" (Fort Sill, Okla.: 25 August 1964); and Col. James M. Dubik, USA, "Military Force in the 21st Century" (Washington, D.C.: Army Staff, Pentagon, 11 August 1993).

15. Department of Defense, *JCS Pub. 1,* 81. Quote by General of the Air Force Arnold.

16. General of the Army Omar N. Bradley and Clay Blair, *A General's Life* (New York: Simon and Schuster, 1983), 506–12.

17. Giulio Douhet, *The Command of the Air,* trans. Dino Ferrari (New York: Coward-McCann, 1942), 57–58.

18. For examples of American restrictions on attacking civilians, see Russel F. Weigley, *Eisenhower's Lieutenants* (Bloomington: Indiana University Press, 1981), 62–64; Rick Atkinson, *Crusade* (Boston: Houghton Mifflin, 1993), 290–94; and John Morrocco, *The Vietnam Experience: Thunder From Above* (Boston: Boston, 1984), 184. See also Eliot Cohen, "The Air War in the Persian Gulf," *Armed Forces Journal International* (June 1993): 14. Cohen, who also directed a massive, nine-volume study of Gulf War air operations for the U.S. Air Force, wrote in his article: "Throughout the conflict, coalition forces took exceptional care to avoid civilian casualties, even if this meant accepting lower levels of operational effectiveness."

19. Cohen, "The Air War in the Persian Gulf," 10–14. The Cohen team granted devastating effects against the Iraqi air defense system and the destruction of morale in frontline units. Effects on the more powerful Republican Guard formations, telecommunications, oil, electricity, and rails/roads were significant, but all of those target arrays remained at least partly functional at the war's end. Analysts could find no evidence that any Iraqi Scud mobile missiles were hit. Some nuclear and chemical targets were hit; others were not even located, let alone attacked. Cohen believes that

"dramatic changes were implied by the war's operations, but the reality was less promising."

20. Alfred Thayer Mahan, *The Influence of Sea Power upon the French Revolution and Empire, 1793–1812* (Boston: Little, Brown, 1892), 2: 108, 118, 184–85, 400–402.

21. Alfred Thayer Mahan, *Naval Strategy Compared and Contrasted with Military Operations on Land* (Boston: Little, Brown, 1911), 139, 435.

22. Ray Bonds, ed., *The U.S. War Machine* (London: Salamander Books, 1983), 116, 211. The information in Bonds is somewhat dated and should be considered in light of what is in Secretary of Defense Les Aspin, *The Bottom-Up Review: Forces for a New Era* (Washington, D.C.: Department of Defense, 1993), 15–16. Normally, American naval forces deployed include three to four carrier battle groups (each with a maximum of sixty attack jets) and two to three Marine expeditionary units (battalion landing team, composite air squadron, and service support) embarked on amphibious shipping.

23. Alain C. Enthoven and K. Wayne Smith, *How Much Is Enough: Shaping the Defense Program, 1961–1969* (New York: Harper and Row, 1971), 89–106.

24. David Halberstam, *The Best and the Brightest* (Greenwich, Conn.: Fawcett Publications, 1973), 304. For other trenchant critiques of systems analysis as a form of military strategy, see Eliot Cohen, "Systems Paralysis," *American Spectator* (November 1980): 23–27; and Col. Harry G. Summers Jr., USA, *On Strategy: The Vietnam War in Context* (Carlisle, Pa.: Strategic Studies Institute, 1981), 27–32. Secretary Les Aspin's background as a systems analyst is noted in Bruce B. Auster and Greg Ferguson, "Caught in the Crossfire," *U.S. News and World Report* (6 December 1993): 30.

25. Philip D. Zelikow, "Force Without War, 1975–1982," *Journal of Strategic Studies* (March 1984): 29–54. Zelikow based his work on Barry M. Blechman and Stephen S. Kaplan, *Force Without War* (Washington, D.C.: Brookings, 1978). Blechman and Kaplan found that in 215 crises from 1945 to 1975, seapower alone addresses 47 percent of the crises, airpower proved useful in 10 percent, and a joint force acted in 42 percent. The bulk of the "seapower only" cases occurred prior to the 1962 Cuban Missile Crisis and the final collapse of the stability provided by the remaining European colonial systems.

26. Department of the Air Force, *Global Reach—Global Power*, 3. For the reasons behind the D day claim, see W. Frank Craven and James L. Cate, eds., *The Army Air Forces in World War II*, vol. 3, *Europe: Argument to VE*

Day (Chicago: University of Chicago Press, 1951), 166. U.S. forces did not endure a single daylight air attack on D day.

27. Department of the Navy, *From the Sea,* 5.

28. Department of the Army, *FM 100-5,* 2-0 to 2-4.

29. Russell F. Weigley, *History of the United States Army* (Bloomington: Indiana University Press, 1984), 84–88.

30. Aspin, *The Bottom-Up Review,* 11–12, 14–16; Rosemary Sawyer, "Combat Gear Loaded Aboard First of Eight Vessels," *European Stars and Stripes* (18 November 1993): 3. For an analysis of typical force requirements for major and minor conflicts, see Maj. Daniel P. Bolger, USA, "A Power Projection Force: Some Concrete Proposals," *Parameters* (Winter 1992–93): 59–60, n. 11.

31. DOD, *JCS Pub 1,* 24.

32. U.S. Department of Defense, *Joint Publication 1-02: Department of Defense Dictionary of Military and Associated Terms* (Washington, D.C.: U.S. Government Printing Office, 1989), 243; Whitley Strieber and James W. Kunetka, *War Day* (New York: Holt, Rinehart, and Winston, 1984), 54–63, provides an interesting fictional account of a nuclear conflict, including a launch order sequence, and the image of the undersecretary of the treasury, a survivor, as the acting president (159).

33. DOD, *Joint Pub 1-02: Dictionary,* 350; Bonds, *U.S. War Machine,* 36–47.

34. Mark Perry, *Four Stars* (Boston: Houghton Mifflin, 1989), 328–40.

35. DOD, *Joint Pub 1-02: Dictionary,* 262; Department of the Army, *FM 100-5,* glossary-12.

36. U.S. Department of Defense, *The Conduct of the Persian Gulf War* (Washington, D.C.: U.S. Government Printing Office, 1992), K-8; DOD, *Joint Pub 1-02: Dictionary,* 262, defines "operational control." CINCs by statute exercise "combatant command" (ownership) over their forces (73). They may delegate either operational control (long-term leasing) or tactical control (short-term, single mission renting) (361).

37. DOD, *Joint Pub 1,* 24. See also John Keegan, *The Mask of Command* (New York: Viking, 1987), 164–234, 243–58; Michael Geyer, "German Strategy in the Age of Machine Warfare, 1914–1945" in *Makers of Modern Strategy,* Peter Paret, ed. (Princeton, N.J.: Princeton University Press, 1986), 527–97. For the best description of the army's adoption of the concept called "operational art," see John L. Romjue, *From Active Defense to Airland Battle* (Fort Monroe, Va.: U.S. Army Training and Doctrine Command, 1984), 61, 68–69.

38. Lt. Gen. John H. Cushman, USA (Ret.), "Command and Control in the Coalition," *Proceedings* (May 1991): 74–80. The Somalia evacuation, known as Operation Eastern Exit, occurred on 4–5 January 1991. See Brig. Gen. Edwin H. Simmons, USMC (Ret.), "Getting Marines to the Gulf," *Proceedings* (May 1991): 60–63. A unified CINC can employ six command relations: service component, functional (by mission, like the JFACC), subunified (as in Korea), a joint task force (JTF), single service, or direct personal command. See DOD, *Conduct of the Persian Gulf War,* K-1. Service component and JTF are the most used methods.

39. Gen. Colin L. Powell, USA, "Memorandum to all Joint Activities, Subject: A Doctrinal Statement of Selected Joint Operational Concepts," (Washington, D.C.: Joint Staff, Pentagon, 23 November 1992); DOD, *Joint Pub 1-02: Dictionary,* 199. For Somalia, see Maj. Gen. Waldo D. Freeman, USA, Capt. Robert B. Lambert, USN, and Lt. Col. Jason D. Mims, USA, "Operation Restore Hope: A USCENTCOM Perspective" *Military Review* (September 1993): 66–68.

40. DOD, *Conduct of the Persian Gulf War,* 147–48, F-21 to F-24, K-25 to K-44.

41. John H. Peterson, "Info Wars," *Proceedings* (May 1993): 85–92, provides a good summary of the persent situation.

42. Joseph F. Bouchard, *Command in Crisis* (New York: Columbia University Press, 1991), 96. The speaker was Captain, later Vice Admiral, William D. Houser, USN, who watched the Cuban Missile Crisis unfold in the Pentagon.

43. Gen. Gordon R. Sullivan, USA, "Message to All Army Activities, Subject: Principles Governing Future Arrangements for News Coverage of the U.S. Military in Combat" (Washington, D.C.: Army Staff Pentagon, 27 May 1992). For the corporate account of the CNN phenomenon, see Thomas B. Allen, F. Clifton Berry, and Norman Polmar, *CNN: War in the Gulf* (Atlanta, Ga.: Turner Publishing, 1991), 232–36.

44. Gen. George S. Patton Jr., USA, *War As I Knew It* (New York: Pyramid Books, 1970), 303.

45. Department of the Army, *FM 100-5,* 2-2, depicts the current range of military operations. The chart shows three levels: war, conflict, and peacetime, with combat restricted to the first two levels and operations other than war to the last two. "Noncombat operations can occur during war, just as some operations other than war might require combat." It's somewhat confusing, but then again, so is America's modern military environment.

46. Keegan, *The Mask of Command,* 140.

CHAPTER 3
Dirty Work

Let me speak proudly; tell the constable
We are but warriors for the working-day;
Our gayness and our gilt are all besmirch'd
With rainy marching in the painful field . . .

William Shakespeare
Henry V

When brutal Somali gunmen and their grinning cronies dragged the battered bodies of Sgt. Thomas Field and MSgt. Gary I. Gordon through the streets of Mogadishu on 4 October 1993 for the edification of Cable News Network watchers worldwide, average Americans reacted with horror. Cheryl Lister of Wellesley, Massachusetts, spoke for many. "Feeding food to starving people is one thing," she said. "Feeding our soldiers to bloodthirsty guerrillas is another. Bring our troops home."[1] Like their angry constituents, political leaders from the president down to local mayors all had sharp comments. Most acted as if the sky had fallen. Somalia was supposed to be benign, clean, and easy. The refrain sounded: "We did not sign up for this."

Of course, we signed up for exactly this. To read the newspapers, listen to the radio, or watch television in America in late 1993, you would think that American troops in Somalia had been just running soup kitchens and spreading good cheer when the disgruntled locals emerged from some unforeseen hellhole. Maybe it seemed that way, especially given America's gross ignorance about life in the grim Somali capital. Downtown Mogadishu certainly does not get much airplay on *Lifestyles of the Rich and Famous.*

But what happened to the two unfortunate soldiers is what happens in wars. They and their comrades had no illusions as they choppered into battle with weapons primed. "War is cruelty and you cannot refine it," said Gen.

105

William Tecumseh Sherman.[2] Having wrecked the Confederate Army of Tennessee, devastated Georgia and the Carolinas, and crushed several tribes of Plains Indians, Sherman knew what he was saying. He had been there.

So have many others. The things lumped together today as operations other than war are not new. Americans in uniform have been doing them since 1775, and these little wars, these OOTWs, have been the rule between the exceptional spasms we normally call wars. We have fought ten major wars, lasting a total of about thirty-eight years, since 1775. But over the span of that same two-plus centuries, the United States conducted hundreds of other combat missions, and the men (and some women) killed in small wars are just as dead as those killed in big ones.[3] It has always been a savage peace out there past the stockade gates. The work is never clean or easy.

They did not have CNN back in 1866 when Col. Henry Carrington and his regiment found the shredded physical remnants of Capt. William Fetterman's massacred eighty-four man column on a knoll near the modern town of Sheridan, Wyoming. We must make do with Carrington's laconic list of atrocities: "Eyes torn out and laid on rocks; noses cut off, ears cut off, chins hewn off, teeth chopped out, joints of fingers cut off, brains taken out and placed on rocks, entrails taken out and exposed, hands cut off, feet cut off, arms taken out from socket, private parts severed."[4] That's what can happen out in the Great Gulp. It isn't pretty.

If you go to the average bookstore today and consult the racks of business literature, you might be amazed to see how much of it follows the "business is war" motif. You can learn to run with the wolves, swim with the sharks, and take the high ground. Books tout the leadership and tactical secrets of George Patton, Norman Schwarzkopf, Gus Pagonis, Attila the Hun (made-up and freely admitted as such), and other famous generals. Even Sun Tzu has a following among those seeking insight into "the Oriental mind" (whatever that is) prior to cutting deals in Seoul or Tokyo. Authors counsel inside tricks, using military jargon like "outflanking the competition," "penetrating his market," and "seizing his assets." Hard, cutting phrases predominate: "be ruthless," "dog eat dog," "cut-throat," "win at all costs," and "show no mercy."

Now this is all harmless when taken as it is intended, as argument by analogy. But the business as war analogy breaks down at its most fundamental level. The average stockbroker, executive vice president, or corporate attorney may blow a deal. He could bankrupt his firm. He might even lose his job. But he will not get his stomach ripped open by a trench knife or his face torn off by a white phosphorus grenade, not unusual consequences in that other dirty world where war is the only business.

This could well explain why Carl von Clausewitz has not been very popular in the community of business writers. Clausewitz, who actually got shot at a good bit during the Napoleonic Wars, addressed the real face of war in his massive master work, *Vom Krieg* (On War), which was still not fully edited at his death. Like the Bible, another volume not carefully edited and not likely to be, *On War* has something for everyone. And like the Bible, it gets quoted out of context on a regular basis.

Clausewitz has a style all his own, and some parts are easier going than others. The more interesting and often-quoted sections discuss war as a continuation of state politics by other means, the importance of battle, and the qualities of military genius. There are also lesser-known stretches on mountain warfare, march order, and partisan warfare. These are all fine and full of useful ideas. But the real reason Clausewitz will never take his place in a *One-Minute Conqueror* compendium has to do with his absorbing interest in the gruesome realities of combat. Like a gawker at a bloody car wreck, Clausewitz stares and tells.

Clausewitz explained that all military operations feature the opposition of at least two human groups, facing off in an environment of time and space. When you rub two sticks together you get friction, and in the broadest sense, the same thing happens when folks with weapons go after each other. Friction arises regardless of the scale of effort; rifle squads in the Korean DMZ know it as well as any squad that fought at Hue City in Vietnam. The guys at the pointy end, however few, always find the intensity high enough in their neighborhood, and some armed conflicts are worse than others. But every one, of every type, produces friction.

Clausewitz noted four of the chief characteristics of what he termed "general friction": physical exhaustion, incomplete information, things that just go wrong, and danger. All cause trouble. That last item on the list, danger, explains why war is war, not to be confused with advertising, football, or chess.

Physical exhaustion affects many human activities, although war intensifies exertion. A good portion of the military still lives outdoors in the wind, rain, cold, and heat. Even relatively cozy airmen and sailors endure industrial age warrens of screaming engines, dripping pipes, and sparking wires in the bowels of some flying giant or storm-tossed leviathan. Staying safe, dry, warm, and cool—indeed, just staying alive—on a pitching, icy destroyer deck or in a monsoon torrent can take a lot out of a person.

Exposure is only part of the story; sweating, grinding physical labor is the rest. Marine and army riflemen still walk, often under excruciating loads of nearly a hundred pounds. Gunners in tanks, on howitzers, in some ship turrets, and even aboard AC-130H Spectre flying gunships manhandle long, slick rounds of ammunition as big and heavy as full ten-gallon coffee urns, one after another for hours on end, and often on a pitching, rolling deck as their vehicle, ship, or aircraft jinks and accelerates to evade enemy fire. Most everyone on land digs holes and trenches; most everyone afloat chips paint and moves heavy chains and lines. Marines get to do both, which may explain their unusual aggressiveness.

You may think that modern conveyances help, and they do. But high, medium, and low technology takes its own toll. Mechanics, drivers, crew chiefs, and technicians swap out huge, greasy metal things for other unwieldy, slimy metallic objects. No robots exist that can extract and replace helicopter engines, refuel landing craft, load thousand-pound bombs, or change cargo truck tires. Just moving the parts, fuel, and ammunition occupies entire regiments. There never seem to be enough forklifts or time, but there are always plenty of strong backs.

Only a few people in uniform push buttons for a living. Even they tend to get rousted out for guard duty, damage control parties, and other entertaining diversions out in the unforgiving elements. Heavy lifting, brute force, and backbreaking labor are still required in almost all segments of the armed forces, and those who airily dismiss war as a video game suitable for the frail would do well to keep that in mind. Lack of sleep and missed meals don't help. It's a recipe for miscalculations and oversights as tired brains and aching bodies try to gut it through one more event. Sooner or later, the fuel tank runs dry.[5]

One way to hedge against fatigue involves getting more and/or better information on which to base decisions—at least that's the theory. In practice it doesn't pan out. Clausewitz, who had the operator's traditional disdain of intelligence officers, summarized rather brutally, "Many intelligence reports in war are contradictory; even more are false, and most are uncertain."[6] The intelligence guys can always tell you exactly what just hit you. That's not much comfort.

Tired and surrounded by ambiguity, Clausewitz subscribed early to Murphy's Law ("What can go wrong will go wrong"). He explained it this way: "Countless minor incidents—the kind you can never really foresee—

HOTEL Crescent Court
DALLAS

ROSEWOOD HOTELS & RESORTS

combine to lower the general level of performance, so that one always falls far short of the intended goal."[7]

This is not some mystical property of armed conflict. You do not have to be in the armed forces to experience this brand of friction. Membership in the human race will do. Given the myriad of variables in human reason and emotion, compounded by numbers of people and the wonders of today's machinery, any complex human activity, even a relatively benign one, displays this annoying tendency.

Anyone who has ever planned and conducted a wedding understands this. The flowers arrive late and, despite what the catalog showed, the genuine items don't quite match the bridesmaids' dresses. The reverend reads the wrong selection. Aunt Tilly gets lost and never does show up. Little Johnny the ringbearer elects to take a ninety-degree turn halfway up the aisle. We've all been there. We do not expect our lives to be perfect, and military endeavors are working with the same blunt instruments.

Physical exhaustion, inadequate information, and "countless minor incidents" are bad enough, and the realities of combat exaggerate these aspects. But by far the greatest cause of friction is outright danger. "Without an accurate conception of danger, we cannot understand war," said Clausewitz.[8] Amen to that.

Danger means a lot more than having a bad hair day. It means being scared that at any minute a Scud rocket, a shell, a bullet, a bayonet, or the creeping blorch will arrive unbidden and send you to the next world, and you may or may not be able to do anything about that. Many occupations are hazardous, construction work for one, but you can take preventive measures to limit predictable outcomes. Tall buildings and suspension bridges tend not to hide, run around, or shoot back. Only the most awful police work includes a thinking, stalking killer as a central concern. For those on patrol somewhere out there, danger is a constant companion. It is the unifying cord that binds together every other aspect of friction.

Danger does come in degrees. Few would argue that the riflemen on patrol in the Korean DMZ are in as much danger as the 5th Ranger Battalion clambering up Pointe du Hoc under machine-gun fire on 6 June 1944. But the potential is there in both cases, and stress comes with that. If it's coming your way, it takes only one round to put you at war.

Whatever its perceived degree, danger increases the highs and depresses the lows. It can keep a man alert when dead-tired, and then leave him drained and useless when he needs to be ready again. Danger causes intelligence people to hedge every bet, to overreact, to jump to conclusions, then jump back. It makes things already going wrong go more wrong. Fears of maiming, death, capture, and failure gnaw at the back of the mind—they circle through the subconscious, waiting like rabid dogs, licking their chops, ready to pounce when exhaustion, rumors, or frustration cut the leashes.

Sometimes, unbridled fear brings on panic, but that is not the worst. At least a panicked unit does something, even if it's wrong. In its ultimate state, danger gives birth to fear so great—piss-your-pants fear—that it causes utter paralysis of the individual, of the small unit, or of a vast command. Such people just stand there like rabbits caught in the headlights: dumbstruck, inert, doomed. That doesn't happen in Madison Avenue executive suites. But it happens in war, and in OOTW, too.

"Friction is the only concept that more or less corresponds to the factors that distinguish real war from war on paper," wrote Clausewitz.[9] It is an ugly, uncomfortable concept, a thing that will not go away. No technology on earth can banish friction. The best the military can hope to do is acknowledge it, accept it, and work around it. The best the American armed forces can do about friction is train to live with it.

You can learn a lot about friction on the island of Aragon. There's almost always fighting going on there—OOTW, war, and the blurry mix of the two ideas that Americans have been running into lately around the world. The island crawls with friction: fatigue, smart enemies and the resultant dearth of solid intelligence, and all the little Murphys that you can imagine. There is some danger, what with live rounds going off all the time, high-performance aircraft, parachute and heliborne assaults, and complex night operations. But people do not die on Aragon, because most of the bullets are eye-safe laser beams, courtesy of the army's version of Laser Tag, MILES (multiple integrated laser engagement system).

Aragon is, in reality, Fort Polk, Louisiana, and the surrounding states. The army's Joint Readiness Training Center (JRTC) makes its home at Fort Polk. Its exercises also sprawl out to encompass outlying areas: Fort Sill in Oklahoma, Little Rock Air Force Base and Pine Bluff Arsenal in Arkansas, and England Air Force Base in Louisiana. But most of the action occurs on the Polk reservation.[10]

The fact that Aragon is mythical should not take away from its value as a learning experience, a chance for American forces to experience friction. The danger of death and wounding cannot really be replicated, but the boys at Polk are clever. Stealing a page from the army's demanding Ranger

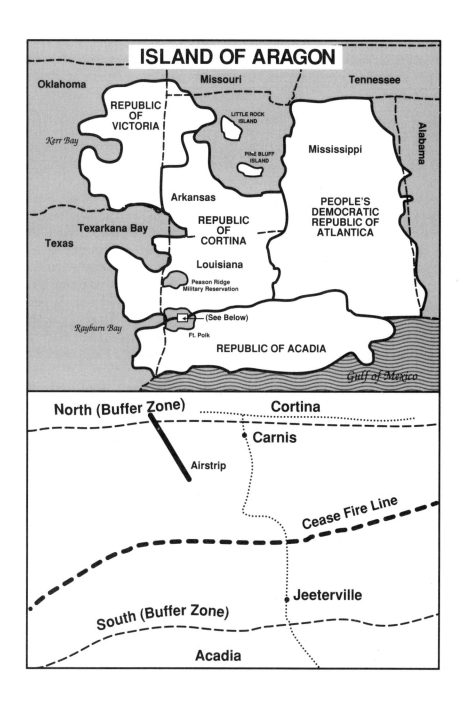

School, they substitute relentless assessment, a brutal pace of operations, a highly skilled enemy, and a very murky battlefield situation to increase the stress levels on the player units. They ratchet up the other aspects of friction and substitute for mortal peril the danger of professional failure—not to be taken lightly in a shrinking military eager to cast off its weaker constituents. It works. Friction abounds.

And units, individuals, and especially leaders learn. The bloodless nature of the instruction offers one big bonus not found in real life. In Aragon, you can make mistakes today and live to do better tomorrow.

Aragon is designed as true Indian country, badlands to the nth degree. It has a history not unlike a lot of places that concern Americans. It may be made-up, but in the case of the military's training, art definitely imitates life. Supposedly located on the northeastern fringes of the Caribbean Sea about a thousand miles southeast of the United States, Aragon hosts four small, jealous states: nonaligned Victoria, pro-Cuban Atlantica, pro-American Cortina, and an upstart country, Acadia, made up of a quartet of southern departments that seceded from Cortina. Although exercises can key on any of the four countries, a particularly interesting one in November 1993 focused on a peace enforcement operation along the raw new border between Cortina and Acadia.

Cortina, a typical lesser-developed country, exhibits all of the usual problems: a colonial past, per capita income of less than three hundred U.S. dollars a year, population pressures, less than a 50 percent literacy rate, and a lot of weapons lying around (thankfully no nuclear or biological, but perhaps some chemical stuff). By the summer of 1993, Cortina had been wracked by brutal internal conflict for almost a decade. The ethnic Acadians of southern Cortina, the island's native population, had long since squared off against the British-stock Cortinian majority. With the founding of their breakaway state, the Acadians gained a firm base to help their ethnic relatives.

During recent American administrations, America backed its small Cortinian ally. Marxist Atlantica had funneled arms to the Acadians during the Cold War. Once the Soviet Union fragmented, the Cuban spigot shut off, and Atlantica ceased active support to the Acadians. The Cortinians closed in for the kill. The Acadian government recognized that without Atlantican aid, their movement lacked the armed might to defeat Cortina. Acadia began making noises about a settlement.

Here, the United Nations came in. In response to Acadian demands and concerns on both sides about ethnic cleansing, the UN arranged a cease-fire and separation of forces. Negotiators convinced the belligerents to pull back from an agreed cease-fire line (CFL), which bisected a buffer zone to be manned by UN peacekeepers, including Americans. The normal DMZ terminology had been rejected by the Acadians in Cortina, who proved willing to pull back but did not plan to disarm anytime soon.

The Cortinian leadership did not like any of this, but with America backing the UN, they had to accept the inevitable. The Acadians in Cortina, who might well have gone the way of the dodo without UN intervention, were quite pleased. Along with stopping the slow but inexorable Cortinian campaign of extermination, the agreement appeared to permit enough food to get through another winter. The constant civil strife had long since ravaged local agriculture.

International publicity attended the pressing need to get food to the populace, especially the Acadians. Nongovernmental aid organizations and private charities had been in country for years, but the cease-fire gave them hope this winter might be different. The International Rescue Committee, Interaction, the International Red Cross, Save the Children, World Vision, and CARE leaders in Cortina thought they had enough supplies. They trusted that the peacekeepers, led by the Americans, could provide enough stability to permit distribution.

So, with television cameras whirring and winter closing in, the United Nations interceded in force. Along with token units from other countries, America offered the 21st Infantry Division (Light) (a notional unit played by the JRTC exercise group), which included the "All-American" 82d Airborne's 2d Brigade (a very real unit, the focus of the rotation). The UN command hoped to get between and disarm the warring parties, a tricky interposition mission.[11] It would not be easy. The JRTC designed it to be hard, to re-create the pain and friction of doing it for real.

In that respect, the exercise labeled JRTC Rotation 94-2 reflected the way Americans learn about their dirty work. Soldiers, sailors, airmen, and Marines do not become educated in their profession primarily by reading books, especially not the dull warehouse loads of service doctrine. That's hardly the American way. Books are for nerds and couch potatoes. Action guys, the sort you need to pilot F-15E Strike Eagles or jump out of a landing craft under fire, get to work. Hands-on folks start punching buttons on microwaves, computers, and videocassette recorders with hardly a glance at the obtuse instruction manuals. They take apart car engines to see how they're put together. America, and especially its military, brims with action guys, type A personalities with "make it happen" written all over their chiseled faces.

The JRTC and its many analogs in the army and the other services recognize that strain in fighting men, as have all good militaries through the ages.[12] You can read about OOTW and friction all day, but how much better to live it, feel it, and be it. JRTC 94-2 allowed just such a total immersion experience, minus the blood.

This laboratory of OOTW allows a good look at the full-blown phenomenon. Military professionals often size up their conditions using the time-honored "estimate of the situation," marked by the mnemonic METT-T: mission, enemy, terrain, troops available, and time. It can serve as a decent framework to consider a generic OOTW, JRTC 94-2.

The mission drives everything, and one of the first challenges in OOTW involves translation of political aims into military tasks. In the Cortina situation, the UN voted to "enforce, supervise, monitor, and verify the cease-fire" in order to "stop the hostilities."[13] Those are fairly clear goals for policy makers, but you cannot hand them verbatim to a fighter squadron commander or rifle platoon sergeant. At that level, "enforce" and "stop" can mean anything or everything.

The chain of command, starting with the theater commander and the head of Joint Task Force Cortina, had to restate these concepts in more familiar language, the professional tongue of service doctrine. If done right, the tasks should be defined in first-order military euphemisms like attack or defend. When the time came to execute, the trigger pullers would reduce it to the bottom line, brute Anglo-Saxon words of one syllable: kill, break, shoot, hold.

Because JRTC is a training environment, the scenario builders decided to do the job only partway, as so often happens in reality. It would be up to the brigade chain of command to resolve the remaining ambiguities, and that in itself is an important aspect of OOTW. Thus, the paratroopers headed into Aragon as part of the mythical 21st Infantry Division received this mission:

21st Infantry Division (Light) conducts airborne assault commencing 081000Z November 1993 to seize Objective GRANT (grid coordinates WE033420), conducts peace enforcement operations, protects relief efforts and the civilian population, and demilitarizes the UN Buffer Zone. On order, conducts combat operations to defeat hostile elements.[14]

That's a real mouthful and no easier to do than say. For the 2d Brigade of the 82d Airborne Division, a subordinate command of the 21st Infantry Division on this operation, the mission statement specified five tasks. Only two accorded with doctrine, and another came close. The other pair would require interpretation.

First, in a straightforward task right out of the book, the brigade would assault by parachute to take a dirt landing strip (Objective Grant) just north of the CFL. The operation would begin at 1000 Greenwich mean time, which was 0400 local, on 8 November. The jump would not only get the whole brigade into the buffer zone rapidly, it would take charge of an airfield to permit rapid reinforcement by transport plane. The jump also promised an impressive show of force, a warning to belligerents to back off or face the wrath of Uncle Sam's warpower team.

The second task got a lot fuzzier. The brigade was directed to carry out "peace enforcement operations," removing belligerents from the buffer zone. This required the All-Americans to occupy and secure a central strip between the two sides, interposition in peacekeeping verbiage. Of course, saying it was one thing. Doing it is another, especially when parts of both sides choose not to play fair, a typical occurrence in these ventures. The interposition force must stay utterly impartial—it cannot favor one party.

In an ideal situation, all factions agree with those ground rules. But when you put rich and powerful Americans whom everyone loves to hate into the middle of an ethnic dispute, it can be like tossing a bullock into an Amazon tributary teeming with piranha. The little nasties always come biting.

Along with a show of force and interposition, the brigade was directed to protect relief efforts and protect local civilians, to include members of UN and private relief organizations and the usual clutch of official and unofficial American civilians in country, including the news media. This was close to traditional defense and security roles, although the nature of those guarded offered unique challenges. Protecting people who are used to being free agents can be a war in itself; they tend to wander about like unpenned cattle. Everybody, however, seems to dial 911 when the bad guys appear on the scene hunting Yankee hostages and heads.

While doing all of this, the brigade was told to demilitarize the buffer

zone. This term cannot be found in American doctrine. It could mean anything from collecting ammunition caches to dispatching armed recalcitrants
with one between the eyes. How you demilitarize an area by shooting
people remains problematic. (Ask John Mitchell and 1-5th Infantry about
that one.) Still, orders were orders. The paratroopers would give it a try.

Finally, in a what-if situation, the brigade had to be ready for transition
almost instantly ("on order") to fight and finish formed enemy units. This
one matched all of the book language. With the Cortinians and Acadians
keeping an uneasy truce, and the nefarious Atlanticans making bad noises
along the border, one could not assume that things could not get worse.
OOTW can always get worse.

The brigade's five tasks overlapped and in some cases contradicted each
other. How, for example, could one protect a food convoy going to the
Acadians and still appear neutral in Cortinian eyes? To help sort out the
essential from the merely important, the military relies on the commander's
intent, a brief statement of what success looks like. If all else fails, a unit can
work with just a mission (who, what, when, where, and why) and intent
(victory conditions). Note that "how" is preferably left up to subordinates,
although training, experience, written doctrine, and that messy ROE stuff all
crop up at this juncture. It's not a perfect world.

The 21st Infantry Division commander's intent defined success as "the
removal of uniformed forces and hostile elements from the Buffer Zone,
satisfying the UN mandate conditions for handover to UN peacekeeping
forces."[15] In blunt language, when the buffer zone was clear, the paratroopers could leave, to be replaced by the UN troops for the long haul of peace
negotiations to follow. Cleaning out the buffer zone was one of the main
things that would make or break the mission.

The other crucial measure of success involved an implied task, an uninvited but everpresent guest at this and every other OOTW party. Missions
are all fine, but when the roof caves in, survival takes over. And survival,
"force protection," is always a key task, especially in small-scale operations.
You cannot do much if you cannot survive the environment. Self-defense
in the American style can often have drastic effects on the locals. In many
respects, when America deploys an aircraft carrier battle group or a brigade
of airborne troopers, the country anticipates some degree of local compul-
sion simply by the actions of the force to defend itself. The use of destructive force had to be wise and discreet, or the Americans would destroy
Cortina and Acadia in order to save them. Of course, one could not pull

too many punches. There were those hungry schools of piranha lurking out there.

The 2d Brigade's paratroopers had to resolve this dilemma. Along with safeguarding local civilians, they had to prevent casualties, both for their own sakes and those of the American citizenry. Saving Western Europe or blunting world Communism was one thing, and the populace could accept some heavy losses for those kinds of undertakings. But sorting out ugly knife fights in Third World states falls into that tenuous outer ring of American interests. Once all the U.S. citizens are safe, Paul in Peoria often reverts to thinking along the lines of "screw the locals, and a pox on all their squalid houses." So the airborne soldiers could not afford any bloody reverses.[16] The opposing side knew that, which certainly made life interesting.

The opposing forces in Aragon knew a lot of things, and outlasting and embarrassing Uncle Sam's finest would be all in a night's work. Enemy forces in the buffer zone between Cortina and Acadia, as in all OOTWs, were not well defined. But they were there, doing their part to create friction.

On paper, there were two fighting contingents in the disputed area: Cortinian and Acadian armed forces, mainly uniformed armies backed by tiny air and naval forces. Along with these conventional foes, one encountered the unconventional threat, the Cortinian National Militia and the Acadian Freedom Fighters (AFF), both heavily armed and not much concerned with wearing uniforms. All four forces professed public agreement with the UN goals. Under the screen of rhetoric, though, the Cortinian regulars and militia looked for opportunities to continue the war. The Acadian military openly cooperated with the peace process, yet in fact was facilitating a clandestine war by AFF guerrillas. The AFF was merely using the cease-fire, and (it hoped) the ignorant Americans, as new tools in its continuing armed struggle.[17] This sort of force mixture and duplicity typifies OOTW.

The JRTC forces, both those used in Rotation 94-2 and those on hand to create other exercises, intentionally mirror the real world. While every potential adversary, whether a country or a subnational group, fields a distinctive armed force, several generalizations hold true. America's enemies come in three basic flavors: conventional, guerrilla, and police.

Conventional foes practice modern combined-arms warfare, and some even approximate aspects of U.S. warpower. Well-trained, well-led, highly disciplined forces equipped with the latest technology comprise a very dangerous brand of opposition. Examples of such potential enemies include North Korea, an unfriendly China, a resurgent Russia, or such nightmares as Germany, Japan, or France turned violently anti-American. Only a few states fight like this.

Unconventional opponents organize for protracted warfare. They field lightly armed insurgent and terrorist elements and use neutral or sympathetic populations as shields and support networks. They aim to exhaust the Americans in a lengthy war of attrition, usually waged at the expense of unlucky civilians in the area. Skilled propagandists play on fear of foreign Yankee influences and fan ill will in the hamlets that are battered whenever frustrated American units lash out with high-technology firepower in response to guerrilla goading. This method has a lot of potential, and those who have used it against Americans have seldom been disappointed. But it takes time, tremendously disciplined forces, and a willingness to absorb massive casualties from the Americans in the process. It worked for the Vietnamese Communists, but failed miserably for the American Indians and Filipino Insurrectos. Though hard to pull off, insurgent warfare remains the favorite among those determined to derail American OOTW efforts.

Fortunately, the majority of aggressive states lack the capacity to field credible conventional or unconventional forces. Most of the earth's unhappy family rely on what may be described as police armies. They exist to prop up authoritarian regimes, bash in the skulls of troublemakers, and overawe similarly armed and governed neighbors. Although often numerous and sometimes equipped with lavish stocks of top-grade weaponry, these forces are very brittle implements. Police armies suffer from deficient leadership (often chosen for loyalty rather than competence), inadequate or nonexistent training, and weak unit cohesion. In a fight against American warpower, police armies tend to shoot once and then collapse, a pattern seen in Grenada, Panama, Libya, and Iraq. Still, these people have the numbers and weapons to bloody Americans who do not take them seriously. Police armies may be easy foes, but they are not complete pushovers, especially if defending home turf.

In the JRTC scheme, the Cortinians and Acadians fit the police army mold, and their militias obviously filled the guerrilla niche—Americans in OOTW should expect such a heterogeneous force. The JRTC "wider world" could draw upon other made-up countries, analogous to actual hostile states. JRTC's conventional enemy, trained, equipped, and disciplined, were the Atlanticans, who bore some resemblance to the Cubans. Other conventional threats that could be introduced included the Krasnovians (like the Russians) and the Hamchuk forces (a North Korean model). For those who might object to seeing Krasnovians or Hamchukans involved on a Caribbean island, it might be noted that actual Russians and North Koreans were very much in evidence on Grenada in 1983.[18] The JRTC staff could draw on a large and believable cast of characters as they crafted their doings on Aragon.

The only problem at JRTC was that the enemy was always too skilled and disciplined. There was simply no reasonable way to make the Americans portraying police armies reflect their lack of initiative, poor field craft, indifferent marksmanship, and flaky teamwork. The JRTC hostiles, drawn from the paratroopers of the 1st Battalion, 509th Infantry, were very high caliber soldiers indeed, with the added advantage of knowing Fort Polk quite well. The army leadership accepted these qualitative disparities between the JRTC exercise enemy and real American opponents. It only made things harder, adding a little more stress and friction into the soup. Hardbitten Roman legionnaires used to train with double-weight weapons in conformity to the same logic.[19] By comparison, dealing with the actual situations would seem much easier.

Terrain creates the arena of conflict, and it includes both physical and human aspects. Although Fort Polk could not re-create the precise foliage and climate of a tropical island, it had enough thickets, swamps, and sloughs to make things bad enough. The United States Army recognized tough land when it saw it, and trained thousands of soldiers for Vietnam at Polk.[20] Like most military reservations, the post's training areas lacked paved roads, electricity, water and sewage, and telephone service. Dirt roads and a few small, muddy airstrips offered the only links to the outside world. Much of the land was pure wilderness. In short, the back forty at Polk looked like a hundred lesser-developed countries around the world.

Although the post and, by extension, Aragon lacked modern infrastructure, it did not lack people. They added their own complications. Until the last ten years or so, most military exercises occurred in *Field and Stream* settings devoid of inhabitants. But experience in many small scrapes convinced the leaders of all the services that today's battlefields include civilians, their towns, and, in some cases, substantial cities, such as Beirut, Panama City, and Mogadishu. A good simulated battlefield must do likewise. Since its conception, JRTC has always provided civilians. The center brought in contract actors and some detailed soldiers, real humanitarian relief workers, and a mix of real and role-playing journalists. The people on the ground also were outfitted with MILES and, where appropriate (hunters, guerrillas, local firearms enthusiasts), with weapons. It did not take many civilians, perhaps a hundred or so, to peg the old friction meter.

The will of these people figured prominently in the success or failure of the American mission on Aragon. If the Americans gained popular support, they could expect good local intelligence and consequent degeneration of the insurgent information channels. But if the local people turned against the U.S. forces, the guerrillas and terrorists would have it their way, with the stage set for a protracted struggle. Already leery of foreigners, especially the curious and dreadful Yankees, the folk of the area would form their opinions based upon first impressions. To keep their goodwill, the Americans had to be scrupulous about avoiding accidental civilian deaths and property damage, helping with food and medicine without taking over, and treating everyone with dignity and respect. The usual American lack of language facility did not help.

The U.S. armed forces, and certainly the army, had a mixed track record in winning hearts and minds. There had been many successes on the American frontier and overseas, to include the eventual resolution of the Philippine Insurrection, the Marine interventions in Haiti and the Dominican Republic, counterinsurgent efforts in South Korea, the 1965 Dominican Republic operation, the cleanup in Grenada, and the aftermath of the Panama campaign of December 1989. The postwar recoveries in Germany and Japan reflected admirably on those prostrate societies' GI occupiers. American soldiers, after all, are not the Mongols or the Visigoths.

But against many fine performances, one must consider the blots and failures. Few in uniform want to talk about Washita and Wounded Knee, water torture and refugee relocation in the Philippines, or the policies that led to My Lai and free-fire zones in Vietnam. In every case, the local commanders justified their actions in terms of protecting their troops.

In some ways, the situation created at Fort Polk showed how much Americans had learned in the doomed fight for Vietnam. By almost any measure, the war in Southeast Asia represented a nadir in the balancing act between protecting a region's population and preserving American military lives. American use of firepower was prodigious, so much so that South Vietnam remains the most heavily bombed and shelled country in history.[21] And they were on our side.

That spasmodic employment of firepower is no longer American military practice. American forces accept risk to their lives to preserve the lives of the civilians around them. It is not just chivalry. As Mao Tse-tung cautioned, it is essential in this type of war.[22] But coupled with concerns to keep U.S. casualties low, protecting the people creates another contradiction to throw into an already full bag. The tension is always there, and JRTC replicated it.

In the buffer zone, one could find two small villages. Carnis, with forty souls, lay to the north of the CFL. It hosted a refugee camp of forty others, run by humanitarian groups. Carnis also incorporated a secret AFF guerrilla underground element. Jeeterville, with a population of sixty-two, was to the south. This town had seen horrific civil slaughter, with the AFF actively besieging ethnic Cortinians and their desperate militiamen in one corner of the built-up area. Nongovernmental organizations distributed food and gave medical care in Jeeterville.[23]

These nongovernmental aid groups, supplemented by U.S. and UN aid agencies, intermixed freely with the local population. They had been there for a long time, knew the land and its people, and felt some degree of immunity from the fighting. Some believed that the arrival of American forces ruined that moral protection and imperiled their relief programs. Others welcomed the stability that could accompany the arrival of American airborne soldiers.[24] These relief workers could be allies, adversaries, or inert impediments, depending upon how the American forces worked with them. Aid people required special handling.

Along with the villagers and the relief workers, one other group of civilians can be found on any battlefield, including JRTC. These are the ladies and gentlemen of the press, the all-seeing, all-commenting news media, determined to get the real story. Once more, the JRTC scenario designers did not shy away from this uncomfortable bit of modern warfare. Invited members of the press and some role players suited up and joined the fray.[25] But in observing these operations-other-than-war correspondents at their trade, one must keep in mind that Ernie Pyle is dead in every sense of the word.

Today's effervescent media looks at the military as a mysterious, clannish organization left over from an earlier era (the nineteenth century or, perhaps, the Dark Ages). Hounded by inexorable deadlines and the need to fill column space and airtime on dull days as well as exciting ones, journalists find the military stupid, petty, overly optimistic, and, frankly, boring. Most only have time to blow in and blow out. They come for "bang, bang" and tend to see guys filling sandbags. Plus, everything is a secret, or seems to be, and accessible information is cloaked in impenetrable jargon and acronymia. Getting to the bottom of all this strange stuff is a story in itself.

With only about 1 percent of the American population in any kind of military service (including reserves), the armed forces are terra incognita to a lot of the press. The very idea that a young man would willingly take a rifle and go hunting for enemy men in these enlightened days of the late twentieth century strikes most well-heeled reporters as bizarre—man bites dog, for sure. Social critic Tom Wolfe noted that, like "the consummate hypocritical Victorian gent," the press was always looking for "the proper emotion," "the seemly sentiment," "the fitting moral tone" to frame its stories.[26]

Military events in the press reflect a certain sameness, that proper mood Wolfe mentioned. With deadlines looming, with little time for originality, and with the experience of draftee service but a memory, younger reporters turn to past works and Hollywood to set the appropriate imagery. Everybody seems right out of central casting. For example, senior flag officers, unless they become press mascots like Schwarzkopf, are often perceived as highly decorated (routine service awards), cautious (in no hurry to kill themselves or others), and hiding something. Fliers are always "jocks," practicing "push-button warfare"; lieutenants often seem "green," and "just kids"; and sergeants are "leathery" and "hard-bitten" (this even though most buck sergeants are twenty-two years old, the same age as lieutenants). The service's biggest bunch, the enlisted ground troops, often come across as a faceless proletariat, a little dull and seedy. There is always a sense that nobody worth his salt would actually join the military.

But once shooting starts, the mood adjusts, at least with regard to the privates. In the World War II tradition, these folks metamorphose into devil-may-care GI Joes (and sometimes Janes). These long-suffering, fresh-faced heroes from Main Street, USA, are invariably portrayed as brave and decent and "fed up with this chickenshit outfit." So goes the usual line. Wolfe's Victorian gentleman has spoken.

The objects of these caricatures have their own views, rarely disclosed but fiercely held. Uniformed Americans tend to see the press as at best a nuisance and at worst agents of Satan. Many, especially older officers and NCOs, stand firmly convinced that the press undermined public support for the Vietnam War and would do the same for any other operation given half a chance. The attitude of most soldiers is: The press wants to screw you, so you better be very careful around them. Tom Wolfe has an applicable opinion here, too. For those in the armed forces: "there was only one way to play it: with a salute stapled to your forehead."[27] Anything else can mean trouble.

The press is part of modern combat, however. It has become the American people's way of looking over the fighting man's shoulder. Hiding things or doing the wrong things does not cut it. The press will find out. And the American population, whose will is also important in sustaining foreign military adventures, can turn sharply when they feel betrayed. So JRTC rightly plays the news media. It is part of the landscape.

The presence of private and government civilians and press people in combat areas creates one final complication for U.S. forces. At some point, these unarmed American citizens will have to be rescued, secured, or pulled out—a noncombatant evacuation operation, or NEO. Carrying out a NEO under nonpermissive conditions (i.e., the bad guys are blazing away) cannot be cooked up on the back of an envelope. Throughout their operations, prudent commanders create and update a contingency plan to gather up and extract Americans and other civilians if and when that becomes necessary.[28] NEO is another reality of today's fighting, and JRTC allows for it.

While terrain, particularly with all its human facets, greatly affects matters, the key variable in the formula always comes down to troops available. As in most OOTW, ground forces carried most of the load in the Aragon scenario, although their cooperating air and sea arms made vital contributions, too. What do American warriors bring to this kind of fight?

The All-American order of battle at JRTC showed a fairly good example of a joint "team of teams" totaling about 4,050 personnel. Most were 82d Airborne soldiers, but the troop list included many special operations troops, airmen, and some sailors and Marines too.[29] Combat forces, actual trigger pullers, bomb droppers, and belly stickers, amounted to about seventeen hundred.

Casual observers may find it strange that an airborne brigade and its joint comrades organized for combat in a distant land employ only about a third of their strength as riflemen, combat sappers, pilots, field medics, frontline leaders, and the like. The other people are not simply "clerks and jerks" but the real sources of the firepower, mobility, and resilience of the team. The nonfighting portion of the U.S. armed forces may be thought of as a strong, sturdy shaft, ramming home the spearpoint formed by combat units. They allow Americans to bring devastating fires to bear at extended ranges, to fight in all weather at the end of a tether thousands of miles long, and to keep piling it on.

Indeed, these support troops, not the fighters, reflect the advanced nature of American warpower. Every country's armed forces have fighters. But only the most sophisticated have the combat support and service support that allow for effective, prolonged joint operations. Archimedes of Syracuse bragged about finding a lever strong enough to move the world. America's supporting arms and services are that lever.

The Team of Teams
Joint Readiness Training Center Rotation 94-2
2d Brigade, 82d Airborne Division

Combat
1st Battalion, 325th Airborne Infantry
2d Battalion, 325th Airborne Infantry
Team C, 1st Battalion (Mechanized), 18th Infantry
Company A, 3d Battalion (Airborne), 73d Armor
Task Force 2-82 Aviation (Airborne)
2d Battalion, 319th Airborne Field Artillery
Battery B, 3d Battalion (Airborne), 4th Air Defense Artillery
Elements, Long Range Surveillance Detachment, 82d Airborne Division
Special Forces Detachment, 3d Battalion, 10th Special Forces Group (Airborne)
Elements, Sea/Air/Land Team 2 (Navy)

Combat Support
Company B, 307th Engineers (Airborne)
Team B, 313th Military Intelligence Battalion (Airborne)
82d Military Police Company (Airborne) (-)
2d Platoon, 21st Chemical Company (Airborne)
Direct Support Team, 450th Civil Affairs Battalion
Elements, 9th Psychological Operations Battalion (Airborne)

Combat Service Support
407th Forward Support Battalion (Airborne)

Command and Control
Headquarters and Headquarters Company, 2d Brigade
Company B, 82d Signal Battalion (Airborne)
Tactical Air Control Party (Air Force)
Elements, 2d Air/Naval Gunfire Liaison Company (ANGLICO) (Navy/Marine)

Source: U.S. Department of the Army, Headquarters, Joint Readiness Training Center, *Peace Operations* (Fort Polk, La.: Joint Readiness Training Center, 7 December 1993), 1.

The 2d Brigade, as organized for JRTC Rotation 94-2, comprised four principal types of forces: combat, combat support, combat service support, and command and control headquarters. Combat units included a few Special Forces A-Teams, some Navy SEAL sections, two airborne infantry battalions, a mechanized infantry company team (including M1A1 Abrams tanks), and a light armor company armed with M551 Sheridans, small tanks capable of being dropped by parachute. An aviation task force capable of lifting a rifle company into battle and simultaneously flying attack helicopter missions, a 105-mm howitzer battalion, and an air defense battery of shoulder-fired Stingers completed the army portion of the combat strength. Joint battle power, including air force attack jets and the gunfire of two destroyers offshore, was available through liaison teams.[30] In all, 2d Brigade possessed the firepower of several World War II infantry divisions, and had on tap the joint destructive capacities of the planet's mightiest air and naval forces, if it came to that. Sometimes it did.

Combat support brought this sharp spearpoint to the right spot to influence the action. Combat engineers, airborne sappers who trained to fight as infantry when necessary, cleared mines, built bridges, improved rutted roads, and constructed field fortifications. Intelligence units gathered and analyzed human, imagery, and electronic data to feed the fighting units the latest readouts on where the hostiles had gone. Military police moved traffic (including refugees and civilian traffic), guarded prisoners and detainees, and secured key sites, responding to minor insurgent threats. Civil affairs teams interacted with relief organizations and local village leaders, and psychological operations teams spread the American word through the area by radio broadcasts, loudspeakers, and leaflets. Air force flying psyops planes helped with the latter efforts.[31]

Combat service support units kept the spearpoint sharp and ready to go around the clock. Logistics organizations, like the forward support battalion, manned, fueled, fixed, armed, and moved all forces, including the service support elements themselves. Medical units treated injuries and casualties, not neglecting civilians. Personnel sections processed in replacement troops as needed. Helicopters, jets, and tanks swallowed fuel in thousands of gallons and required much tinkering and parts swapping to stay fully ready. And everything had to move, and quickly, which required trucks, helicopters, and air force transports, all of which needed to be manned, fueled, fixed, armed, and moved. It is cyclical, endless when done right, and grinding in any case.

The cycle of sustainment becomes a journey, not a destination. It is never finished, but it can be halted by determined enemy action or internal friction. When it works, soldiers go into battle stripped for action, lean and mobile, certain that their supply lines will not fail them. When it falters, American warpower degenerates to a level about even with that of the local opposition.[32]

Headquarters tie everything together for the chain of command. Army battalions, brigades, divisions, and corps (and their air force, navy, and Marine equivalents) all possess headquarters capable of integrating teams of teams, connected by a signal backbone of radios, satellite communications, and microwave radiotelephone systems. In Rotation 94-2, the JRTC staff, playing JTF Cortina and the 21st Infantry Division, did most (but not all) of the joint integration. Most of the battlefield integration, to include tying in to the chain of command, local battlefield civil government, and relief teams, fell to the brigade headquarters. The book told the brigade commander how to tie together his joint team. Unfortunately, one cannot write enough books to hook up all of the other loose screws rolling around a place like Aragon.

The chain of command in OOTW should be clean: Washington to the theater CINC to the JTF to the fighting units. But in fact there are many extraneous actors, all with their own agendas: the UN, the relief groups, the Department of State and its local ambassador or other emissary, the Drug Enforcement Agency, the Central Intelligence Agency, and the U.S. Information Service, to name a few. In theory, the ambassador coordinates the "Country Team," working directly for the president under the courtly traditions of the foreign service. In practice, the top military officer and the ambassador (or ambassadors—borders do not contain most conflicts) reach an agreement about who does what. It is very messy, and that's before injecting foreign powers and their ministerial hodgepodges.

In Aragon, the 2d Brigade commander had to meet almost daily with the U.S. Country Team at the embassy. Then, to resolve Acadian-Cortinian flareups in the buffer zone, the U.S. commanders hosted mixed military working groups.[33] In between negotiating and meeting, the colonel had to lead his brigade against AFF guerrillas. It was war at the graduate level, not for amateurs.

Fortunately, the paratroopers in 2d Brigade were not amateurs—not in the least. Many had combat experience in Grenada, Panama, the Gulf, or Somalia. Their commander, in fact, was Col. Tom Turner, the same man who commanded the JSA Battalion the night 1-5th Infantry had their brush with danger in Korea's DMZ. After two years of patrolling Panmunjom and its environs, not to mention service as a Ranger officer in Panama, Colonel Turner knew a thing or two about OOTW.[34] Though he was the most experienced, there were people like him throughout his team of teams.

Men like Colonel Turner are more typical than you may think. Although the news media finds it expedient to paint today's soldiers as Willie and Joe, and the army sometimes prefers not to use the term to avoid offending prickly National Guardsmen, the reason the 82d Airborne could cope with this hellish puzzle box was simple: they were Regulars, hardened troops. They were not conscripts or the scraped-up catch of press gangs but volunteers. Rome and Britain built empires with relatively small militaries manned by volunteers; America is using the same proven technique.

Regulars man our fleets, fly our aircraft, and carry our Marine and army rifles. Even the numerous reservists who serve on active duty today are more like regulars: they're certainly not bumbling, stay-at-home militiamen with dusty squirrel guns mounted over their fireplaces. Contrary to some images, the military consists of a fairly decent caliber of men and women. Basic American antimilitarism sometimes causes people to think of those in uniform, especially those who enlist in peacetime, as Lord Wellington's "scum of the earth . . . enlisted for drink." Senior defense leaders, afflicted with can-do hyperbole, often go to the opposite extreme and leave one with the impression that their services brim with individuals with the patriotism of George Washington, the strength of Arnold Schwarzenegger, the brain of Albert Einstein, and the sensitivity of Mother Teresa.[35]

In truth, the people wearing the uniform today are neither demons nor angels. They sign up for many reasons, and they come from many walks of life. The army recruits represent a good median for all the services. Almost all have high school diplomas, clean disciplinary records, decent health, and enough gumption to sign up for the military. Most are the children of the lower middle class, the kids of fathers who served in Vietnam without complaint. Some come from the urban jungle, some from the shacks of Appalachia. Only a few enter from privileged suburbia.[36] They are not, in short, the society's so-called best and brightest, but that is probably just as well. Service life is not for the effete. "Single men in barracks," warned Rudyard Kipling, "don't grow into plaster saints." That injunction still describes today's armed forces.[37] Contemporary troops may not be choir boys, but they have shown themselves to be solid citizens, good stock, the same kind of volunteers the Romans, British, and frontier American militaries recruited.

What has made these good people better have been the changes in the services themselves, a revisitation of fundamental military ethics: sacrifice, discipline, duty, and honor. Training like the JRTC typifies the new emphasis upon professionalism, on hard work, and on self-discipline. It exemplifies the shift from a draftee military run by a career cadre, which Herman Wouk acidly called a "master plan designed by geniuses for execution by idiots," to a true regular establishment, where all are professionals.[38]

Under the draft, picayune rules and close order drills worked to break down the recruits, to stop them from independent thought, to make them cogs in the green machine. "Thinking weakens the team," shouted the drill sergeants of that time. Today, the military challenges its people to think, and, moreover, demands it. Privates at checkpoints, junior sergeants in the Korean DMZ, and ensigns in Tomcat fighter jets make decisions daily that determine the success or failure of American foreign policies. The service is not easy—nobody will ever ask to go through Parris Island's Marine boot camp twice. But it lacks the arbitrary, negative brutality that once marred its methods. Today, peer pressure and group ethos, not the whack of a sergeant's fist, keep order.

And it cannot be any other way. On a dark night, in a firefight with everyone armed, camouflaged, and widely dispersed, a leader cannot bully his men to close with the foe. What good would it do to threaten to shoot a soldier when he and his comrades all carry loaded rifles too? The sanction of a court-martial, with its legal niceties in a distant, clean courtroom, would seem like a blessing, a welcome respite. No, the driving methods do not suit the modern, extended battlefield. They have not really worked for a century, but militaries are nothing if not traditional and slow to alter their ways.

Instead of pushing, the military employs the pulling approach, emphasizing leadership by example. The American armed forces carefully choose and school leaders from among the strongest, smartest, and most aggressive. Only those of recognized competence and character can give orders to groups trained since induction to follow their leaders, even unto death. "Such orders," noted combat veteran T. R. Fehrenbach, "cannot be given by men who are some of the boys. Men willingly take orders to die only from those they are trained to regard as superior beings."[39] Every order is another referendum on the leader's ability and charisma.

This is why JRTC scrutinizes and stresses leaders ruthlessly and without respite. The entire unit depends upon the chain of command and its ability to bring the rest of the force into the fight, despite the waves of friction pumped into the scenario by diabolical JRTC planners. While even this sort of realistic training exercise cannot pinpoint the next Matthew Ridgway or George Patton, it can flush out the weaklings and croakers. A few unhappy people, almost always leaders, actually break down, become catatonic, or begin spouting gibberish. If you cannot handle JRTC, you surely cannot handle combat.

As any corporal can tell you, doing anything once in the military can be hard. Doing it over and over, again and again, in fair weather and foul, becomes the real challenge for leaders and units. Time is the final factor that affects OOTW. It normally favors the enemy, as Americans have little patience with extended overseas commitments, especially when political aims do not appear vital and casualties start to mount. It takes time to get in, get the lay of the land, and establish stability. The bad guys know that if they can keep the pain level high enough for long enough, the Yankees may go home. That's why Mao called it protracted war.

The funny thing about OOTWs is that, when they work, Americans get stuck for a long haul. When things go well, the U.S. can look forward to reducing its forces gradually over the years, until all that stays behind is a small advisory group. This pattern has applied in Korea, the Philippines, and the Dominican Republic. It is developing right now in Kuwait.

So the best that can come of most of these small wars is a tar baby. Those hoping for instant gratification will not be satisfied. The quick in and out "surgical strike" exists only in dreams—every intervention, even by air or by sea, has human costs and repercussions. High-technology reprisal raids resemble a Chinese dinner; they taste good going down but they are not satisfying, and all sides tend to come back for more.

Mission, enemy, terrain (including population), troops available, and time—these considerations, laden with half-truths, ambiguities, and unpleasant choices, framed the situation in Aragon. Colonel Turner's brigade and its joint partners enjoyed a full-contact workout during their rotation to Fort Polk. They did not resolve the dispute between Cortina and Acadia, and they could not stabilize the fragile buffer zone, although they came close. In fact, midway through, the Acadians launched a conventional invasion of Cortina just to demonstrate that they were sore losers and to provide some additional training. The exercise ended with a counterattack by the

All-Americans. The people involved learned a great deal, every bit of it without spilling any blood. That kind of training has already paid off in actual OOTWs around the world.

Aside from the lack of physical fear of death or wounding, the only other artificiality in JRTC Rotation 94-2 involved the length of the exercise. Due to fiscal constraints and the need to schedule other brigades, the JRTC scenario lasted only twelve days "in the box," with some additional planning, special operations reconnaissance, deployment, and redeployment days tacked on at either end.[40] Some would argue that twelve days cannot possibly be long enough to learn all the nuances of keeping the peace in the globe's more treacherous snakepits. Maybe that is so. But at least JRTC veterans sent to OOTW would know the job was dangerous before they took it.

JRTC is a military form of art imitating life. It and its fellow, similar institutions throughout the American armed forces reflect a lot of lessons learned the hard way. For an armed force that learns by doing, such measures can pay great dividends.

There was no JRTC when Americans began patrolling the barren Sinai Desert or when they pushed ashore into hostile Beirut back in 1982. Those interventions occurred during the final years of the Cold War, seemingly a lifetime ago but in truth, not so far back. As at JRTC, the Americans learned by doing, but in these venues, everyone played with real bombs and bullets, not eye-safe Laser Tag systems. Trial and error produced various outcomes—some good, most ambiguous and incomplete, and a few tragic. Just as every OOTW today includes a piece of JRTC-style corporate wisdom, so every American peacekeeping venture in these times asks for a glance into the rearview mirror at what went right in the Sinai and what went wrong in Beirut.

Notes

The epigraph is from William Shakespeare, *Henry V,* as found in Hardin Craig, ed., *The Complete Works of Shakespeare* (Chicago: Scott, Foresman, 1961), 760.

1. Cheryl Lister in "Reader Feedback: Should the United States Continue to Keep Troops in Somalia?" *Boston Globe,* 7 October 1993. For the official identification of the dead soldiers, see "Dead Soldiers Now Identified," *Washington Times,* 12 October 1993, in which the Department of Defense identified the casualties as MSgt. Gary Gordon and Sgt. Thomas Field. In Arlene Levinson, "Somalia Mission's Unknown Soldier," *USA Today,* 20 December 1993, the reporter advances the belief that the dead soldiers could also be Sgt. First Class Randall Shugart, SSgt. William Cleveland, or CWO Ray Frank.

2. Burke Davis, *Sherman's March* (New York: Random House, 1980), 21. This famous quote comes from a response Sherman sent to Mayor James Calhoun and the aldermen of Atlanta, Georgia.

3. See Appendix A for a listing of American conflicts of all types.

4. Evan S. Connell, *Son of the Morning Star* (San Francisco: North Point Press, 1984), 131–32. Fetterman's column included soldiers of the 2d Cavalry, 18th Infantry, and 27th Infantry.

5. Carl von Clausewitz, *On War,* ed. and trans. Michael Howard and Peter Paret (Princeton, N.J.: Princeton University Press, 1984), 115–16. See also U.S. Department of the Army, Headquarters, Joint Readiness Training Center, *JRTC Update* (Fort Polk, La.: Joint Readiness Training Center, 10 November 1993), 27, which shows typical infantry soldier equipment loads in excess of one hundred pounds.

6. Clausewitz, *On War,* 117.

7. Ibid., 119.

8. Ibid., 114.

9. Ibid., 119.

10. JRTC, *JRTC Update,* 12.

11. U.S. Department of the Army, Headquarters, Joint Readiness Training Center, *Peace Operations* (Fort Polk, La.: Joint Readiness Training

Center, 7 December 1993), 12–23. Note that scenario planners chose the words "Cease Fire Line" intentionally to increase ambiguity when used as the acronym CFL. That acronym is a standard doctrinal fire support coordination measure, the "coordinated fire line," beyond which surface to surface fires may be conducted without coordination (i.e., across a doctrinal CFL, you can shoot ground weapons at ground targets without checking friend and foe). The Aragon CFL, obviously, meant something completely different, and the last thing desirable would be U.S. free fires across it. This intentional confusion was injected to create just more grit in the machinery.

12. Aside from JRTC, the army also runs the National Training Center (NTC) at Fort Irwin, California, specializing in armored warfare in a desert environment, and the Combat Maneuver Training Center (CMTC) at Hohenfels, Germany, which runs both conventional, OOTW, and mixed scenarios for U.S. and NATO battalions. American forces tagged for possible use in Bosnia train at Hohenfels. Other services sponsor similar joint training efforts, to include the Marine Corps's very challenging urban OOTW area at Camp Lejeune, North Carolina, and the navy's Strike Warfare Training Center ("Strike U") at Fallon Naval Air Station, Nevada, which includes a tough OOTW-style reprisal mission in its repertoire. Larger joint exercises, such as U.S. Atlantic Command's Ocean Venture series, have included OOTW tasks, to include noncombatant evacuations and peacekeeping elements. The May 1992 scenario placed army and Marine troops in the Lejeune "OOTW city." In May 1993, Atlantic Command orchestrated a massive joint seizure of Puerto Rico involving numerous civilians, media, and State Department role players. All services and joint commands also run computer-driven map wargames on OOTW missions.

13. JRTC, *Peace Operations*, 25–26.

14. Ibid., 14–18.

15. Ibid., 30.

16. For a contemporary analysis of the relationship between political aims and losses, see Harvey M. Sapolsky, "War Without Killing" (Boston: Massachusetts Institute of Technology, September 1992), 1–3, 11–15.

17. U.S. Department of the Army, Headquarters, 1st Battalion, 509th Parachute Infantry, *Mission 94-2-1 Peace Enforcement* (Fort Polk, La.: Joint Readiness Training Center, 30 October 1993), 1–3.

18. Anthony Payne, Paul Sutton, and Tony Thorndike, *Grenada: Revolution and Aftermath* (New York: St. Martin's Press, 1984), 162, 178, 185.

19. Vegetius, *The Epitome of Military Science,* trans. N. P. Milner, (Liverpool, England: Liverpool University Press, 1990), 12.

20. Leroy Thompson, *The U.S. Army in Vietnam* (Newton Abbot, UK: David and Charles, 1990), 29.

21. Thomas C. Thayer, *War Without Fronts* (Boulder, Colo.: Westview Press, 1985), 57, 79.

22. Mao Tse-tung, *Basic Tactics,* trans. Stuart R. Schram (New York: Frederick E. Praeger, 1967), 57–59, 133–37.

23. JRTC, *Peace Operations,* 37.

24. U.S. Department of the Army, Headquarters, Joint Readiness Training Center, 2d Brigade, 82d Airborne Division, *JRTC 94-2 Peace Operations After Action Review (PAUSEX)* (Fort Polk, La.: Joint Readiness Training Center, 10 November 1993), 9–13.

25. Maj. Joe McCaskill, USA, SSgt. Jim Connel, New York Army National Guard, and Spec. Larry R. Butterfas, USA, "Media on the Battlefield" *Soldiers* (October 1993): 21–22.

26. Tom Wolfe, *The Right Stuff* (New York: Farrar, Straus, Giroux, 1979), 121–22.

27. Ibid., 158.

28. U.S. Department of the Army, *FM 100-5 Operations* (Washington, D.C.: U.S. Government Printing Office, 1993), 13-9. See also U.S. Department of the Army, Headquarters, 101st Airborne Division (Air Assault), *NEO Handbook* (Fort Campbell, Ky.: 101st Airborne Division (Air Assault), 1 May 1990), 2, H-1.

29. JRTC, *Peace Operations,* 1, 46.

30. U.S. Department of the Army, Headquarters, Joint Readiness Training Center, *Forging the Warrior Spirit* (Fort Polk, La.: Joint Readiness Training Center, 10 November 1993), 15–17. The quote from Archimedes may be found in Emily Morison Beck, *Bartlett's Familiar Quotations* (Boston: Little, Brown, 1980), 93.

31. JRTC, *JRTC Update,* 14.

32. Department of the Army, *FM 100-5,* 12-18 to 12-22.

33. JRTC, *Peace Operations,* 32–33, 39.

34. Col. Thomas Turner served as battalion executive officer, 3d Battalion, 75th Ranger Regiment, during the Panama intervention of 1989–90.

35. Wellington in John Keegan, *The Mask of Command* (New York: Viking, 1987), 126. For a very pointed critique of the quality of today's volunteer force, see Col. William Darryl Henderson, USA (Ret.),

The Hollow Army (Westport, Conn.: Greenwood Press, 1990), 1–10, 29. Henderson refers to a concerted public relations effort aimed at "selling a mythical Army" of high quality, and explains that these are "inflated claims." He argues that recasting test categories, rather than upgrading actual recruit quality, accounts for most of the perceived qualitative increases reported in the 1980s, and includes a wealth of statistical data to buttress his case.

36. George C. Wilson, *Mud Soldiers* (New York: Scribner's, 1989), 43–66. Wilson followed a company of riflemen from induction to service in an infantry division. He reported that the new men shared lower-middle-class or working-class origins, not any degree of affluence. Sons of privilege were not represented at all. Wilson characterized the soldiers as typical of a "youth underclass" who had "joined the Army in the belief it would get them somewhere in life and provide them with some fun and adventure along the way."

37. Rudyard Kipling, *Rudyard Kipling's Verse: Definitive Edition,* ed. Elsie Kipling Bambridge (Garden City, N.Y.: Doubleday, 1940), 397. The line is from the poem "Tommy." For a controversial but interesting look at the daily life of American soldiers, see Lt. Col. Larry H. Ingraham, USA, *The Boys in the Barracks* (Philadelphia: Institute for the Study of Human Issues, 1984). Ingraham's depiction of extensive narcotics use among the lower ranks has been hotly disputed. His broader commentary on socialization in an army unit is less contentious.

38. Herman Wouk, *The Caine Mutiny* (New York: Dell, 1951), 116.

39. T. R. Fehrenbach, *This Kind of War* (New York: Macmillan, 1966), 434.

40. JRTC, *JRTC Update,* 45.

CHAPTER 4
Getting It Right:
The Multinational Force and Observers—The Sinai

It's not a soldier's job, but it takes a soldier to do it.
Heard among U.S. soldiers in the Sinai

The All-Americans' adventures in Cortina lasted only a few days, but the paratroopers' frustrations underscore an important aspect of these difficult operations. Trying to keep warring factions in their corners takes a sustained effort, and only the best can do it without suffering the death of a thousand cuts (or one big whack) in the process. Simply bringing in American forces guarantees nothing, unless the political aims, the chosen means, and the potential or actual hostile forces fall into line. And even if everything else works out, Americans in country dare not suffer any significant number of casualties during the operation, or public sentiment may demand withdrawal. That was the lesson drawn after the 1982–84 Beirut debacle, and events a decade later in Mogadishu appear to reinforce this conviction.

Americans will endure casualties rather stoically, however, if the effort appears to be in the country's interests, and if it is working.[1] The best example of a successful American peacekeeping operation in the mid-1990s is in the Sinai Desert, under the supervision of the Multinational Force and Observers (MFO). This small-scale operation, never employing more than twelve hundred Americans and a thousand or so more from ten other countries, has kept peace between perennial opponents Egypt and Israel since 1982, quite an achievement in light of enmities tracing back to biblical times.

The mission has been anything but cheap or bloodless. One homebound Sinai battalion suffered more killed in a single day than the United States lost in Beirut to the infamous suicide truck bombing, and the MFO's founding civilian director general, a senior American diplomat, fell to terrorist bullets in Rome. There have been other minor incidents in and around the Sinai. Yet despite the pain, the MFO has endured and prospered.

Most Americans know very little about the quiet, daily triumph of the MFO. That's too bad. The MFO deserves more attention, especially these days as our country's opinion leaders scramble around trying to figure out how to deal with peacekeeping. A lot has been going on right in the Sinai.

The MFO is the child of the Camp David Accords, brokered by President James E. Carter and signed 17 September 1978 by President Anwar Sadat of Egypt and Prime Minister Menachem Begin of Israel. In the first formal agreement between Israel and an Arab state, the Israelis relinquished control of the Sinai Peninsula. In return, the powerful Egyptians, always the most dangerous of Israel's panoply of foes, agreed to live in peace with their tough Israeli neighbors.

Essentially, Begin traded the desolate Sinai for security, land for peace, as the formula goes. But the cautious Israeli leader wanted something between his small state and the Egyptians, just in case. After several surprise attacks and numerous raids, who could blame him? The Egyptians had gotten their share of unexpected bloody noses, too. Both parties hoped for United Nations forces to interpose themselves between the former belligerents.

At the time of the Camp David Accords and the follow-on peace negotiations, there were UN troops and American civilians stationed between the two sides in the Sinai. The forty-five-hundred-man UN Emergency Force (UNEF-II) had been in country since the aftermath of the 1973 October War. Since 1976, UNEF-II had worked in tandem with the civilian technician teams of the American Sinai Field Mission, who operated electronic warning sensor systems similar to those in the U.S. sector of the Korean DMZ. The Sinai Field Mission monitored movements on the primary invasion routes, the Gidi and Mitla passes, with complete readouts furnished to both sides. The final Egyptian-Israeli Peace Treaty of 26 March 1979 envisioned a continuation of this UN contingent and its American technical associates; its language clearly refers to "United Nations forces and observers."[2]

That was not to be. Other than Egypt, most of the Arab countries and the wider community of states with Islamic majority populations rejected any deals with Israel. Most denounced the Camp David process as treasonous to the anti-Zionist cause and the long-held dream of a Muslim Palestinian state. This determination to derail the Camp David Accords took many forms, leading eventually to Anwar Sadat's assassination in 1981, continued terrorism, and escalating violence against the United States as Israel's strongest ally.

All of this vitriol spilled into the United Nations as the Security Council deliberated its role in supporting the Israeli disengagement from the Sinai. The Soviet Union, the erstwhile Evil Empire, was at the peak of its game back in 1979. In a successful effort to curry favor with the Islamic world, Moscow's delegation blocked a U.S. attempt to formalize UNEF into a more permanent force. The best the Americans could salvage was a small increase to the ineffectual UN observer element that had been in place for years, ostensibly to monitor the Egyptian front.[3] The rebuff in the United Nations greatly upset the Israelis, who had already completed much of their withdrawal. It looked like the agreement with Cairo might come apart thanks to Arab intransigence and Soviet opportunism.

At this juncture, America stepped up to the plate. Carter had foreseen the possibility of a UN bailout. He had guaranteed Begin and Sadat in writing that if the UN failed to create an interposition force, America would "ensure the establishment and maintenance of an acceptable alternative multinational force." Begin called in this marker, and the United States began negotiations to assemble a viable multinational team outside the UN fold.[4]

America made the MFO—of that there can be no doubt. America's determination to keep the peace between Egypt and Israel, already expressed in massive foreign aid to both countries, would be underwritten by flesh and blood, too. As Secretary of State Alexander M. Haig informed the foreign ministers in a missive of 3 August 1981, America pledged to furnish a senior diplomat as director general, one of the three infantry battalions proposed for the Multinational Force, a logistics unit, civilians to verify treaty compliance (the Observers), a third of the annual cost (and three-fifths of the start-up price), and diplomatic efforts to find replacements for any states that withdrew from the MFO. Egypt and Israel agreed to pay the remaining expenses.[5]

Given the huge U.S. subsidies to both parties though, America basically paid the whole bill. By the early 1990s, Japan and Germany gave token contributions, about a million dollars apiece, against a total budget of $55 million. The Egyptians had dropped several million dollars into arrears. And Uncle Sam continued to pick up the tab.[6]

America assembled its MFO by early 1982, convincing its allies to pony up. Colombia and Fiji contributed the other two infantry battalions, and a shifting array of traditional U.S. friends has filled the other roles over the years. Effective 1300 on 25 April 1982, Israel officially returned the last of the Sinai Peninsula to Egypt, and the MFO began operations.[7]

"The mission of the MFO can be stated very simply: observe and report." So says the director general in the organization's official publications. "Observe and report" is a bit vague, so the MFO has defined things a bit more carefully for its multinational conglomerate of soldiers, sailors, and airmen.

The MFO carries out four "essential tasks" in the Sinai, in constant cooperation with the Egyptians and Israelis, whose peace the force guarantees. The MFO's uniformed units, principally the three infantry battalions, man observation posts (OPs), conduct reconnaissance patrols, and run vehicle checkpoints (CPs) along the international boundary, on the line demarcating its zone of action, and throughout the force's assigned area. The Civilian Observer Unit carries out periodic verification tours of Israeli and Egyptian forces in and around the Sinai, as well as upon report of a violation or at the request of either former belligerent. Finally, the Italian Coastal Patrol Unit, cooperating with the southernmost American OPs, uses three converted minesweepers to ensure free navigation of the Strait of Tiran at the south end of the Gulf of Aqaba.[8] The rest of the MFO provides command and control, combat support, and combat service support for these efforts. Force protection, as in all OOTW, is an unstated but important part of the overall mission.

The MFO operates in a strip of the Sinai known as Zone C, the easternmost of the three zones established in the 1978–79 accords and treaty process. Almost three hundred miles from north to south, Zone C ranges from ten miles wide in the south to about twenty-five miles wide in the north, opposite the Palestinian hotbed of the Gaza Strip. It is MFO country, though a few Egyptian civil police do work in this sparsely populated area, mainly to exercise Egyptian sovereignty. Overlooking the Strait of Tiran, one finds the growing resort center of Nama Bay, a satellite of the larger town of Sharm al-Sheikh. This dual community forms the only substantial populated area in Zone C.

The Multinational Force and Observers (MFO) as of 1 June 1993

MFO Headquarters (Rome, Italy)
  Leamon R. Hunt (assassinated 15 February 1984)
  Victor H. Dikeos (15 February 1984 to 1 September 1984)

Peter D. Constable (1 September 1984 to 1 July 1988)
Wat T. Cluverius IV (since 1 July 1988)

Force Headquarters (North Camp, Sinai)
Lt. Gen. Fredrik V. Bull-Hansen (until 27 March 1984)
Lt. Gen. Egil J. Ingebrigtsen (27 March 1984 to 30 March 1989)
Lt. Gen. Donald S. McIver (30 March 1989 to 1 April 1991)
Lt. Gen. J. W. C. Van Ginkel (since 1 April 1991)

The Force

At North Camp, El Gorah, Sinai:

Headquarters Unit (HQ)
Britain (25 April 1982 to 1 October 1992)
Australia (since 1 January 1993)
Norway (since 25 April 1982)
Canada (since 25 April 1982)
United States—Civilian Observer Unit (COU) (since 25 April 1982)
New Zealand—Training and Advisory Team (TAT) (since 25 April 1986)
Fiji—infantry battalion (FIJIBATT) (since 25 April 1992)
Colombia—infantry battalion (COLBATT) (since 25 April 1982)
France—Fixed-Wing Aviation Unit (FWAU) (since 25 April 1982)
France—Rotary-Wing Aviation Unit (RWAU) (since 25 April 1982)
Australia/New Zealand—(25 April 1982 to 25 April 1986)
Canada—(25 April 1986 to 25 April 1990)
Netherlands—Force Signal Unit (FSU) (since 25 April 1982)
Netherlands—Force Military Police Unit (FMPU) (since 25 April 1982)
United States—1st Support Battalion (-) (since 25 April 1982)
    including aviation company (rotary-wing) (-)
Uruguay—Motor Transport Unit (MTU) (since 25 April 1982)
Uruguay—engineer unit (since 1 March 1983)

At South Camp, Sharm al-Sheikh:

United States—infantry battalion (USBATT) (since 25 April 1982)
Italy—Coastal Patrol Unit (CPU) (since 25 April 1982)
United States—Company A, 1st Support Battalion (since 25 April 1982)
    including aviation platoon (four helicopters)

Sources: Multinational Force and Observers, *The Multinational Force and Observers: Servants of Peace* (Rome, Italy: MFO Office of Personnel and Publications, 1993), 18–25; U.S. Department of the Army, Headquarters, Task Force 1-327, "OPORD 25-93 (DESERT RENDEZVOUS)," (Fort Campbell, Ky.: 15 June 1993), 2.

To the west, Egyptian combat strength increases as one gets closer to the Suez Canal. The central Zone B includes four Egyptian border guard battalions, amounting to four thousand soldiers. Zone B stretches across most of the Sinai, forming an irregular triangle some sixty miles wide. Zone A, just east of the Canal, has an overstrength mechanized division of 22,000 personnel, 230 tanks, 480 armored personnel carriers, and 126 artillery pieces. Mount Sinai, crowned by St. Catherine's Monastery and the Gidi and Mitla passes, can be found in Zone A. The MFO's observers check Zones A and B at least twice a month to ascertain treaty compliance and on other occasions as required by events or requested.

There is a Zone D, stretching just over two miles into Israel's Negev Desert and parallel to the international boundary. Four Israeli Defense Forces battalions, with up to 4,000 men and 180 armored personnel carriers, garrison Zone D. The observers also verify activities in Zone D.[9]

The MFO organizes for its tasks under a fairly clean command structure. Political leadership emanates from MFO headquarters in Rome, home of the director general, his planning staff, and supporting administrative offices for diplomatic activities, finances, logistics and contracting, international law, public affairs, publications, and clerical support. The director general, always an American, usually of ambassadorial rank, reports to the leaders of those countries that compose the MFO as well as to Egypt and Israel. The MFO maintains permanent representation in both Cairo, Egypt, and Tel Aviv, Israel, to facilitate treaty supervision efforts and more mundane matters like local contracting and tours for off-duty MFO personnel. Finally, the director general coordinates his peace operations with the United Nations, which also has small observer elements in and around the Sinai.[10]

Under orders from Rome, the force commander directs military operations from his headquarters at North Camp (El Gorah, formerly Eitam Israeli Defense Force air base). To strengthen the international composition of the force, the commander comes from one of the non-American participating states. For those currently wringing hands over whether Americans should be placed under foreign command, it should be noted that the MFO has intentionally featured such an arrangement for over a decade.

The force commander's principal maneuver units occupy Zone C. These comprise, from north to south, the Fiji battalion (Sectors 1 and 2), the Colombian battalion (Sectors 3 and 4), the U.S. battalion (Sectors 5, 6, and 7), and the Italian naval unit sailing the Strait of Tiran. Other than the

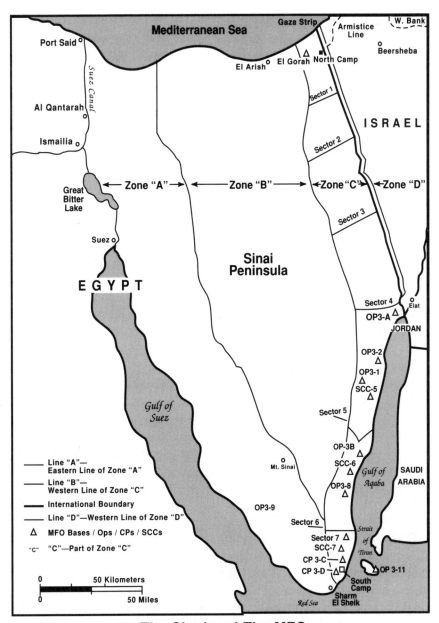

The Sinai and The MFO

American infantry battalion, the Italian sailors, and small support elements, most of the MFO works out of North Camp. The Americans and Italians stage from South Camp near Sharm al-Sheikh (formerly known as Ophira, another Israeli facility).

In addition to his uniformed troops, the force commander employs about fifteen or so civilian observers to investigate suspected violations and look at Egyptian and Israeli treaty implementation activities, units, and military installations in Zones A, B, C, and D. Drawn from American citizens with previous diplomatic, military, and intelligence experience, small verification teams move throughout the Sinai in concert with Egyptian (Zones A, B, and C) and Israeli (Zone D) liaison teams.[11] In a sense, the observers relate to the line units much as detectives backstop police on the beat.

Liaison with both sides, an international brigade in interposition, and a handful of civilian observers suffice to help Egypt and Israel avoid war in the Sinai. The MFO appears to represent a classic peacekeeping situation— an impartial force, working with the consent of all parties, and not engaged in hostilities. But in the Sinai, as in all OOTW, appearances of calm and safety can be deceiving, mirages shimmering in the distance, beckoning the complacent into peril and woe.

The mechanics of American peacekeeping in the Sinai bear a strong resemblance to the setup employed for years in the U.S. sector of the Korean DMZ. In both places, the soldiers carry out defensive tasks under conditions that mandate strict ROE. In Korea and in the Sinai, Americans rely on a network of fortified fixed sites with foot and vehicular patrols monitoring the gaps. Soldiers who have served in both theaters cannot help but recognize familiar patterns.

And yet, despite pronounced physical similarities, the Sinai is different, a pale, objectively less frightening cousin of the DMZ near Panmunjom. Compared to the situation in Korea, Zone C seems diluted and diffused in effort, space, hostile pressure, and especially time—less Americans doing less things over more terrain and under less threat, all done to a tempo that meanders along at a biblical, cosmic pace, suggesting eons and epochs, not hours or days. The Sinai is the DMZ re-created by Salvador Dali—distorted, dilated, stretched in all dimensions. Yet, as in any surrealist landscape, there is a hard core of truth, that same nugget of sharp danger that stares up from the bottom of every OOTW. It can sometimes be hard to see, but it is there.

The danger seems distant because of the limited mission. American MFO troops observe and report military activities in their areas. Unlike Colonel Turner's paratroopers in mythical Cortina, Americans in the Sinai do not try to prevent potential treaty violations. Instead, they make notes, call in to headquarters, and wait for the observers to come and adjudicate.

Transgressions rarely occur. When they do, they are not targeted against the Americans or, indeed, against anything other than the dictates of friction and human nature. Now and then, an Egyptian supply convoy motors toward Sharm al-Sheikh or aircraft from either side accidently stray into the MFO sectors. During the 4th Battalion, 87th Infantry's six-month tour in 1991–92, for example, the Americans recorded four confirmed violations—hardly a breakneck pace of incidents.

Such rare events comprise the sum total of interactions between the U.S. battalion and the uniformed forces of the two former belligerents. Even in these cases, the observers, not the soldiers, get to investigate, negotiate, and resolve any potential disputes. The Egyptians and Israelis police themselves, and the MFO watches them do it. The result can be ceaseless, mind-numbing, repetitive boredom, seemingly waiting for Godot at the battalion level.

As they keep their dull vigil, the Americans have responsibility for the three southern sectors of Zone C, nearly a hundred twenty-five miles of godforsaken wilderness. After seeing the Sinai, the wonder is not that Moses and his followers wandered for four decades, but that any Israelites emerged sound, sober, and sane at the far end. A classic rocky desert, scored by deep crevasses and crisscrossed by jagged peaks, the Sinai enjoys little rain, sports scrawny and stunted vegetation, and endures daytime temperatures above one hundred degrees Fahrenheit. Fog on the coasts and sandstorms in the interior complete the sterile tableau. A few Bedouin nomads and a smattering of Egyptians in decrepit hamlets live in the U.S. portion of Zone C. At the extreme southern end, some ten thousand people dwell in the town of Sharm al-Sheikh and an average of five thousand more play at the Nama Bay resorts, but these folks stay put. You could spend years in the Sinai without seeing another living human being.

While both North and South Camps have jet-capable airstrips in close proximity, these tend to be used to receive flights from outside the Zone. For most internal transportation, the MFO depends upon light aircraft, helicopters, and trucks to keep its forces supplied and in touch. Two major north-south connections, an unpaved MFO-built road in Zone C and a 1990-vintage paved highway looping through Zone B, ensure ground links between North Camp and South Camp. On the MFO road, a truck column takes about ten hours to make the run between the camps at convoy speeds of twenty-five miles per hour, although the Uruguayan drivers have been known to shave that time. The Sinai has also scraped off a good number of reckless drivers, both MFO and locals. Force medics have plenty of highway traumas to keep them busy.[12]

One U.S. battalion must cover this desolate expanse. To do this, over the years U.S. battalions have divided their area into three sectors, and each territorial subdivision falls under the supervision of a Sector Control Center (SCC). To the north, Sector 5 fronts on Eilat, Israel, and includes three OPs, with OP 3A overlooking the road into the Jewish state. In the center, Sector 6 controls one OP and CP 3B, which watches a road that enters the U.S. battalion's area from Zone B. Finally, Sector 7, around South Camp and above the Strait of Tiran, has two CPs along roads coming from Zone B, plus two OPs. One of these, OP 3-11, stands on a small island in the Strait of Tiran itself and typically resupplies and exchanges personnel by helicopter. Sector 7 coordinates closely with the Italian patrol ships in the strait. In all three sectors, the troops also conduct both foot and vehicle reconnaissance patrols, sallying forth at intervals from the SCCs, CPs, and OPs on lonely sojourns through the Sinai hills and boulder fields.

Less than three hundred Americans actually keep watch, strung thin as a wisp across a daunting frontage—in the Gulf War, America occupied a similar stretch, along much flatter terrain, with the entire VII Corps, five-plus divisions and nearly 150,000 soldiers. But the mission in the Sinai is different. To observe and report, a few scattered positions seem like enough.[13]

Each of the twelve remote sites, sprinkled across the rocky expanse of the U.S. area like rice grains on a broad beach, hosts a rifle squad of six to twelve souls, and perhaps a platoon or company headquarters. These small facilities center around two huts, each about the size of a contractor's office trailer at any American construction site. One of the structures provides rather tight living quarters, bunk beds stacked up like those in a U-boat's torpedo room. The other hut allows for communications, a kitchen, supply stockage, and a dining-meeting area. Outside these utilitarian containers, depending upon the exact site, one sees a varied collection of observation towers, sentry boxes, and field fortifications, sandbagged and protected by rolls of razor-sharp concertina wire, with fields of fire cleared of obstructions and scrubby vegetation all around, out to a distance of several football fields. A tall microwave tower marks the SCCs, and lesser antennae festoon the smaller outworks. These isolated posts make for cramped, hard living, Spartan and austere in every sense of both words. There is not much to do but attend to duty.

That part of the U.S. battalion not marooned at the twelve remote sites resides at South Camp, where the men secure that facility, provide a quick reaction force to respond to emergencies, train on various individual and unit tasks, and participate in recreation programs. Compared to the OPs, South Camp is relatively plush, but it too lacks amenities, even to those with tastes long dulled by garrison life at places like Fort Bragg, North Carolina, or Fort Campbell, Kentucky.[14] The phrase "middle of nowhere" inevitably springs to mind. Isolation and detachment, lack of meaningful stimuli, assail the Sinai peacekeeper, gnawing at his self-discipline, wearing him down. Only the best units hang in there all the way.

The idea that field operations lack drama is nothing new. Many military analysts, S. L. A. Marshall prominent among them, have commented upon the emptiness and inaction of the modern battlefield, "the lonesomest place which men share together." Far from the busy scenes painted by patriotic artists or conjured by motion picture directors, the principal activities in most fights appear to be nothing, the major actors nobody. As Marshall describes it, the soldier in battle "had expected to see action. He sees nothing. There is nothing to be seen."[15] Not by accident do combat veterans describe war as 99 percent boredom and 1 percent sheer terror.

In OOTW, with the most lethal, unconventional enemies working according to leisurely protracted time scales, the ratio may be more like 99.9 percent to .1 percent, and in the barren Sinai, maybe down to .01 percent. But the threat remains. That hint of death explains why boredom is an enemy, as remorseless and deadly as the scorching desert sun. Apathy can kill people or, more correctly, lull them into circumstances that bring on death. Lassitude favors the terrorist, the guerrilla, the man with a decade to wait and waste, looking for the right opportunity to act.

There were such people in and around the Sinai, and they did not wear uniforms, though they certainly did not lack for arms. The various anti-American terror factions of the Middle East never approved the Camp David process, and they never saw a U.S.-dominated MFO as impartial or benign.

Rather, they judged the MFO, and its Americans in particular, as potential targets, marks growing softer every time they cut another corner due to the corrosion of tedium.

That slow slide into entropy will get any unit sooner or later, which is one reason that Sinai battalions change out every six months and remote sites swap over every three weeks or so.[16] Well they should. The average day on an MFO outpost could bring a Zen Buddhist to tears, let alone an eighteen-year-old paratrooper itching to see real action.

Sinai days start early, with wake-up well before dawn as all soldiers stand-to, prepared to repel any dawn raids. Once secured from stand-to, some soldiers provide a guard and man the radio while others conduct physical training, wash up, and eat. Then those on duty take their turn. Weapons training, military classes, preparations for patrols, and recreation take up the rest of the day, with another stand-to at dusk. Researcher David R. Segal, who has spent many days in the Sinai studying the MFO, said it best: "Every day is a carbon copy of the day before."

Housekeeping, training, and guard duties aside, it is not as if lookout efforts allow for a lot of stimulation. Those watching have little to see. Private Alfredo Hudson of the 101st Airborne Division described his experiences in 1984 this way: "I have been on this OP for five days now. I observe this road to see if any military or Egyptian police vehicles pass by. If they do, I report it to the tactical operations center. I don't worry about ships in the gulf, unless they are military. About the only people I've seen so far are some Bedouins down in that village riding their camels."[17] Given this kind of stultifying routine, it is no wonder that soldiers eagerly look forward to patrols, searching cars at road checkpoints, and helping Egyptian civilians with medical emergencies—anything other than scanning the empty stoneyards.

By and large, nothing happens in the Sinai, and there appears to be no threat. There have been suspected and real violations of the treaty and incursions into Zone C, but none has resulted in a firefight. MFO patrols have now and then encountered minefields left over from the many Arab-Israeli conflicts; some of these minefields have caused U.S. casualties. The Fijians to the north have tangled with arms smugglers going in and out of the Gaza Strip, although only sporadically, as smuggling is the responsibility of the Egyptian authorities. And in the U.S. sector, at least one light infantry squad has engaged Bedouins it claimed fired first, although subsequent investigation fingered an overly aggressive U.S. sergeant as the actual cause of the incident.[18] Even these minor scrapes amount to very unusual occurrences. Most rotations go by without running into anything out of the ordinary.

This dreary daily routine can take its toll, even on crack outfits—some would say especially on crack outfits, like the American paratroopers, air assault infantry, and lightfighters that conduct the Sinai mission. The superb French Foreign Legionnaires, posted in the wastes of the western Sahara, complained of *le cafard,* depression and listlessness leading to violent feuding within small units, even murders and mutinies. It all arose from prolonged inactivity, an endless succession of unvarying sentry duty overseeing a timeless horizon, and feelings of profound alienation exacerbated by the harsh, boundless, empty desert vistas. Heavy drinking of cheap Legion wine stocks did not help. A company that gave in to this malady of morale might not react when Arab foes finally boiled up out of the distance, bent on mayhem. The ravages of *le cafard* supposedly explained the erasure of several tiny Legion outposts and camps. Legion leaders considered the phenomenon a true medical disease, like smallpox or typhoid fever, with relentless hard work, strenuous training, and campaigning the only sure innoculations.[19]

As it went in the Legion, so it also went in the Sinai. Soldiers stuck out on the CPs and OPs can surrender to what the men call "creeping Bedouin syndrome," losing track of the days of the week, gradually winding down to a clockwork, tunnel-vision universe of wordless staring, eating, sleeping, and eliminating. Back at South Camp, between tours out on the line, some have found solace and escape in beer and, occasionally, in illicit narcotics.

Strong chains of command in the great majority of America's MFO battalions have responded to the perils of boredom with well-oiled programs of physical labor (sandbagging, digging bunkers, and laying concertina wire), meaningful collective training emphasizing live fire, recreational sports and tours, and constant emphasis on the importance of doing the difficult MFO mission correctly, especially with regard to force protection. Yet without any active counterinfiltration role, bound by purely defensive ROE, there is only so much the officers and sergeants might do to keep their men keen to observe, report, and protect the force.[20]

Soldiers are not stupid, and only a foolish chain of command would attempt to manufacture a bogeyman just to keep the boys on their toes. Troops know the deal, and experiences upon arrival confirm their suspicions. Again,

David Segal captures the impressions: "Soldiers stand guard but expect no fire fights. They build bunkers but do not anticipate having to use them." They become, as one author called them, "soldiers without enemies."[21]

Superficially, this is true. The MFO leadership does not seriously expect an Egyptian or Israeli attack, and would be hard-pressed to survive such an onslaught, let alone stop it with its flimsy necklace of squad outposts. Every indicator demonstrates that no attack will ever come, and relations with both sides stay cordial. Egypt acts as host to the MFO, and many soldiers visit Israel on trips. The idea that an Egyptian armored brigade or Israeli mechanized task force might materialize outside a checkpoint would strike most MFO veterans as ludicrous.

Of course, the real hostile elements work hard not to be obvious. Terror cells take their time and do things their way, and, naturally, hitting an alert, heavily armed U.S. rifle squad appeals to few, especially when there are easier things to strike. Still, the possibility is very real, and the solitary American posts invite a spectacular effort. Some day, some way, it will probably come.

American MFO battalions, mindful of the terrorist threat, do not intend to invite the bad guys in. This explains why the remote sites have been hardened and why they keep sentinels and stand-to at the witching hours of dawn and dusk. American commanders caution their people to stay alert: "Attacks, if any, will be against an isolated or vulnerable target." Over the years, U.S. MFO units have increased their readiness posture in response to warnings or local events, such as the Marine barracks bombing in Beirut in 1983, the naval skirmishing in the Persian Gulf in 1987–88, and the Gulf War of 1990–91.

Concern with terror tactics underlies the MFO's rules of engagement. Although substantially more restrained than those used in the Korean DMZ, the Sinai ROE clearly and prominently permit acts of self-defense. But to prevent incidents with lost Israelis and Egyptians, to protect innocent Bedouins, to keep the focus on "observe and report," even this punch is pulled, just enough to encourage complacency among the unwary.

Soldiers carry live ammunition but do not load magazines into their weapons. Unlike Sergeant Duffy in the Korean DMZ, nobody in the Sinai is authorized to jack the first bullet into his rifle's chamber, ready to shoot. The MFO Use of Force Instruction Card carried by every soldier reminds him that he can fire "only as a last resort" and "whenever possible, request orders from your commander before you use force."[22]

Around Panmunjom, in the face of the implacable North Koreans, that kind of hesitation would probably cost heavily. It definitely crippled the Marines in Beirut in 1983 with horrific results. Yet in the Sinai, given the low level of tensions, caution might make sense, as long as the MFO troops do not mistake a minimal threat for none. You can rest assured that a private first class who should have fired first will be frantically calling for instructions when the satchel throwers and drive-by shooters really do show up. Some think they already have.

A recent U.S. MFO battalion summarized the common view of the present danger to the MFO thus, "Since the inception of the MFO, there have been no attacks directed against the force. This includes terrorist activities."[23] It would be very comforting if true.

The bloody reality suggests otherwise. The MFO has sustained one certain terrorist blow, and a second that, if truly the work of a hostile group, represents a massive strike against the United States military contribution to the Sinai mission. Both events happened outside Zone C, which may explain why the force does not acknowledge them as attacks on the MFO.

Without a doubt, the brutal slaying of the MFO's founding director general reflected the handiwork of terrorists. Though the murder occurred in Rome, Italy, the perpetrators clearly intended to influence American resolve and that of participating states of the MFO, especially Italy. They stalked their prey carefully, and when they struck, they knew what they were doing.

Ambassador Leamon R. "Ray" Hunt had surely made himself a prominent target, at least among those obsessed with U.S. intervention in Arab-Israeli affairs. A career foreign service officer with experience in Syria, Jerusalem, and as chargé d'affaires in Beirut, Lebanon, in 1976, Hunt crowned his diplomatic portfolio by heading the civilian Sinai Field Mission from 1977 to 1979. At the request of President Reagan, Hunt emerged from retirement to became the MFO's first director general in August of 1981, with the full approval of the governments of Egypt and Israel. Along with his extensive Middle Eastern resume, Hunt's year as an exchange student at the U.S. Army War College gave him some unique insight into military aspects of his new role.

Hunt formed the Multinational Force and Observers largely by dint of his own initiative, working from a temporary office in Alexandria, Virginia. He had eight months to select his force and observers, build an infrastructure of camps and remote sites, conduct training, and position his people. Hunt and his chosen team accomplished these feats and began operations on schedule. With the mission under way, Hunt left his temporary offices and, in response to an Italian invitation, formally opened MFO Headquarters in Rome in November 1982.

At 1945 on the cool winter evening of 15 February 1984, Hunt was returning home from MFO Headquarters. As usual, he rode in the rear seat of his blue Alfa Romeo, driven by his sixty-four-year-old chauffeur, Antonio Mazzioli. Things had been going well in the Sinai proper, but not in the unhappy land north of Israel. In fact, that morning the MFO was again on heightened alert following the sequence of gruesome bombings and shellings that had prompted the ongoing withdrawal of American, French, and Italian forces from shattered Beirut. With those same three countries intimately involved in MFO operations, few would be cavalier enough to discount the likelihood of reprisal raids by anti-Western, anti-Israeli factions. What better target than the MFO, strung out in its isolated little huts and bunkers across the eastern Sinai desert?

Instead, the target proved to be Hunt himself. When Hunt's car paused in the driveway in front of his handsome two-story house on Rome's fashionable Via Sud-Africa, Mazzioli activated a remote control system, opening the metal gates. It was the usual routine at the usual time.

As the gates slowly began to move, a trio of swarthy young men jumped out of a blue Fiat 128 parked across the street and ran toward Hunt's automobile. One man opened fire with some sort of submachine gun. "Get down!" Mazzioli hollered as he gunned the engine and tried to back up. Bullets ricocheted off the armored car body and reinforced glass.

The bespectacled, portly Hunt squirmed low into the backseat, but the gunman was not to be denied. He clambered onto the trunk and pressed his weapon's muzzle against the seam between the bulletproof window and the hardened roof. The hitman fired, a long, mean burst that skittered and sparked off the car's roof and window. One bullet worked its way through, smashing into Hunt's head.

The director general sagged across the backseat, leaking brains and blood. He would be declared dead on arrival at San Giovanni Hospital. Their butchery done, the shooter and his associates fled on foot, into the anonymity of the Eternal City.[24]

Some previously unknown band called the Fighting Communist Party claimed responsibility, calling a Milan radio station within thirty minutes after the shooting. "We must claim the attempt on General Hunt," the caller said, "the guarantor of the Camp David agreements." He also bellowed something about "imperialist forces out of Lebanon," then, just for good measure, demanded that Italy leave NATO and refuse to allow the U.S. to emplace cruise missiles in Sicily.

Over the next few days, various persons sent letters to newspapers and made calls to other journalists, claiming the killing for the Red Brigades, Italy's best-known practitioners of political violence. Italian authorities, who had jurisdiction in the case, initially accepted this proposition. But something sounded strange. The Italian security people knew that the Red Brigades had been decimated in a major crackdown following the 1981 kidnapping, and subsequent rescue, of U.S. Army Brig. Gen. James L. Dozier. Some of the Red Brigade types who were taking credit for the murder had made their boasts from prison or en route to court appearances.

As their investigation proceeded, Italian police began to suspect a Lebanese group had been involved. Within a week, the Italians suggested that Red Brigade remnants probably had provided local support for a visiting Lebanese gunman and his comrades. While no arrests or convictions ever resolved the Hunt killing, vigorous Italian police and security agents, motivated by the director general's execution, uncovered and foiled a planned Islamic Jihad truck bombing of America's Rome embassy on 27 November 1984.[25]

Interestingly, while the killing spurred greater concern for security in the Sinai, an awareness that persists to this day, it set off few alarm bells in the U.S. military and intelligence establishments. At the time, U.S. intelligence and security organizations quite reasonably were concentrating their assets on the Soviet Union. What little could be spared from watching Moscow's moves and serving in the Middle East went toward trying to find Americans held in Lebanon, tracking the Iran-Iraq War, and keeping an eye on Syrian aggression. The Hunt incident was perceived as a matter for the Rome authorities, another Red Brigade eruption. Possible Lebanese connections raised little interest. The Italians would handle it. America had bigger fish to fry.

Hardly anyone outside of the MFO community itself, even those who dealt routinely with the activities of American Sinai units, knew who Hunt was, let alone that he had been assassinated. In a hearing before the House of Representatives Subcommittee on Crime that specifically concerned terrorism directed against the MFO, a senior representative of the Defense

Intelligence Agency (DIA) when asked about Hunt's death responded, "I don't know to whom you refer, sir." He could not say for sure if the U.S. even had personnel in the MFO in 1984. An army general at the same hearing, who had worked closely with the MFO, responded with conviction that Hunt was "a Brit," and he, too, was not quite sure if Americans were assigned to the force in 1984.[26] These men were experts, responding on congressional invitation to prepared questions about the MFO and terrorism. Their ignorance indicates that perhaps the creeping Bedouin syndrome extended beyond the Sinai.

The lack of awareness, let alone reaction, to the Hunt murder could not have pleased the terrorists trying to send the MFO the way of the Western powers who had entered Beirut in 1982 and left so ignominiously in early 1984. Terror only works when it gets noticed, when it draws attention to "the cause" (in this case, opposition to U.S. intervention in the Arab-Israeli struggle). Obviously, it would take something even more dramatic than killing the MFO's senior leader—a mass slaughter of MFO soldiers, perhaps. Many think that is exactly what happened just past the end of Runway 22 at Gander International Airport, Newfoundland, early on the morning of 12 December 1985.

The crash of Arrow Air charter flight MF1285R, a McDonnell-Douglas DC-8-63, killed 8 aircrew members and 248 U.S. soldiers (four of them women), part of the 101st Airborne Division's Task Force 3-502d Infantry en route back from the Sinai. In the stark words of the Canadian Aviation Safety Board (CASB) report, "the aircraft was destroyed by impact forces and a severe fuel-fed fire. All 256 occupants on board sustained fatal injuries."[27]

By any measure, this was a tragedy of immense proportions. The Arrow Air flight ended in the worst military air disaster in U.S. history, the largest single-incident death toll inflicted on any American battalion task force (exceeding the Beirut truck bombing of 1983, the Custer massacre of 1876, and even the most horrendous battle casualties), and the most costly aviation accident ever to occur on Canadian territory. The numbers tell their own grim story of the heart torn out of the 3d Battalion, 502d Infantry: 110 soldiers comprising almost all of Company A, an antiarmor platoon of 22 men from Company D, 55 other soldiers from the battalion's headquarters company, the battalion commander, two company commanders, the battalion command sergeant major, and numerous other officers and senior NCOs.[28] The unit had to be thoroughly rebuilt and reorganized.

That much of the story is not disputed. The big question involves why? Despite a lot of loose talk alleging poor maintenance of the Arrow Air jet, all serious investigations quickly discounted these early rumors. The DC-8 was in good shape and, by all accounts, ably crewed. It had to be something else. Since that cold morning in 1985, two schools of thought have developed. These can be summarized as ice and fire.

The Canadians, who had jurisdiction in the case, officially endorsed the ice thesis. They investigated and determined that freezing buildup on the wings had caused the aircraft to stall and crash. This had been the preliminary suspicion of many, and, given the tough winter weather associated with Newfoundland, seemed perfectly reasonable. Many of those first to reach the scene recall snow and ice hampering the sad tasks of recovering charred bodies, personal effects, and military property.[29] Icing at Gander had a visceral sense of rightness about it. It certainly could have explained the crash, and the American law enforcement and safety agencies that reviewed the case publicly agreed with the CASB's final report.

This finding came after almost three years of agonizing and acrimonious debate, some carried on in public, among members of the CASB. Adoption of the icing idea split the CASB, with four members issuing a formal "Dissenting Opinion" two weeks after the official report emerged. They discounted the presence of ice buildup on the ground or in the descent through surrounding weather fronts, carefully scrutinizing meteorological records and interviewing ground crewmen, none of whom had seen any ice accretion on the wings or control surfaces. Records showed there had been no sleet at Gander that morning nor icing conditions. Subsequent analyses by the Aviation Group of Canada's Department of Transport, the Union of Canadian Transport Employees, and Judge Willard C. Estey (appointed by Canada to resolve the arguments dividing the CASB) all rejected the icing theory. It did not hold up.

The fire hypothesis did. By any measure, the CASB's dissenting quartet's credentials as pilots and engineers demanded attention to their informed opinions, especially since the majority report reflected the views of members with considerably less flight and engineering expertise. After demolishing the ice argument, the four gentlemen attributed the crash to "an on-board fire and massive loss of power" which "may have been associated with an in-flight detonation from an explosive or incendiary device."

Sifting through the bits of blackened wreckage, the dissenters found evidence of "simultaneous multiple systems failures" overlooked or attributed to impact damage in the official CASB report. These included engines exhibiting power loss and possible deployment of thrust reversers (used to brake on the ground), flaps set at various improbable angles inconsistent with an ice-induced stall (but quite in line with several major, coincident hydraulic failures), and landing gear still extended (again suggesting hydraulic trouble). Controls and lines for all of these systems pass through the cargo bays, where a detonation likely occurred.

Eyewitness accounts, although often notoriously inaccurate in describing rapidly developing accidents, include several reports of a glow or fire on the underside of the aircraft as it struggled to gain altitude during its brief flight. Nobody reported a nose-up stall, and the four members assessed that none had occurred. Flight data recorder and cockpit voice recorder outputs both proved inconclusive, despite attempts in the official report to correlate these damaged records with an icing stall. Medical data disclosed during identification of the dead (there was no formal coroner's autopsy) indicated the inhalation of chemical toxins produced by burned plastic, which could only have been inhaled before the smashing, traumatic, lethal effects of impact.[30] All in all, the fire thesis had much to recommend it.

There is more. Almost as soon as the crash was announced, Islamic Jihad claimed responsibility for the downed aircraft. One man talked to a Reuters office in Beirut. Another phoned French journalists in that same city, saying the explosion proved an "ability to strike at the Americans anywhere." A third Islamic Jihad caller contacted the U.S. consulate in Oran, Algeria. A fourth told the Italian ANSA news service that the Organization for the Liberation of Egypt, a previously unknown group, had done the deed. Finally, in January of 1986, the U.S. embassy in Port Louis, Mauritius, reported a letter from the "Sons of Zion," thought to be a Mossad (Israeli intelligence) front group. The writer blamed the air disaster on disgruntled Egyptian mechanics, aided by Libyans and "other anti-U.S. and anti-Israeli individuals." It looked like some of the usual suspects, all right.

Islamic Jihad and its running partners surely had cause to want to hit the MFO. They had the capability to build sophisticated devices that would go off following a set number of compression-decompression cycles in the baggage hold as the plane took off and landed. And they had shown an ability to infiltrate commercial airports to plant their awful seeds.[31] So the motive and competence to act were there.

Even so, Canadian and American government officials immediately and completely refuted these claims. Governmental skepticism might well have been founded on certain intelligence. The bad actors of Islamic Jihad had definitely attracted attention through previous mischief. Maybe the Reagan administration knew for sure.

More likely, though, there was no smoking gun, no definite proof beyond a few telephone statements. Unable to verify the Islamic Jihad claims and hence unwilling to react forcefully as public opinion would no doubt demand, America and Canada ignored the whole issue. Both governments normally avoided stirring the terrorist pot in the absence of any corroborating evidence. Considering that Reagan was vilified at home and abroad for bombing Mu'ammar Gadhafi's Libya in April 1986, even with ample evidence that the Libyans had attacked U.S. soldiers in Berlin, this caution was not misplaced. As a minimum, it denied the terror bombers the limelight they craved. If America is not ready to reply in force, silence looks like the smartest policy.

After all, these days a few phone calls does not a terrorist act make. Every calamity brings in a raft of messages from those eager to advance their beliefs and gain free publicity, seeking to reap the benefits of terrorism without the work. In this vein, some groups even took credit for the explosion that destroyed the space shuttle *Challenger,* even though ample immediate evidence pointed to a mechanical malfunction, later proven. With the shuttle accident, nobody took boasts of sabotage seriously.

The same sort of thing happened regarding Gander. The Canadians became convinced early on that ice was the culprit, not mad bombers. With Ottawa's people in charge, Americans would have sparked friction in relations by leaping in to allege a terrorist tie, especially when all they had to go on were some telephone calls. Initial American reports indicated that icing made as much sense as anything, and that the roasted scraps of evidence would be very hard to piece together anyway. The main thing was to get the dead soldiers home.[32] So the terrorist claims received short shrift. In this way, the Arrow Air event has become known as an accident, not an act of political violence.

But for those convinced that something beyond confusion and predisposition toward the ice theory were at work, this only whetted appetites. Certain people—several of the same stripe that have populated the grassy knoll in Dallas with renegade CIA gunmen bent on killing President John F. Kennedy in 1963 or accused the U.S. government of abandoning hundreds of live Americans in Hanoi's labor camps in 1975—have seized upon the dismissal of the terrorist calls as evidence of yet another government conspiracy. This one supposedly covers up the real purpose of the Arrow Air flight. Not satisfied that terrorists might want to attack the MFO itself, certain folks have attempted to tie the returning flight to Lt. Col. Oliver L. North's notorious arms-for-hostages transfers with Iran or concurrent U.S. special operations in Lebanon, both still secret at the time of the crash.[33] These charges have only muddied the fairly reasonable idea of a terrorist strike against American troops. They do little credit to those who advance them.

The Iran-Contra connection coincides in timing, but that is all. The convoluted American-Israeli initiatives to supply weapons to the Tehran government in return for Americans held in Beirut went their own way. They displayed no link whatsoever with the MFO. Although Arrow Air flew some CIA contracts in its time, it did not participate in the three shipments of antitank and air defense missiles that had gone to Iran by December of 1985. Arrow Air had nothing to hide in Gander.

By the time of the crash, the first few armament consignments had spurred the release of one American held in Lebanon, thereby beginning the clandestine arms-for-hostages transfers. Thorough investigations by Sen. John Tower's Special Review Board and the joint Senate-House Congressional Committee, as well as the published autobiographies of North and his cohort, retired Air Force Maj. Gen. Richard Secord, make no reference to the Gander crash one way or the other.[34] If Arrow Air's return flight had something to do with the Iran-Contra effort, the documentary record does not reflect it, nor does such a linkage make all that much sense. Things were going into Iran, not coming out through the Sinai. The Iran enterprise was running according to its own strange course.

The special operations ties are a bit more suggestive, although by no means as intriguing as some would charge. Some have argued that the plane's manifest included a nebulous "Company E" of TOW missile trainers, recently returned from advisory duty in Iran. Others think that six crates loaded in Cairo contained contraband arms or even corpses of men killed in an abortive hostage rescue attempt in Lebanon. Finally, a few believe that special operators were using the cover of the MFO flight to return to the United States.

All of these allegations except the last can be discounted out of hand. The twenty-two TOW gunners aboard were from 3-502d Infantry's Company D. The Iranians were at war and well aware of how to employ TOWs, as they had been using them in combat since 1980. The six crates loaded in Cairo contained tools, records, unit machine guns, and training aids—one held a resuscitation dummy, hence the dark hint of a concealed body.[35] Suggestions that the U.S. would ship sensitive intelligence materials through Cairo, Cologne, and Gander International Airports, subject to inspection all the way, defies all experience of such secretive operations.

The same logic explains why elite counterterrorists of 1st Special Forces Operational Detachment–Delta (Delta Force), SEAL Team 6 (ST-6), and especially the shadowy Intelligence Support Activity (ISA) would never travel in uniform aboard a chartered unit flight. These forces go in and out under deep cover. If coming from a mission, they would leave Egypt by far more covert means, and they have many at their disposal. Suggestions that terrorists tracked Delta operatives aboard Arrow Air and then blew up the plane in retaliation for unnamed outrages impute too much to the terrorist types and too little to the Delta people.

And yet, accounts of that period, as revealed in Iran-Contra documents and related stories, paint a picture of an intensive U.S. special operations mission under way in Lebanon, searching for captive Americans and setting up potential hostage rescues. Here the MFO might have gotten involved, albeit peripherally and in a very minor way. But for those who think U.S. peacekeepers can ever really be impartial in regional conflicts, there is a lesson here.

One of America's lesser-known special operations episodes culminated in November 1985, when meticulous U.S. reconnaissance and surveillance efforts, led by the ISA, pinpointed five of six American hostages held in Lebanon by the Hezbollah faction. Detailed preparations for a rescue raid began, to include construction of scale models of the buildings where the terrorists held their prisoners. North at one point prepared an option paper that included the choice of a raid "to execute NLT [not later than] next Saturday," either 7 or 14 December 1985.

All of this was put on hold when President Reagan's advisers chose to pursue less violent options, including a Syrian inclination to free the Americans themselves and the growing promise of more arms for hostages deals with Iran. Although the raid was off, the ISA apparently maintained its network in Lebanon, in league with the CIA. Indeed, in June of 1986, North referred to "one ISA officer in Beirut."[36] Dismantling the raid support structure and scaling back to mere surveillance did, however, require removing some support troops. And here the MFO might have come in.

The army described eleven of the soldiers on the ill-fated flight as being "from Forces Command," at that time the umbrella organization for all Stateside army units, including special warfare outfits. The army labeled "*most* of those that were not in the 101st [Airborne Division]," (emphasis added), as troops deployed to assist TF 3-502d. It should be noted that the MFO mission's support requirements can be filled completely by the troops in any army division, in concert with the in-place MFO 1st Support Battalion, without resort to help from other Forces Command units. In any event, eleven Forces Command troops passed through the Sinai in December of 1985, perhaps en route back from other business.

These individual augmentees may have been Joint Special Operations Command (JSOC) support and service support troops, or perhaps ground crewmen of the 160th Special Operations Aviation Regiment (160th SOAR) located at Fort Campbell, Kentucky.[37] While not as stimulating as whispers of ninja-suited triggermen aboard, it would explain persistent rumors. And whatever their actual identity, which may be exactly as reported, their deaths were simply a bonus if, indeed, hostile actors destroyed the TF 3-502d aircraft.

Unfortunately, the more bizarre secret warfare allegations have served mainly to divert attention from the very real opportunities presented for terrorists to gain access to the Arrow Air charter. Several of the various postcrash analyses have identified numerous security lapses that might have allowed entry to a determined agent trying to rig a bomb. Throughout its ill-starred transit, the flight was treated more like a tourist junket than a military transport returning from one of the more violent regions in the world. Regardless of what knocked down Arrow Air flight MF1285R, no military professional can take comfort in the porous security arrangements that characterized the flight.

Typically, the American charters had come and gone from Ras Nasrani Airfield, a facility right near South Camp. But ongoing runway repairs there required TF 3-502d to redeploy through Cairo International, obviously a place more open to trouble. In accord with MFO protocol, the U.S. commanders deferred to the Egyptians to secure the flight. There were MFO transportation staff present, as well as military customs inspectors and unit equipment guards. Most security, however, was handled by the Egyptians, who parked the plane in a relatively isolated portion of the airport.

American guards in Cairo were mainly interested in keeping track of military baggage and cargo, leaving surveillance of the servicing of the DC-8 to one languid Egyptian sentry, who now and then wandered off during the five hours the plane stayed in the parking area. Several groups of Egyptian civilians approached the aircraft, and certain individuals entered the four cargo bays, which were open. Although U.S. troops normally load baggage on MFO flights, this time they let the Egyptian workers do it. No American entered the cargo bays.

The slipshod Egyptian security was a model compared to that at Cologne. Upon arrival, the jet pulled up to a commercial air terminal in Cologne, right alongside all the other airliners. No guard was posted on the ground during the ninety-odd minutes the plane stayed there. Various personnel had access to the charter aircraft, and no particular attempt was made to observe them or control their movements. The B cargo bay door, under the forward edge of the wing and therefore hard to see from the flight deck, remained open throughout the stay on the ground. Ground personnel placed six food containers in bay B, a process carried out without anyone watching. The plane's crew changed over during this stop, which further concentrated their attentions inside as they did their swapover. TF 3-502d personnel left guards in the aircraft when they deplaned through the covered jetway, but these soldiers did not go outside or check the baggage compartments.

Any one of the unknown people who entered the DC-8's cargo bays could have left behind a nasty surprise. One experienced pilot, Capt. Art Schoppaul, who flew the leg from Egypt to Germany, told the CASB members, "Ground security was *very poor* in Cairo and Cologne" (his emphasis). He made similar comments to American FBI agents.[38]

As if this was not sobering enough, it is possible that the Americans themselves might have inadvertently done the job. Soldiers have been known to carry home training ammunition, and a trip flare or explosive grenade simulator in the wrong place could prove as lethal as any Semtex time bomb. The unit chain of command is supposed to verify that these items do not come aboard, but after six months in the Sinai, the creeping Bedouin syndrome could have taken over.

TF 3-502d did not thoroughly inspect baggage, and the rather sketchy cargo manifest was never approved by the customs inspector at Cairo. Postcrash investigation shows that the unit brought home medical and dental records on the same conveyance as their owners, contrary to army regulations and good sense—this shortcut impeded attempts to identify the dead. As the doomed battalion commander, Lt. Col. Marvin Jeffcoat, told Captain Schoppaul, "I don't know what these men have in their baggage. It could be anything from hand grenades to night vision scopes to classified equipment—who knows?"[39] Perhaps a trip flare came too, did its own thing, and Islamic Jihad merely jumped on the bandwagon. We will never know.

There is irony here. What may be Islamic Jihad's greatest hit of all time might not ever receive its due. And that can only lead to another attempt. MFO soldiers, and all Americans concerned with today's military expeditions, should not forget what went wrong on the fatal flight that ended so tragically in the snowy woods of Newfoundland.

What is going right in the Sinai has allowed the U.S. commitment to weather the Gander disaster and the murder of Ray Hunt. Some thirty battalion task forces, in concert with their MFO allies, have done their six-month tours and thereby helped guarantee peace in the Sinai. They have done their duty without fanfare but with thorough professionalism and skill enough to deter those anxious to kill Americans. As the saying goes, eternal vigilance is the price of peace. It can also keep you alive.

The MFO works because America is willing to pay the price for peace in the Sinai. Prior to the Camp David Accords, the successive waves of Egyptian-Israeli wars and their ancillary terrorist strains threatened American lives and imperiled the country's access to Middle Eastern oil. A two-battalion investment to guarantee stability seems reasonable enough, especially since costs appear to have been small. Here, the fact that terrorists were not blamed for Gander has certainly helped.

But even if Gander had been officially ascribed to Islamic Jihad right on the spot, America would likely have remained in the Sinai. The mission is worth doing. Equally important, the MFO has become, in the prescient words of the late Ray Hunt, "the Middle East peace force that works."[40] Tranquility prevails between Egypt and Israel, despite the best efforts of the malcontent factions that infect the Middle East. By any measure, in the Sinai, the gain has been worth the pain.

Notes

The epigraph comes from David R. Segal et al., *Peacekeepers and Their Wives* (Westport, Conn.: Greenwood Press, 1993), 53. This is the best single-volume study of American participation in the Sinai MFO.

1. For a complete development of this idea, see Benjamin C. Schwartz, *Rand Briefing: The Influence of U.S. Public Opinion on American Intervention* (Arroyo, Calif.: RAND Corporation, 1993).

2. Mala Tabory, *The Multinational Force and Observers in the Sinai* (Boulder, Colo.: Westview Press, 1986), 1–9; U.S. Department of State, Sinai Support Mission, *Watch in the Sinai* (Washington, D.C.: U.S. Government Printing Office, 1980), 21; Multinational Force and Observers, *The Multinational Force and Observers: Servants of Peace* (Rome, Italy: MFO Office of Personnel and Publications, 1993), 31–46; Segal et al., *Peacekeepers and Their Wives*, 30–31.

3. Tabory, *The Multinational Force and Observers in the Sinai*, 3–7.

4. Ibid., 7, 11–12, 19–20; MFO, *MFO: Servants of Peace*, 7–8.

5. Tabory, *The Multinational Force and Observers in the Sinai*, 21; MFO, *MFO: Servants of Peace*, 58.

6. Wat T. Cluverius IV, *Annual Report of the Director General 1990–91* (Rome, Italy: MFO Office of Personnel and Publications, 1991), 8–12; MFO, *MFO: Servants of Peace*, 27.

7. Tabory, *The Multinational Force and Observers in the Sinai*, 15.

8. Maj. Tom Williams, USA, "MFO: Border Buffer," *Soldiers* (January 1985): 8; Victor H. Dikeos, *Annual Report of the Director General 1983–84* (Rome, Italy: MFO Office of Personnel and Publications, 1984), 13; Cluverius, *Director General 1990–91*, 5; MFO, *MFO: Servants of Peace*, 13.

9. Governments of Egypt and Israel, "Treaty of Peace," in *MFO: Servants of Peace*, 33–34.

10. Maj. Cornelis Homan, Royal Netherlands Marine Corps, "MFO: Peacekeeping in the Middle East," *Military Review* (September 1983): 4. Major Homan served as a staff officer at North Camp. See also Segal et al., *Peacekeepers and Their Wives*, 27–28, 32–33.

11. U.S. Department of the Army, Headquarters, 1st Battalion, 327th Infantry, "OPORD 25-93 (DESERT RENDEZVOUS)," (Fort Campbell, Ky.: 15 June 1993), 2–5; Homan, "MFO," 7–9; MFO, *MFO: Servants of Peace,* 20.

12. 1st Lt. Robert L. Bateman, USA, "U.S. Battalion Operations in the Multinational Force and Observers," *Infantry* (July–August 1992): 9; Segal et al., *Peacekeepers and Their Wives,* 81–82; Homan, "MFO," 9, 12; MFO, *MFO: Servants of Peace,* 6, 10, 24.

13. 1-327th Infantry, "OPORD 25-93," 3–5; Richard Jupa and Jim Dingeman, *Gulf Wars* (Cambria, Calif.: 3W Publications, 1991), 76, 81.

14. Segal et al., *Peacekeepers and Their Wives,* 84–85.

15. S. L. A. Marshall, *Men Against Fire* (Gloucester, Mass.: Peter Smith, 1978), 44, 47.

16. U.S. Department of the Army, Headquarters, 1st Battalion, 327th Infantry, "MFO Rotation 25 July 1993 Thru January 1994 Rotation Schedule" (Washington, D.C.: Army Staff, Pentagon, 15 June 1993). To date, MFO battalion task forces have come from the 82d Airborne Division, 101st Airborne Division (Air Assault), 7th Infantry Division (Light), 9th Infantry Division (Motorized), 10th Mountain Division (Light Infantry), and 25th Infantry Division (Light). The 7th and 9th Divisions have been recently inactivated. Note that MFO troops have not been drawn from mechanized infantry battalions.

17. Segal et al., *Peacekeepers and Their Wives,* 84–85; Maj. Tom Williams, USA, "Sandmen of the Sinai," *Soldiers* (January 1985): 11–12.

18. Ibid., 53–54, 96–97; Holman, "MFO," 13; 1-327th Infantry, "OPORD 25-93," 2, 9; Michael Ross, "Troops Never Fired on in 3 1/2 Years of Duty," *Los Angeles Times,* 13 December 1985. For a discussion of Islamic Jihad gun-running into the Gaza Strip from Egypt, see Ian Black and Benny Morris, *Israel's Secret Wars* (New York: Grove Weidenfeld, 1991), 463, 481.

19. Douglas Porch, *The French Foreign Legion* (New York: Harper Collins, 1991), 306–8.

20. Williams, "Sandmen of the Sinai," 11–12; Segal et al., *Peacekeepers and Their Wives,* 90–91, 100; U.S. Congress, House Committee on the Judiciary, *Fatal Plane Crash in Gander, Newfoundland, December 12, 1985: Hearings Before the Subcommittee on Crime,* 101st Cong., 2d sess., 4–5 December 1990, 895 (hereafter cited as Congress, *Gander Hearings*).

The congressional hearings refer to a U.S. Army Criminal Investigation Division (CID) agent carrying hashish seized from a soldier at South Camp.

21. Larry R. Fabian, *Soldiers Without Enemies* (Washington, D.C.: Brookings Institution, 1971); Segal et al., *Peacekeepers and Their Wives*, 87.

22. Segal et al., *Peacekeepers and Their Wives*, 38–39, 99–100; Holman, "MFO," 13; 1-327th Infantry, "OPORD 25-93," 1, 9.

23. 1-327th Infantry, "OPORD 25-93," 1.

24. Henry Kamm, "U.S. Diplomat Slain by Gunmen on Rome Street," *New York Times*, 16 February 1984; "Ray Hunt Dies; Was U.S. Aide on Middle East," *Washington Post*, 17 February 1984; "Alive and Well," *Time* (27 February 1984): 46; MFO, *MFO: Servants of Peace*, 9–14.

25. "Alive and Well"; "Red Brigades Claim Killing of American," *New York Times*, 18 February 1984; "Red Brigades Threaten Another U.S. Diplomat," *New York Times;* Sari Gilbert, "7 Charged with Plot Against U.S. Embassy," *Washington Post*, 28 November 1984.

26. Congress, *Gander Hearings*, 194. The DIA representative was William J. Allard, General Counsel of the DIA. The U.S. Army representative was Lt. Gen. John S. Crosby (Ret.), who had been Assistant Deputy Chief of Staff for Personnel in December 1985.

27. Canadian Aviation Safety Board, "Aviation Occurrence Report: Arrow Air, Inc., Douglas DC-8-63, N950JW, Gander International Airport, Newfoundland, 12 December 1985, 28 October 1988," in Congress, *Gander Hearings*, 772.

28. Segal et al., *Peacekeepers and Their Wives*, 113; Richard Halloran, "Army Replacing Men Killed in Crash," *New York Times*, 20 January 1986. The 1st Minnesota Regiment lost 215 on 2 July 1863 at Gettysburg (Harry W. Pfanz, *Gettysburg: The Second Day* [Chapel Hill, N.C.: University of North Carolina Press, 1987], 414). The Custer massacre of 25 June 1876 cost 212 lives from Custer's provisional battalion of the 7th Cavalry Regiment (Robert M. Utley, *Frontier Regulars* [New York: Macmillan, 265–69]. The Marines in Beirut lost 236 Marines and sailors from Battalion Landing Team 1/8 Marines on 23 October 1983 (Daniel P. Bolger, *Americans at War, 1975–1986* [Novato, Calif.: Presidio Press, 1988], 228).

29. CASB, "Aviation Occurrence Report," Congress, *Gander Hearings*, 766–882; U.S. Army, "Gander After Action Report," Congress, *Gander Hearings*, 333–39; Congress, *Gander Hearings*, 165.

30. Norman Bobbitt, Les Filotas, David Mussallem, and Ross Stevenson, "Dissenting Opinion," 14 November 1988, Congress, *Gander Hearings,* 67–88. Bobbitt and Stevenson were experienced pilots, the former a test pilot. Mussallem was an aeronautical engineer and an experienced airline pilot. Dr. Les Filotas, an aeronautical engineer and professor of aeronautics, also wrote *Improbable Cause* (Toronto, Ontario: McClelland-Bantam, 1991), a detailed account of his role in the Gander investigation, as well as the internal disputes among members of the CASB. Unfortunately, Dr. Filotas also takes a brief excursion into half-baked Iran-Contra and special operations possibilities, which detract from his otherwise convincing technical arguments against the CASB official report.

31. "Claims by Two Groups Discounted," *New York Times,* 14 December 1985; U.S. Department of State, "Cable, AmEmbassy Algiers to SecState, Subject: Claimed Responsibility for Canadian Air Disaster," 18 December 1985; "Cable, AmEmbassy Port Louis to SecState, Subject: Purported Letter from 'Sons of Zion' on Crash of U.S. Military Transport in Canada," 17 January 1986, Congress, *Gander Hearings,* 662–64; Union of Canadian Transport Employees, "Gander Crash," Congress, *Gander Hearings,* 27. For a description of aircraft bomb technology, see Filotas, *Improbable Cause,* 130–31.

32. Union of Canadian Transport Employees, "Gander Crash," Congress, *Gander Hearings,* 29. See also testimony by Robert M. Pines, deputy assistant secretary of state for European and Canadian Affairs, Congress, *Gander Hearings,* 290. Pines termed the terrorist claims "frivolous."

33. For a typical example of conspiracy allegations regarding Gander, see Roy Rowan, "Gander: Different Crash, Same Questions," *Time* (27 April 1992): 33–34.

34. U.S. Congress, Joint Special Committee, *Report of the Congressional Committee Investigating the Iran-Contra Affair,* 100th Cong., 1st sess., 17 November 1987, 159–64; Senator John Tower, Senator Edmund Muskie, and Lt. Gen. Brent Scowcroft, USAF (Ret.), *Report of the President's Special Review Board* (Washington, D.C.: U.S. Government Printing Office, 26 February 1987), B-40 to B-49, B-174 to B-180; Lt. Col. Oliver L. North, USMC (Ret.) with William Novak, *Under Fire* (New York: Harper Collins, 1991), 26; Maj. Gen. Richard Secord, USAF (Ret.) with Jay Wurts, *Honored and Betrayed* (New York: John Wiley and Sons, 1992), 219–26. Under a legal subcontract from Southern Air Transport, Arrow Air flew several

resupply runs to the Nicaraguan resistance in early 1985, and one former Arrow Air pilot may have flown a cargo jet into Iran. Neither of these activities imply any wrongdoing regarding Arrow Air. As it was, the company was thoroughly investigated during attempts to determine if maintenance problems downed the Gander flight.

35. Iran's skill and experience with TOW missiles is discussed in Anthony R. Cordesman and Abraham R. Wagner, *The Lessons of Modern War*, vol. 2, *The Iran-Iraq War* (Boulder, Colo.: Westview Press, 1990), 442–43. For the contents of the crates, see the testimony of Lt. Col. Ronald W. Carpenter Jr., USA, former MFO liaison officer in Cairo, Egypt, Congress, *Gander Hearings*, 158. Carpenter was present when the aircraft was loaded.

36. Steven Emerson, *Secret Warriors* (New York: G. P. Putnam's Sons, 1988), 225–32. For another popular account of U.S. counterterrorist units, see Terry Griswold and D. M. Giangreco, *Delta: America's Elite Counterterrorist Force* (Osceola, Wis.: Motorbooks, 1992). Curiously, one ISA man was aboard Pan American Flight 103, destroyed by a bomb over Lockerbie, Scotland, in 1988. In pursuing the idea that terrorists might have traced him aboard from Lebanon, Steven Emerson discounted the possibility. He demonstrated just how hard it was for terrorists to tail such individuals. He also explained why the ISA and similar outfits do not fly with U.S. military units. See Steven Emerson and Brian Duffy, *The Fall of Pam Am 103* (New York: G. P. Putnam's Sons, 1990), 75–76. The U.S. Armed Forces awarded posthumous Purple Hearts, issued for hostile fire deaths and wounds, to include those inflicted by terrorism, to the members of the services who died in the Lockerbie crash.

37. Congress, *Gander Hearings*, 163, quoted from Major General Crosby's testimony. Although in 1985 army special operations units reported officially to Forces Command, since 1987 all U.S. special operations forces, including army elements, have been assigned to the United States Special Operations Command (USSOCOM). For a description of modern U.S. counterterrorist forces, see Emerson, *Secret Warriors*, 26, 38, 45–48, and 81–84. For a typical MFO task force drawn from divisional units, see 1-327th Infantry, "OPORD 25-93," A-1. TF 1-327th included forty-seven augmentees; one of these came from the CID command, as with TF 3-502d. The remainder were divisional troops.

38. U.S. Department of Justice, Federal Bureau of Investigation, "Memorandum Relating to the Interview of Arthur Schoppaul," 3 March 1986,

Congress, *Gander Hearings,* 418, 420–25. For comments on the loading process in Cairo, see the Carpenter testimony, Congress, *Gander Hearings,* 181–82.

39. Filotas, *Improbable Cause,* 150–51; Bobbitt et al., "Dissenting Opinion," Congress, *Gander Hearings,* 78–79; FBI, "Interview of Arthur Schoppaul," Congress, *Gander Hearings,* 419.

40. "Talk of the Town: Notes and Comment," *New Yorker* (12 March 1984): 39.

This rusty sign is one of 1,291 markers erected to separate hostile forces in the Korean Demilitarized Zone. There is no fence or wall dividing North from South Korea.

As seen from United Nations Command Guard Post Collier, the great flag tower and low buildings are Ki-jong Dong ("Model Village"), North Korea's showplace hamlet in the Demilitarized Zone.

President William J. Clinton visits United Nations Command Guard Post Ouellette in June, 1993. The soldiers are assigned to the U.S./South Korean United Nations Command Security Force—Joint Security Area (the JSA Battalion). *Department of the Army*

On a little-used road in the Sinai Desert, a fire team of paratroopers from the 82d Airborne Division returns from a foot reconnaissance patrol. *Department of the Army*

American infantrymen in the Sinai Multinational Force and Observers man a watch tower overlooking the Strait of Tiran.

On guard in the Sinai, a soldier awaits the landing of a Multinational Force and Observers UK-1H Huey helicopter.

Manning a lonely post in the Sinai wilderness, Pfc. Randall Brock of the 1st Battalion, 502d Infantry serves as sentry at the front gate to Observation Post 3–9.

Capt. James G. Breckenridge snapped this remarkable photograph while under a barrage on the morning of 4 September 1983. The dirt puff is an enemy shell landing in the joint Army/Marine Combat Post 39, near Khalde. *Captain James G. Breckenridge*

The tension is obvious as two Marine jeeps halt enroute to the Embassy in dangerous downtown Beirut, September 1983. Weapons are loaded, and the men scan their assigned sectors for anything unusual.

The battered Battalion Landing Team Headquarters building appeared this way on 1 October 1982, more than a year before the bombing. Two armored amphibious assault vehicles are parked to the left.

The wreckage of the Battalion Landing Team Headquarters building looked like this by 15 November 1983, about three weeks after the truck bombing.

A Light Armored Vehicle (LAV-25) from Battalion Landing Team Marines drives past a deserted Iraqi Army compound in Dihok, Iraq in May of 1991. This LAV is armed with a 25-mm automatic cannon.

Marine riflemen dig in along the limit of the Coalition advance, not far from Dihok, Iraq, May, 1991.

A U.S. Army UH-60A Blackhawk helicopter brings in a vehicle by sling near a Kurdish refugee camp in Northern Iraq, April, 1991.

Marines in Somalia gather in front of a television camera near the Joint Task Force Headquarters in Mogadishu. The press is a full participant in almost every aspect of modern American military operations.

Early in Operation Restore Hope, an AAV-7A1 Amphibious Assault Vehicle from Battalion Landing Team 2/9 Marines returns from a mounted patrol on the outskirts of Mogadishu.

Men of 2/9 Marines patrol near Mogadishu, Somalia, in January, 1993. Note the distance between the riflemen—snipers had been active.

Safe behind cover, a wary Marine fire team talks about their next move during a firefight in Mogadishu in January, 1993.

A U.S. Marine AH-1W Super Sea Cobra engages Somali gunmen with 70-mm rockets. Army AH-1F Cobras played major roles in later phases of the Somalia mission.

A 2/9 Marines Quick Reaction Force truck stands by to be called forward during a street battle in Mogadishu in January of 1993. Note the armored amphibious assault vehicle to the left of the 5-ton truck. Truck-mounted, similarly equipped Army light infantry formed the core of the Quick Reaction Force that attacked in order to link up with Task Force Ranger on 3–4 October 1993.

American 10th Mountain Division soldiers aboard three Army High-Mobility Military Wheeled Vehicles (HMMWVs) negotiate the narrow streets of Mogadishu, Somalia, in February, 1993. To the left of the trucks, dismounted riflemen stand guard. *Department of the Army*

American Army traffic drives along a dusty road skirting Mogadishu late in 1993. An armed military police Humvee, with the gunner ready in the hatch, heads into town. Oncoming traffic includes an unarmed cargo Humvee and a 5-ton truck. *Department of the Army*

This is the University Compound from which Task Force 2-14 Infantry moved out to link up with Americans encircled in downtown Mogadishu on 3 October 1983. The Quick Reaction Force 5-ton trucks and Humvees can be seen in the parking lot. *Department of the Army*

A Moroccan patrol cruises the ravaged streets of Mogadishu aboard a UN-marked light-armored personnel carrier based on a South African design. Similar Russian-built BRDMs, manned by Malaysians, carried American light infantrymen into a raging street battle late on 3 October 1993. *Department of the Army*

An unmodified Army OH-6A Cayuse waits at a remote desert site in the United States. Army special operations aviation units employ heavily modified "Little Birds" in operations such as those conducted in Mogadishu in August through October of 1993. *Department of the Army*

This is the Army MH-60K Special Operations Blackhawk, the primary aircraft of the 1st I Battalion, 160th Special Operations Aviation Regiment. It has an aerial refueling boom, long-range tanks, satellite communications capabilities, and special infrared navigation and optics systems on the bow (the small ball-shaped turrets). Armament includes two 7.62-mm Gatling guns.

During Operation Sharp Guard, the USS *McInerney* (FFG-8) works with the Turkish destroyer TCG *Aniteppe* as part of the NATO blockading force in the Adriatic Sea.

An F/A-18D from the 312th Marine Fighter Attack Squadron lands on the USS *Theodore Roosevelt* after a Deny Flight mission over Bosnia. The Marine jet is fully loaded for battle, less fuel expended. This type of aircraft conducted a bombing raid near Gorazde, Bosnia, in April, 1994.

The Aegis cruiser USS *Normandy* (CG-60) provides awesome antiaircraft capability for a naval battle group. Aegis ships off the Adriatic coast, linked to orbiting aerial radar planes, monitored all air traffic in and around the former Yugoslavia as part of Sharp Guard and Deny Flight.

An American C-130E Hercules transport lands at Sarajevo, Bosnia, as part of the Provide Promise airlift.

White-painted United Nations vehicles take American-delivered humanitarian supplies into the streets of Sarajevo, Bosnia.

With a United Nations blue beret on his head and a radio on his back, a rifleman of the 6th Battalion, 502d Infantry walks a security post near Skopje, Macedonia. *Department of the Army*

CHAPTER 5
Getting It Wrong:
Beirut, Lebanon, 1982 to 1984

But you got nothing to brag about being in Beirut. We were just there, that's all. When I got home, I didn't want anyone to ask me about it. I just wanted to get in my car and drive and forget the whole thing.

LCpl. Gordon Brock
Company E, 2d Battalion, 8th Marines

Given how well things went in the Sinai right from the outset, it was only natural for intelligent Americans to think that a superpower capable of enforcing peace on Arabs and Jews in the Sinai could certainly work a similar miracle between Arabs and Jews in Lebanon. The analogy seemed obvious. Egypt and Israel had long warred over the Sinai, and putting Americans there had helped guarantee the end of that fighting. Syria and Israel had long contended over Lebanon, a rivalry peaked by the war of 1982. In the wake of that Israeli-Syrian combat, could a Sinai-style effort in Lebanon do the trick? After all, Lebanon was a tiny country, easily invaded by Syria in 1976 and again by Israel in 1982. A few Yankees on the ground in this pretty little place should have sufficed.

Things in Lebanon went wrong. In retrospect, the failure seems as preordained as any Greek tragedy, but that misses the essential nature of the acts of omission and commission that scuttled American policy in this turbulent corner of the Mediterranean. Each move, each choice made or deferred, pushed the force toward trouble, yet every act or decision done or undone reflected a logic that made sense at the time. One thing led to another, imperceptibly at first, then a bit faster, the whole situation gathering momentum into a whirling, seemingly inevitable death spiral that culminated in the horrific truck bombing of 23 October 1983. It could have happened thus around Panmunjom, or in the Sinai, or in the Arizona

Territory a century before. Indeed, it could happen on any OOTW. Failure and death are always nearby, patiently waiting for an opening. In Beirut, Americans provided that opening and paid for it with blood.

Almost everything went wrong in Beirut. By any measure, it was a debacle, one that has cast a long shadow of hostages taken, doubts reinforced, opportunities missed, and peace deferred. During its eighteen months ashore, the U.S. intervention force made little or no progress toward creating a stable, independent Lebanon capable of holding apart its jealous Israeli and Syrian neighbors, let alone holding together its own fractious, violent social fabric. And as the wheels gradually came off of the U.S. mission, the price went up and up—239 Americans dead in the great truck blast alone. Unlike the Sinai, none of this was worth it, and everybody knew it.

Lebanon happened almost a decade before anyone invented the term operations other than war. But it was OOTW, all right, OOTW of the worst kind. The Americans walked right into it, eyes open, hoping for the best. This time, they got their heads ripped off. And as in the Sinai, there are lessons here.

Lebanon was and is a land of trouble, the Sinai with an attitude, full of unruly people. Largely thanks to its militant population, Lebanon has become one of the most dangerous countries in the world, even compared to its unhappy neighbors in the volatile Middle East. Its green hills still feature the famous cedars of biblical lore, and white beaches front on the azure eastern Mediterranean. That very beauty is a cruel deception, a lovely lure that hides the bitter, sputtering struggle for control of a small country not much bigger than Connecticut. The three million quarrelsome inhabitants occasionally acknowledge a weak central government and an inexperienced army of at most twenty thousand men. But neither the government nor the army is unified. Although Syria's heavy hand crushed many factional forces in 1990, no single authority really controls Lebanon, and there is no "safe" district. Things may be a bit better than in 1982, but just barely.

In June 1982, the jewel of the Levant was split among local militias, a Syrian occupation army, vicious Palestinian squatters, Iranian Revolutionary Guard volunteers, and the ineffectual United Nations Interim Force in Lebanon (UNIFIL). Lebanese religious factions also controlled chunks of the small state army. Their private militias squabbled for turf like American ghetto street gangs, but this was not some Arab version of *West Side Story*, with switchblades and zip guns. These people meant business. The Muslim Druze Progressive Socialist Party (4,000 under arms), Maronite Christian Phalange (10,000), Christian South Lebanon Army (3,500), Amal Shiite Muslims (2,000), Iranian-backed Hezbollah and Islamic Jihad groups (at least 1,000 total), not to mention numerous smaller splinters, all employed stolen, borrowed, and bestowed Sagger antitank missiles, 122-mm rockets, 130-mm guns, armored personnel carriers, and even tanks. The groups formed loose alliances on occasion, often crossing religious lines for the sake of expediency. Splits in the militias created new conflicts and constant reshuffling of this deadly deck.

As if this was not bad enough, foreign forces stirred the pot, playing the suspicious militias against each other. When Jordan's King Hussein ejected Yasir Arafat's Palestine Liberation Organization (PLO) in 1970, the PLO moved to south-central Lebanon, aided by Syrian units. Arafat continued attacks into Israel and manipulated Lebanese Muslim groups; Israel countered by influencing and arming Christian militias. Civil war erupted in 1975, urged by the PLO and Israelis. Fearful that the turmoil might encourage an Israeli military move, Soviet-armed Syrians entered in June 1976 and occupied much of northern and central Lebanon. They actually fought and disarmed many PLO elements. Although Christians, the ruling Lebanese Gemayel clan welcomed the Syrians, then promptly contacted Israel to complain about the Syrian incursion. By the summer of 1982, the Syrians were still there, pressing to install a puppet Lebanese government. Meanwhile, Arafat's heavily armed raiders and rocketeers had long since returned to business as usual, and their strikes took a heavy toll in Israeli Galilee. Israel responded with occasional air bombardments, limited ground raids, and assorted special operations.

Supposedly, UNIFIL existed to prevent the constant Israeli-PLO strife. The United Nations deployed more than six thousand soldiers from Finland, Fiji, France, Ghana, Ireland, Italy, the Netherlands, Norway, Senegal, and Sweden. The troops patrolled the Israeli-Lebanese border, and not exactly to Korean or Sinai standards, either. The PLO routinely infiltrated these positions, often with UNIFIL approval or at least "official" ignorance.[1] By the summer of 1982, Israeli Prime Minister Menachem Begin, spurred by his pugnacious defense minister, Ariel Sharon (hero of the 1973 Suez Canal counterattack), decided to solve the problems to the north once and for all.

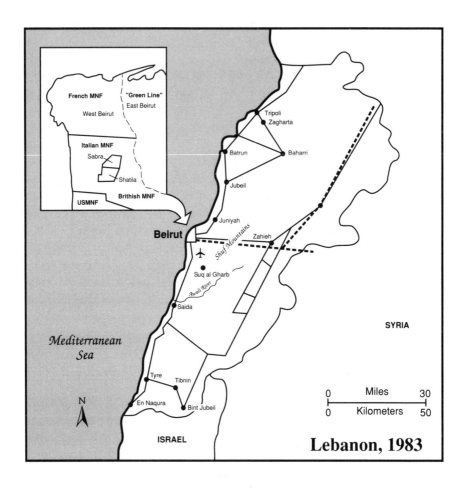

Lebanon, 1983

Operation Peace for Galilee commenced on 6 June 1982, with the stated goal of pushing the PLO fighters about twenty-five miles into Lebanon, to shove back and destroy Palestinian rocket and gun batteries menacing the Jewish state. This massive operation involved eight division-sized units, and they made short work of the befuddled, unprepared PLO, punching deep into Lebanon on three major axes. The rapid Israeli advance into the Bekaa Valley soon slammed into the Syrians, who fought hard but suffered grievous losses in the air and on the ground. To avoid a major Israeli-Syrian war, a cease-fire went into effect by 11 June 1982, although Israel continued to hunt down and destroy shattered fragments of Arafat's PLO.

Encouraged by their initial successes, and having stunned the Syrians, the Israelis pressed well beyond their twenty-five-mile limit to the outskirts of Beirut. With Yasir Arafat and the frantic, bedraggled remnants of the PLO trapped in Muslim West Beirut, Begin and Sharon saw an opportunity to smash the PLO utterly. Israeli troops pressed into the populous city of Beirut, bombing and shelling their way toward the desperate Palestinians. Taking advantage of the Beirut operation, the Israeli-backed Christian Phalange entered the Muslim Druze stronghold in the Shuf Mountains to eradicate their rivals.[2]

Supporting the PLO is a knee-jerk Arab reaction, even in the more moderate states. Faced with the imminent extinction of Arafat's unsavory following, an unlikely pair from pro-American Saudi Arabia and pro-Soviet Syria joined together on 16 July 1982 to ask President Reagan for U.S. help in arranging a PLO withdrawal. The Arab ministers wanted American troops and warships to ensure a safe extraction. Thanks to the efforts of American special envoy Philip Habib, the Israelis grudgingly agreed. Most of the PLO would leave by Greek charter shipping for Tunisia. Well aware that some Syrian units had also been trapped in the tightening Israeli noose, the Syrians agreed to permit some of their Palestinian allies to move by highway to Damascus, Syria.[3]

The United States Sixth Fleet landed part of Col. James Mead's 32d Marine Amphibious Unit (MAU—today known as a Marine expeditionary unit, or MEU) as early as 23–24 June to evacuate American civilians from Juniyah, Lebanon. From 24 August until 10 September, Battalion Landing Team 2/8 Marines (BLT 2/8) joined with a French Foreign Legion paratroop battalion to secure the port of Beirut. An Italian unit protected the road to Damascus. Multinational force (MNF) troops—organized like the Sinai MFO outside the official and, to the Israelis, discredited UN umbrella—cooperated to escort more than eight thousand PLO soldiers safely out of West Beirut by ship, plus another six thousand or so over land. The Israelis glowered, rival militias celebrated and demonstrated, and Americans cordoned off the hostile elements. Marines guarded Arafat himself as the PLO leader went aboard a steamer.

Intentionally, the Marines carried only personal arms. Mortars, tanks, and artillery remained offshore, to avoid any appearance that the Americans had joined the conflict. Given that the United States is Israel's staunch ally, the Marines had to go out of their way to appear entirely neutral. It was a risky step, but it worked just as Philip Habib had promised. Everything went well. The Palestinians departed, and Mead reembarked his men without incident.

It was just another noncombatant evacuation, as at Juniyah. No longer needed, the MNF disbanded.[4]

Four days later, a Syrian-backed assassin blew up Bashir Gemayel, charismatic Phalange chief and duly elected president of Lebanon. Factional clashes seemed unavoidable. Israeli troops moved into West Beirut to ensure order. Vengeful Phalangists took advantage of Israeli negligence (perhaps calculated) and conducted systematic massacres in the Palestinian Sabra and Shatilla refugee camps. The butcher's bill came to 460, including 15 women, 20 children, and Syrian, Iranian, Algerian, and Pakistani volunteer fighters. Bashir's brother Amin Gemayel, chosen as the new Lebanese president, appealed for help from America and Europe. On 20 September 1982, President Reagan joined the French and Italians and announced the reconstitution of the Multinational Force, to replace the Israelis and Phalangists in Beirut until the Lebanese army could take charge.[5]

On 29 September, Colonel Mead's men returned to the shattered Paris of the Middle East. Some Marines probably remembered a "temporary" expedition on behalf of Saigon, once known as the Paris of the Orient. And with that unpleasant analogy noted, the Marines dropped into the Lebanese maelstrom.

Colonel Mead's mission on his second insertion into embattled Beirut was not as clear or finite, but it did not seem overly threatening. As President Reagan put it, the Marines landed as an interposition force to separate the staggering Lebanese government from the feuding religious militias and their powerful Syrian and Israeli associates, at least in the vital capital of Beirut. Obviously, prevention of further factional bloodbaths constituted the immediate goal. The same sort of thing later brought Americans into northern Iraq, Somalia, and the former Yugoslavia. The urge to do something can become overwhelming, even when something may be rather fuzzy. Unfortunately, with troops on the ground for uncertain ends, the Americans in country can quickly become part of the problem rather than part of the solution.

American objectives in Lebanon went beyond a transient sense of order in part of Beirut, about all that a MAU could really accomplish. U.S. intentions remained simple and yet maddeningly difficult to achieve: pullout of all foreign forces, restoration of a stable Lebanese government in charge of its own country, and removal of threats to Israel from Lebanese territory. No American leaders were willing to put a time limit on the Marine deployment, but Reagan himself told Congress that the mission would last a "limited period." Finally, the president insisted that "the American force will not engage in combat," although he warned that the unit "may, however, exercise the right of self-defense and will be equipped accordingly."[6]

Real fighting seemed a remote possibility indeed. Reagan told America's legislators that "all armed elements in the area have given assurances" that they would respect the MNF contingents. The first Americans ashore found themselves treated as welcome protectors by rejoicing Lebanese Christians and grateful Muslims alike. The locals were fairly certain that the Marines and their European allies had no territorial ambitions, unlike the Syrian and now Israeli "liberators," who had overstayed their welcome. Surrounded by a relatively friendly city, the Marine commanders agreed with their president's assessment.

Aside from matching conditions on the ground, defining the interposition role as a noncombat mission avoided the timetable linked to any congressional War Powers Resolution oversight, a great bugbear back in the 1970s and 1980s, and occasionally invoked even these days. For this reason, and to avoid unwelcome comparisons with the lackadaisical UNIFIL elements, American political and military leaders emphasized that the MAU was not in Beirut for peacekeeping. Of course, they were doing exactly that, thus foreshadowing the "not war" line regarding the nature of OOTW. It sure looked, smelled, and felt like peacekeeping, because, of course, it was.

The Marines occupied ground, but the Joint Chiefs of Staff and Gen. Bernard C. Rogers (commander in chief of the European Command, the responsible CINC) distinctly excused the MAU from direct responsibility for any sector of the Lebanese capital. Recalling Vietnam, the U.S. generals and admirals winced at the image of Americans trying to police a restive alien city, fighting as necessary to maintain order. This would be like the Sinai—be there, observe and report, and protect the force, with impartiality itself a form of defense. As Chief of Naval Operations Adm. James D. Watkins told a congressional committee, "We are not in a peacekeeping mission. Peacekeeping could well be a combat operation. This is not a combat operation." If things turned sour, U.S. Navy amphibious transports remained just off the beach to withdraw the Marines. Intentionally, command never passed ashore, the amphibious squadron commanders retaining overall authority throughout the American deployment, just in case an extraction became necessary.[7]

The Marines preferred to call their role "presence," seizing upon a line in the JCS mission statement of 23 September 1982 that described "a multinational force presence in the Beirut area." The only problem was succinctly summarized by Marine Corps Commandant Gen. Paul X. Kelley: "It is not a classic military mission." So Colonel Mead approached his deployment with special care. He directed his men to prominently display the U.S. colors on vehicles and tactical positions, and all Marines wore a flag patch on their camouflaged battle dress uniforms. The superbly conditioned and disciplined Marines presented a terrific military spectacle, a show of force, an unmistakable American military presence. Mead might just as well have chosen to emphasize the "occupy and secure" portion of his assignment, or the "combined defensive operations with other MNF contingents" and the Lebanese army prescribed by General Rogers. But the colonel judged that the situation in Beirut hardly necessitated a bona fide defense. So it seemed in those early days.

The Mission in Lebanon

• President Ronald W. Reagan, message to Congress, 29 September 1982: "Their mission is to provide an interposition force at agreed locations and thereby provide the multinational presence requested by the Lebanese government to assist it and the Lebanese Armed Forces. In carrying out this mission, the American force will not engage in combat. It may, however, exercise the right of self-defense and will be equipped accordingly."

• Secretary of Defense Caspar Weinberger: guidance incorporated in JCS message.

• JCS Alert order to CINC, U.S. European Command (USCINCEUR), 23 September 1982: "In order to establish an environment which will permit the Lebanese Armed Forces (LAF) to carry out their responsibilities in the Beirut area, when directed, U.S. Commander in Chief Europe will introduce U.S. forces as part of a multinational force presence in the Beirut area to occupy and secure positions along a designated section of the line south of the Beirut International Airport to a position in the vicinity of the Presidential Palace; be prepared to protect U.S. forces; and, on order, be prepared to conduct retrograde operations as required."

Additional guidance:
1. U.S. forces would not be engaged in combat.
2. Peacetime Rules of Engagement would apply (fire in self-defense and defense of collocated LAF units).
3. Be prepared to extract U.S. forces if required by hostile action.

• USCINCEUR OPREP-1 to CINCNAVEUR (Naval component, U.S. European Command), 24 September 1982 (as modified and approved by JCS, 25 September 1982):

1. Commander, Task Force 61 (TF-61, the Amphibious Task Force) designated Commander, U.S. Forces, Lebanon.

2. Land U.S. Marine Landing Force in Port of Beirut and/or vicinity of Beirut Airport. U.S. forces will move to occupy positions along an assigned section of a line extending from south of Beirut Airport to vicinity of the Presidential Palace. Provide security posts at intersections of assigned sections of line and major avenues of approach into city of Beirut from the southeast to assist LAF to deter passage of hostile armed elements in order to provide an environment which will permit LAF to carry out their responsibilities in city of Beirut. Commander, U.S. Forces will establish and maintain continuous coordination with other MNF units, EUCOM liaison team, and LAF. Commander, U.S. Forces will provide air/naval gunfire support as required.

Additional missions:

1. Conduct combined defensive operations with other MNF contingents and the LAF.

2. Be prepared to withdraw on order, in event of hostile action.

• CINCNAVEUR to Commander, Sixth Fleet: defined locations for U.S. positions.

• Commander, Sixth Fleet to Commander, TF-61: designated the Commander, TF-61 as the on-scene commander and the MAU Commander as Commander, U.S. Forces Ashore in Lebanon.

Formal modifications: Change 1 (undated) altered intelligence data concerning the Israelis; Change 2 (6 October 1982) defined the time to occupy/secure; unnumbered change (2 November 1982) ordered U.S. patrols in East Beirut; Change 3 (7 May 1983) directed the MAU to secure the temporary U.S. embassy facilities in Beirut; unnumbered change (16 September 1983) added protection of LAF positions at Suq-al-Gharb to the U.S. mission.

Sources: U.S. Department of Defense Commission on the Beirut International Airport Terrorist Act, October 23, 1983, *Report of the Department of Defense Commission on the Beirut International Airport Terrorist Act, October 23, 1983* (Washington, D.C.: U.S. Government Printing Office, 1984), 35–38; President Ronald Reagan, "Message to Congress: War Powers Resolution and U.S. Troops in Lebanon," in *Department of State Bulletin* (December 1982), 42; House Armed Services Committee, *Review of the Adequacy of Security Arrangements for Marines in Lebanon and Plans for Improving That Security*, 98th Cong., 1st sess., 15 December 1983, 605.

The Multinational Force divided troubled Beirut into three sectors. By choice, French paratroopers assumed control over the port and downtown Muslim West Beirut. Colonel Mead wanted access to his amphibious shipping by sea and air and requested beachfront positions at Beirut International Airport (BIA), the sort of site preferred by any deployed U.S. force. This conveniently placed the Marines near the wary Israelis, their erstwhile allies. Initially, the MAU commander wanted to expand his outer perimeter to the high ground a few miles to the east (the Suq-al-Gharb spur of the Shuf Mountains). The U.S. chain of command said no, probably for fear of involving the Marines in the ongoing Druze-Phalange struggle for control of the Shuf. The Italians chose last and shouldered the unpleasant duties of occupying central Beirut, including the gutted Sabra and Shatilla Palestinian refugee camps.

There was no central MNF command; the French objected to probable American domination, and the Americans refused to countenance overall French authority. Instead, the MNF commanders met regularly to exchange information and formulate combined policies, coordinating with their respective ambassadors and the Lebanese government. Each force ran its own area in its own way. Americans maintained their presence bound by a variant of the same peacetime rules of engagement in use in Korea and the Sinai. The Americans avoided combat in an attempt to keep a strictly neutral stance among the squabbling urban factions. The French and to a lesser extent the Italians were much more assertive about keeping order in their more populous areas.[8] In any event, the "temporary" MNF structure existed long beyond its expected lifetime.

The 32d MAU's second stop at Beirut went by relatively quickly, marred by one death while Marines were clearing unexploded munitions left over by the summer's fighting. Significantly, Colonel Mead and his subordinates chose the basic positions used throughout the Lebanon intervention, sending one rifle company south to the Khalde neighborhood, spreading another along the eastern rim of BIA, and placing the third company out to the east at the Lebanese Scientific and Technical University. These units deployed tactically, although they did not prepare major field works.

The Marine colonel decided to concentrate his MAU, BLT, and Marine Service Support Group (MSSG) command posts in the airport proper, presumably to facilitate coordination and strengthen rear-area security. The MAU commander approved use of the cluster of stout airport buildings for the headquarters and service units. Mead took a risk by putting these key elements within a few hundred yards of each other, but he judged that the threat of massive artillery barrage or ground attack was not great. In any event, the troops assigned to these outfits remained in dispersed bivouacs. The designated BLT command post, destined for a tragic demise, particularly impressed Mead. The blocky, chipped, pocked, battered four-story edifice once served the PLO and Syrians, withstanding heavy bombardments. An Israeli field hospital had been set up in the solid building during the summer. Presence had nothing to do with Mead's choices, nor did any political or chain of command pressures. As Colonel Mead said, "It was simply logistics."

Mead's men left on 30 October, replaced by Col. Thomas M. Stokes's 24th MAU. If the 32d MAU had set the scene, Stokes and his force defined the tactics that came to characterize the U.S. portion of the Multinational Force. The only real excitement occurred immediately. On 1 November, a small car bomb blew up harmlessly just beyond the supply parties at work on Black Beach. Which disgruntled faction set the charge remained a mystery. The failed attempt, rated as "clumsy" and "amateurish" by Stokes' intelligence officers, represented the first direct attack on the Americans.[9] It would not be the last.

Within days of his arrival, Stokes received authorization to begin jeep patrols into the Phalange strongholds of Christian East Beirut, a bold move that strengthened the MNF's claims of impartiality among suspicious Muslims. Over time, Battalion Landing Team 3/8 Marines instituted foot patrols in the Hay-es-Salaam slums and the Khalde area, lairs of the Shiite militiamen. These uneventful sweeps showed the flag, and the rifle squads gathered valuable intelligence about activities around the long, fragile Marine perimeter. Although the situation remained calm after the initial car explosion, Stokes went beyond his predecessor's restraint. The 24th MAU commander landed his six howitzers and his platoon of five M60A1 main battle tanks to supplement security arrangements.[10]

During December, 24th MAU began training the Lebanese army, in coordination with the Office of Military Cooperation (OMC), an American advisory outfit drawn mostly from the U.S. Army. Training the Lebanese had always been a MAU mission, closely tied to the attempt to create a sovereign Lebanese government capable of ruling its own territory. The effort gainfully employed Marine expertise, and the Lebanese soldiers received USMC-style camouflage uniforms to mark them as Marine products.

The significance of this seemingly sensible program cannot be under-rated. The Lebanese president, Christian Phalange leader Amin Gemayel, controlled his fragmented Christian-Muslim army through Gen. Ibrahim Tannous, another Phalangist. Traditionally, Lebanon's army served Chris-tian purposes. Muslims in Beirut thought they endured undue military attentions compared to Christians, which helped germinate the Muslim militias. Although the Americans encouraged recruitment of Islamic sol-diers and trained all Lebanese alike, many Muslims preferred to trust their own armed bands rather than government forces.[11] By training the Chris-tian-dominated Lebanese army, the Marines inadvertently compromised the neutral image they had tried so hard to build.

Interestingly, Stokes's Marines tried to keep their impartiality intact by dealing harshly with an unanticipated source of hostility—the Israeli De-fense Force (IDF). The Israelis pressed regularly at the Marine boundaries, challenging U.S. patrols, sending tanks toward American positions, and they were careless about stray shots and projectiles primarily directed at fiesty Muslims. Marines stopped patrolling south of Khalde to avoid these un-pleasant encounters, but the IDF persisted in its probes and provocations. Despite command conferences and establishment of a MAU-IDF radio link, incidents continued. On 2 February 1983, the bullying went too far. Ma-rine Capt. Charles B. Johnson at the Lebanese University drew his pistol to stop an Israeli tank platoon, announcing that the Israelis could advance at their peril. The confrontation received extensive and favorable coverage in the local Muslim press. It took direct coordination by Stokes and the Israeli commanders to prevent more serious scrapes between the Americans and their presumed allies.[12] Even so, sporadic IDF actions continued to test and endanger the Marines, and American diplomats stayed busy soothing Israeli pride. Apparently, the IDF expected special treatment by the Marines. To Stokes's credit, he did not deviate from his nonpartisan stance.

On 15 February, Col. James Mead entered Lebanon for the third time. Mead's 22d Marine Amphibious Unit (his headquarters had been renum-bered) took over from 24th MAU. The temporary expedition had obviously lasted longer than expected. BLT 2/6 Marines occupied the usual locations, and Mead trusted that this stay would be as quiet as his previous landings. After all, Stokes's MAU had suffered no casualties despite all of the tus-sling with the unruly Israelis.

At first, all seemed quiet. Following a late February blizzard, the Ma-rines made many friends by using helicopters and track-laying amphibious assault vehicles (AAVs) to rescue snowbound villagers, motorists, and even a few Syrian soldiers in the drifting ravines of the Shuf Mountains. In Beirut, Mead's men and U.S. Army Special Forces (Green Berets) assigned to the OMC continued to train the reorganizing Lebanese army. Shortly after landing, Mead tested his new partners by developing a regular program of joint USMC-Lebanese army patrols. At the same time, Mead extended this reconnaissance and "show the flag" effort throughout the neighborhoods of Beirut. The Marines and their newly schooled comrades demonstrated their close ties for all to see. Apparently, not everyone was impressed.

The Israelis expressed their discontent with renewed incursions, random rounds, and diplomatic objections about supposed Marine slights. The Marine Corps commandant at the time, Gen. Robert H. Barrow, complained in writing to Secretary of Defense Caspar Weinberger about the incidents, which he suspected were "orchestrated and executed for obtuse Israeli political purposes." Weinberger intentionally released the letter to the U.S. press, and American diplomats expressed serious concern to Begin's government. The fact that America supplied the bulk of Israel's arms, including F-16 fighters embargoed since the Israelis had destroyed an Iraqi reactor site in June 1981, surely played a part. Menachem Begin wanted his fighter jets. The IDF got the message and backed off.[13]

In mid-March, the urban Muslim militias reacted to perceptions that the MNF was getting too friendly with Gemayel's Christian-oriented military. On 15 March, an Italian squad hit a minefield and took sniper fire; one soldier died and two fell wounded. The next day, someone dropped a grenade off a rooftop onto a Marine fire team in West Beirut, injuring five Marines. A day later, a French paratrooper was hit. Mead prudently strengthened his defenses by erecting some concertina wire, adding and reinforcing bunkers, placing snipers on rooftops, and allowing patrols to move through Beirut with loaded magazines and rounds chambered. He accepted some resultant accidental shootings and the pain that went with them.[14] Mead kept his men dispersed and employed his patrols carefully, searching for indicators of trouble. But the various enemies of the MNF chose not to test the improved USMC perimeter beyond an odd round or two.

In the early afternoon of 18 April 1983, a pickup truck laden with a ton of high explosives detonated inside the American embassy compound. The driver parked the vehicle and left before it blew. The explosion shattered the eight-story main building, killing seventeen Americans and forty-four Lebanese. Four Marine guards were among the dead.

Colonel Mead reacted forcefully and immediately. He sent all of Company F and a rifle platoon from Company E, 2/6 Marines, to cordon off the blast site and pick up the numerous classified materials scattered by the disaster. The Marines went in loaded for bear, with bullets locked in their rifle chambers. Once the American diplomats had moved to temporary facilities at the Durafourd Building and the British embassy, a reinforced rifle platoon from the MAU remained on guard to prevent another attack. Barricades, earthen berms, and amtracs (AAVs) with .50-caliber machine guns stiffened the Marine defense. There was no room to be polite. At 0220 on 28 April, a Lebanese car ran past a Marine AAV, and the American gunner loosed a burst of wicked slugs that sent the light vehicle careening into a barrier. Two drunks emerged, panic-stricken. But Mead refused to compromise the harsh rules of engagement. At the temporary embassy, Marines shot first and asked questions later.

At BIA, Mead took further precautions. He increased the frequency of patrols to improve his feel for the changing situation in the local slums, doubled the sentries twenty-four hours a day, added observation posts, emplaced AAVs to protect the closely spaced headquarters facilities, and directed construction of the first full-scale field fortifications, to include major wire entanglements and sandbagging efforts around positions and occupied structures. When questioned later about possible political implications, Mead stressed that he considered defensive actions well within his command prerogatives: "I had full authority. I could have put tanks in there, .50 calibers there, and if I needed more weaponry, it would have been flown out from the States." U.S. diplomats stood aside. Special envoy Philip Habib agreed with Mead, because "policymakers at the civilian level don't make the rules of engagement."[15] These measures evidently worked; 22d MAU completed its tour without further incident, despite receiving additional stray rounds that appeared to be intended for others.

As Colonel Mead prepared to depart Beirut, U.S. Secretary of State George Shultz personally intervened to expedite rambling negotiations for an Israeli troop withdrawal, hoping that Syria would soon do likewise. The bilateral Gemayel-Begin Agreement, signed on 17 May 1983, favored the Israelis. They were allowed to keep a buffer zone held by their clients, the Christian South Lebanon Army. Moreover, two days later, President Reagan resumed F-16 sales to the IDF, an obvious sweetener for the deal. The

Syrians were expected to follow suit and pull out completely, abandoning seven years of effort and leaving numerous Muslim associates to their fate. Aware of Israeli domestic discord sparked by the Lebanon incursion, Syria's President Hafiz Assad knew that the IDF would probably leave regardless of Syrian actions. With his Bekaa Valley units refitted from their June 1982 mauling, Assad rebuffed the agreement and dug in to stay.[16] The next Marine contingent faced a novel, more deadly situation.

Colonel Timothy J. Geraghty's 24th Marine Amphibious Unit assumed the MNF mission on 30 May 1983. During the relief in place, Colonel Mead explained the local tactical situation, offered views on the Lebanese army (at least a year to go toward real proficiency), and reminded Geraghty that the Multinational Force commitment was "not open-ended," especially in the face of an increasing threat. With Capt. Morgan R. France and his Amphibious Squadron 8 centered around USS *Iwo Jima* steaming majestically just off the beach, Geraghty had help on call. Captain France retained overall command in Lebanon, because he might have to pull out 24th MAU anytime things got too hot ashore.

Although the 24th MAU had just been to Lebanon under Colonel Stokes, few men remained from that recent excursion. The revamped headquarters and assigned subordinate units reflected their new commander, who had worked with Lt. Col. Larry Gerlach's BLT 1/8 Marines (BLT 1/8), Lt. Col. L. R. Medlin's Marine Helicopter Squadron 162 (Reinforced) (HMM-162), and Maj. D. C. Redlich's 24th Marine Service Support Group (MSSG 24) in predeployment training to prepare the force for Beirut. Like Mead before him, Colonel Geraghty's perceptions of his mission and situation proved critical. On his shoulders rested much of the heavy burden of American foreign policy in Lebanon, and the Marine commander thought twice before acting. He was determined to meet the challenge of carrying out his perceived mission in the treacherous Lebanese capital.[17]

Colonel Geraghty was an experienced infantryman, described by a major on his staff as "a poster Marine." He inspired confidence in subordinates, and he demanded high standards. Given the stress on presence, Geraghty insisted upon a disciplined, combat-ready appearance. He worked on proper media relations, a forerunner of the sort of training that is now routine at places like Fort Polk's JRTC. During the Atlantic transit, a special duty officer from Headquarters Marine Corps instructed the young men on how to deal with journalists. Major Robert Jordan, MAU public affairs officer, remembered, "The thrust was to prepare them so they wouldn't embarrass themselves by voicing inappropriate or seemingly insensitive comments." Geraghty himself proved adept at handling the press. He wanted his men to present themselves well.

At least one junior enlisted member of the MAU S3 (operations) staff section sensed something more. "I realized he was a consummate politician. The enlisted troops knew the colonel was bucking for a star," wrote Cpl. Michael Petit, "and being the on-site commander in Lebanon was a big chance for recognition and to advance his career. Colonel Mead had commanded the 32d and 22d MAUs in Lebanon. He was now a brigadier general."[18] There was nothing wrong with this; healthy ambition has fueled many a great commander, from Washington to Patton to the Marines' own Lewis B. "Chesty" Puller. Geraghty must have recognized that, like John Mitchell in the U.S. sector of the DMZ in October 1990, he was "the man," responsible for everything his Marines did or failed to do. In Lebanon, as in most OOTW, a colonel was on the hot seat when the music stopped.

Although Geraghty's military chain of command remained clear and accorded with normal procedures, circumstances in Beirut definitely influenced the MAU commander's view of his role. Geraghty found himself bombarded by conflicting opinions and suggestions from a wide range of sources. He held scheduled meetings with the other MNF commanders (now including a small British unit). Each of the MNF components maintained liaison officers in each others' headquarters. Additionally, Geraghty met regularly with the U.S. Country Team in Lebanon, to include Captain France, U.S. Army Col. Arthur T. Fintel of the OMC, Ambassador Robert Dillon, Special Envoy Habib (replaced on 27 July by Robert McFarlane), plus a variable array of embassy staff advisers. The 24th MAU had emergency liaison with the Israelis, in the event of confrontations. Finally, Geraghty maintained a day-to-day working relationship with General Tannous of the Lebanese army.[19] Sometimes it was probably hard to remember that Captain France and Sixth Fleet, not well-meaning foreign service officers and allies, guided 24th MAU's fate.

By Colonel Geraghty's interpretation, "The mission of the MAU in Lebanon is a diplomatic mission." He elaborated later, "It was important to me, in the interpretation of that mission, that there was a presence mission. That means being seen. It was a mission where we were not to build up any permanent-type structures because to emphasize the temporary nature of our mission, which is my understanding as to why the Marine Corps went in and not the Army to start with, and that is why we maintained ships offshore." By delineating a noncombat mission—an operation other than war in its narrowest sense, if you will—the colonel planned to avoid combat and, hence, casualties. If fighting flared, Geraghty expected to leave.

But this version of his role was not the only or even the most likely mission concept implicit in his orders, and it was by no means intended to be unalterable in the face of increasing threats. Significant offensive operations were ruled out; aggressive patrolling and solid defenses were not. Geraghty himself derived the idea that his mission precluded "permanent-type structures," based upon his attempt to fulfill a nonmilitary role. After his deployment, the colonel told investigators, "I never felt there was undue influence to retard any type of action felt necessary for the rules of engagement in the light of the mission." Asked if superiors ever refused greater defensive measures, Geraghty's response was a painfully brief "No, sir." That was up to the commander on the ground.

Because the 24th MAU commander did not think his mission was military in nature, he did not consider standard battlefield defensive tactics applicable, although Marine units certainly train such tasks, and have defended well in storied actions like Wake Island and Khe Sanh. Like other Marines, Geraghty chafed at being tied to a static perimeter. He considered it innately nontactical, unmilitary, proof positive that this was no war. He stated that he would have acted differently "if we were on a solely military, an offensive mission, more Marine-oriented." Unable to influence his surroundings by the offensive action inculcated into Marines (a hollow possibility without significant U.S. reinforcements), Geraghty could either erect sturdy defenses or employ presence to try to affect his unwelcome situation.

Geraghty's diplomatic interpretation made him extremely cautious about changing or enforcing the airport perimeter he had inherited. Eager to strengthen the Lebanese government's power in accord with American strategic goals, Geraghty deferred to the Lebanese Civil Aviation Administration's desires to keep BIA operational, and ceded official security duties in the area to the Lebanese army. He thought the Marines should be careful not to interfere with Lebanese airport activities, even at the expense of their own security. Geraghty knew this was tricky; he called the tactical situation "terrible," because he was stuck at the active international airport, where "you don't have security." He concluded that vulnerability went with the presence task, "but you accept that."

Like Colonel Mead back in September 1982, Geraghty would have preferred to hold Suq-al-Gharb, the high ground overlooking his force. Instead he was stuck at the seaside airport, with a reinforced battalion of strung-out, partially dug-in Marines. The position was good for resupply or rapid withdrawal; only a prodigious fortification effort could render it suitable for prolonged defense. Geraghty probably figured that a successful defense was unlikely, regardless of the amount of dirt turned or guns sited. He recognized the numerous potential factional enemies and knew that the Marines conceded the initiative by defending. As he stated later, "Our location has been relatively static . . . and they [the enemy] are going to find vulnerabilities."

Colonel Geraghty believed that, much like the MFO in the Sinai contemplating an Egyptian or Israeli tank assault, the Marines' best defense in Lebanon was their visible neutral image. In this view, the optimum way to preclude losses was to be seen. The commander trusted that impartiality and showing the flag could accomplish the mission as he understood it, to include protecting his force. By taking an active, fearless posture and avoiding involvement in militia feuds, the Marines might achieve a degree of protection that sandbags could never furnish.

Certainly it had worked previously. As the colonel explained, "We walked a razor's edge to maintain our neutrality and treated all Lebanese factions alike, showing no favoritism toward one group or another, and it was in this context, I think, that successes were made." Despite a steady rise in dangers around BIA, Geraghty did not want to resort to combat actions: "I was very adamant to maintain that neutrality that I think we had built up—and goodwill—for over a year."[20]

The impartiality that Geraghty so prized was tentative at best, and was soon to dissipate altogether. The 24th MAU inherited a mission poisoned by a built-in contradiction: "interposition," which required an even hand, and "combined defensive operations" with the Christian-controlled Lebanese army, an organization that was anything but neutral in the continuing civil war. In effect, the Marines simultaneously chose not to fight and then took sides anyway. The enemy, unencumbered by such contradictions, simply engaged.

Colonel Timothy Geraghty, however, made the conscious choice to eschew defense in favor of presence. Whereas Stokes and Mead had responded to increased threats with beefed-up protection, Geraghty would attempt to alleviate danger to his men by trying to restore the benign circumstances of early 1983. It was a risky course of action, a bluff based on the belief that no defense could be airtight. Guts, grins, and the U.S. flag replaced interlocking fields of fire, and a Marine colonel did his best to handle a tough mission. Presence became defense.

*   *   *

The first weeks of 24th MAU's operations in Beirut passed quietly. Battery C, 1/10 Marines, pulled its new M198 155-mm howitzers to a knoll just north of the MAU-BLT-MSSG complex. Marine gunners and Lebanese soldiers manned checkpoint 74 along the main airport access road. Company C established positions at the Lebanese Scientific and Technical University and combined USMC–Lebanese army combat posts 35 and 69. These isolated posts strung across Hay-es-Salaam, tying in the university Marines with Company B. Fronting on Hay-es-Salaam to the north and Ashuefat to the south, Company B guarded the easterly BIA runways. This unit manned combined American and Lebanese combat posts 11 and 76, almost smack in the center of the slender Marine line. Company B's riflemen linked in with Company C to the north and Company A to the south. Most of Company A held the south end of the airport (combat post 39) near Khalde, and a detached rifle platoon protected the temporary U.S. embassy in downtown Beirut.

Since the immediate threat appeared slight, some of Colonel Mead's security measures were relaxed. The amtrac moved away from the BLT building, to join its dozen or so mates as supply and reaction force transports. After a nervous Marine shot two Lebanese joggers, Geraghty prohibited insertion of magazines by Marines on certain headquarters guard posts and on most patrols. The wartime atmosphere of early May dissipated. In the words of Major Jordan, "Life within the Marine compound varied little from any normal deployment."[21]

Geraghty tried to make the Marines' stay bearable and at the same time show his Lebanese friends how Americans lived. Off-duty time provided rather typical military entertainments. Corporal Michael Petit remembered the Marines' recreation: "The officers and senior enlisted men were watching a videotape. The tapes came from Habibi's Video in the Shuf, and one of the Arabic-speaking Marines from the Interrogator-Translator Team picked up a supply once a week on 'intelligence gathering' trips. While the enlisted troops were prohibited from drinking hard liquor, the officers' club served both mixed drinks and beer." Visits to the other MNF contingents (with the requisite toasts and swapping of memorabilia), intramural sports, relaxing runs out to USS *Iwo Jima,* and occasional liberty trips to Egypt rounded out Marine free hours.

Colonel Geraghty ensured that even recreation contributed to 24th MAU's mission. On 4 July, the Marines celebrated Independence Day in a grand style, with a combined U.S.-Lebanese marathon run and a barbecue,

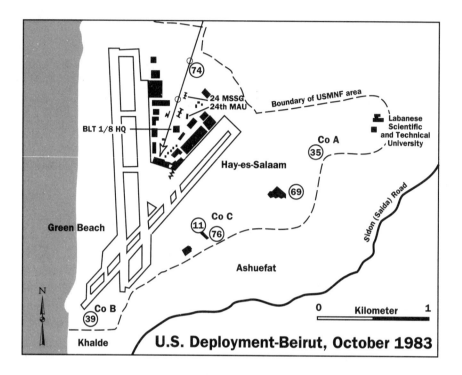

U.S. Deployment-Beirut, October 1983

all before a massive press corps. On Sunday mornings, except for a few sentries, the MAU slept late. Sunday afternoons, most of the Marines enjoyed a pleasant barbecue, often with Lebanese friends and French MNF comrades in attendance. At these parties, games within the MNF and with the Lebanese provided diversions, although Colonel Geraghty's subordinates went a bit overboard one day when they created an elaborate wooden and steel regulation basketball court, complete with a scoreboard and proper markings, for a single USMC-Lebanese contest.[22] It was all in the name of presence.

But even as the Marines attempted to make the best of their Beirut sojourn, the situation around them began to change. On 6 July, Syria formally rejected the Israeli-Lebanese withdrawal plan of 17 May 1983. Their allies of the moment, the Muslim Druze, began a major effort to eject the Christian Phalange from the Shuf Mountains. The Syrians expected Israel to withdraw unilaterally; the Druze and Amal Shiites prepared to fill the resultant gap. Unfortunately, so did the Lebanese army, many resplendent in their new Marine-type camouflage battle dress uniforms. Their comrades walked, rode, and manned combat posts with the Americans every day.

On 22 July, eleven 122-mm rockets arced into the Beirut International Airport, rattling the Marines and chasing them into their shallow fighting holes. The Americans went to full alert, but nothing else happened. After ten anxious minutes, the Marines emerged to check the damage. One round dug a crater between the BLT and MAU buildings. Fragments injured three Americans. The Marines hopefully dismissed the projectiles as an accident.

The supposition was mistaken. On 8 August, two more rockets struck near the USMC bunkers, and Colonel Geraghty's operations log noted, "The rocket attack on 22 July was no longer an aberration, and these impacts signaled that more attacks were likely and, in fact, were becoming standard operating procedure." In agreement with Lieutenant Colonel Gerlach, Geraghty gathered almost all of Gerlach's BLT 1/8 Headquarters and Service Company, Weapons Company, and landing team attachments into the massive BLT command post structure to provide protection from further barrages.[23] Meanwhile, out on the perimeter, the line companies prepared for more trouble. They had rotated on 1 August, with Company B sent to the university, Company A to the eastern BIA line, and Company C to the south end of the runway, less one platoon downtown at the embassy.

Early on 10 August, more than two dozen rockets smashed into BIA, closing the airport and battering the Lebanese training camp and aircraft flight line directly adjoining the MAU-BLT command post compound. Another Marine fell wounded.

But this time, the Americans found out who was tormenting them. A few days prior, a provisional U.S. Army Target Acquisition Battery (TAB) had arrived in Beirut, a test unit assembled and sent directly from the Army Field Artillery School at Fort Sill, Oklahoma. The soldiers set up their two new AN/TPQ-36 Firefinder radars, one down near Khalde, the other with the Marine artillery battery. Although the army devices could detect mortars and artillery by tracking the rounds as they decelerate after firing, the Firefinders lacked the software modifications to trace rockets, which actually speed up after launch. Deprived of electronic help, the dogged army survey section examined the rocket impact points and calculated the enemy locations the old-fashioned way, by crater analysis. Soldiers estimated that the rockets had come from Walid Jumblatt's Druze Progressive Socialist Party (PSP) militia area in the Shuf.

Geraghty authorized a unique response. He directed the BLT's 81-mm mortar platoon to fire illumination rounds (parachute flares) above the identified Druze launch site, a clear warning. Lance Corporal Brian Parkin recalled his amazement as he scrambled to conduct his first combat fire mission: "I saw the guys 'halfload' the tubes and then fire. It was only illumination, but I couldn't believe it."[24] The Druze apparently understood, and ceased fire. Although more rounds landed over the next few days, there were no other U.S. casualties.

Over the next two weeks, Colonel Geraghty assessed the deteriorating situation. President Reagan's new special envoy and his team had arrived. Robert McFarlane (a retired Marine lieutenant colonel and a participant in President Gerald Ford's planning efforts toward recovery of the *Mayaguez*) took charge dramatically between the 22 July and 8 August shelling incidents. In an attempt to buttress Christian President Amin Gemayel, McFarlane decided to sever all U.S. contacts with Walid Jumblatt's Druze forces since these militiamen opposed Gemayel's army and government. Gemayel's staff was elated as they plotted to destroy their many enemies with America's supposed blessing. Gemayel's defense adviser Wadia Haddad snorted, "We have the United States in our pocket."

Although McFarlane later reversed his harsh measure, the damage was done. The wily Jumblatt turned toward his old mentors, the Syrians. Meanwhile, counting on U.S. support, Gemayel and Tannous prepared to send their refurbished brigades into the Shuf when Israel withdrew. The Lebanese army intended to clear the Shiite Amal from Hay-es-Salaam as well.[25] The American forces, who undoubtedly would have paid anyway, paid more and sooner on behalf of their Lebanese army proteges.

It was a critical time for 24th MAU. Nobody seriously considered withdrawal, certainly no one who spoke to the energetic McFarlane. Yet the mission had reached a crossroads. The Marines had taken sides, at least in the eyes of the Druze, Shiites, and Syrians, and their opinions counted since they owned the guns. If impartiality was the 24th MAU's defense, that defense had been breached. The neutral interposition mission had failed, leaving only the commitment to back the Lebanese army and, as always, protect American lives. Like it or not, the Marines were in the fight.

American forces that back into major hostilities in this way, whether through situational decay (as in this case) or "mission creep" (taking on a succession of significantly broader tasks, as in Somalia), have two choices: destroy the opposing forces or go home. If the cost of fighting to win looks like it will be too high relative to the interests involved, then there is only one decision to be made. The U.S. must swallow pride and get out.

Nobody in Washington's leading circles much liked that idea with regard to Lebanon. They did not like it in Vietnam, nor would they like it in

Somalia. But once Americans come under fire, it is only a matter of time before the blood really starts flowing. If the U.S. troops stay, they will fight with whatever they have on hand, one battalion or a hundred. Leaving small units adrift in the middle of a building war invites catastrophe. But that was exactly what America chose to do in Beirut.

After all, despite harbingers, things had not yet gone over the edge. Colonel Geraghty did not think he had joined the fray in Lebanon; on the contrary, he stressed that the Marines could not permit the shellings to stop their presence duties. His solution to decaying conditions was not defense, but an attempt to re-create the old circumstances by sticking to the familiar rituals and routines. It was like trying to restore virginity by wearing white. The 24th MAU stuck to the game plan.

Major Jordan noted that "visibility was still the order of the day." Training of the Lebanese army increased, to include hand-to-hand combat, repeated combined patrols, artillery drills, and a night infiltration course. The rest of the usual schedule, the athletics, the barbecues, the lazy Sundays, persisted without change. The thoughtful Jordan summarized the mood quite well: "The seriousness of the situation still had not registered on many of the Marines despite several of their mates suffering minor wounds."[26] Like it or not, 24th MAU was about to become a full participant in Lebanon's long civil war.

The Israeli Defense Forces planned to withdraw south to the Awali River for their own reasons. At America's request, the Israelis postponed their pullout twice during August, buying time for the Lebanese army to get ready. But the cacophony of protest in Israel grew louder and louder, demanding an end to the IDF intervention. Phalange elements beefed up to meet the counterattacks that would surely follow any IDF withdrawal. The Druze and Amal readied for a finish fight against the Phalangists and their presumed allies, the Lebanese army. On Sunday, 28 August, long-extant rumors took concrete form as Israel commenced the first portions of their major troop movements. Without warning the Americans, the IDF turned over the northern Shuf range and Christian East Beirut to the half-trained Lebanese army.[27] Within hours, it became evident who had really been providing order around Beirut.

By early afternoon, the Marines found themselves in the line of fire as shooting escalated around them. Most of the Marines were at the usual Sunday barbecues when the MAU declared a Condition I Alert. Probably, the incoming rounds were not actually aimed at the Marines, but Druze and Amal fighters must have had a hard time distinguishing between the identically uniformed Marines and Lebanese soldiers crouching in their combined force combat posts. As Marine 1st Lt. Gregory Balzer explained it, "When the IDF pulled out of the area, the Lebanese Armed Forces began using our lines as protection for movement up and down the coast road, which put us in direct fire of forces hostile to the Lebanese Armed Forces, trying to control the positions that the IDF withdrew from."[28]

Regardless of Colonel Geraghty's diplomatic intentions, the Marines on the perimeter soon found that mere hunkering down would not suffice. Stray lead ricocheted around the isolated Marine positions. About 1610, machine-gun fire concentrated on combat post 69, held by 1st Lt. David Hough and his 1st Squad, 2d Platoon, Company B. As the Marines hugged their bunkers, Amal fire grew more intense. Rocket-propelled grenades caromed off the sandbags, 106-mm recoilless rifles punched into the field fortifications, and a half-dozen AK-47s blazed away on full automatic. Hough took it for ten minutes as his men pleaded to return fire. "I knew we had to fire back," said Hough. "The rules of engagement applied, but I called the company headquarters anyway." Approval came swiftly.

For the first time, the Marines shot back, at first to scare, and then to kill. Unfortunately, weeks of complacency had caught up with the Americans. They had only about 175 rounds per man, with no backup stocks on hand. Worse, their powerful M60 machine gun turned out to have a defective bolt, permitting only single shots. Husbanding their precious ammunition, the Marines shot back until nightfall, when the firing slackened.[29]

Lieutenant Hough was merely the first Marine leader among many who found himself and his men under direct, intentional attack over the next week. While Hough shot at his fleeting targets, Company A also opened fire with selected marksmen. Unlike Lieutenant Hough in the urban strongpoint of combat post 69, Capt. Paul Roy's Company A occupied sites along the wide-open airfield that analyst Eric Hammel later called "more ceremonial than real." The Marines lived in tents that rose high above the sagging knee-high sandbag blast walls intended as shielding. On the morning of 29 August, a mortar barrage killed Roy's 1st Platoon leader and platoon sergeant in their tent. Five Marines were wounded. Sporadic 82-mm fire injured three more before Colonel Geraghty authorized Battery C's mighty 155-mm pieces to hit back at the Druze mortar crew spotted by the busy army TAB radar teams. The first 155-mm volley sprinkled illumination rounds over the Druze crew near Khalde. The Druze mortar kept shooting. Geraghty authorized a battery sheaf of six high-explosive rounds, and that erased the troublesome enemy tube. Meanwhile, the rest of Company A was blazing away, covering three amphibious assault vehicles sent from the BLT headquarters to remove U.S. casualties.[30]

Company C to the south remained unengaged, thanks to the Israelis still in the vicinity. But Company B was not so lucky. Marines at combat post 35 opened fire on their own initiative. Lieutenant Hough's ordeal at combat post 69 continued at dawn on 29 August. Druze officers approached Hough and demanded a surrender. They threatened a ground assault. The Marine refused.

Shortly thereafter, an extensive 122-mm rocket and artillery barrage rained around the reinforced buildings and trenches, raising a pall of smoke, dust, and splinters. Small-arms fire kept the Marines ducking, and Hough watched with dismay as the Muslim troops of his affiliated Lebanese army units debated with their Christian officers about returning fire on core-ligionists. At least one Lebanese deserted outright. Hough inventoried his meager ammunition stocks: a few hundred rounds, ten M203 40-mm grenades, and three light antitank weapons (LAWs), unguided rockets in disposable launchers. Fortunately, the Druze bluster about a ground attack proved empty, despite heavy fire all afternoon. Perhaps a pair of AH-1T Cobra attack helicopters that flew over late in the day made a difference. Although ordered not to shoot, Cobra pilot Capt. John Kerr did not hesitate to blast a Druze .50-caliber machine gun that dared to open up on his aircraft. Kerr's rocket fire quelled the Druze, at least for the night.

Alarmed by the situation at combat post 69, Colonel Geraghty and BLT commander Gerlach readied a tank and amtrac relief column to rescue the beleaguered outpost. Instead, dawn on 30 August saw the Lebanese army mount a clumsy armored thrust to protect its forces at combat posts 35 and 69. A great deal of haphazard tank fire and spraying machine-gun bullets ripped up the shacks of Hay-es-Salaam, sending the Amal and Druze scampering for their bomb shelters. But as incredulous Marines watched and fired at the few militia troops still bothering with the combat posts, the Amal captured one M113 armored personnel carrier (APC) intact and destroyed two others. Hough tried to hunt down the captured APC over the next few days with his LAWs, but the slippery Amal men repeatedly drove away too quickly. Finally, on 2 September, another platoon from Company B relieved Hough's tired Marines, who rotated back to the relative comfort of the university area.[31]

As the fighting slackened, Colonel Geraghty faced an unpleasant quandary. His bluff of presence had been called in a major way. Geraghty and his superior afloat, Captain France, controlled everything ashore, from rifles up to 155-mm howitzers and Cobra gunships. The commanders devised "a postured response"—first pointing gun tubes and launching attack choppers, then popping illumination flares over active hostile firing sites, and finally engaging any defiant shooters. As France said, "We were very concerned with remaining neutral. That was the linchpin of our mission and the linchpin of Tim's [Geraghty's] survival."[32]

But the Americans had fired small arms, machine guns, mortars, artillery, and even Cobra rockets at both Amal Shiite and Druze PSP people. Geraghty, Gerlach, and their subordinate commanders tried desperately to contain the violence. Even so, friction and danger soon caused things to escalate out of control. Like Captain Kerr in his helicopter, other privates, corporals, sergeants, and lieutenants boldly elected to defend themselves, which was certainly permitted by the rules of engagement.

Although he supported the decisions of the men on the ground, especially after the deaths on 29 August, Geraghty acted as if he thought he could somehow put the lid back on the hideous Pandora's box. He hoped to return to the seemingly halcyon days of June and July. The MAU commander delayed fire support missions and continued to use the intimidation and illumination routine even as outlying posts came under heavy fire. As he later explained, "I think a lot of the shelling and the casualties that we took there over the months were really directed to—as bait to force us to have a large response into the village and we didn't do that." He added, "I think we earned the respect of the people."[33] Local civilians, no doubt, were grateful. Opponents saw this as a sure sign of American weakness.

So now, as the troops would say, the shit had hit the fan. What were the American options as they waited for the full Israeli withdrawal and the fire storm sure to accompany it? Planners examined the usual three possibilities: pull out the MAU, reinforce or reposition the MAU, and maintain the status quo. Only Gen. Bernard Rogers, CINC at European Command (EUCOM), wanted to withdraw, even though the noncombat line was obviously and irretrievably breached. There were those in Washington who wanted to expand the U.S. contingent of the MNF, pushing the enlarged force as far south as the Awali River to fill the space opened when the Israelis departed. But President Reagan had promised to ask Congress before altering the American role in the MNF or reinforcing the Marines. Indeed, Public Law 98-43 (27 June 1983) required such consultation. What if Congress said no? Where would that leave Gemayel and his fragile army?

Instead, the president decided not to decide. He let events follow the path of least resistance, doing nothing, leaving 24th MAU in place. Encouraged by the forceful McFarlane, Reagan risked the American troops as a shield for the Lebanese. The IDF pullout required America to choose between the last remaining shreds of truly neutral interposition and direct support for Gemayel's government. Having already tilted toward Gemayel, the U.S. found its hand forced by the aggressive Shiite Amal and Druze. Every time the Marines shot back, they identified themselves as Lebanese army—and hence Christian—allies. The impartial interposition role was through.

But rather than admit the changed circumstances, commanders in Washington on down to Colonel Geraghty insisted that the U.S. force's mission had not altered, though the situation was far different than it had been when that mission was designed. That doomed the Marines to continued hostilities and mounting losses. Reagan specified, however, that "U.S. forces be prepared to exercise their right of self-defense should such attacks recur."[34]

The growing violence made an impression on 24th MAU's chain of command. To protect the Marines, General Rogers delegated authority to VAdm. Edward H. Martin of Sixth Fleet to employ aircraft carrier reconnaissance jets and naval gunfire. Offshore, on "Bagel Station," the carrier USS *Eisenhower* and its battle group prepared for action. Additionally, the navy moved the helicopter carrier USS *Tarawa* and Amphibious Squadron 1, with 31st MAU embarked, toward Lebanon, as potential reinforcements. The French, who also had sustained casualties in the militia skirmishing, readied their air wing aboard the carrier *Foch*. Italian destroyers moved in for fire missions. If the simmering situation blew up again, the militiamen could expect heavy retribution.

Colonel Geraghty's reaction during the lull was quite curious. In order to prevent casualties, on 31 August he ended all but a few local security patrols. Even these were not run when gunfire endangered the Marines involved. Concerned about losses, Geraghty intended to close the vulnerable combat posts 35 and 69. He even considered evacuating the university, because if a man was wounded, "the only way we could have gotten him out is to have an armored force [go] through a hostile village in order to get them." But after consultation with his commanders and McFarlane, who urged him to reconsider, Geraghty found his idea overtaken by events on the ground. The Marines in the combat posts remained fully engaged until the next significant break in the fighting. These initiatives might have cut losses in the short run, but, given the suspension of almost all patrols, removing the combat posts from the airport approaches would have torn open 24th MAU's only early-warning cordon.

Even as the colonel cut his links to the Beirut streets, he clung to the viability of his mission as he saw it. Geraghty's performance at a memorial service during the first days of September reveals his thinking at the time. With a crowd of news media in attendance, Colonel Geraghty went well beyond the traditional eulogy for the dead Marines. Geraghty said only a few words about the deceased. Instead he focused his talk on how "we must help Lebanon maintain her sovereignty." He did not acknowledge the vicious fighting that had flared around the airport. As witness Cpl. Michael Petit said, "This isn't a memorial service to the dead. It's a justification to the press on why we're here." Another Marine said to Petit, "And of course we haven't been in combat. [2d Lt. Donald George] Losey and [SSgt. Alexander] Ortega dropped dead from boredom, not massive shrapnel wounds to the head."[35] The Marine commander was drawing his unit into a shell, but the shell was paper-thin.

On Sunday, 4 September, the Israelis withdrew their main forces from Khalde. As expected, fierce fighting broke out. Company C, which enjoyed IDF protection until that day, found itself involved in major firefights with the denizens of Khalde. Fortunately, SSgt. Joe Curtis woke his 1st Platoon before dawn, suspicious of heavy vehicle noises to the south and east. They were ready when the first shells detonated at about 0930.

Unexpectedly, two sloppy Lebanese army armored columns drove south into the middle of this shooting. They hoped to replace the departing Israelis. One went down the BIA runway and ran right through Company C. The other went down the coast road. The unit on the runway planned to clear out Khalde and then swing north through Ashuefat and finally Hay-es-Salaam. Although Tannous never talked to Geraghty, it must have looked as if the Marines were providing a base of fire for the Lebanese attack.

By the time Lieutenant Colonel Gerlach authorized Company C to return fire, Curtis's platoon was already in action, shooting up pesky rocket-propelled grenade (RPG) gunners. Heavy supporting fires were not permitted, although SSgt. Richard Smith's conveniently placed tank ravaged a hostile 106-mm recoilless rifle position with one "beehive" round. This projectile belched a hot cloud of steel flechettes that eliminated the militia crew. Curtis worked with Smith to direct tank machine-gun fire onto the RPG gunners. The rifle platoon sergeant blew open a building with a precise LAW shot. His men cut down the fleeing enemy with bursts from an M60 machine gun. Captain Roy's Company A on the airfield line received permission from Gerlach at BLT headquarters "to support the LAF [Lebanese Armed Forces] by laying down some screening [suppressive] fire."

The fighting exceeded the late August eruption. At nightfall, 1st Lt. Leo Lachat of 24th MSSG looked south from his supply point at Green Beach (formerly called Black Beach). He watched Company C's Khalde action: "Thousands of tracer rounds, the wiggling tracks of RPGs, and the flash of numerous rocket and artillery exchanges blazed through the sky." When Company C called out of this inferno for artillery support, however, Geraghty okayed only illumination.[36] The exchanges of gunfire ebbed and flowed all night around the southernmost Marines, gradually dying down early on 5 September.

But the Druze gunners were not finished. Indirect fire continued to crash into and around several MAU positions. The army Target Acquisition Battery tracked the Druze shots, and Geraghty prepared to reply in force to end the long-range sniping.

The TAB data indicated that the offending pieces squatted behind a ridge. Although Battery C's howitzers used high-angle fire to blast the enemy position, Geraghty and France decided to employ added combat power to eliminate the threat. Attempts to locate the source more precisely led to the commitment on 7 September of *Eisenhower*'s F-14A Tomcat fighters rigged with reconnaissance pods. The French carrier jets were already up, looking for Druze batteries that had shelled their headquarters.

The American jets quickly found their quarry. The USS *Bowen* sailed slowly south, just past the intervening ridge. When on line with the Druze position, the navy frigate fired four 127-mm (5-inch) high-explosive rounds, which silenced the site.[37] There could be little doubt that the Americans had intentionally destroyed the Druze battery.

Despite the strong U.S. response, shelling intensified. In the Shuf, the Druze, their Shiite Amal associates of the moment, Syrian advisers, Syrian-backed Palestinians, and even some Iranian volunteers cooperated to assail the Phalangists. Fearful of a threat to Beirut, Tannous rushed his shaky

Lebanese army 8th Brigade into the mountains to save the endangered Christian fighters. By 10 September, fighting centered on Suq-al-Gharb, the high ground overlooking BIA. Battered by more than sixteen hundred artillery rounds, the 8th Brigade barely held its own. Robert McFarlane judged that Suq-al-Gharb was a test. If it fell, Gemayel's coalition and U.S. hopes for a true central government in Lebanon might go with it.

On 12 September, General Rogers of EUCOM authorized Sixth Fleet to use carrier air strikes to support 24th MAU as necessary. McFarlane immediately asked for air support at Suq-al-Gharb, but Captain France and Colonel Geraghty demurred. Geraghty strongly reminded the special envoy that this kind of active intervention on behalf of the Lebanese army "clearly changed our neutral role, our mission, our peacekeeping role, and that our vulnerabilities were not unknown, since we were in static locations and so on." In other words, helping the Lebanese at Suq-al-Gharb definitely placed the Americans in combat alongside the Gemayel forces and, hence, the Christian factions. The militant Muslims would react.

On 16 September, the cruiser USS *Virginia* and destroyer USS *John Rodgers* fired to support Geraghty's Marines. The ships plastered six different targets, including suspected Syrian positions, with seventy-two rounds. The sniping and shelling continued at the airport.

Meanwhile, at nearby Suq-al-Gharb, a Lebanese army counterattack miscarried, and Walid Jumblatt's Druze tanks and troops menaced the 8th Brigade. Tannous reported that his men were running out of ammunition, a report verified by U.S. Special Forces advisers in the mountain stronghold. Given the deteriorating situation, Captain France and Colonel Geraghty received orders from Washington that added fire support for the Lebanese foothold (including U.S. advisers) at Suq-al-Gharb to the MAU's force protection tasks. The MAU could help if three things transpired: the mountain spur was in danger of capture, non-Lebanese forces (Syrians) were attacking, and the Lebanese asked for the help. Although the change reflected McFarlane's influence, it came through the chain of command, and it reserved the final call for Geraghty.

The desperate hill struggle flared over the next few days. Despite pressure from McFarlane, Geraghty refused to approve support. He expressed concerns that innocent Druze civilians might die. Tannous screamed for help, claiming his men were under heavy pressure. One Lebanese officer had been hacked apart by a hatchet in a hand-to-hand struggle, and the 85th Artillery Battalion ran out of 155-mm ammunition. Geraghty held firm to his three criteria. But when American Green Berets on the scene reported Syrian tanks closing on Suq-al-Gharb around 0730 on 19 September, Geraghty relented. Americans were in trouble, and that demanded action.

Accordingly, USS *Virginia* and USS *John Rodgers* pummeled the Shuf with 368 rounds. Two Syrian or Druze tanks exploded, and numerous enemy infantrymen died. Geraghty waved off an orbiting air strike from USS *Eisenhower* as overkill. The 8th Brigade stiffened and held. Curiously, the Lebanese suffered only eight dead and twelve wounded in their last-ditch defense. Perhaps the fog of war had exaggerated the danger.

Although later analysis keyed on the Suq-al-Gharb incident as the critical shift in the American role in Beirut, the importance of this use of naval gunfire is probably overstated. Marines had killed and wounded plenty of Muslim militiamen before 19 September, had employed naval guns twice before for their own defense, and had intentionally and unintentionally supported Lebanese army operations for weeks before the Suq-al-Gharb battle. How or why the Marines shot probably mattered little to the Druze, Amal, and Syrians. For them, any suggestion that the Americans were impartial had become a hollow joke.

Was Geraghty pressured? Yes, he was. But he had the final say, and he made the decision to fire. When he authorized the engagement, he believed in what he was doing: "It would have been unconscionable for us to stand by and not provide support for them at that moment." He thought that if Suq-al-Gharb fell, American Special Forces men would die, and Lebanon's nearly impotent government would fall.[38] But as he predicted, the Marines had now become fair game in the Lebanese civil war.

After 19 September, the Marines and the militias traded unpleasantries of all varieties and calibers, to include more naval gunnery. Skirmishing erupted along the entire perimeter. But the blunting of their Shuf attack evidently stymied the Druze and Amal. The arrival on 25 September of the massive battleship USS *New Jersey,* with its nine 406-mm (16-inch) main guns and brace of 127-mm secondary cannons, triggered a cease-fire the next day. In one of the final acts of the September War, Geraghty ordered Gerlach to withdraw combat posts 35 and 69. Under heavy fire, Company B's men pulled back to the university. Then the shooting died down for a week or so. In the words of Major Jordan, "It appeared that presence and a good salvo or more of naval gunfire had indeed made peace a possibility."

On 3 October, BLT 1/8 switched its line company positions for the last time, with the arrival of 22d MAU and BLT 2/8 only weeks away. Company

C moved from exposed Khalde to even more exposed combat posts 11 and 76 and the line of airport bunkers. Company A went to the consolidated university site. Company B redeployed to the south end of the runway and sent a reinforced platoon downtown to the embassy. Offshore, USS *Tarawa* and 31st MAU sailed away, seemingly unnecessary. Even USS *Eisenhower* slipped off to Naples for a well-deserved port call. The men of 24th MAU were on the home stretch, grateful for the cease-fire and anticipating their relief at the start of November.

Although Geraghty rightly predicted that there would be retaliation for all of the recent Marine shooting, no serious defensive improvements occurred. Patrolling did not resume, outside a bare minimum of foot routes right around occupied sites. More than three hundred Marines, plus attached sailors and soldiers, remained jammed into the stout BLT headquarters. In a gesture of faith in the Lebanese army, Geraghty removed the USMC guards from checkpoint 74 on the main airport entry road. On 7 October, some subordinate officer pulled the two TOW antitank missiles out of their rooftop emplacements on the BLT building. Things seemed to be returning to a tense routine similar to late July.

But all was not well. There were indicators that the danger had merely altered, not abated. Frustrated in their attempts to shell or intimidate the stolid Marines, the Amal and their comrades resorted to random sniping, particularly in the northeast corner of the Marine sector, around the university. Marines noticed some hard-looking characters in Soviet-pattern camouflage fatigues, sporting red headbands. Two Americans died over the next few weeks, victims of the nerve-racking rifle shots, but USMC snipers took out their share of tormentors. On 15 October, 24th MAU proudly announced four confirmed kills, and Geraghty's men demonstrated their precision night sights to interested journalists. Presence was not discussed.

The arrival of the camouflage-uniformed types and the coincident widely publicized sniper dueling might have been the most critical developments leading to the eventual destruction of the BLT building. It appears that the new breed with their red headbands were members of the Hezbollah group, a small but fanatical Shiite splinter group with direct ties to Iran. These same people, intimately linked to the Islamic Jihad, would earn plenty of U.S. attention as hostage takers and bombers—Gander was still to come.

In these initial encounters, Marine shooters claimed four dead and fourteen wounded, a significant number for this tiny faction. In the words of TAB commander Capt. James G. Breckenridge, "There was just no way this act could go unavenged. The problem was that this group did not have the resources like artillery and rockets available to exact but token revenge. To kill the commander responsible for this disaster would be meaningful retribution. When this failed on 19 October, they resorted to a contingency plan or merely an idea that was to supplement Geraghty's death—the bombing of 23 October." Unfortunately, nobody recognized the importance of the sniper struggle at the time.

While sniping and countersniping continued, the real omen of things to come occurred on 19 October, during a routine supply run to the temporary embassy. Colonel Geraghty rode along, bound for a conference. The sniping incidents had encouraged the MAU commander to ride in the back of his jeep, rather than in the right front seat as usual. He carried an M16A1 rifle and wore no rank. The precautions might have saved him. As the American truck and its three escort jeeps passed through the Italian sector, a white Mercedes car parked along the street exploded into a sheet of boiling flame. Geraghty's lead vehicle had just passed. The truck was hit hard, showering the road with chunks of metal as it swerved to a halt. The blast wave threw the trailing jeep into a telephone pole. Four Americans lay dazed and injured. A Marine reaction force arrived quickly aboard hulking AAVs, weapons at the ready. All that remained of the white car was a smoking chunk of transmission.[39]

Evidently, Geraghty did not let the near miss shake him. He took no special precautions, nor did he increase security around the Marine positions. The car bomb was dismissed as an isolated act, largely unsuccessful, a spike in the relative calm prevailing after the September outbreaks. On the afternoon of Saturday, 22 October, the United Services Organization (USO) presented two shows by Megaband, a country-western group, right in the BLT compound. A liberty party left for Alexandria, Egypt. Trans-Mediterranean Airlines managed about ten flights from half-repaired Beirut International. A gathering with the French paratroopers was on tap for Sunday, a return to the traditional barbecues of earlier days. Although first light would come at 0524, reveille for Marines was set for 0630, typical for a Sunday in 24th MAU.

There were tremors of trouble on 22 October, had anyone noticed. Guards were warned to watch for a blue Opel rigged as a car bomb; American intelligence agencies had furnished the Marines with many such tips, probably too many. Without patrols, it was the only information available. A remote-controlled mine destroyed a French jeep to the north. Finally, after dark, the routine foot patrol from the BLT headquarters down the runway to Company B at Khalde got pinned in the south by rocket and artillery fire. Some rounds sparked off the pavement around the BLT building. Rockets crumped in nearby. After a tense hour or so, the American guards relaxed to a lesser alert state. Even that condition was not fully enforced. Although a sentry noticed a suspicious yellow Mercedes truck in the exterior airport parking area about 0500, he made no report. Another Marine observed a white Mercedes car stop out front about 0618. The driver took two photographs of the USMC complex and sped off.

Sergeant Stephen E. Russell, in charge of the guards at the BLT headquarters, had just stopped a jogger from going out to run about 0600. At 0622, he was at his post in the door of the BLT building when he saw, to his horror, a big yellow five-ton truck smash through the concertina wire and head straight for his sandbagged position. The small inside gate was wide open, as usual. Two nearby sentries did not open fire. They could not load their magazines fast enough. The truck gunned its motor, the driver smiled, and the speeding vehicle easily careened past the flimsy metal pipes lying in front of the BLT doorway. Russell ran out, yelling, "Hit the dirt!"[40] It was too late.

The truck hit the opening and exploded into a bright yellow-orange flash. A throaty, cracking roar thundered out and up, knocking Russell to the ground. The four-story building lifted up, shrugged apart, and caved in with a tumbling crash. Dust hung like a funeral shroud over the ruins. Reagan, McFarlane, and Geraghty, among others, had gambled and lost. Now it was only a matter of time before the plug was pulled for good.

The devastation was massive. FBI explosives experts later estimated that the truck bomb had delivered the equivalent of twelve thousand pounds of TNT into the enclosed atrium of the Marine BLT building. Even if the bomb had blown well outside the structure, FBI scientist John W. Hicks estimated that "there would be considerable injury and quite possibly loss of life, just simply from the shrapnel, flying glass, and things like that." But the Hezbollah suicide driver had punched home his lethal cargo, and the gas-enhanced detonation utterly wrecked the building. The carnage was tremendous: 218 Marines, 18 sailors, 3 soldiers, a visiting French paratrooper, and a Lebanese civilian died. Eighty Americans were wounded and evacuated; 32 other U.S. troops were treated and returned to duty.[41] No other Marine battalion, not even in the meat grinders of Belleau Wood, Tarawa, Iwo

Jima, Okinawa, the Chosin Reservoir, or Khe Sanh, suffered this many dead in one day.

The United States military responded vigorously and immediately to the barracks explosion. A tremendous medical effort rescued the injured and recovered the dead. As in any military operation, despite the trauma, the mission went on. The MAU greatly strengthened its defenses, digging in, tightening the perimeter, dispersing forces, and cleaning up ambiguities in the ROE. Nobody talked about presence anymore.

Beyond Beirut and its embattled U.S. contingent, the military chain of command immediately sent in individual replacements and several formed units by air, thereby reconstituting Geraghty's outfit, pending the imminent arrival of the next MAU. This interim force persisted a while longer than expected, as the 22d MAU was diverted en route to participate in the Grenada intervention. They did not take over the Beirut positions until 19 November. The locals, who had been somewhat quiet after the bombing, welcomed 22d MAU with a hail of gunfire, rockets, and artillery. The U.S. responded in kind, to include carrier air strikes and barrages from the battleship USS *New Jersey* and its escorts. The gloves were off.

Naval gunfire and air strikes bolstered the Marines, but did not convince the Syrians to leave and did very little to support the disintegrating Lebanese army. One reinforced American battalion, regardless of its floating backup, could not hold off the swelling ranks of Druze and Amal fighters. The powerful Syrians even deflected a U.S. Navy air strike on 4 December, shooting down a pair of carrier-based jets, killing one aviator and capturing another (later released). Worst of all, despite all of these measures, 22d MAU suffered twelve killed and three wounded in action, far in excess of the price paid for victory in Grenada.[42] It was becoming obvious that Lebanon was never going to end up in the "win" column.

Even before the tragedy of 23 October, the agitation to put a time limit on the Lebanon venture produced Public Law 98-119 (12 October 1983). This limited the American participation in the MNF to eighteen more months without further congressional agreement, mandated regular reports by President Reagan to Congress, and necessitated congressional approval of any increase in the American forces or changes in mission.[43] By January 1984, another eighteen months looked very unlikely. The standard trio of options faced the American president and his men: add forces, stand pat, or go home. With Lebanon in utter disarray, nobody was pushing much for options one or two.

Two investigations of the BLT truck attack, one by the House Armed Services Committee released on 19 December, and the other by a Defense Department commission of senior officers issued on 20 December, reached similar conclusions. Both reports censured the chain of command for errors of omission and commission. More to the point, as Reagan and his advisers reconsidered American policy in Lebanon, the reports warned of increased vulnerability and further losses. The defense commission, chaired by retired Adm. Robert L. Long, concluded that "There is an urgent need for reassessment of alternative means to achieve U.S. objectives in Lebanon."[44] In plain English, the two investigations urged Reagan to pull out.

The end proved painful and embarrassing. The firefights sputtered along the airport perimeter, the American warships fired more rounds ashore, and the carrier air wings launched a night precision air strike—like everything else by this point, the laser-guided bombs went awry. By early February, the bedraggled Lebanese army lost control of the Shuf to the Druze and gave up most of Beirut to the Amal Shiites. That did it. The Marines finally withdrew to their ships offshore on 26 February, remaining nearby as a show of force to back the tottering Gemayel government, which by this point governed almost nothing.

Even this limited commitment proved hollow. On 5 March 1984, after a trip to Damascus to grovel before Assad, Gemayel abrogated the 17 May agreement with Israel. It was as if the Americans had never even been there. Syria entrenched for the long run, Israel remained watchful in the south with its new buffer strip, and the militias went crazy in the no-man's-land between, presided over by the pathetic shell of Gemayel's impotent government. On 30 March 1984, Reagan broke up the unneeded USN flotilla on Bagel Station, leaving a few wary OMC trainers in Lebanon to patch together the bits of Tannous's army still on duty. Thus ended America's direct role in Lebanon.[45]

Like Syria and Israel, America could not exert its will over tumultuous Lebanon. It was overly optimistic to think that the weak Gemayel government could extend sovereignty over the fractured country in a few months or, indeed, ever. The Syrians and Israelis refused to leave unless that mess was sorted out in accord with their contradictory intentions. Although the American goals in Lebanon were probably unattainable from the start, the truck bombing of the Marine headquarters precipitated and heightened the eventual U.S. failure. The bombing was the single most critical event that derailed any remote chance for success and ensured a frustrating withdrawal. American influence and prestige in Lebanon went up with the blast. The resultant spate of hostage taking and terrorism, coupled with the machinations of the Iran-Contra project, only served to underscore the magnitude of the disaster.

What went wrong?

For a military professional, there were three possible explanations. The first, associated with President Reagan, Secretary of Defense Caspar Weinberger, and Marine Commandant Gen. Paul X. Kelley, explained the event as an unconventional bolt out of the blue, unanticipated by rational men who had done their best to prepare themselves for more ordinary direct and indirect fire threats. These leaders did not think that the Marines could have done anything to halt or avoid the mobile bomb. General Kelley, who had visited the Marines just prior to the attack, told a congressional committee, "No one that I talked to in Lebanon or anywhere else could ever show me a thread of evidence that would show this kind of massive assault where you are actually penetrating a position with a five-ton truck going sixty miles an hour. This has just never been conceived of before."[46] A definite case can be made that the suicide truck bombing was an utter surprise to the Americans at the airport, and the 24th MAU leadership can be well satisfied with the vigorous support of their chain of command. In such a view, the exceptional nature of the attack made defense impossible, and, hence, no officers were held accountable.

Despite the president's assumption of responsibility, another explanation arose. Some Marines who served in Lebanon believed that they had been handed "mission impossible," with unworkable ROE to boot. Eric Hammel, a historian who has written several detailed accounts of Marine Corps campaigns, interviewed many of the participants. He summarized their views: "Rather, I believe, the bombing was the direct outgrowth of our leaders having made available a target of unprecedented magnitude in the center of a chaotic situation. That our combat force was declawed and placed in a static position with no clear mandate or any clear means for eluding the wishes of a maniacal anti-American regime or regimes was a bonus."[47] In this interpretation, the MAU leadership had been placed in a hopeless situation, fraught with perils, with both hands tied. Diplomats, civilian security advisers, and other nonmilitary decision makers and staffers—the ever-present "they"—supposedly hung the Marines out on a limb and then allowed "terrorists" to saw off that branch. Most of the popular press critiques of the Lebanon episode reflected this view.

Although each of these versions of the truck bombing has merit, neither goes far enough toward explaining the event. Both the first (blaming the enemy) and the second (blaming the civilian leadership) explanations assign full culpability to circumstances external to the MAU command structure. A careful examination of the available facts, buttressed to a large extent by the Department of Defense commission and congressional studies of the explosion, indicates that a third interpretation is in order. Although the enemy was crafty and circumstances were hardly ideal, it appears that the greatest part of the responsibility for this unfortunate incident rests squarely on the shoulders of the 24th MAU and BLT 1/8 commanders. Their misapprehension of the mission, incomplete defensive preparations, and permission of deviations from established security regimens certainly exacerbated difficult conditions and expedited the work of a resourceful enemy.

The 24th MAU and BLT 1/8 commanders misinterpreted their assigned mission. This conceptual error produced a misunderstanding of the military environment in the Beirut area and placed the American troops at risk. How did these capable Marine officers make such a mistake?

Fundamentally, their misperceptions were a function of trying too hard to translate overarching political objectives into military terms, always a risk when national policy rides on the backs of tired colonels far from home. The mission in Lebanon was multifaceted and complex, and evolving circumstances on the ground clouded the issue even more. Nevertheless, the chain of command assigned defensive tasks within the military capability of the U.S. forces, albeit not always in language that would earn high marks from the faculty at the Marine Corps University at Quantico, Virginia. Combat was not anticipated, but the Marines were explicitly ordered to defend themselves, other MNF contingents, and their Lebanese allies. The designated tasks were military in nature, not diplomatic. Had the 24th MAU done as ordered, things might have turned out better, at least as far as casualties.

Unfortunately, the Marine commanders allowed State Department rhetoric about showing the flag, stiffening Lebanese government resolve, and the symbolic need to keep the airport open to affect military judgments about the tactical situation. This occurred even though such tasks were never assigned to the Marines, and Department of State personnel were not in the chain of command.

Senior military, naval, and political officials also created ambiguity. Many of them described the Marines' duties to the American public as "peacekeeping," "interposition," "visibility," or "presence," and these thoughts were widely known in Beirut. Trying to please allies, ambassadors, envoys, and the press, it was easy to get sidetracked and forget exactly what the mission was.

Yet the original mission was always there, in stark black and white. The chain of command spoke in terms familiar to any Marine rifleman: "occupy," "secure," and "defend." Those things can be done regardless of whether the Druze, Amal, and Syrians love you or hate you—and when they hate you, you had better be doing them. For all the use and abuse of the word, presence was never a designated mission.

The commanders in Beirut failed in their defensive role because they attempted to produce direct diplomatic outcomes intended as second-order consequences of successful accomplishment of the assigned military tasks. By failing to protect their force, the Marine leadership sustained losses that jeopardized the very policy they had been sent in to support.

The 24th MAU slipped into their odd mode of operations under the full view of their higher headquarters. Superior civilian defense officials, the JCS chairman, responsible commanders and staff officers (from USEUCOM, USNAVEUR, Sixth Fleet, and the Amphibious Task Force), two Marine Corps commandants, the Chief of Naval Operations, and other senior leaders visited the 24th MAU in Beirut. Two dozen generals and admirals visited between the April embassy bombing and the October barracks explosion, and presumably witnessed how the Marines were doing business. Yet no corrective actions occurred. The Long Commission, itself heavy with flag officers, found this disturbing. Their final report charged a "lack of effective command supervision throughout the chain of command," and recommended "that the Secretary of Defense take whatever administrative or disciplinary action he deems appropriate."[48]

But there is another way of viewing this development. These ranking officers allowed the local commanders to assess and react to the situation as they saw fit. The excesses of the Vietnam era had taught that much, and U.S. officers are properly sensitive to what they perceive as too much help or micromanagement. Given their mission, the Lebanon commanders were obviously more restricted than U.S. generals in Desert Storm. Yet to its credit, the Reagan administration let the MAU perform its professional duties without too much meddling. The military (and civilian) chain of command approved every Marine request for liberalization of rules of engagement, and trusted that the on-scene commanders knew best.[49] Rather than take advantage of the opportunity for local initiative, the Marines in Beirut accepted the chain of command's noninterference as a blessing of the MAU's nonmilitary activities.

The 24th MAU's "semitactical" appreciation of its mission influenced and sustained an incomplete and eventually inadequate defensive perimeter. Although the Marines had been in the same positions for more than a year by October 1983, defensive arrangements featured limited dispersion, a dearth of barriers and protective reinforcements, and a contraction of local patrols in the face of an increasing threat. These halfhearted defenses were justified by the allegedly diplomatic mission, although complete dispersion, solid defenses, and aggressive patrolling were well within the original concept of operations. Asked if stronger fortifications affected political goals, Special Envoy Philip Habib stated, "It would not have impaired the diplomatic mission."[50] The attempt to perform a self-designated nonmilitary role created unnecessary risk. The failure to prepare adequate defenses heightened the danger.

The Marines occupied precisely the sector they had requested in the first days of the MNF mission, and the Americans stayed there for the entire expedition. The Marines had bitten off a big hunk, in that the 4-mile frontage, much of it adjoining congested urban slums and streets, surpassed the 2.8 miles usually assigned to a Marine battalion in uninhabited, rolling terrain.[51] Defending this long perimeter well would take a lot of skill, hard work, and constant attention.

That level of effort did occur along most of the forward trace, at least after some early scares. These locations proved suitable for self-defense, and some decent positions were built. Given the terrific volume of shooting into these emplacements, the few losses sustained on the front line reflect favorably on the bunkers, trenches, revetments, and barriers eventually erected.

The real weakness in the Marine scheme was in the crowded rear, almost a part of the northern perimeter and hence near the U.S.-Italian boundary— allied force boundaries are textbook soft spots for infiltrators. Here, the majority of the attachments, the service support units, and both the MAU and BLT headquarters elements occupied a few buildings within a five-hundred-yard radius of the Beirut International Airport terminal. By 23 October, the BLT building alone sheltered 350-odd men. This contingent included engineers, medics (with their aid station), TOW crews, the BLT reconnaissance platoon, a liaision team from the army target acquisition battery, air and artillery spotters, sniper teams, and the entire battalion staff and command section. Many of these men could have been profitably employed to bolster the thin, isolated segments of the perimeter or to conduct local security patrols.

The BLT building epitomized the business-as-usual nature of Marine activities in Beirut. Colonel Geraghty and Lieutenant Colonel Gerlach stated that they concentrated their men to protect them from enemy gunfire. True, the building was solid enough, but it was also the only four-story structure left standing in the area and a perfect landmark for enemy artillerists. Using the edifice as an observation post or even a forward command post was reasonable. Employing it as a barracks for hundreds of vital Marines, sailors, and soldiers in key duty positions was not. In the harsh words of Admiral Long's commission, "While it may have appeared to be an appropriate response to the indirect fire being received the decision to billet approximately one-quarter of the BLT in a single structure contributed to the catastrophic loss of life. The commission found that the BLT commander must take responsibility for the concentration of approximately 350 members of his command in the BLT headquarters building thereby providing a lucrative target for attack. . . . The MAU commander shares the responsibility for the catastrophic losses in that he condoned the concentration of personnel."[52]

The large grouping of personnel in the BIA terminal area was dangerous enough, but the general absence of obstacles throughout the sector did much to facilitate the eventual enemy approach. The BLT building was treated like a sturdy fortress, but it lacked the necessary outworks and redoubts. Secretary Weinberger observed that the BLT commander had the authority to employ barbed wire, trenches, or even concrete barriers as he deemed fit. General Kelley explained that the Marines had used a large quantity of engineer materials, more than twenty tons (10,000 feet of concertina, 1,000 engineer stakes, and 500,000 sandbags) by one estimate.[53]

This sounds like a lot, until one consults the relevant engineer manual and discovers that it amounts to just over a thousand yards of triple-strand concertina fence and about a mile and a half of six-foot-high sandbag breastworks (or a much lesser frontage of thicker walls, fully covered bunkers, or trenches). Much of this material went into reinforcement of the BLT and ancillary headquarters and support buildings. Although tank ditches and mines were permissible, Geraghty decided that they should not be used around the BLT building "in view of the threat existing at the time and the commercial nature of the airport."[54] This was despite repeated experiences with car bombs and a known Syrian and Druze armor capability.

In truth, the few Marine barriers were weak and largely symbolic. Much of the engineer effort was directly devoted to the congested MAU-BLT rear area in the midst of the Lebanese airport facilities. The resulting projects appeared to be mainly for traffic control, not defense. Given the lengthy period ashore, the Marine infantry and engineers could have done much more in the way of obstacles. The time was available; 24th MAU engineers spent some of it building an elaborate basketball court. As for defensive wire, General Kelley summarized the USMC building effort: "The wire that was put in, in the estimation of those who put it in, was sufficient to stop a car, not a five-ton truck, obviously."[55] The BLT barriers proved incapable of halting a commercial vehicle. Their anticipated effectiveness under determined infantry or armored assault was extremely questionable. In brief, the Marines had just enough protection to create a false sense of security.

Finally, the Marines intentionally stripped themselves of their organic intelligence-gathering capability in late August 1983. Fearful of possible losses on foot and jeep patrols around Beirut, the MAU contracted patrol routes to the immediate vicinity of USMC positions. This was not long after the BLT commander relocated most of his Headquarters and Service Company, Weapons Company, and attached combat forces in the four-story BLT headquarters. In essence, the Americans created a very big target even as they curtailed their early-warning network. JCS chairman Gen. John Vessey stated flatly that while he understood Geraghty's desire to cut casualties, "I would have knocked him [Geraghty] for not patrolling for security reasons."[56]

Once the Marines abandoned most infantry patrols and idled their capable reconnaissance platoon, they had to rely on vague national intelligence service reports. There were indicators of what was in store, as there always are—Clausewitz's acid dismissal of most intelligence reports as outright bunk comes to mind. Numerous bulletins warned of shelling, sniping, car bombs, and terrorism without specifics. Additionally, the Marines had firsthand experience with the methods of their Muslim adversaries. The MAU beach had been unsuccessfully car bombed in November 1982, the

American embassy ravaged by a light truck munition in April 1983, and a 24th MAU convoy nearly missed by an exploding car on 19 October 1983. In order to foil the busy militia demolition teams, the MAU commander thought it necessary to remove his rank insignia and sit in the backseat when traveling by jeep. Though the danger of both conventional and unconventional attack was evident, 24th MAU elected to prevent patrolling casualties at the expense of seeing the battlefield. The final costs of this caution, tacked onto loose defenses, proved to be much higher.

Even with their misperception of the military mission and their defensive shortcomings, the U.S. commanders still had a final means of protection, typically a capable one: the ingenious, courageous U.S. Marines. Had the established security structure functioned as designed, the consequent American losses might have been markedly reduced. Although a nonmilitary state of mind, lack of dispersion, weak defensive works, and imprecise intelligence increased the scale of the eventual enemy success, intentional and unintentional deviations from security procedures proved to be the immediate cause of the disaster.

The Marine rules of engagement were certainly restrictive, although they permitted a wide range of options for self-defense. Individual Marines received cards that commenced with these points:

1. When on post, mobile or foot patrol, keep a loaded magazine in the weapon; weapons will be on safe, with no rounds in the chamber.
2. Do not chamber a round unless told to do so by a commissioned officer unless you must act in immediate self-defense where deadly force is authorized.[57]

Vehicular intruders were not addressed. After the U.S. embassy was bombed in April 1983, MNF Marines were sent to guard the temporary facilities. Separate embassy rule of engagement cards specifically identified attempts by vehicles or people to breach the embassy perimeter fence as "hostile acts." Unfortunately, due to choices made within Geraghty's headquarters, the Marines around BIA kept their old ROE cards.[58]

Still, the old ROE cards did permit firing in immediate self-defense. The BLT guard force was small but theoretically able to deal with a single vehicle. At full strength, the BLT building guards consisted of a sergeant of the guard, a corporal of the relief, and twenty-two sentries. Two additional reliefs (forty-six men) were off duty but immediately available. Aside

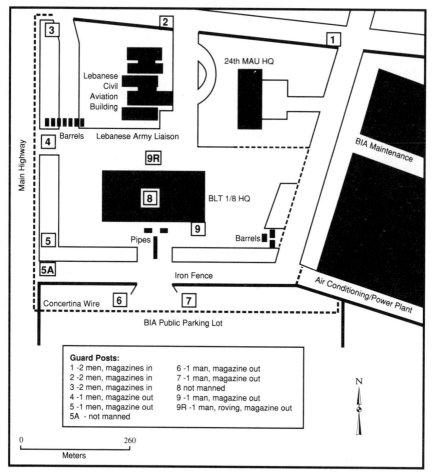

Guard Posts:

1 -2 men, magazines in	6 -1 man, magazine out
2 -2 men, magazines in	7 -1 man, magazine out
3 -2 men, magazines in	8 not manned
4 -1 men, magazine out	9 -1 man, magazine out
5 -1 men, magazine out	9R -1 man, roving, magazine out
5A - not manned	

24th MAU/BLT 1/8 Compound

from these, the building mounted four machine guns on the third floor (the fourth story). Until early October, there were two TOW antitank launchers on the roof. The rooftop offered superb 360-degree observation. A vehicle would have to brave potentially devastating fires while negotiating a concertina fence, an iron post gate, a lengthwise sewer pipe, and smaller pipes athwart the BLT headquarters entrance. Four alert conditions were prescribed, with Condition I meaning full readiness for imminent enemy attack and Condition II including loading of all weapons, full manning of all positions, and issuance of LAW antitank rockets to sentries on post. The guards were supposedly at Condition II at 0622 on 23 October 1983.

The situation in Beirut by October 1983 was pregnant with known and suspected dangers. The MAU commander, however, made substantial modifications to his security methods, including "a conscious decision not to permit insertion of magazines in weapons on interior posts, to preclude accidental discharge and possible injury to innocent civilians." All of the sentries interviewed by investigators after the bombing expressed grave reservations about this decision. Only three of the posts were permitted to keep their weapons loaded. Additionally, the interior posts were reduced to one man (with magazine out) in daylight. Some went unmanned. Finally, LAWs were removed from the guard posts, even when the compound was at Condition II.[59]

As a result, at dawn on 23 October 1983, the Marines were operating with a hamstrung, half-strength guard, without LAWs, and by and large without loaded weapons. Some of the sentries, in the middle of two-week tours of alternate four-hour stints and eight-hour breaks, had "frankly lost track of what day it is." The Headquarters and Service Company commander, designated the permanent guard officer, was asleep in the barracks, as were the rooftop observers and the reaction force. After many months of duty in Lebanon, the Americans had seen plenty of evidence that Sunday was the start of the Muslim work week, "Beirut's traditional day of war." But 24th MAU continued to sleep late on Sundays, as if they were snug in their racks at Camp Lejeune.

About 0500, a large yellow Mercedes truck was observed circling suspiciously just outside the BLT wire. The Marine compound had gone to Condition I during shooting during the night and was supposedly at Condition II at 0622. Later investigation established that the Marines were not even at Condition III. Weapons were unloaded, LAWs not issued, posts not augmented, and machine-gun bunkers left unmanned. The front gate was not even shut.[60]

The actual attack was over so swiftly that not a shot was fired. The big yellow truck crushed the flimsy concertina wire, ran through the open gate, and rammed into the BLT building. The truck's passage had been eased by the MAU's modifications of the standing guard instructions. It was merely the culmination of a series of understandable small decisions that aggregated to engender a tragedy.

Did the Marines really have any alternatives? It appears that they did. The French MNF component suffered a similar incident on 23 October in Beirut and lost fifty-eight men; the Israelis had twenty-nine soldiers killed by a truck explosion in Tyre on 4 November 1983. These injuries were serious, but well short of the toll inflicted on the less numerous U.S. forces. Situational awareness, adequate dispersion, and better security proved to be the major differences.

Yet the Americans need not have looked to foreigners for other approaches to security in Lebanon. Colonel James Mead's actions in late April offered a good model for what might have been done as things turned ugly. During the September clashes, the army TAB had established a solid and secure system of field fortifications. At sea, the carrier battle groups and amphibious ships had maintained a high level of combat vigilance, to include armed sentinels, strict control of local aircraft and boat traffic, and constant, unpredictable motion. In a similar vein, the OMC, the joint service advisory element, had reacted strongly to the increased threat following the April embassy bombing: advisory teams were dispersed in order to reduce the attractiveness of the potential target.[61] While the OMC dispersed, the MAU concentrated.

Admiral Long and his fellow investigators were harsh: "The Commission recommends that the Secretary of Defense take whatever administrative or disciplinary action he deems appropriate, citing the failure of the BLT and MAU commanders to take the security measures necessary to preclude the catastrophic loss of life in the attack on 23 October 1983."[62] But in truth, the Marine officers did their duty as they saw fit. They guessed wrong, and their men paid. Reagan spared them and their superiors from the further pain of court-martial proceedings. There already had been enough suffering in Beirut, and as in most genuine fiascos, there was plenty of blame to go around.

The story of Beirut casts a long shadow within military ranks. The tragedy has long since slipped from the public eye, lumped into the long list of terrorist outrages that marred the 1980s. But those in uniform remember. The specter of Beirut has been invoked in every operation since, but especially the small, messy ones. In the Korean DMZ, in Panama, in the Sinai, and in the Persian Gulf, commanders recall what happened to the 24th MAU. In the words of an army battalion commander deployed to Operation Provide Comfort in northern Iraq, "Any American force committed to peacekeeping must keep in mind the Marine barracks bombing in Lebanon."[63] Far more than the positive lessons from the Sinai MFO, the awful denouement at the BLT building offers a sharp prod not to take such things lightly.

The examples of the Sinai and Beirut—how to do it, how not to do it—echo through the JRTC cycles at Fort Polk and MEU training at Camp Lejeune's mock city, reverberate through the navy's Strike University in Fallon, Nevada, and in air force exercises at Hurlburt Field in Florida. The Sinai and Beirut, after all, serve as reminders of how these things can turn out, OOTW bright and dark. We love the light, but do well to fear the darkness. For therein lurk the demons.

Notes

Epigraph from Thomas L. Friedman, "America's Failure in Lebanon," *New York Times Magazine* (8 April 1984): 33.

1. International Institute for Strategic Studies, "The Military Balance 1984–85,"*Air Force* (December 1984): 121, 124; International Institute for Strategic Studies, "The Military Balance 1985–86," *Air Force* (February 1986): 108; Ze'ev Schiff and Ehud Ya'ari, *Israel's Lebanon War* (New York: Simon and Schuster, 1984), 19–22, 94; U.S. Department of Defense Commission on the Beirut International Airport Terrorist Act, October 23, 1983, *Report of the Department of Defense Commission on the Beirut International Airport Terrorist Act, October 23, 1983* (Washington, D.C.: U.S. Government Printing Office, 1984), 24–29 (hereafter cited as DOD Commission, *DOD Report).*

2. Chaim Herzog, *The Arab-Israeli Wars* (New York: Random, 1982), 385–93; DOD Commission, *DOD Report,* 29.

3. Schiff and Ya'ari, *Israel's Lebanon War,* 210; DOD Commission, *DOD Report,* 29; Eric Hammel, *The Root: The Marines in Lebanon, August 1982–February 1984* (San Diego, Calif.: Harcourt Brace Jovanovich, 1985), xxvii. Hammel's account is the definitive story of the daily Marine actions in Beirut.

4. Christopher C. Wright, "U.S. Naval Operations in 1982," *Proceedings* (May 1983): 63, 225; Schiff and Ya'ari, *Israel's Lebanon War,* 228; Hammel, *The Root,* 15, 26–28.

5. Schiff and Ya'ari, *Israel's Lebanon War,* 247, 253, 282.

6. President Ronald Reagan, "Message to the Congress, 29 September 1982," *Department of State Bulletin* (December 1982): 42; House Armed Services Committee, *Review of the Adequacy of Security Arrangements for Marines in Lebanon,* 98th Cong., 1st sess., 15 December 1983, 348, 349, (hereafter cited as Congress, *Review of Adequacy).*

7. Senate Armed Services Committee, *Use of U.S. Military Personnel in Lebanon,* 98th Cong., 1st sess., 28 September 1983, 71; Reagan, "Message to the Congress, 29 September 1982," 42; Hammel, *The Root,* 47; Congress,

214

Review of Adequacy, 433, 479; DOD Commission, *DOD Report,* 36, 37, 39.

8. Nathan A. Pelcovits, "The Multinational Force in Beirut: What Went Wrong?" *International Workshop on the Multinational Force in Beirut* (Oslo, Norway: Norwegian Institute of International Affairs, 30 October 1985), 22, 23; Hammel, *The Root,* 35, 36; DOD Commission, *DOD Report,* 35, 36, 74; Congress, *Review of Adequacy,* 29, 407, 408, 419, 430.

9. Congress, *Review of Adequacy,* 408; DOD Commission, *DOD Report,* 72.

10. Congress, *Review of Adequacy,* 32, 430; Hammel, *The Root,* 54, 55; Ann A. Ferrante and Col. John G. Miller, USMC, "Chronology: Marines in Lebanon," *Proceedings* (May 1984): 300.

11. Friedman, "America's Failure in Lebanon," 37; Michael Petit, *Peacekeepers at War* (Boston: Faber and Faber, 1986), 92, 93.

12. Friedman, "America's Failure in Lebanon," 37; Ferrante and Miller, "Chronology," 300; Hammel, *The Root,* 62–66.

13. Lt. Col. David Evans, USMC, "Navy–Marine Corps Team in Lebanon," *Proceedings* (May 1984): 135, 136; Hammel, *The Root,* 68–71.

14. Congress, *Review of Adequacy,* 410–14; Hammel, *The Root,* 74, 75. Col. Ralph A. Hallenbeck, USA, "Force and Diplomacy: The American Strategy in Lebanon" (dissertation, Pennsylvania State University, 1986), 322–24. Hallenbeck provides a most authoritative account of the Lebanon expedition as viewed from the operational level at U.S. European Command.

15. Congress, *Review of Adequacy,* 347, 410–12, 416; Evans, "Navy–Marine Corps Team in Lebanon," 136; Hammel, *The Root,* 78–80.

16. Roy Gutman, "Battle Over Lebanon," *Foreign Service Journal* (June 1984): 32; Maj. Robert T. Jordan, USMC, "They Came in Peace," *Marine Corps Gazette* (July 1984): 57; Friedman, "America's Failure in Lebanon," 40; Hallenbeck, "Force and Diplomacy," 324–26.

17. Jordan, "They Came in Peace," 56, 57; Hammel, *The Root,* 89, 90.

18. Jordan, "They Came in Peace," 57, 58; Petit, *Peacekeepers at War,* 65–66.

19. Pelcovits, "The Multinational Force in Beirut," 22; Congress, *Review of Adequacy,* 358.

20. DOD Commission, *DOD Report,* 69; Congress, *Review of Adequacy,* 259, 260, 262, 263, 283, 304, 531, 536–38. Colonel Geraghty's testimony offers his views of the mission and the Beirut environment.

21. Congress, *Review of Adequacy,* 380, 381, 564; Jordan, "They Came in Peace," 58, 59; Petit, *Peacekeepers at War,* 68, 86; DOD Commission, *DOD Report,* 69.

22. Jordan, "They Came in Peace," 59, 62; Congress, *Review of Adequacy,* 376, 382, 385, 386; Petit, *Peacekeepers at War,* 71, 74, 75, 84, 85; Hammel, *The Root,* 101, 102.

23. Hallenbeck, "Force and Diplomacy," 326, 327; Ferrante and Miller, "Chronology," 300; Jordan, "They Came in Peace," 59, 60; Petit, *Peacekeepers at War,* 108, 109, 114. Petit quotes the unit operations journal.

24. Jordan, "They Came in Peace," 59, 60; Petit, *Peacekeepers at War,* 113–15; Ferrante and Miller, "Chronology," 300; Eric C. Ludvigsen, "Army Weaponry," *Army* (October 1983): 379, 380; Capt. James G. Breckenridge, USA, interview by author, West Point, N.Y., 1 September 1987. Breckenridge commanded the Field Artillery School Target Acquisition Battery in Beirut.

25. Patrick J. Sloyan, "U.S. in Lebanon: Anatomy of a Foreign Policy Failure," *Newsday* (8 April 1984): 34; Friedman, "America's Failure in Lebanon," 37.

26. Jordan, "They Came in Peace," 60; Petit, *Peacekeepers at War,* 118–20.

27. Schiff and Ya'ari, *Israel's Lebanon War,* 298; Sloyan, "U.S. in Lebanon," 34.

28. Congress, *Review of Adequacy,* 450.

29. Hammel, *The Root,* 149–52; Jordan, "They Came in Peace," 60.

30. Ferrante and Miller, "Chronology," 300; Hammel, *The Root,* 120, 121, 126, 131, 132, 134, 135.

31. Ferrante and Miller, "Chronology," 300; Hammel, *The Root,* 155, 167.

32. Petit, *Peacekeepers at War,* 137; Congress, *Review of Adequacy,* 234, 609.

33. Congress, *Review of Adequacy,* 554.

34. Pelcovits, "The Multinational Force in Beirut," 16; Hallenbeck, "Force and Diplomacy," 327, 328; President Ronald Reagan, "Message to Congress, 30 August 1983," *Department of State Bulletin* (October 1983): 79, 80; U.S. Congressional Research Service, *Digest of Public General Bills and Resolutions,* 98th Cong., 1st sess., 1983, 17.

35. Ferrante and Miller, "Chronology," 300; Congress, *Review of Adequacy,* 539, 609; Hallenbeck, "Force and Diplomacy," 327, 328; Petit, *Peacekeepers at War,* 136, 137; DOD Commission, *DOD Report,* 40; Chris-

topher C. Wright, "U.S. Naval Operations in 1983," *Proceedings* (May 1984): 59.

36. Hammel, *The Root,* 173–75, 177, 178, 180–84; Breckenridge, interview.

37. Hammel, *The Root,* 191; Evans, "Navy–Marine Corps Team in Lebanon," 136; Congress, *Review of Adequacy,* 234; Ferrante and Miller, "Chronology," 300; Petit, *Peacekeepers at War,* 138–41; Breckenridge, interview.

38. Sloyan, "U.S. in Lebanon," 34, 36, 38; Hallenbeck, "Force and Diplomacy," 328, 329; Congress, *Review of Adequacy,* 485–87, 529–31, 564, 609; Evans, "Navy–Marine Corps Team in Lebanon," 137; Friedman, "America's Failure in Lebanon," 42; Ferrante and Miller, "Chronology," 303; Petit, *Peacekeepers at War,* 142.

39. Hammel, *The Root,* 249, 251, 276, 277, 281; Ferrante and Miller, "Chronology," 303; Congress, *Review of Adequacy,* 391, 585; Petit, *Peacekeepers at War,* 158–61; Jordan, "They Came in Peace," 61; Hallenbeck, "Force and Diplomacy," 330; Breckenridge, interview.

40. Congress, *Review of Adequacy,* 169, 177, 207–9, 257, 307, 309, 327, 381, 583, 584; Hammel, *The Root,* 292; Petit, *Peacekeepers at War,* 161–64; Jordan, "They Came in Peace," 61, 62.

41. DOD Commission, *DOD Report,* 99, 106; Congress, *Review of Adequacy,* 75, 402; "Bloody Beirut: Trading in Lives," *U.S. News & World Report* (9 February 1987): 27.

42. Evans, "Navy–Marine Corps Team in Lebanon," 139; Hallenbeck, "Force and Diplomacy," 245–47; George Wilson, *Supercarrier* (New York: Macmillan, 1986), 118, 124–55. George Wilson's eyewitness accounts of the air strikes are exhaustive.

43. Congress, *Public General Bills,* 98th Cong., 1st sess., 22.

44. DOD Commission, *DOD Report,* 1, 7, 20–21. The DOD Commission consisted of chairman Adm. Robert L. Long, USN (Ret.), Robert J. Murray (formerly of the Departments of State and Defense), Lt. Gen. Lawrence F. Snowden, USMC (Ret.), Lt. Gen. Eugene F. Tighe, USAF (Ret.), and Lt. Gen. Joseph T. Palastra, USA (still on active duty at that time). For details on the conduct, composition, summarized findings, and recommendations reached by the congressional investigation, see House Armed Services Committee, *Full Committee Consideration of Investigations Subcommittee Report on Terrorist Bombing at Beirut International Airport*, 98th Cong., 2d sess., 31 January 1984, 3.

45. Friedman, "America's Failure in Lebanon," 37; Evans, "Navy–Marine Corps Team in Lebanon," 139; Ferrante and Miller, "Chronology," 303; Hallenbeck, "Force and Diplomacy," 331–35; Christopher C. Wright, "U.S. Naval Operations in 1984," *Proceedings* (May 1985): 45. "Lebanon Cancels Agreement with Israel, 5 March 1984," *Department of State Bulletin* (April 1984): 61; President Ronald Reagan, "Letter to the Congress, 30 March 1984," *Department of State Bulletin* (May 1984): 68.

46. House Committee on Appropriations, *Situation in Lebanon and Grenada: Hearings before a Subcommittee of the House Committee on Appropriations,* 98th Cong., 1st sess., 8 November 1983, 19.

47. Hammel, *The Root,* xxvii.

48. DOD Commission, *DOD Report,* 56; Senate Committee on Armed Services, *The Situation in Lebanon: Hearings before the Senate Committee on Armed Services,* 98th Cong., 1st sess., 25 and 31 October 1983, 32. Twenty-four flag rank general officers and admirals visited the 24th MAU, along with numerous civilian leaders. The referenced page includes the complete list.

49. Congress, *Full Committee Consideration,* 3; DOD Commission, *DOD Report,* 44–51.

50. DOD Commission, *DOD Report,* 43; Congress, *Review of Adequacy,* 358.

51. U.S. Department of the Navy, Headquarters, Marine Corps, *FM 6-2 Marine Infantry Regiment* (Washington, D.C.: U.S. Government Printing Office, February 1978), paragraph 3,407.

52. DOD Commission, *DOD Report,* 6, 7.

53. Ibid., 73; Congress, *Situation in Lebanon and Grenada,* 48, 49; Congress, *Situation in Lebanon,* 11, 12.

54. Congress, *Situation in Lebanon and Grenada,* 49; Congress, *Situation in Lebanon,* 65; U.S. Department of the Army, *FM 5-34 Engineer Field Data* (Washington, D.C.: U.S. Government Printing Office, 24 September 1976), 93, 109; U.S. Department of the Army, *FM 5-15 Field Fortifications* (Washington, D.C.: U S. Government Printing Office, June 1972), 4–15.

55. Hammel, *The Root,* 102, 103; Congress, *Situation in Lebanon and Grenada,* 16.

56. Congress, *Situation in Lebanon,* 51, 52; Hammel, *The Root,* 280; Congress, *Review of Adequacy,* 611.

57. Congress, *Situation in Lebanon ond Grenada,* 48; Hammel, *The Root*, 281, 282; Evans, "Navy–Marine Corps Team in Lebanon," 136; DOD Commission, *DOD Report,* 49–50. The view that the Beirut bombing was an act of terrorism is well argued in Maj. Jeffrey W. Wright, USA, "Terrorism: A Mode of Warfare," *Military Review* (October 1984): 35–45. The opinion that the truck attack was merely an unusual enemy assault method, not a terrorist act, is cogently presented by Lt. Col. Frederic C. Hof, USA, "The Beirut Bombing of October l983: An Act of Terrorism?" *Parameters* (Summer 1985): 69–74.

58. DOD Commission, *DOD Report,* 74, 85–88; Congress, *Situation in Lebanon,* 65, 66.

59. DOD Commission, *DOD Report,* 88, 89; Congress, *Situation in Lebanon and Grenada,* 28, 29.

60. Hammel, *The Root,* 116, 264, 289, 292. Particularly violent Sundays included 28 August 1983, 4 September 1983, and 24 September 1983; DOD Commission, *DOD Report,* 88, 89, 94, 95, 99; Congress, *Situation in Lebanon,* 65, 66.

61. DOD Commission, *DOD Report,* 130–32; Capt. Don G. Palen, USN, "Close-in Battle Plan," *Proceedings* (January 1987): 67–73. The OMC benefited from an ISA team's visit and situation assessment. For details, see Steven Emerson, *Secret Warriors* (New York: G. P. Putnam's Sons, 1988), 185–192.

62. DOD Commission, *DOD Report,* 10.

63. Lt. Col. John P. Abizaid, USA, "Lessons for Peacekeepers," Military Review (March 1993): 18.

PART TWO

◆

Between Gog and Magog

I come not to bring peace, but the sword.
                              Matthew 10:34, the Bible

CHAPTER 6
Shelter from the Storm—
Success in Northern Iraq, 1991 to the Present

We no longer wage the same sort of war as you, colonel. Nowadays it's a mixture of everything, a regular witches' brew of politics and sentiment, the human soul and a man's ass, religion and the best way of cultivating rice, yes everything, including the breeding of black pigs. I knew an officer in Cochin-China who, by breeding black pigs, completely restored a situation which all of us regarded as lost.

Jean Larteguy
The Centurions

British soldiers often jest that, without fail, the most crucial operations always occur where four map sheets come together. Something like that happened in America's first major OOTW after Desert Storm, right on the boundary that separated the CINCdom of Gen. John R. Galvin's U.S. European Command (USEUCOM) from the area under the sway of Gen. H. Norman Schwarzkopf's victorious U.S. Central Command (USCENT-COM). Up there, on the border, in the snowy mountains that divided Turkey from beaten Iraq, some 500,000 Kurds had fled into the desolate uplands. Their revolt aborted, they were dying by the score, pressed by vengeful Iraqis exacting a price for their humiliation in Kuwait. If nothing was done, the freezing weather and relentless Iraqi pursuers would finish off the Kurdish people.

Riding the crest of its smashing triumph in Kuwait, America led a coalition force into northern Iraq to save the Kurds. The success of Operation Provide Comfort, in the face of daunting odds, proved that the U.S. warpower that had devastated the Iraqi armed forces could also be used to set the conditions for humanitarian efforts. In the process, the undertaking demonstrated the versatility of America's armed forces. The strength shown in the Gulf War could do more than patrol Korea's DMZ or keep watch from a few outposts in the Sinai. The mission to Kurdistan seemed to indicate that the lessons of Beirut—inaction in the face of changing circumstances, insufficient force, and inattention to self-defense—had been learned.

By arriving in great strength on the heels of a blitzkrieg, American forces rescued a half million Kurds from annihilation and thereby offered a model of how to save others. So it appeared to many at the time. In view of what happened later in Somalia and what almost happened in Bosnia, one might argue that Provide Comfort succeeded too well.

From the outside, the whole project looked well oiled, straightforward, cheap, and almost bloodless—a piece of cake in every respect. But as always, the reality differed from these rosy impressions. To paraphrase Carl von Clausewitz's famous observation, everything in Provide Comfort was very simple, but the simplest thing was difficult.[1] Fatigue, misinformation, Murphy's Law, and looming danger—every aspect of the friction of war—applied in spades in the mountain fastness of Iraqi Kurdistan. Images aside, this one did not come easy.

Where the Kurds are involved, nothing ever comes easy. The Iraqi offensive of March 1991 was only the latest in a long, dreary record of outrages. That the Kurds suffered slaughter and atrocities hardly seems remarkable—things like that happened to them with depressing regularity. The amazing thing was that this time, somebody took notice.

About eighteen million Kurds live in the irregular expanse marked by the Lesser Caucasus Mountains of Armenia and Azerbaijan to the north, the upcountry near Tabriz, Iran, to the east, the Hilgurd Highlands above Mosul (Assyrian Nineveh of the biblical era) in Iraq to the south, and the rugged area south of Mount Ararat in Turkey to the west. Kurds reside in the six countries that contain parts of their mountain homeland: Turkey (9 million), Armenia (50,000), Azerbaijan (200,000), Iran (4 million), Iraq (3 million), and Syria (1 million).[2]

The Kurds are definitely a people set apart. They speak an Indo-European tongue akin to the Farsi spoken in Iran and a unique, written Kurdish language has been extant since the early medieval period. Unlike the Iranians, most of whom adhere to the uncompromising Shiite branch of Islam, 99 percent of the Kurds follow the more accommodating Sunni version. Throughout most of the last millenium, the Kurds have remained on their slopes and in their high-country valleys, eking out lives as herders of cattle, sheep, and goats, supplemented by subsistence farming on the rocky hill-sides. Tribal life prevails as it has from the beginning, organized around small, intimate villages and a few larger towns, all set like islands among the frozen waves of the lower mountains.[3]

Kurds have little in common with the flatlanders and outsiders who seek to rule them. Like mountain folk from the Balkans, Scotland, Afghanistan, and Appalachia, the Kurds have an independent, suspicious streak, a large stock of weapons, and a tradition of resistance. As they used to say to government agents determined to come "up holler" in West Virginia, you enter at your own risk. These people definitely shoot back.

Over the centuries, the Kurds' spirited distrust of external constraints has prompted different reactions. For centuries, they were ignored, left as a hole on the map by settled peoples more interested in dominating easier prey. After a few one-sided ambushes up in the icy passes, few had the stomach to fight these ferocious highlanders.

When the Ottoman Empire finally established a long-term claim to Kurdistan, they chose another path. Always shrewd about such matters, the empire gave up trying to pacify the Kurds. Instead, the Ottomans enlisted Kurdish warriors in the sultan's armies and granted some autonomy to the hill folk in return for their service. Given that the Kurds were fairly autonomous regardless of whatever Constantinople decreed, this seemed like a good bargain. Unfortunately for the Kurds and their neighbors, this arrangement fell apart in 1918 when the Ottoman Empire finally collapsed.

The successor states to the Ottomans turned to oppressing the Kurds, or trying to do so. This has been a popular pastime in all the host countries and a convenient focus for new states struggling to create nationalist sentiments. The Kurds have the dubious distinction of ending up on the receiving end of repression and outright liquidation campaigns in all six of their host countries, with the Iraqis resorting to particularly odious means, including widespread use of poison gas.[4] Yet the Kurds are tough. They have hung in there.

A close second to bashing one's native Kurds involves stirring up the neighbor's bunch. Examples abound. After World War II, the Soviet Union bankrolled and advised a short-lived Kurdish Republic in northwest Iran. The Iranians, both under the shah and the Ayatollah Khomeini and his ilk, have often agitated the Iraqi Kurds into rebellion or sustained ongoing insurrections—this was one of the causes of the Iran-Iraq War of the 1980s. The Iraqis have returned the favor. Syria has fomented troubles in Turkey. The list goes on and on.[5] Sometimes, it looks like anyone with arms and money can get the Kurds to rise up, if only briefly. They are itching to do it anyway.

Iraqi policy has included all of these measures. Dismissal, accommodation, repression, and agitation have characterized various phases of Iraqi behavior. Saddam Hussein, who took over in 1970, ended a long Kurdish revolt (1961–75) by ceding limited home rule (or as much as one could enjoy under a dictatorship) and cutting a deal with the shah of Iran to cease meddling with each other's Kurdish minorities. Iranian adventurism in the wake of the 1979 revolution scuttled that brief interlude of calm, leading directly to the horrific anti-Kurd campaigns of the mid-1980s, replete with eradication of entire villages by fire and toxic chemicals. By 1988, the lid was back on, at least until the Gulf War preoccupied Saddam Hussein's men.[6] The Kurdish uprising in the wake of Desert Storm merely reopened this old, remorseless struggle.

American interest in the plight of the Kurds has been, at best, inconsistent. At times, the U.S. has supported attempts to ignore, succor, quash, or inflame the Kurds, usually to influence the countries in which they live. For Iran under the shah and staunch ally Turkey, Americans either accepted the Kurdish plight or actively supported attempts to suppress insurgencies. Turkey has been afflicted by Marxist leaning Kurdish Workers' Party (PKK) guerrillas since 1984, with over thirty-five hundred lives lost in this continuing conflict. America actively sponsored Kurdish separatists against Saddam Hussein's Iraq in the early 1970s, joining with Reza Shah Pahlavi of Iran.[7] America mostly sat by during the bloody Iraqi reprisals of the 1980s, confining its responses to rhetoric as U.S. policies gradually hardened along a pro-Iraqi line. The Kurds amounted to a few more pawns on the big board.

Until Provide Comfort, Americans dealt indirectly with the Kurdish question, if at all. Kurds were just another unhappy nation without a state, more members of the globe's frustrated four billion have-nots. But in 1991, the Kurds in Iraq finally enjoyed a little luck. Their nemesis, Saddam Hussein, picked a fight with America and lost. Encouraged by American psychological operations calling for Saddam Hussein's demise and addressed generically to the Iraqi people, the Kurds thought they heard their cue. They rose up.[8] As usual, they miscalculated. This time, unexpectedly, America bailed them out.

*   *   *

When Iraqi armored forces invaded Kuwait on 2 August 1990, Saddam Hussein and his commanders expected an easy victory. They surely did not count on the American-led warpower juggernaut that swept his men out of Kuwait seven months later. Operation Desert Storm outflanked and eviscerated Iraq's military in a brilliant display of warpower in all its awesome splendor—battleships, cruisers, and submarines firing waves of lethal cruise missiles, stealth fighter-bombers ranging at will to hit Baghdad, Marines breaching obstacles and knocking out bunkers, and racing tanks spitting deadly accurate long-rod death. It was blitzkrieg Yankee style, with the appropriately named Wolf Blitzer of CNN prominent among the flocks of excited news people on hand to call the action. On-scene commanders, military historians, students of warfare, and even the bedraggled Iraqis recognized that the lopsided American-Coalition triumph had devastated Saddam Hussein's armed forces and rendered him incapable of threatening any further significant cross-border adventures for years to come.[9]

However, the allied triumph was not complete. As with Germany in November 1918, although Iraq clearly gave way, it did not surrender unconditionally, nor did Saddam Hussein's regime cease to be—far from it. Less than two years later, bitter jokers in America would heckle outgoing President George Bush with taunts that "Saddam Hussein still has his job—how about you?" The wily Iraqi dictator persisted and persists today because he managed to save enough of his armed power to keep a grip on his country, no mean accomplishment in light of his crushing defeat. Not unlike his Kurdish foes, Saddam Hussein is a survivor.

Operation Desert Storm almost destroyed the Iraqi armed forces and its politically reliable *corps d'elite,* the Republican Guard. But the key word in that statement is almost. About a third of the tanks and heavy equipment, and at least half of the men, made it out of the American pincers intact. Arguments continue about this. Some charge the Americans and their allies ceased firing too soon, and thereby let the Iraqis escape. Others applaud the Coalition for having the humanity and political sense to suspend attacks on the retreating foe along the "Highway of Death" heading north out of Kuwait City. The Coalition effort, after all, was limited to liberating Kuwait and smashing up Saddam Hussein's forces. For those purposes, almost destroyed was good enough.[10]

What did Iraq salvage from its beating? An exact accounting is difficult because sources disagree upon what the Iraqis really had at the outset.

Sources range from a high estimate of 630,000 Iraqi troops engaged to as low as 183,000, with no way of knowing the truth. This much is known: the Coalition took 86,000 prisoners and destroyed 3,847 of Iraq's 4,280 tanks in and around Kuwait, along with sundry other arms. Reliable postwar U.S. estimates determined that Iraq lost 20–22,000 troops killed in action, plus about twice that number wounded (although here the figures start to over-lap with prisoners).

It appears that five of seven Republican Guard divisions emerged at some level of effectiveness, including the 1st "Hammurabi" Armored Division at about one-third strength (the U.S.-British VII Corps pretty much destroyed the 3d "Tawakalna" Mechanized Division and nearly finished off the 2d "Medinah" Armored Division as well). Republican Guards special forces brigades made it through the conflict largely unscathed, and they turned out to be well positioned to meet the domestic unrest that convulsed Iraq in the wake of Desert Storm. Much of the Republican Guard Corps, including most of the remaining armored elements, coalesced in a ragged pocket around Basra.

Like the Guards, the rest of the Iraqi army was badly smashed up on the way out of Kuwait. Even so, thirteen divisions were still fully capable, as they had not been committed to the war. Of the thirty-five that did fight, most were badly beaten up, although individual battalions and brigades survived as relatively cohesive forces.[11] The Iraqi military surely endured terrific punishment. But though down, it was not out. Any way you mea-sured it, Iraq ended the war with hundreds of thousands of men under arms, thousands of tanks and armored vehicles, plenty of artillery, and dozens of aircraft and armed helicopters. Since they did not expend much ammunition against the Americans and their allies, these forces did not lack for bullets and shells as they turned to settle scores in the Iraqi interior.

Saddam Hussein's mauled army faced two massive problems: a Shiite revolt in and around Basra, and, hard on its heels, a Kurdish uprising in the Mosul area. Both necessitated immediate and ruthless responses. Saddam Hussein's soldiers were just the guys for that.

The Shiite rebellion erupted right under the withdrawing Iraqi forces, yet beyond the zone of southern Iraq controlled by the allies. The Shiites in the lower marshlands of the Euphrates and Tigris Rivers did not have a long history of revolt like the Kurds, but this uprising was very serious. Shiites constitute a majority in eastern Iraq and a plurality in the country. Unlike the suspect Kurds, excluded from conscription, Shiites are well represented in all ranks of the military. Anti-Baghdad sentiments among the Shiite populace, fanned as always by Shiite Iran's ayatollahs, gravely endangered Saddam Hussein's secular Baathist Party dictatorship, which depended upon Sunni Arabs and a heavy hand to keep it solvent. Within days of the allied cease-fire, the Shiites seized control of Basra and several towns along the lower Euphrates River Valley.[12] This insurrection gained momentum as the Iraqi senior commanders gathered at Safwan airfield on 3 March 1991 to discuss armistice arrangements with General Schwarzkopf.

The American and allied units, halted at the Euphrates and in a wide arc around Basra, held Kuwait and the southeastern fifth of Iraq itself. The Safwan talks formalized the Coalition's current forward trace as a temporary military demarcation line (MDL, as in Korea), with the understanding that each belligerent would stay on its side from this point onward. There had been some trouble with this as Iraq jockeyed its troops to react to the spreading Shiite disturbances. The Hammurabi Division had tried to fight through the forward battalions of the U.S. Army's 24th Infantry Division (Mechanized) on 2 March. The Americans stopped the Iraqis cold, killing hundreds of Guardsmen and knocking out 30 tanks, 147 other armored vehicles, and some 400 trucks just to make their point.[13]

At Safwan, the Iraqi generals wanted to prevent similar costly incidents. They meekly aquiesced to refraining from military provocations and honoring the proposed MDL, especially after Schwarzkopf assured them it would not be permanent. The allies would withdraw once Iraq signed the formal cease-fire agreement. When the Americans and their friends left, UN troops and observers would police a DMZ along the Iraq-Kuwait border.

Territorial matters settled, the men quickly resolved other issues: prisoner exchanges, marking and clearing of minefields and abandoned munitions, and the return of corpses for proper burials. Finally, the top Iraqi present, Lt. Gen. Sultan Hashim Ahmad, raised one point. "You know the situation of our roads and bridges and communications," he said, alluding to the extensive damage caused by allied air attacks. "We would like to fly helicopters to carry officials of our government in areas where roads and bridges are out," he explained. "This has nothing to do with the front line. This is inside Iraq."

The request sounded reasonable. American and allied bombs had smashed up much of Iraq's highway and rail systems. Schwarzkopf thought about the request, then responded carefully. "As long as it is not over the part that we are in, that is absolutely no problem. So we will let the helicopters fly." He turned to the stenographers, saying, "That is a very important point, and I want to make sure it's recorded that military helicopters can fly over Iraq. Not fighters, not bombers."

"So," Ahmad asked, "you mean even helicopters that are armed can fly in Iraqi skies, but not the fighters? Because the helicopters are the same, they transfer somebody—"

"Yeah," Schwarzkopf interrupted. "I will instruct our Air Force not to shoot at any helicopters that are flying over the territory of Iraq." That settled it.[14] The Safwan meeting ended with this apparently meager U.S. concession.

Schwarzkopf's gesture, seemingly a small thing in the aftermath of the great American triumph, made no difference with regard to the safe withdrawal of American and Coalition forces. But it pretty much sealed the fate of the Shiite rebels. That same day, Iraq marshaled its hundreds of armed and troop transport helicopters for action. The effort was spearheaded by forty or so Soviet-made Mi-24 Gorbach (Hunchback—known as Hind to NATO) armored gunships, the same type of flying monsters that scourged Afghanistan for a decade. Lifted by helicopters, backed by Mi-24s and surviving armor, Republican Guard riflemen plunged into the streets of Basra. Other heliborne battalions assaulted into the towns along the Euphrates, restoring tranquility the hard way, with bullets and high explosives.

On 4 March, as the Republican Guards started to gain a measure of control in the south, the Kurds rose up, probably encouraged by Syria. Kurdish timing, as usual, proved awful. What might have worked superbly at the height of Desert Storm proved to be disastrous after the cease-fire. The Kurds enjoyed a false spring, almost a month of free reign in the north, before the Iraqi military turned to settle accounts.

While Saddam Hussein shifted his shrunken armored brigades and helicopters south to defeat the Iranian-backed Shiites, Kurds established control over half of Kurdish Iraq. Several local defense regiments defected with their arms and ammunition, which assisted the cause. Jalal Talabani, leader of one Kurd nationalist group, claimed to have engineered the surrender of the entire Iraqi 24th Infantry Division, to include its generals. On 13 March, Kurdish bands even seized the great oil center of Kirkuk, eastern terminus of the pipeline to Turkey.[15]

Yet these achievements did not last. They could not last. To hold their gains, the Kurds needed a lot of help. They did not get it. The allies did not intervene—with Kuwait liberated, they were leaving. Near the end of

March, the 82d Airborne Division and parts of other large combat units departed. The rest followed in short order. By 8 May, all Coalition forces had left southern Iraq.

The Shiites did not even hold out that long. By late March, their uprising collapsed in blood and flames. Basra fell, houses gutted by Republican Guard tank and mechanized battalions, roofs caved in by aerial rocket barrages from orbiting helicopters. The other Shiite centers succumbed in quick succession. Thousands of refugees streamed into the Euphrates marshes. Others headed overland, toward the rapidly thinning allied lines.

Waiting to go home, American troops witnessed this sad sequence unfold. In the words of the U.S. Army's history of the Gulf War, "In full view just across military demarcation line, American forces watched helplessly as Republican Guard soldiers killed thousands of their countrymen."[16] It looked gruesome, and it was, yet nobody seriously proposed armed intervention on behalf of the Shiites. The Coalition was looking homeward, toward getting out, not going in deeper.

Coalition troops could not entirely avoid the repercussions of Iraq's internal mayhem. In southern Iraq, mechanisms created for postwar reconstruction in Kuwait were stretched to accommodate the people displaced by civil strife. The U.S. forces provided safe havens for thousands of fleeing Iraqis, to include basic services such as food, water, medicine, and, in some cases, shelter and transportation. In one area, the U.S. 2d Armored Division (Forward), a reinforced brigade, built Camp Rafha II, which served up to twenty thousand refugees at various times in April and May. But for the departing Americans, this was a transitory effort. Aided by the Saudis, nongovernmental agencies (the Red Cross and the Red Crescent, for example) took over this entire program by May.[17] Once the revolt ebbed, most of the displaced Iraqis went home anyway. For the Shiites, there would be no liberation from Baghdad's yoke.

America had joined the war to secure Kuwait and, in the south, continued to focus on that objective. By the mid-1990s, some American forces still remained in the liberated emirate, to include periodic deployments of armored battalion task forces under the Intrinsic Action exercise program. In the summer of 1992, America and its allies decreed and began to enforce a "no-fly" zone south of the thirty-second parallel, a measure announced on behalf of the Shiite refugees still tormented by Saddam Hussein's security units. This included a succession of small-scale punitive air strikes against active enemy surface-to-air and aerial targets. While these operations did prevent some aerial massacres of the Shiites, they actually served even better as an air extension of Kuwait's DMZ and, hence, Kuwaiti defense.[18] At best, like the refugee camps, it all seemed to be a relatively indirect form of support, the least America might do. The Shiites were pretty much on their own, then and now.

The collapse of the Shiite insurrection and America's evident inaction appeared to doom the Kurds. The Shiites had risen near allied front lines— but there were no sizeable American or Coalition elements in Iraqi Kurdistan, and hence no real prospect of indirect assistance. Encouraged by the decisive results in the south, free to operate without even the threat of nearby U.S. units, Saddam Hussein turned on the Kurds with a vengeance. He shuttled his heliborne and armored fire brigades north, determined to break the back of the rebellion.

It did not take long. On 29 March, after only a three-hour fight, Iraqi forces retook the important oil center of Kirkuk, then began moving north, laying waste to villages and encampments. Kurdish morale shattered, a million and a half Kurds began fleeing north, heading into the forbidding mountains along the Turkish and Iranian borders. The majority, about two-thirds, headed toward Iran. The rest went straight for Turkey.

Men, women, and children, hounded by the pitiless Iraqi helicopter gunships, climbed into the gray slopes, seeking safety. About a half million continued beyond prudence, well past the works of man, above the snow line, right into the teeth of the late mountain winter gales. Huddled like pathetic sheep in the exposed hollows, unprotected from the violent winds, snow squalls, and bitter cold, they waited for the end. Two thousand or so died every day in this freezing white hell, nature finishing off Baghdad's bloody work.[19] It looked like Saddam Hussein's men and the up-country blizzards would soon exterminate Iraq's Kurdish problems once and for all. The unblinking eye of the world news media showed it all, in living—and dying— color, perspectives rather lacking during the ugly Basra episode. This time, enough was enough. The Americans went in.

It has become popular to claim that the United States intervened in Kurdistan because of the horror story unfolding hourly on the CNN feeds. If life was a Hollywood production, there would be a nice little screenplay here: America inadvertently causes a revolt, America tries to walk away from the consequences of its efforts, America has pangs of conscience, and then, America acts. The moral—We must take responsibility for what we have done.

That sort of narrative frame appealed to the news media's Victorian gentleman, ever in search of the seemly sentiment and only too pleased to exaggerate the influence of journalism on policy makers. A facile explanation does not, however, tell the real story. There were concrete U.S. interests that spurred intervention, and they went beyond the urge to help. After all, people suffer all over the world, and the U.S. cannot and does not jump in to save all of these folks. America, in company with its allies, intervened for reasons best summarized in three words—Turkey, 688, and feasibility.

Turkey, a staunch ally of America since the onset of the Cold War back in the late 1940s, wanted action to stem the Kurdish flood. The Turks were still caring for some thirty thousand Kurds left over from the nerve gas horrors of Saddam Hussein's 1988 campaign of brutality, not to mention contending with that nasty PKK insurgency among Turkey's own Kurdish population. The prospect of half a million more unwelcome Kurds, many armed and all frustrated, did not excite the Turkish leadership. Not surprisingly, it was Turkish president Turgut Ozal who first raised the idea of safe havens for Iraq's threatened Kurds, leaving no doubt that these havens were to be carved out of northern Iraq.

Ignoring Ozal's scheme was not an option for America. During the Gulf War, led by Ozal, the Turks had reluctantly allowed U.S. airmen to stage fifty-five hundred sorties from Incirlik Air Base, an effort the Americans called Operation Proven Force. The Turks also shut down the pipeline out of Iraq (the one that originated at Kirkuk), thereby enforcing the UN economic embargo aimed at Saddam Hussein. This favor to America cost Turkey some $9 billion in lost oil revenues, a major blow to the country's economy. Few Turks appreciated that.

The deal with Washington also greatly dismayed the military, none too pleased with Ozal anyway. The Turkish armed forces' chief of staff, Gen. Necip Torumtay, resigned in protest. The generals did not relish the possibility of ground incursions by Iraqi brigades and the probability of more Kurdish trouble, likely fomented by Americans. Indeed, sensitive to these concerns, the commanders of U.S. Army Special Forces that infiltrated into Iraq to establish downed aircrew recovery networks during the war were strongly cautioned to "avoid the K-word" by the local U.S. ambassador, Morton I. Abramowitz. Beyond pilot pickups, no other special operations were permitted to be launched from Turkish soil.

By early April 1991, circumstances indicated that General Torumtay and his uneasy comrades in arms had been at least half right. As predicted, hundreds of thousands of Kurds were on the run, destination—Turkey. President Bush owed Ozal, and the Turkish president let it be known that he expected help from all his NATO allies, including the superpower across the Atlantic.[20] Keeping the Iraqi Kurds in Iraq was the biggest reason America joined the fray.

United Nations Resolution 688 was another. This pronouncement condemned "the repression of the Iraqi civilian population in many parts of Iraq, including most recently the Kurdish populated areas, the consequences of which threaten international peace and security in the region." The UN demanded that Saddam Hussein "immediately end this repression" and begin an "open dialogue" with the Kurds and others (the already broken Shiites). The UN bound the United States to "contribute to these efforts." Promulgated by the Security Council on 5 April 1991, Resolution 688 opened the way for what would become Provide Comfort.[21]

America had little choice but to join and, as usual, lead, even though Prime Minister John Major of Britain had most strongly championed UN action to aid the Kurds. Having prosecuted the Gulf War with the carefully engineered consent of the United Nations at every turn, to the tune of thirteen hand-crafted UN Security Council resolutions, President George Bush could ill afford to begin distancing himself at this point. The cease-fire was barely a month old, more than half of the American troops were still in Iraq and Kuwait, and postwar inspections of Iraq's nuclear and chemical programs were just getting started. War crimes tribunals might be held. And, of course, Kuwait's new DMZ had to be manned, and the emirate rebuilt and secured. The Coalition still had a lot of work to do. (It officially remained on call years later, as there was no formal peace treaty to end the Gulf War.) Bush had played the UN game, and now it was playing him.

Now you do not become president by being stupid. Popular opinion in America, already registering discomfort over Saddam Hussein's persistence in power, favored U.S. intervention to help the Iraqi Kurds. The million or so that entered Iran had passed beyond the realm of practical U.S. influence, and nobody dared to suggest plunging into that fundamentalist maelstrom. By comparison, jumping into shell-shocked Iraq seemed worth a try.

Bush bowed to the inevitable and had the good sense to make it look like his idea. He even sent his secretary of state, James Baker, to scout the area at the opening of a previously scheduled Middle Eastern trip. Bush said later, "We simply could not allow 500,000 to a million people to die up there in the mountains." But he also warned, "We will not intervene in Iraq's civil war."[22] Those two ideas rather neatly framed the scope of the operation that Bush ordered to begin on 7 April.

Bush gave those directives because sending a small expeditionary force into northern Iraq to protect the Kurds appeared to be feasible, largely thanks to Desert Storm. Already beaten badly, the Iraqis would likely shrink back from allied forces. In addition, the wartime arrangements with Turkey still held, and the Ankara government was more than willing to back this initiative, as were several other U.S. allies, most notably the old reliables from the Sinai, Beirut, the Gulf War, and many other conflicts and undertakings: Britain, France, and Italy. Provided the United States and its partners limited themselves to scaring off the already Yankee-shy Iraqis and creating enough security for the Kurds to go home, the whole thing might work, and at minimal cost. Security was a precondition, food critical, shelter important, and medical aid a must. The key point, though, would be avoiding intervention in the ongoing civil war. It would be delicate, but in the vacuum created by Desert Storm, some pretty special people could pull this one off. Luckily, those people were available.

The Americans did not go into Kurdistan blindly. There had been Americans on the ground in northern Iraq up until mid-March. Operational detachments (made up of a dozen Green Beret unconventional warfare specialists) of the 10th Special Forces Group (Airborne) had been active throughout the region. Supported by the MC-130E Combat Talon transports and MH-53J Pave Low III helicopters of the air force's 39th Special Operations Wing, the American teams had established a rescue and recovery system to find and retrieve downed allied airmen.

The pilot recovery network fell under the authority of Brig. Gen. Richard W. Potter Jr., normally the head of Special Operations Command, Europe (SOCEUR), the special warfare component of Galvin's USEUCOM. SOCEUR regularly commanded joint operations with the 10th Special Forces and 39th Wing, and Potter maintained a deployable forward headquarters configured for just such tasks. During the Gulf War, he worked for Maj. Gen. James L. Jamerson, commander of JTF Proven Force, the air combat and support forces that flew out of Incirlik Air Base in southern Turkey. In order to get a long reach into Iraq, Potter had created a forward operating base for his heliborne contingents on an eastern Turkish airfield at Batman, a real place with a name better than anything even Green Berets could cook up.

Batman was a bare-bones facility, consisting of a lone airstrip, a helipad, and a fresh water source. Jamerson gave Potter a composite air force base emergency engineering force (known as Prime BEEF) to build a modicum of decent facilities, and these people went to work with a vengeance. Sustained and directed from Batman, Potter's forces roamed throughout Kurdish Iraq, ready to react if any Incirlik planes went down. During the entire air effort, only one such mission was mounted, and that for an aircraft flying out of Saudi Arabia. Even so, the SOCEUR pilots and special operators gained a good feel for the mountainous area and made contact with many of the Kurdish clans around Mosul.[23] This experience greatly expedited events during the opening days of Operation Provide Comfort.

Jamerson and Potter were alerted on 6 April to begin supply airdrops to the Kurdish camps the next morning. By 1900 that night, the two commanders were en route back to Incirlik, accompanied by small staffs. They reopened their respective headquarters. By 1100 the next morning, the first two MC-130Es of 39th Wing kicked out the first bundles to the Kurds just north of the Turkish border.[24] Provide Comfort had begun.

Fighter and attack aircraft from Europe flew into Incirlik, followed by several C-130 Hercules air transport squadrons, some from NATO allies. Ungainly A-10A Thunderbolt IIs, the armored tank-killing Warthogs that had scourged the Republican Guards's vehicle columns during Desert Storm, flew ahead of the transports to scout out drop zones for the slower airlifters. Turkish RF-4C Phantom IIs rigged for reconnaissance aided this effort. By 9 April, the allies had flown thirty-nine sorties (thirty-one by Americans) and dropped eighty-six tons, an impressive amount. But this was not enough.

Feeding a half million refugees by parachute drops might barely do the job, given a steady commitment of airpower, favorable weather, and rapid reaction by the receiving parties. It took approximately 340 tons a day, about sixteen C-130 sorties, to deliver less than a pound and a half of food to each Kurd in the camps—obviously, the allies were finding it tough to deliver that much. Even this minimal level of sustenance did nothing to solve the growing problems of exposure, disease, and security from Iraqi attacks. Worse, the bundles blew here and there in the high winds, rolled down mountain slopes, broke apart among sharp rocks, and, in a few unfortunate instances, crushed crowds of people running to meet the descending food pallets. One assessment rated the attempts as having "minimal impact on the suffering."[25]

Secretary of State Baker's personal tour of Turkish refugee camps on 9 April confirmed that the parachute deliveries were not effective. The Americans could not just stand off and drop things on mobs of freezing, starving people. To succeed, U.S. forces had to go in on the ground, and though that would start in Turkey, there could be little doubt that matters would draw Americans into hostile Iraq—pure Indian country. Baker knew it, and so did Galvin at EUCOM. Circumstances demanded action. Galvin acted.

Orders changed that same day. Jamerson was told to insert his Special Forces (SF) troopers to assist airdrops, organize camps, supervise food and water distribution, and help with sanitation and medical care. This expanded role went to the arriving teams from the 1st Battalion, 10th Special Forces. The SF A-Detachments had the expertise to enter Iraq, talk to the refugees in the Kurdish tongue, and establish drop zones for aerial resupply. Additionally, 39th Special Operations Wing MH-53J helicopters, backed up initially by navy special-duty helicopters that had brought in the Baker party, began ferrying supplies to makeshift landing zones marked and secured by the Green Berets.[26]

As the special warfare units moved into the Turkish mountains, three things became obvious: the mission had to be defined, more forces brought in, and a reasonable chain of command set up. Trying to wing it with the lightly armed residue of JTF Proven Force courted disaster in the face of advancing Iraqi Republican Guards brigades, and the Kurds might not survive long enough for the United States to try various experiments. Provide Comfort could not accomplish its purpose on the cheap. Between 9 and 16 April, therefore, the Americans, in concert with their allies, got organized to do the job the right way.

General Galvin did not receive much of a mission initially, being told over the telephone little more than "stop the dying." Of course, more carefully formulated instructions followed. But if any general could function with almost no guidance, Galvin was that man. A thoughtful soldier whose record reflected both combat experience in Vietnam as a battalion commander in the 1st Cavalry Division (Airmobile) and a succession of solid books and articles on topics ranging from air assault operations to the American Revolution, Galvin had come to Europe after a stint as commander in chief of U.S. Southern Command, steward of American interests in perenially unsettled Latin America. He knew a thing or two about the relationship between policy goals and warpower, and so the CINC did not wait for the paperwork. He assessed his situation and went at it.

Throughout the Gulf War, Galvin had carefully monitored developments in Iraq, and his performance as both USEUCOM and NATO commander in support of USCENTCOM ensured the timely arrival of combat-ready American and allied units of all services. JTF Proven Force, mounted rapidly and carried out professionally, typified USEUCOM's dedication to giving Schwarzkopf everything he needed to defeat Iraq. The Kurdish uprising and its grim aftermath, though, fell into Galvin's sphere. And these developments did not catch him or his USEUCOM or NATO staffs napping.

Galvin realized early on that he had his work cut out for him: "Stopping the dying and the misery up in the mountains and then find a workable scheme to relocate the refugees to places still unknown to us at that time where we would be able to sustain them. Then, as rapidly as we could, to transition this operation to the United Nations High Commissioner for Refugees or some other similar organization."[27] Here, in embryo, was the concept for Provide Comfort.

Galvin eventually codified the mission in these terms: "Combined/Joint Task Force (CJTF) Provide Comfort [on deployment] conducts multinational humanitarian operations [in Turkey and Iraq] to provide immediate relief to displaced Iraqi civilians until international relief agencies and private voluntary organizations can assume overall supervision." The complete text of the order specified the humanitarian tasks, which included delivery of relief supplies by air and land, development of transit camps near relief sites, movement of displaced Kurds back to their homes, and withdrawal of the force.

Yet Provide Comfort was not just a portable NATO soup kitchen. Right from the outset, Galvin believed that moving the Kurds out of the mountains was essential. Because they could not go deeper into Turkey, the refugees had to go back to Iraq, back toward those bent on killing them. With this in mind, the CINC displayed no illusions about the nature of the environment and the potential for violence. Galvin spelled out the use of warpower in Provide Comfort. He directed creation of a secure zone in Iraq around the Kurdish camps and villages, mandated establishment of a strong combat air patrol to deny Iraqi flights over the security zone, and told his commanders to be ready to fight Iraqi forces as necessary to keep the Kurds and their zone safe.[28] Security and force protection came first, then relief. The allied forces would go in with their eyes open and their powder dry, loaded for bear.

Given that Iraqi forces in the area totaled three fresh divisions and at least one Republican Guard brigade, the allies could not be expected to intervene with a token troop strength. Accordingly, America and its partners assembled a large force. The organization grew to greater than division strength by 1 June, totaling twenty thousand personnel from eleven countries, aided (and sometimes hindered) by the Turks, an occasional twelfth associate. More than half of those involved were Americans.

CJTF Provide Comfort drew its fighting battalions from the cream of units remaining in Europe in the wake of Desert Storm. All of the ground maneuver units were elite, worthy reinforcements for the 10th Special Forces already in country. From the Sixth Fleet in the Mediterranean came the U.S. 24th Marine Expeditionary Unit (MEU), complete with the usual array of air and service support elements; it had been designated "special operations capable," which meant the unit had been trained specifically for OOTW. By air from its post at Vicenza, Italy, came the 3-325th Airborne Battalion Combat Team, built around the paratroopers of the 3d Battalion, 325th Airborne Infantry, who had served for years as part of NATO's mobile reaction force. Great Britain contributed 3 Commando Brigade, including 40 and 45 Commandos of the Royal Marines, the latter battalion-sized organization direct from patrols in Northern Ireland. France sent its renowned 3d Paramarines, veterans of fighting in Chad. The Netherlands provided its 1st Airborne Commando Group, and Spain and Italy also contributed reinforced paratrooper battalion task forces. Many of these battalions had trained together on previous NATO exercises or on bilateral exchanges. While CJTF Provide Comfort featured a thoroughly mixed force, its line battalions shared a warrior ethos that overcame many differences in language, tactical style, and experiences.[29]

It was well known that the Iraqis feared allied air attacks, so a powerful air armada backed up the ground combat units that would need to enter Iraq. Built around the U.S. Air Force 7440th Composite Wing, the air combat organization formed for Proven Force, the Americans assembled an impressive array of airpower. The American aircraft included F-16 Fighting Falcons and F-15 Eagles for air superiority, A-10A "Warthogs" for close air support, EF-111A "Spark Varks" to jam enemy radars and communications, F-4G "Wild Weasels" to attack hostile air defenses, and E-3A Airborne

Warning and Control System (AWACS) planes to sort all of it out. In addition, aircraft launched by the aircraft carrier USS *Theodore Roosevelt* contributed their share of combat sorties. Finally, large numbers of army, Marine, and allied attack helicopters supplemented this air umbrella, among them swift U.S. Army AH-64A Apaches equipped with high-resolution thermal sights.[30]

Combined/Joint Task Force Provide Comfort (as of 1 June 1991)

CJTF Headquarters (Incirlik, Turkey)

Task Force Alpha (Silopi, Turkey)

10th Special Forces Group (Airborne) (Silopi, Turkey)
1st Battalion, 10th SFG (A)
2d Battalion, 10th SFG (A)
3d Battalion, 10th SFG (A)
40 Commando, Royal Marines [Britain]
Infantry Platoon [Luxembourg]
Elements, 4th Psychological Operations Group
39th Special Operations Wing (+)

Task Force Bravo (Zakho, Iraq)

24th Marine Expeditionary Unit (Dihok, Iraq)
Battalion Landing Team 2/8 Marines (-)
3-325th Airborne Battalion Combat Team (-) (ABCT)
Marine Medium Helicopter Squadron 264 (+)
24th Marine Service Support Group
418th Civil Affairs Company
79 Battery, Royal Artillery [Britain]
Detachment, 9th Special Forces [Italy]

3 Commando Brigade [Britain] (Sirsenk, Iraq)
45 Commando [Britain]
1st Airborne Commando Group (-) [Netherlands]
29 Royal Artillery Regiment (-) [Britain]
Commando Aviation Battalion [Britain]
96th Civil Affairs Battalion (-)
59 Company, Royal Engineers [Britain]
Logistics Company [Australia]

Airborne Task Force [France] (Suri, Iraq)
3d Regiment de Parachutistes d'Infanterie de Marine [France]
Logistics Battalion [France]
Hospital [France/Spain]
Company E, 2/8 Marines
Team, 96th Civil Affairs Battalion
Detachment, 9th Special Forces [Italy]

Airborne Task Force [Italy] (Zakho, Iraq)
5th Airborne Battalion [Italy]
9th Special Forces (-) [Italy]
Logistics Battalion [Italy]
Field Hospital [Italy]
Company A, 3-325th Airborne
431st Civil Affairs Company (-)

Airborne Task Force [Spain] (Zakho, Iraq)

18th Engineer Brigade (Zakho, Iraq)
94th Engineer Battalion (Combat, Heavy)
133d Navy Mobile Construction Battalion
39th Civil Engineering Squadron
Air Force Prime BEEF (5 teams)
11th Engineer Battalion (+) [Netherlands]
51 Field Squadron [Britain]
Platoon, 6 Field Squadron [Britain]
524 Detachment, Royal Engineers [Britain]

18th Military Police Brigade (Silopi, Turkey)
709th Military Police Battalion (-)
284th Military Police Company
527th Military Police Company
Elements, 36th Security Police Squadron

Combined Support Command (Silopi, Turkey)

51st Maintenance Battalion (-)
65th Maintenance Battalion
66th Maintenance Battalion
70th Transportation Battalion
72d Signal Battalion
Contingency Marine Air-Ground Task Force 1-91
39th Tactical Group Hospital

48th Tactical Fighter Wing Air Transportable Hospital
Field Hospital [Netherlands]
Ambulance Platoon [Canada]

Civil Affairs Command (Incirlik, Turkey)

353d Civil Affairs Command
354th Civil Affairs Brigade (-)
432d Civil Affairs Company
Elements, 96th Civil Affairs Battalion (-)

Combined Air Forces (Incirlik, Turkey)

7440th Composite Wing (Incirlik, Turkey)
Elements, 20th Tactical Fighter Wing (EF-111A)
Elements, 36th Tactical Fighter Wing (F-15)
Elements, 52d Tactical Fighter Wing (F-4G)
Elements, 81st Tactical Fighter Wing (A-10A)
Elements, 86th Tactical Fighter Wing (F-16C)
Elements, 302d Tactical Airlift Wing (C-130)
Elements, 552d Airborne Warning and Control Wing (E-3A)
Elements, 37th Tactical Airlift Squadron (C-130)
Elements, 61st Tactical Airlift Squadron (C-130)
Elements, European Tanker Task Force (KC-135R)

JTF-A Army Aviation Task Force (Diyarbakir, Turkey)
Company D, 502d Aviation (CH-47D)
Company E, 502d Aviation (CH-47D)
Troop S, 11th Armored Cavalry Regiment (UH-60A)
4-81st Helicopter (UII-60A) [Gcrmany]

JTF-B Army Aviation Task Force (Zakho, Iraq)
Aviation Brigade Headquarters, 3d Infantry Division (Mechanized)
6th Squadron, 6th Cavalry (AH-64A)
Company G, 6th Cavalry (OH-58D)
159th Medical Detachment (Air Ambulance) (UH-60 medevac)
Rifle Platoon from 3-325th ABCT
Antiarmor Section from 3-325th ABCT

Airlift Element [Belgium]
Royal Air Force Element [Britain]
Air Transport Group [Canada]
Airlift Element [France]
Airlift Element [Italy]

Aviation Element [Spain]
Aviation Element [Germany] (restricted to Turkish airspace)

In support: (Mediterranean Sea)

Task Force 60: USS *Theodore Roosevelt* Carrier Battle Group

Task Force 61: Navy Amphibious Group 8

All units are U.S. except as noted.

Sources: Lt. Gen. John H. Cushman, USA (Ret.), "Joint, Jointer, Jointest," *Proceedings* (May 1992): 80; Sid Balman Jr., "Wing Shifts to Refugee-Relief Flights," *Air Force Times*, (22 April 1991), 16; John T. Fishel, *Liberation, Occupation, and Rescue: War Termination and Desert Storm* (Carlisle Barracks, Pa.: Strategic Studies Institute, 31 August 1992), 53–56; Lt. Col. Gordon W. Rudd, USA, "Operation PROVIDE COMFORT: One More Tile in the Mosaic," (unpublished manuscript U.S. Army Center of Military History, 1991), 6–22; Donna Miles, "Helping the Kurds," *Soldiers* (July 1991): 13–20.

Equally important, perhaps more important in the trackless high country, the Americans and their friends brought in a large number of transport aircraft and cargo helicopters. Most of the airlift elements relied on varied models of the Lockheed C-130 Hercules, a rugged turboprop transport eminently suited for parachute drops and dirt strip landings. The French used their similar C-160 Transall. Helicopters employed included the brawny H-53 series (U.S. Marines, Air Force, and Navy) and twin-rotor CH-47 Chinooks (U.S. Army and some of the Europeans), plus an assortment of smaller troop-haulers and utility models that included the impressive, sturdy U.S. Army UH-60A Blackhawk and venerable U.S. Marine CH-46E Sea Knights, usually called Frogs.[31] Airpower in all its forms offered the great equalizer in Provide Comfort, granting the allies lethality, mobility, and speed that could not be matched by the Iraqi opposition.

The CJTF also included combat support and combat service support elements drawn from all services, with some augmentation from America's partners. Engineers and military police would be especially handy in creating and securing transit camps. Civil affairs organizations, trained to run military governments and interact with local officials and community leaders, created links to the Turks, the various Kurd factions, the U.S. Department of State, and nongovernmental organizations like CARE International.

They also built and administered refugee transfer facilities and oversaw reoccupation of Kurdish villages when that became possible. Mostly drawn from the U.S. Army Reserve, these small but unique units came in directly from work with the Kuwaitis and Shiites in the south.[32]

To put this joint, international effort into motion, Galvin chose Lt. Gen. John M. Shalikashvili, at that time the deputy commander of U.S. Army forces in Europe. It is standard military practice to meet contingencies by forming ad hoc units using deputies or chiefs of staff as temporary commanders. This preserves the basic chain of command for the ongoing, primary mission.[33] In Galvin's USEUCOM, he could not afford to part with his only remaining deployable U.S. headquarters, V Corps. With VII Corps still in southern Iraq cleaning up after Desert Storm, somebody had to hold the line against the Soviets, still a threat of sorts in those final days of the Gorbachev era. So Galvin turned to his most available army lieutenant general, Shalikashvili.

Shalikashvili was the right man for the job for other reasons more important than his relative availability. If anyone understood the plight of refugees and grasped the nuances of thorny political-military situations, especially dealing with European allies, it was this extraordinary soldier. Born in Warsaw, Poland, in 1936 to a Polish mother and a Georgian father who had fled the Russian Bolshevik upheaval, Shalikashvili and his family emigrated to Germany when Poland fell under Nazi rule at the start of World War II. The boy attended school under the Third Reich while his father fought in the German armed forces. By 1945, the Shalikashvilis, like many other Europeans, had nowhere to go—Poland and a third of Germany had fallen under Russian Communist domination, and Communist Georgia was, of course, out of the question. Shalikashvili knew what it was like to be chased from a home by ruthless armed men. He was not a Kurd, but he had been in their shoes.

Like so many other people uprooted by the war, the Shalikashvilis came to America, to Peoria, Illinois, no less. Young John joined the army as a private and was selected for Officer Candidate School, from which he received a commission in the field artillery. Shalikashvili served in Vietnam as a senior district adviser in 1968–69, getting a good look at the spasmodic, bloody village war. Along with the usual succession of unit commands from battery to division, Shalikashvili also served on the joint staff in Korea during the tense times of the early 1970s, and as the G3 (senior operations chief) of the Southern European Task Force, the headquarters that owned the American airborne battalion task force that had joined his Provide Comfort team. He headed up political-military sections in the Army Staff and the strategy segment of the Joint Staff. Shalikashvili's several tours in Europe, reinforced by his fluency in German, Polish, and Russian and crowned by his service as the deputy commander of the army component of Galvin's NATO forces, ensured that he had the talent to assemble and command a multinational force.[34] He had done well in his basic soldiering, and he had both skill and experience in wrestling with issues exactly like those transpiring in northern Iraq. So "Shali" got the nod.

Shalikashvili was at Incirlik by 16 April. He found that Jamerson and Potter had essentially reestablished JTF Proven Force, built around the 39th Wing and 10th Special Forces, along with a good-sized assortment of fighters and attack planes. The progression to heliborne supply deliveries would suffice to stop the dying along the border, but it was at best a Band-Aid to the overall question of Kurds in Turkey. Now the challenge was to keep the mountain relief going, quickly move the Kurds into a cleared area, and then get out (or at least get back to Turkey). That required a more complex CJTF structure.

The new commander rearranged things accordingly. Ideally, Shalikashvili would have taken a corps level headquarters from Europe, but thanks to Desert Storm, the cupboard was bare. So he improvised. He pulled up the senior air force general, Jamerson, to be his deputy and designated the senior Marine Corps officer, Brig. Gen. Anthony C. Zinni, as his chief of staff. These officers drew together a staff, bringing in individuals from USEUCOM, the various service component headquarters in Europe, and augmentees and liaisons from the allied forces. All of these people coalesced around Jamerson's Proven Force structure, already in place.

With his headquarters forming up, Shalikashvili settled upon a CJTF with five subordinate pieces, designated by function, and each also joint and combined in nature. He renamed Potter's special warfare team Task Force Alpha, with the mission to contact and care for the Kurds, then move them south when so ordered. He created a Task Force Bravo, made up of his pastiche of elite NATO infantry battalions, and directed them to carve out a secure zone in northern Iraq so that the Kurds could go home. All airpower, less the Marine aviation habitually associated with 24th MEU, came under a combined air force; this air component promised mobility and firepower on call. A combined support command handled all logistics. Finally, the civil affairs command, built around units hastily transferred from Kuwait and southern Iraq, orchestrated all ties to the Turks, the UN relief agencies, the other humanitarian organizations, and the various Kurdish leaders.

Interestingly, the soft-spoken Shalikashvili never allowed the usual who's-on-first debates to start up. He signed no memoranda of understanding, nor did he indulge the various flag officers leading the U.S. service and foreign national contingents. Shalikashvili simply announced the command arrangements, assumed tactical control of all forces, and got on with it. CJTF Provide Comfort worked directly for Shalikashvili, and he reported solely to Galvin. It was neat, clean, and workable, a tribute to years of NATO cooperation and exercises even though it violated many painstakingly negotiated alliance agreements on who should be in charge, reporting channels, and the like.[35] Confronted with people dying by the thousands and a once-beaten opponent waiting to pounce, the allies dared not waste time on bureaucratic wrangling. It was time to act.

The allies were hopping into murky waters in Kurdistan—a polyglot stew of friends, foes, and not-sures. The scenario writers at Fort Polk's JRTC borrowed liberally from this lineup as they cooked up their peace operations exercise in the autumn of 1993, but they could not hope to do justice to the confused situation that confronted CJTF Provide Comfort in late April of 1991. This one redefined the term "ambiguity."

Some things were relatively known. At the friendly end of the spectrum were all the humanitarian groups, each with its own portfolio, and none particularly amenable to Shalikashvili's authority. Most helpful and responsive to military requirements was the U.S. Agency for International Development's Disaster Assistance Response Team (DART), headed by Fred Cuny, a former Marine. The DART took the lead, in concert with the CJTF's Civil Affairs Command, in sorting out and coordinating nearly sixty disparate sources of volunteer assistance for the Kurds. The DART worked closely with the various UN groups, such as the World Food Program, World Health Organization, the Office of the High Commissioner for Refugees, and the International Children's Education Fund, all of which provided general humanitarian relief beyond their basic charters.

Private organizations addressed more specialized concerns. For example, CARE International worked on staple food distribution, Save the Children did just that, and the French-based Medicines sans Frontiers (Doctors without Borders) handled medical matters. Full of energy and goodwill, but suspicious of soldiers, these people became converts to Shalikashvili's cause and, as planned, eventually assumed the follow-on support to the Kurdish communities.[36]

The hostile end of the spectrum was also clear. The Iraqis were the Bad Guys. Just for extra friction, they came in three varieties: the Special Police, the Republican Guards, and the regular forces, each a bit more hard-nosed than the next. A deal made with one set of Iraqis did not necessarily affect the others. And though they had weapons and the desire to use them, they were not always ready to fight. At times, they preferred to negotiate rather than shoot back.[37]

In the middle somewhere were the Turks and Kurds, more friends than enemies to CJTF Provide Comfort, but with little tolerance for each other. Steeled by years of firefights with the PKK faction, Turkish forces had no love for Kurdish refugees. Like American frontier troopers trying to sort out reservation Indians from renegade braves, many Turkish soldiers thought the only good Kurds were dead Kurds. The Turks would help the Americans shoo these people back across the border and had few qualms about weakening Iraq.[38] If the allies were hoping for wholehearted Turkish assistance and humanitarian largess, they could forget it.

The displaced Kurds, the object of this whole endeavor, featured three major subgroups: a few from the left wing PKK, most from the Kurdish Democratic Party (KDP), and some from the Patriotic Union of Kurdistan (PUK). Each bunch had its own armed *peshmergas* (guerrilla fighters), more than willing to fight each other whenever the Iraqis and Turks backed off. Of the three factions, the PKK were by far the most dangerous, vociferously anti-Western with ties to the Hezbollah terrorists in Lebanon. The KDP had worked with the American CIA in the 1970s, but the failure of that Kurdish revolt left no happy memories on either side. Finally, the PUK leadership was for whatever the KDP was against, except for occasional alliances of convenience. The rather regimented PKK leaned toward the Syrians, remaining resolutely opposed to the Turks and Iraqis. The other two groups, though, swayed alternately toward the Turks, Syrians, Iranians, or even the Iraqis, in a confusing minuet.[39]

Starving and freezing, the Kurds were willing to put aside their squabbles and cooperate. But with full bellies and warm bodies—well, then the fun would start, and the allies be damned. With the Kurds, Shalikashvili's forces could not afford to take anything for granted.

*   *   *

Surrounded by this highly charged atmosphere, Task Force Alpha set up its headquarters at Silopi, closer to the border than the old base at Batman. The task force expanded quickly as April went on, gradually extending its network of Green Beret teams to the east, toward the Iranian border. All three 10th Special Forces battalions, with eighteen A-teams each, had entered the theater by late April, with the 3d Battalion crossing into Iraq proper to make its linkups.

These twelve-man teams, commanded by a captain with a warrant officer as his deputy, also included a senior team sergeant (the top NCO), two weapons sergeants, two demolitions experts, two communications sergeants, an intelligence NCO, and two highly trained medical corpsmen. All held sergeant rank, earned by hard experience in line battalions. All had passed through grueling special warfare selection and qualification courses. Along with being expert in his own field, each soldier had been cross-trained in each other's skills.

In most situations, the Green Berets would organize their own guerrilla force, up to a battalion per team. But training Kurd guerrillas was not the mission. Gaining their trust, helping them survive and then return home, and protecting them as necessary comprised the special forces' tasks. Mao Tse-tung would have understood and approved.

The A-teams had the right mix of talents to accomplish this mission, especially in concert with the hard-charging pilots of the 39th Special Operations Wing, their comrades on many missions, including those conducted throughout Desert Storm. Some teams spoke the Kurdish dialects, but most did not. The 10th Special Forces had responsibilities across Europe, mostly on the far side of the old Iron Curtain, so languages like German, Polish, and Hungarian predominated. The teams brought in additional linguists, medics, and physicians from the Army National Guard's 20th Special Forces to buttress their efforts.[40]

There was nowhere to go but up. The first Green Berets to arrive encountered a pathetic tableau. Major Lloyd Gilmore, commanding Company C, 2d Battalion, 10th Special Forces, described the first camp he entered near Pirinceken, Turkey, as "Woodstock without the music": twenty thousand listless, shivering, hollow-eyed people squatting in the sleet and snow, ankle-deep in the churned swill of their own fetid waste. The only active area was the cemetery, which gained about fifty new graves every day. Gilmore and his men had their work cut out.

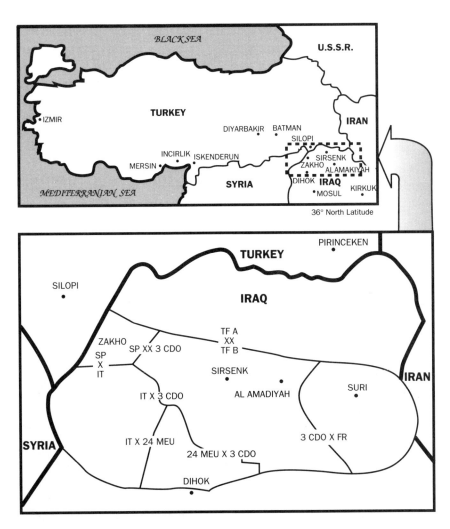

24 MEU   24th Marine Expeditionary Unit (United States)
3 CDO   3 Commando Brigade, Royal Marines (Britain)
FR   French Airborne Task Force
IT   Italian Airborne Task Force
SP   Spanish Airborne Task Force

Operation Provide Comfort, 1991

Step one involved getting the Kurds to take charge of their own survival. A few dozen individuals, even highly trained Green Berets, cannot save twenty thousand souls without some help from the victims. Gilmore and his men shared tea with the Kurd elders and gained their confidence. The fact that the Americans came to stay, carried weapons, and could summon armed helicopters and jets impressed the Kurds, both by appealing to their warlike strain and implying a legitimate counter to the hated Iraqi tanks and attack helicopters.[41] With evidence that a security umbrella was going up, the Americans and the Kurdish elders started right at the basic level: food, shelter, and sanitation.

Food came first. Initially, hungry refugees ate whatever they got, to include calorie-rich Meals, Ready-to-Eat (MREs), the standard U.S. military fare. American manufacturers did not adhere to Islamic dietary prescriptions, lacing these rations with lots of pork, ham, and similar items offensive to Muslims but popular with American consumers. Once the Kurds had enough to eat and access to other foods, they avoided MREs, preferring traditional staples like rice, wheat flour, lentils, and vegetable oil. These provisions came through organizations like CARE, often purchased from Turkish markets and transported by leased Turkish commercial trucks. Bulk stocks were available by late April.

The Green Berets were also given other food products to pass out, which they and the relief workers issued to mixed reviews. Candy entranced and delighted Kurdish children, and adults also sampled approvingly. Potatoes generated some interest, especially when cooking oil was available to fry them. Canned peas and meat were big hits.

On the other hand, certain commodities did not work at all. Attempts to give the people corn left over from Desert Shield Thanksgiving feasts proved especially unpopular. The Kurds would not touch the stuff, which to them was fit only to feed livestock. They also refused to try a shipment of excess Thanksgiving cranberry sauce or a large consignment of puffed cheeseball snacks—this particular junk food could not even entice teenaged American Marines and soldiers. By early May, Kurdish families who once rioted over access to pallets of MREs rejected them out of hand and demanded rice.[42] Pickiness was actually a good sign. Satisfied, healthy Kurds could afford to be discriminating.

Shelter was as important as food. Persistent cold rains, sleet, and even a few late snows took a toll on the Kurds. Until they could be returned to their homes in northern Iraq, they needed to get out of the weather. Tentage and used parachutes allowed for expedient protection, but the best materials turned out to be heavy plastic sheets supplied by the Germans. Provided in great profusion, nearly indestructible, and easy to roll up and move, this material did the job until full-scale transit camps were ready to support the move out of the mountains.[43]

Finally, along with sustenance and shelter, something had to be done about the unrelenting filth. Hungry and weak from exposure, the Kurds had ceased to care about rudimentary sanitation. Most were longtime village dwellers unaccustomed to roughing it. Garbage and animal carcasses had been strewn around the living areas and near water sources. Careless refugees even eliminated their bodily wastes in the running water, then drank, cooked, and washed in the same streams. The resultant diarrhea accelerated the disease cycle, leading to dehydration, weakness, and death—people literally defecating themselves into oblivion. The Special Forces sergeants went right to work.

In company with the village elders, Major Gilmore's team collected and burned trash, buried dead animals, and taught boiling and cleaning techniques, as well as how to dig, use, and close down field latrines. Green Berets gave candy to children who brought back full garbage bags—trash and treat. Engineers assisted with drilling new wells and piping in fresh water as required. Coupled with food and shelter, these efforts had immediate effects. "We know we're doing some good," said Sgt. Mike Conlon.[44]

The experiences of Gilmore's team occurred over and over again along the border, with minor variations. Tough Special Forces sergeants, reinforced by British Royal Marines of 40 Commando, made common cause with the refugees. The men splinted fractured arms, taught English, assisted in births of babies and goats, and even sang lullabies to tired children. Well, Mao had told his guerrilla cadres to become one with the people. The Kurds learned to trust the Green Beret soldiers and Royal Marines, as well as their heliborne flying comrades who delivered the goods. When the Americans and British told them it was safe to go home, they believed, packed up, and moved out.

With full stomachs, access to shelter, and good health, not to mention cars, carts, and hoofed stock mended by the American Green Berets and their British allies, the Kurds headed for home. The first groups started south as early as 2 May. Proceeding smoothly along cleared routes, fed and housed in sturdy transit camps, and succored by military and civilian agencies, the returning populace displayed a festive mood far different from the desperation that marked their original flight into the mountains. The temporary camps emptied out rapidly as May wore on.

Things went so well that Task Force Alpha closed up shop on 8 June, mission accomplished.[45] The Kurds were home or en route. The reason they had a safe place to go related to Task Force Bravo. Like the special warriors, they had not been idle. And unlike most of the Green Berets, Task Force Bravo had met the Iraqi military face to face, muzzle to muzzle.

During Desert Storm, Coalition airpower had paved the way into Iraq. The roving attack jets set the conditions that allowed for a swift ground advance. CJTF Provide Comfort entered northern Iraq with memories of that allied aerial might, a recollection enhanced by a bold foray of a more personal variety. On 19 April, Lt. Gen. John Shalikashvili, accompanied by a small staff element and a U.S. Marine armed escort, flew to Habur Bridge, a border crossing into Iraq not far north of Zakho. The American came to parley with the Iraqi senior military officials in the region. Shalikashvili intended to inform and warn, not negotiate.

Waiting for Shalikashvili was Brig. Gen. Danoun Nashwan, the senior Iraqi military representative in the area. Nashwan listened in uncomfortable silence as Shalikashvili dictated the terms for allied entry into Iraqi Kurdistan. CJTF Provide Comfort was there to help the Kurds get home, not fight Iraqis—but if the Iraqis wished to test the allies, they could expect a fight, and the ever-present air force warplanes left little doubt how that contest would turn out. Allied forces intended to enter Iraq the next morning to secure a zone centered on Zakho, a Kurdish city of 150,000 reduced to a few thousand by the March exodus. The Iraqis must withdraw some twenty miles from Zakho in all directions (out of the range of most tube artillery) and offer no resistance. Over the security zone, soon clarified to extend as far south as the thirty-sixth parallel of latitude, the CJTF reserved the authority to destroy any Iraqi flying machine of any type not expressly cleared by the allies. Brigadier General Nashwan grudgingly acknowledged these points.

To help prevent unintended incidents and hostilities as CJTF Provide Comfort entered Iraq, Shalikashvili directed the formation of a Military Coordination Center composed of allied, Kurdish, and Iraqi representatives. U.S. Army Col. Richard Naab headed the allied team, and Nashwan spoke for the Iraqis. The resultant committee resembled the Korean peninsula's often contentious Military Armistice Commission. As in Korea, the forum was only as effective as the allied willingness to use warpower to back up their challenges.[46] Shalikashvili was willing to act, and he and his forces left no doubt about that over the next few days.

On 20 April, as promised, Task Force Bravo entered Iraq under the command of Maj. Gen. Jay M. Garner, deputy commander of the U.S. Army's V Corps. Like Shalikashvili, Garner had deployed to meet the contingency. Now, with only a five-man staff to call his own (V Corps could spare no more), Garner piggybacked onto Col. James L. Jones's 24th MEU headquarters.[47] The Marines were ready to go.

Organized into their usual balanced air-ground team, 24th MEU spearheaded the allied push south. Launching from Silopi, covered by screaming air force Warthogs and fighters and their own AH-1W SuperSeaCobra attack choppers, the Marines helicoptered into a landing zone east of Zakho, then fanned out to the south and west to isolate the city. Iraqis of the 44th Infantry Division watched from the heights. Unbeknownst to the enemy, hidden Marine Force Reconnaissance and SEAL teams were keeping Jones fully informed about Iraqi reactions.

Over the next few days, a tense showdown ensued. Garner and Jones had several face-to-face meetings with stubborn Iraqi officers. The Iraqis did not want to fight, but they did not want to leave either. Some three hundred Iraqi Special Police filed into town to maintain law and order in the event the Iraqis withdrew. As unproductive talks and evasive excuses continued, the American Marines patiently and methodically improved their positions on the outskirts of Zakho, scaring off several Iraqi outposts. Garner wanted the Iraqis out and the road back to Silopi open. Would he have to fight a pitched battle to achieve that?

On 22 April, two superb battalions arrived to beef up 24th MEU's 2/8 Marines: 45 Commando of the British Royal Marines and the 1st Airborne Commando Group of the Royal Netherlands Marines. The British had just left Ulster and were in no mood to play games in city streets. These welcome, timely reinforcements raised the allied strength to some thirty-four hundred Marines, backed by strong and very evident airpower. That same day, Garner told his counterpart in no uncertain terms to get out of town. Early the next morning, the Iraqi soldiers began withdrawing.[48]

The heavily armed Special Police battalion remained, and, clearly, that could not be tolerated. The Kurds would never come home to face those people. Garner again sent word through the Military Coordination Center— Iraqis out of Zakho. He backed up his demand with warpower, sealing off all routes with his American Marines to the east, south, and southwest and with the Dutch Marines to the northwest, astride the road back to Silopi, Turkey. American air force and navy fighters and attack planes roared low across the valley in a continual show of force. With Zakho ringed and targeted by aerial firepower, Garner sent the elite British 45 Commando into the city, accompanied by U.S. Marine Light Armored Vehicles (LAVs), wheeled personnel and weapons carriers, most of them armed with the same wicked 25-mm Bushmaster chain gun found on the army's tracked Bradley infantry fighting vehicles.

The Royal Marines rapidly established a firm grip on the streets, running off the remaining Iraqi soldiers and sending the Special Police scurrying to their blockhouses. There was scattered shooting and some dicey moments; the British commander, Lt. Col. Jonathan Thompson was captured at one juncture, but managed to "brass it out" at gunpoint and get away. The Royal Marines were about to finish off the recalcitrant Special Police the hard way when the Iraqis gave up and left on their own. Only a few dozen actual police, armed only with pistols and cleared by the Coalition forces, were allowed to remain in town.[49]

With Zakho in hand, the Iraqis cowed, and more forces arriving daily, Garner began looking south and east, determined to take advantage of his initial success and regain control of most of the Kurdish home region in Iraq, thereby paving the way for resettlement. Moving down out of the mountain foothills, Garner intended to extend the security zone east to Suri and south to Dihok, an eighteen-fold expansion in territory. He intended to do this within days by a truck and helicopter blitz backed by strong and consistent air support. The A-10A Warthogs and a newly arrived battalion of Army AH-64A Apaches would play a big role in expediting the advance.

The British 3 Commando Brigade, Brig. Andrew M. Keeling commanding, took charge of the Dutch Marines and most of the U.S. Army 3-325th Airborne Battalion Combat Team, which was just coming into the theater. These troops organized to push well east, starting before dawn on 2 May. The attack aimed to secure Sirsenk and its small airstrip, then press onward to Suri. Assembling international forces on the fly to conduct an immediate attack was not easy. In the words of 3-325th commander Lt. Col. John P. Abizaid, who had jumped into Grenada in 1983 as one of John Mitchell's fellow Ranger company commanders, "At 1400, the battalion (-) was placed under operational control of 3 Commando, relieved in place at night by units from 24th MEU, and began what was essentially a 120 kilometer [almost 75 miles] movement to contact in a driving rainstorm at 0300 hours the next morning. Even the most sadistic planners at one of our training centers would have refrained from dreaming up that scenario."[50] Reflective of the quality of his paratroopers, Abizaid's battalion and the British moved out on time, headed east. One reinforced rifle company remained behind with the Marines at Zakho.

The drive on Sirsenk met some Iraqi resistance. Abizaid's battalion moved on two axes, with relays of twin-engine Warthogs swooping overhead for immediate backup. When the scouts identified Iraqi companies and battalions, the lead platoons of U.S. paratroopers took up overwatching positions, pointed their weapons at their opponents, and started digging in. As Abizaid put it, "Commanders adopted the motto of the Roman legions: when you stop, fortify." This not only protected the troops, it allowed for extremely heavy, close-in supporting fires from the American battalion's mortars and fearsome U.S. air strikes. Digging in also sent a strong message to the Iraqis—the Americans are serious and they are ready to fight. Abizaid's men grumbled, but they dug. It paid off.

While the lead U.S. Army units faced off and improved positions, the truck-mounted main bodies of the trailing rifle companies probed to outflank and bypass the Iraqis. Officers, accompanied by linguists and loudspeaker teams, attempted to find senior Iraqis and order them to withdraw. Abizaid, who spoke Arabic and had served with the UN in Lebanon, did this chore himself with some success. Pointing to his men and the air force warplanes, the battalion commander told the enemy that he would kill them if they did not back off. Once flanked and presented with the threat from the menacing A-10As and relentless American infantry, the Iraqis pulled back every time.[51]

Led by the Americans and 45 Commando, 3 Commando Brigade secured Sirsenk and Saddam Hussein's nearby resort-cum-headquarters at Al Amadiyah within forty-eight hours of beginning their movement. French airborne forces joined the operation in progress, leapfrogged 3 Commando, and took Suri on 6 May, staking out the easternmost segment of the security zone. There had been no major fighting, just shadowboxing and shows of force.[52] The eastern extension had been won.

To the south, Lt. Col. Tony L. Corwin's BLT 2/8 Marines began their attack toward Dihok, once a city of 350,000 and a major center of Kurdish life. Commencing on 4 May, the Marines pressed south. Behind them, Spanish paratroopers took over security duties near Zakho, and Italian paratroopers followed the advance to secure the Marines' ground routes back to Zakho. From the northeast, Abizaid's 3-325th, freed by the arrival of the French task force, wheeled south to join the Marine attack toward Dihok. One American scout was killed and three others badly wounded in a minefield as the paratroopers drove south to link up with the Marines and pocket Dihok. By 5 May, Americans held the high ground, with the Marines to the north and west and paratroopers to the north and east of the city. The American infantry commenced the usual patrols and attempts to unhinge the Iraqis. One especially bold mounted patrol from Abizaid's battalion even made it into the city before being withdrawn to a safer position just outside. In short order, the Americans cleared and controlled the dominant heights.

Meanwhile, down in the streets, the Iraqis holed up in buildings, preparing for a siege. This time, they refused to budge. Republican Guard tanks started to move into the city from the south. Saddam Hussein had drawn the line. Again, as at Zakho, the question arose: Would there be a battle?

Garner's Task Force Bravo confronted a major problem in Dihok. Most of the Iraqis who had withdrawn from Zakho and points east had congregated in the city, and his Marines and paratroopers lacked the manpower to clear the urban area house to house, which could get very messy. Bombing the town would not do much to prepare a homecoming for the Kurds, who were even then beginning to fill transit camps near Zakho, anxious to go home to Dihok. Garner was willing to try a deliberate attack, convinced the Iraqis had no stomach for a bout with American Marines and paratroopers backed by U.S. airpower. Shalikashvili overruled him, turning instead to the Military Coordination Center to try to negotiate a solution.

By 20 May, a compromise emerged. The Iraqis could leave a few police (again, no Special Police) and the Coalition would limit itself to eighty-one noncombat troops in the city limits, with no limit on civilian relief workers and UN civilians.[53] This opened the door for the Kurds to return. The Americans remained in their positions overlooking the city, just in case.

"Once the security zone was expanded to its limit," noted Abizaid, "the checkpoint war began." The relatively bloodless maneuvering of early May gave way to a three-sided war of nerves, with Kurds, Iraqis, and allies all armed and skittish, trying to defuse misunderstandings face to face or through the Military Coordination Center. Coalition checkpoints and patrols dotted the vast security zone. John Mitchell and 1-5th Infantry would have recognized the situation—the Korean DMZ writ large, with an extra armed contingent tossed in to add to the friction. Americans and other

Coalition forces sometimes had to protect Iraqis from Kurdish guerrillas bent on revenge.

As in Korea, the Sinai, Lebanon, and elsewhere in the wonderful world of OOTW, junior leaders faced many interesting situations: "an Iraqi nuclear scientist wants to defect . . . Kurdish guerrillas want to pass through to attack the Iraqis . . . Iraqi 'civil authorities' are demanding passage to arrest a local Kurd leader . . . armed Kurds are demanding that we confiscate 'stolen' cars from local 'agents' as they pass through . . . a mother brings in a dying child . . . several thousand rounds of ammo is discovered in a secret compartment of a car . . . a gunfight erupts between two armed Kurdish groups . . . the press wants a story and wants freedom to pass into Iraqi-held territory—the incidents were virtually endless."[54] As they say at Quantico and Fort Benning, "What now, lieutenant?" Guess right, protect your men, and do not cause a war crime, an international incident, or a bad spin on the next segment of *CNN Headline News.*

It was not easy. Shooting incidents were rare but they happened; the much-hated allied aircraft often took ground fire from the sullen Iraqi soldiery. The British Royal Marines had a series of especially ugly little scraps in their sector in mid-May. First Sergeant Jock T. McCain of Company A, 3-325th, summarized the twilight struggle: "Should we call our mission in Northern Iraq combat? I don't know, but I sure as hell wouldn't call it a field problem."

Training did continue between operations. Corwin's 2/8 Marines rotated companies every six days to keep their edge and provide some interesting, challenging live-fire training away from the grind. Abizaid's paratroopers jumped near Zakho and also carried out live-fire training on a homemade range complex. The other national contingents joined the Americans and conducted their own proficiency work.[55] This is classic Regular Army behavior and indicative of the caliber of the forces assigned. A good training program, hopefully carried out with an eye on the local security situation, typifies the current American approach to OOTW.

Along with security duties and training, help and assistance had to be provided to the Kurd families moving through the allied sectors. Seeing to their needs offered some respite from the tension of armed confrontation. In Iraq, every Coalition member was also a uniformed relief worker at times, "winning hearts and minds," in the old Vietnam parlance. Like the Green Berets, Task Force Bravo's riflemen did their share.

Still, the bulk of the humanitarian work fell to the engineers, medics, and logisticians, all of whom outdid themselves. The three great camps near

Zakho processed nearly a quarter million Kurds en route home. American army reserve civil affairs specialists acted as mayors for these massive, multinational facilities. Transit Camp 3 was nicknamed "Kampground of Iraq" by its American "mayor," Maj. Ronald Jelks, and he spared no effort to make it a fine habitat for the transients. Relief workers, most of whom had seen many such efforts in their time, were tremendously impressed by men like Jelks and, indeed, all the Coalition forces. "What was incredible to me," recounted team leader Ronald Roome of CARE, "was how the military set up all the detailed and complicated systems at such speed with so little prior experience."[56] The Kurds took advantage of the array of services and then went home. By mid-June, Shalikashvili was ready to do the same.

Getting out was not as hard as getting in, although the Kurds demonstrated and complained bitterly as the allies began to pull out, turning the remaining relief projects over to organizations like CARE. Still, the allies did not depart altogether. Coalition aircraft continued to patrol Iraqi skies as far south as the thirty-sixth parallel, and a residual force remained at Silopi just across the Turkish border.

In the mid-1990s the allies still maintain a presence. The truce remains fragile and negotiations with Baghdad drone on without resolution. The Turks, pleased with the results of the operation, feel free to charge into Iraq to hound their PKK tormentors. The other Iraqi Kurdish factional leaders, now friendlier with Turkey, still enjoy some degree of autonomy from Saddam Hussein, thanks to the maintenance of the no-fly zone. As for the refugees who went to Iran, these unfortunates also filtered back, far worse for the wear, their fate largely ignored by the wider world.[57] Yet all in all, for the Kurds of Iraq, Provide Comfort was a welcome change from their usual miserable run of luck. This time, somebody did something. And even better, it worked.

Operation Provide Comfort succeeded for three reasons: a feasible mission, a combat orientation, and a fine joint and combined command climate. In some ways, these conditions were unique outcomes of Operation Desert Storm, unlikely to be repeated. That acknowledged, there are interesting insights here that offer perspectives on prior and later undertakings of a similar nature.

The Americans led a Coalition that wisely limited itself to relieving Kurdish misery, not reversing centuries of ethnic conflict. Bush refused to join the civil war in Iraq, and his field commanders translated that order into limits on their actions. As a result, the Americans could declare victory and exit, part of the plan from the start. The Americans are not completely out, but that goes with the nature of all successful OOTWs. If PKK terrorists someday assail Silopi, perhaps America might regret getting involved. But as with Egypt and Israel in the Sinai, the Turks deserve the commitment, and so, we stay.

The CJTF's battle focus played a big part in preventing American and allied losses. Nobody entered Iraq thinking they were at Fort Bragg or Camp Lejeune. All allied forces maneuvered and defended as if the next minute might bring on World War III, a combat posture that did much to protect the force. Seeing no exploitable weaknesses, the Iraqis and the feistier Kurds elected not to tangle with Shalikashvili's battle-ready people. "At one point," remembered Abizaid, "when the utterly bedraggled, unkempt Iraqi Army units withdrew through one of our checkpoints, a newsman remarked that you only needed to look at two soldiers from the two nations to predict the outcome of battle between them."[58] With a division's worth of handpicked forces on the ground, veteran pilots overhead, and a strong naval flotilla backing it all up, American prowess in warpower was not presented as a bluff but as a promise. The Iraqis chose not to test that strength.

Much of the CJTF's power came from its strong, cooperative chain of command. Here, most of the credit goes to Shalikashvili, who justified Galvin's faith in him. Joint and combined operations often suffer from niggling turf fights between service components and allies, but Shalikashvili would have none of that. His organization of multiservice and international forces all the way down to mixed battalions and air squadrons demonstrated the full maturity of the American system of warpower, admittedly greatly aided by familiar NATO partnerships.[59] Provide Comfort's command architecture represented a real triumph, achieved on the run, which may well have been beneficial. During the first hectic days, nobody really had the time to raise bureaucratic complaints, and then success and lack of casualties squelched any ex post facto carping.

Strangely enough, Provide Comfort's greatest failing was its success, gained at minimal cost. Those who shape their world view from television sound bites and editorials in the *New York Times* and *Washington Post* drew a set of conclusions from this mission, conclusions so facile as to be laughable had these beliefs not eventually given birth to dire consequences indeed. To some self-inflated opinion leaders, and to more than a few elected and appointed officials who should have known better, the Kurdish relief effort suggested some sort of new world aborning, where soldiers would put down their rifles, pick up plowshares, and go around the globe doing good under the standard of a revitalized United Nations. Nobody bothered to check with the bad guys, an omission that would exact a price on the next major U.S. intervention.

Notes

The epigraph is from Jean Larteguy, *The Centurions* (New York: Avon Books, 1963), 265.

1. Carl von Clausewitz, *On War,* ed. and trans. Michael Howard and Peter Paret (Princeton, N.J.: Princeton University Press, 1984), 119.

2. Gerard Chaliand, ed., *A People Without a Country,* trans. Michael Pallis (Brooklyn, N.Y.: Olive Branch Press, 1993), 39, 96–97, 143, 194–95, 204.

3. Ibid., 4, 248.

4. Ibid., 8–9, 224–26.

5. Stephen C. Pelletiere, *The Kurds and Their Agas: An Assessment of the Situation in Northern Iraq* (Carlisle Barracks, Pa.: Strategic Studies Institute, 16 September 1991), 4–12.

6. Chaliand, *A People Without a Country,* 225–26.

7. Ibid., 170; Ian O. Lesser, *Bridge or Barrier?: Turkey and the West After the Cold War* (Santa Monica, Calif.: RAND Corporation, 1992), 28.

8. Pelletiere, *The Kurds and Their Agas,* 20; John T. Fishel, *Liberation, Occupation, and Rescue: War Termination and Desert Storm* (Carlisle Barracks, Pa.: Strategic Studies Institute, 31 August 1992), 34.

9. Brig. Gen. Robert H. Scales, USA, et al., *Certain Victory* (Washington, D.C.: U.S. Government Printing Office, 1993), iii–iv, vii–viii, 5–6; James F. Dunnigan and Col. Raymond F. Macedonia, USA (Ret.), *Getting It Right* (New York: William Morrow, 1993), 205–12.

10. For a particularly biting critique of American performance in the ground phase of Operation Desert Storm, see Col. James G. Burton, USAF (Ret.), "Pushing Them Out the Back Door," *Proceedings* (July 1993): 37–42. Opposing points of view of the nature and reasons for the suspension of hostilities by the Coalition forces can be found in subsequent issues of *Proceedings* as readers replied to Burton's strong arguments.

11. U.S. Department of Defense, *Conduct of the Persian Gulf War* (Washington, D.C.: U.S. Government Printing Office, 1992), 411; Rick Atkinson, *Crusade* (Boston: Houghton Mifflin, 1993), 340–42, 477.

12. Richard Jupa and Jim Dingeman, *Gulf Wars* (Cambria, Calif.: 3W Publications, 1991), 88–89.

13. Atkinson, *Crusade,* 481; Scales, *Certain Victory,* 312–14.

14. Slightly different accounts of the armistice conference are presented in Atkinson, *Crusade,* 1–10 and Gen. H. Norman Schwarzkopf with Peter Petre, *It Doesn't Take a Hero* (New York: Bantam, 1992), 488–89.

15. Fishel, *Liberation, Occupation, and Rescue,* 34–35; Jupa and Dingeman, *Gulf Wars,* 89–92.

16. Fishel, *Liberation, Occupation, and Rescue,* 44; Scales, *Certain Victory,* 332.

17. Fishel, *Liberation, Occupation, and Rescue,* 28; Scales, *Certain Victory,* 331–32. For a division's view of the relief work among the Shiites, see Maj. Randy J. Kolton, USA, *Historical Summary of 82nd Airborne Division Civil Military Operations and Psychological Operations during Operation DESERT SHIELD/DESERT STORM* (Fort Bragg, N.C.: Headquarters, 82d Airborne Division, 1 July 1991).

18. Atkinson, *Crusade,* 498.

19. Chaliand, *A People Without a Country,* 92, 231.

20. Lesser, *Bridge or Barrier?* 35–37; Michael M. Gunter, *The Kurds of Iraq* (New York: St. Martin's, 1992), 56–57; Stephen J. Blank, Stephen C. Pelletiere, and Lt. Col. William T. Johnsen, USA, *Turkey's Strategic Position at the Crossroads of World Affairs* (Carlisle Barracks, Pa.: Strategic Studies Institute, 3 December 1993), 38–40; Lt. Col. Gordon W. Rudd, USA, "Operation PROVIDE COMFORT: One More Tile on the Mosaic, 6 April–15 July 1991" (unpublished draft, U.S. Army Center of Military History, 15 August 1991), 3, 5. Rudd's account and research notes, based on many interviews and experiences in the theater of operations, will eventually form the core of the U.S. Army's official history of Operation PROVIDE COMFORT.

21. United Nations Security Council, *Resolution 688* (New York: United Nations, 5 April 1991).

22. Fishel, *Liberation, Occupation, and Rescue,* 51; Jupa and Dingeman, *Gulf Wars,* 92; Gunter, *The Kurds of Iraq,* 57.

23. Rudd, "Operation PROVIDE COMFORT," 3–4, 6; Col. James L. Jones, USMC, "Operation PROVIDE COMFORT: Humanitarian and Security Assistance in Northern Iraq," *Marine Corps Gazette* (November 1991): 99.

24. Rudd, "Operation PROVIDE COMFORT," 6; Scales, *Certain Victory,* 341.

25. Lt. Gen. John H. Cushman, USA (Ret.), "Joint, Jointer, Jointest," *Proceedings* (May 1992): 81; Rudd, "Operation PROVIDE COMFORT," 8; Fishel, *Liberation, Occupation, and Rescue,* 51; Sid Balman Jr., "Wing Shifts to Refugee-Relief Flights," *Air Force Times,* 22 April 1991. Food requirements were calculated in accord with Susan H. H. Young, "C-130" in "Gallery of USAF Weapons," *Air Force* (May 1993): 141, and Capt. David S. Elmo, USAR, "Food Distribution During Operation PROVIDE COMFORT," *Special Warfare* (March 1992): 8–9.

26. Rudd, "Operation PROVIDE COMFORT," 7–8; Cushman, "Joint, Jointer, Jointest," 81; Janet D'Agostino, "Incirlik AB is Hub for Expanding Kurdish Relief Efforts," *Air Force Times,* 29 April 1991.

27. Fishel, *Liberation, Occupation, and Rescue,* 52.

28. Fishel, *Liberation, Occupation, and Rescue,* 55; Cushman, "Joint, Jointer, Jointest," 81–82.

29. Headquarters, 3-325th Airborne Battalion Combat Team, *The Blue Falcons Strike* (Marceline, Mo.: Walsworth Publishing, 1991), 16. This was an unofficial publication.

30. D'Agostino, "Incirlik AB is Hub for Expanding Kurdish Relief Efforts," 6.

31. Janet D'Agostino, "Airdrops at Times a 'Real White-Knuckled Ride,'" *Air Force Times,* 6 May 1991.

32. Elmo, "Food Distribution During Operation PROVIDE COMFORT," 8–9; Donna Miles, "Helping the Kurds," *Soldiers* (July 1991): 20.

33. For examples of chiefs of staff and deputy commanders commanding ad hoc contingency organizations, see Maj. Gen. Edward M. Almond's role in the Korean War as reflected in Shelby Stanton, *America's Tenth Legion* (Novato, Calif.: Presidio Press, 1989), 41–42; Gen. George S. Patton Jr., *War As I Knew It* (New York: Pyramid Books, 1970), 66 (Maj. Gen. Geoffrey Keyes's provisional corps in Sicily, 1943); and Lt. Gen. Willard Pearson, USA, *Vietnam Studies: The War in the Northern Provinces* (Washington, D.C.: U.S. Government Printing Office, 1975), 66–69 (Gen. Creighton Abrams's provisional forward headquarters in Vietnam, 1968).

34. Fishel, *Liberation, Occupation, and Rescue,* 52–53; Rudd, "Operation PROVIDE COMFORT," 17; Gen. John M. D. Shalikashvili, USA, "Resume of Service Career" (Washington, D.C.: Department of the Army, 25 October 1993).

35. Fishel, *Liberation, Occupation, and Rescue,* 52–55; Rudd, "Operation PROVIDE COMFORT," 6–7; Cushman, "Joint, Jointer, Jointest," 82–83.

36. Scales, *Certain Victory,* 345, 353; Fishel, *Liberation, Occupation, and Rescue,* 55–56; Rudd, "Operation PROVIDE COMFORT," 35–36.

37. Jupa and Dingeman, *Gulf Wars,* 92; Scales, *Certain Victory,* 342.

38. Blank, Pelletiere, and Johnsen, *Turkey's Strategic Position,* 38–43; Lesser, *Bridge or Barrier?* 28–31; Capt. John Costa, USA, "IPB for Humanitarian Intelligence Support Operations," *Military Intelligence* (October–December 1992): 28.

39. Pelletiere, *The Kurds and Their Agas,* 10–20; Costa, "IPB," 28.

40. Hans Halberstadt, *Green Berets* (Novato, Calif.: Presidio Press, 1988), 22, 110–11; Col. Francis J. Kelly, USA, *Vietnam Studies: U.S. Army Special Forces, 1961–1971* (Washington, D.C.: U.S. Government Printing Office, 1973), 65–67; Maj. (Doctor) John E. Cantrell, ARNG, "The Guard's 20th Special Forces Provided Comfort to the Kurds," *National Guard* (February 1992): 16.

41. Miles, "Helping the Kurds," 17; Rudd, "Operation PROVIDE COMFORT," 11–12; Scales, *Certain Victory,* 343, 345.

42. Rudd, "Operation PROVIDE COMFORT," 13–15; Elmo, "Food Distribution During Operation PROVIDE COMFORT," 8–9.

43. Rudd, "Operation PROVIDE COMFORT," 15; Scales, *Certain Victory,* 343.

44. Rudd, "Operation PROVIDE COMFORT," 13; Scales, *Certain Victory,* 345; Miles, "Helping the Kurds," 17.

45. Rudd, "Operation PROVIDE COMFORT," 19; Miles, "Helping the Kurds," 18.

46. Jones, "Assistance in Northern Iraq," 100–101.

47. Lt. Col. Gordon W. Rudd, USA, "The 24th MEU (SOC) and Operation PROVIDE COMFORT: A Second Look," *Marine Corps Gazette* (February 1993): 21. Drawing on headquarters and units throughout the U.S. European Command and allied contingents, Major General Garner built a coherent joint/combined headquarters for Task Force Bravo by mid-May.

48. Jones, "Assistance in Northern Iraq," 100–101; Scales, *Certain Victory,* 348–49.

49. Rudd, "Operation PROVIDE COMFORT," 18–19; Jones, "Assistance in Northern Iraq," 102; U.S. Department of Defense, Headquarters, Joint Task Force Bravo, "Briefing for General Colin L. Powell" (Washington, D.C.: Army Staff, 1991).

50. Lt. Col. John P. Abizaid, USA, "Lessons for Peacekeepers," *Military Review* (March 1993): 15.

51. Ibid., 13–16; Scales, *Certain Victory,* 349–50; Headquarters, 3-325th ABCT, *The Blue Falcons Strike,* 8–10, 20, 33, 39.

52. Rudd, Operation "PROVIDE COMFORT," 20–23.

53. Ibid, 21, 23–25; Headquarters, 3-325th ABCT, *The Blue Falcons Strike,* 2, 10, 39, 45.

54. Abizaid, "Lessons for Peacekeepers," 16.

55. Lt. Col. Tony L. Corwin, USMC, "BLT 2/8 Moves South," *Marine Corps Gazette* (November 1991): 106; Headquarters, 3-325th ABCT, *The Blue Falcons Strike,* 11–12; Donna Miles, "Leading the Pack," *Soldiers* (May 1992): 15; Joint Task Force Bravo, "Briefing for General Colin L. Powell," 7, 20; Col. E. E. Whitehead, USA, and Capt. Bill Morris, USA, "Operation Provide Comfort: Aviation Operational Flexibility at Its Best," *Aviation Digest* (November/December 1992), 12–15; Lt. Col. Virgil L. Packett II, USA, "Operation PROVIDE COMFORT: The Final Chapter," *Personal Perspectives on the Gulf War* (Arlington, Va.: Association of the United States Army, 1993), 47–48.

56. Elmo, "Food Distribution During Operation PROVIDE COMFORT," 9; Scales, *Certain Victory,* 350–51.

57. Rudd, "Operation PROVIDE COMFORT," 38; Atkinson, *Crusade,* 498–99; Blank, Pelletiere, and Johnsen, *Turkey's Strategic Position,* 45–54. On 14 April 1994, two F-15C Eagles mistakenly engaged two UH-60A Blackhawk helicopters over northern Iraq, killing twenty-six people (fifteen American, five Kurdish, three Turkish, two British, and one French). In the public outcry that followed, many Americans were surprised to find that Provide Comfort was still continuing. See Steve Komarow, "'Screwups' Kill 26," *USA Today,* 15 April 1994.

58. Abizaid, "Lessons for Peacekeepers," 18.

59. Cushman, "Joint, Jointer, Jointest," 83–85.

CHAPTER 7

Down among the Dead Men:
Failure in Somalia, 1992 to 1994

Everyone gets everything he wants. I wanted a mission. And for my sins, they gave me one—brought it up to me just like room service. It was a real choice mission. And when it was over, I wouldn't ever want another.

Apocalypse Now

The American citizenry, even its most sophisticated and world-weary opinion spinners, still accept that people in uniform will get killed doing Uncle Sam's chores in the scummier corners of today's tormented world. The country would have tolerated many more casualties than it took to win the Gulf War, mainly because the majority could recognize some good reasons to fight: a direct link between Kuwaiti and Saudi oil and the quality of their daily lives, the threats to American lives implied by Saddam Hussein's gruesome photo opportunities with innocent hostages, and the conquest and rape of a small, nearly defenseless U.S. ally (that just happened to own massive petroleum reserves). For similar good reasons, America endured losses related to the Sinai effort to guarantee an Egyptian-Israeli peace, and might even have ridden out the Beirut humiliation if only some progress had been evident in defusing the conflict between Israel and Syria. Washington may yet send troops to the Golan Heights and will probably do so to loud and sustained public acclaim, though some peacekeepers might come home permanently peaceful, in shiny aluminum boxes. It should be remembered that America even bore up well in the early days of Korea and Vietnam—as long as there seemed to be some point to the drill.

There was never much point to the Somalia venture, especially once the bulk of those unhappy people had been fed. After all, no one of consequence argued the U.S. had vital interests at stake in Somalia. American state survival was not an issue, nor were American lives in danger (save those inserted during operations). Somalia furnished no special economic treasure, nor could its struggling people support much of a market for American imports. No, this whole thing was pure altruism, Doctor Feelgood making a house call.

As it turned out, not atypically among the less fortunate four-fifths on our planet, some of the patients were not at all grateful. It was Beirut all over again, but there were no excuses available this time. On this iteration, America knew better—or should have. The fact that U.S. forces went in anyway and performed as they did tells us more about the shortcomings of human nature than those of America or its legions. The Greeks used to say it this way: hubris begets nemesis. Well, after the touted triumphs of Just Cause, Desert Storm, and especially the muffled implosion of the USSR, Americans had contracted a very advanced case of hubris. Smart people had begun to believe that they could do OOTW without ever facing the dark cancer of combat ever present in such missions. America's stinging rebuff in Somalia put paid to that conceit.

Somalia is a rather unusual country by any measure. Its seven million people spring from a single ethnic group, the Samaal, who have occupied their present geographic areas since biblical times. Israelites knew the area as the Land of Punt, "God's Land" in the ancient Egyptian tongue, implying a chosen status for the inhabitants. The Somalis certainly think so. Their oral traditions extend all the way back into dim prehistory, tying them to the rulers of antiquity and the family of Muhammed the Prophet. Over the centuries, the Somalis have been the partners of mighty states, the handmaidens of great empires, and the victims of vast disasters—natural, man-made, and often self-inflicted. Examined against the sweep of this epochal continuum, America's brief, ill-fated foray hardly merits consideration. For Somalis, watching a great power come a cropper was nothing new. Such things happen, especially in Somalia. *Inshallah,* they say—as Allah wills.

Almost all Somalis, some 99 percent, adhere to Sunni Islam, speak various dialects of the same Somali language, and share a common cultural heritage. They spring from a common Cushite stock, quite an exception among the mixed peoples of most African states. Freed of the ethnic and tribal hatreds that mar so many other regions, one would expect tranquility in this area.

And yet, homogeneity does not a happy country make. As with the quarrelsome Greeks of the classical age and the Hatfields and McCoys of the

American Ozarks, the Somalis have found that there is no feud like a family feud. Real allegiances have never gone much beyond the six major clans of the Samaal: the herders of Dir, Darood, Isaaq, and Hawiye, and the farmers of Digil and Rahanwein. The clans agree now and then, but disunity and fighting are the norm. It is no wonder that the warrior is the most exalted figure in Somali society. American press references to warlords were not just purple prose.[1]

A steady state of unrest has opened the door for uninvited guests, and the Somalis have seen their share of outside rulers. Lacking any real resources, Somalia attracts invaders because of its position, forming what is known as the Horn of Africa. Somalia dominates the southern entrance to the Red Sea, the Bab al-Mandeb, as well as the southern reaches of the Arabian Sea. These vital trade routes link Africa, the Mideast, and India. To control these important water highways, various interlopers have entered Somalia over the course of the centuries.

The first important wave came in the seventh century, when Arab merchants established coastal stations to facilitate commerce with India and southeast Africa. The capital city of Mogadishu dates from this period. The Arabs also brought Islam, of course, and this great proselytizing faith quickly displaced the old animist strains, or so it seemed. Closer examination reveals that Somali Muslims cling to some interesting remnants of the old ways, to include a thriving belief in primal spirits, a trust in arcane rain-making rituals, and a rather loose interpretation of the Koran's strictures against narcotics. Somalis have long preferred to chew khat, a weed that serves as a natural upper, stimulating conversation and alertness. Islamic law has never had much impact on the khat culture.[2] Added to the combative nature of the people, khat merely made tough fighters even tougher, or at least led them to feel like they were.

In the nineteenth century, however, khat did very little to offset the power of the Maxim gun, at least at first. Europeans had been stopping on the Somali coast for years, but things became serious in the great imperial flowering of the 1880s. Better armed and organized than the relatively backward locals, the European regiments made short work of the rather amorphous Somali clan warriors. France took what would become Djibouti, Italy grabbed the southern area around Mogadishu, and Britain assumed control of the Horn proper (Somaliland) as well as the stretch abutting what is now modern Kenya (known as the Northern Frontier District). The Ethiopians, who had successfully staved off European attackers, snapped up the Ogaden region in the bargain.

Although the takeovers happened quickly enough, not everything went smoothly thereafter. Resistance smouldered and flared, aimed at the traditional African foes and especially the British, who really upset the Somalis by cooperating with the hated Ethiopians. That sort of manipulation of local animosities had served Britain well in other areas of Africa, but not this time. Somaliland proved to be a very expensive and troublesome addition to the vast British Empire.

The British had the bad fortune to take over that part of Somalia marked by the most fanatical devotion to Islam and the national warrior ethos. In a curious foreshadowing of America's eventual frustrations in pursuit of Muhammed Farah Aidid, the British spent twenty-one years chasing Muhammed Abdullah Hassan, whom they tagged "the Mad Mullah." This shrewd opponent and his followers waged a bloody, vicious campaign of night attacks and ambushes. Six major expeditions were mounted, interspersed with fruitless negotiations. Nothing worked to bring him to heel—indeed, the Mullah died in bed, defiant to the last.

The big hammer, however, finally did the job on the Mullah's followers. In 1920, a rain of twenty-pound bombs dumped by the Royal Air Force's Z Squadron finally broke the back of the guerrilla resistance, although violence continued at sporadic intervals. The long war killed off a third of the inhabitants of British Somaliland and discouraged London from any serious investment in improving their spiteful colony. To this day, northern Somalia remains distinct from the southern districts, a direct result of the Mullah's long struggle.

The other two European powers had better experiences, and thus, so did their charges. The Italians around Mogadishu built their portion of Somalia into a showpiece for Benito Mussolini's revived Roman Empire, replete with large-scale banana and sugar plantations, roads, public buildings, schools, and decent sanitation. French Djibouti received similar treatment, and the mother country continues to invest in that economy.[3]

Colonial rule in the area ended in stages, a process accelerated by the general European decline following World War II. In the greater scheme of those years, Somalia was just another colony being unloaded, and, for the harried mother countries, the sooner, the better. The British and Italians pulled out officially in 1960, melding their regions into a single new state under the supervision of the United Nations. So modern Somalia was born with the UN as midwife, leaving behind the usual afterbirth.

It is strange that a people who cannot get along in the parts of their homeland they do control can be so adamant about adding more territory, but the

Somalis made it clear from the first that they believed all their kin should live in one country. Their flag, a five-pointed white star on a light blue field, reflects the pan-Somali desire to gather in their five traditional homelands: ex–Italian Somalia, ex–British Somaliland, Djibouti, northern Kenya, and the Ethiopian Ogaden. Because the borders of modern Somalia were drawn by Europeans, approved by the UN, and included only two of the five traditional territories of Greater Somalia, the locals did not consider these boundaries binding. While other African states agreed to abide by colonial borders, the ever-contrary Somalis demanded unity with their half million countrymen in the Ethiopian Ogaden, quarter million in French-dominated Djibouti, and a similar number in Kenya. Coupled with modern weapons and a warrior heritage, this spelled trouble for all neighbors, at least until the old clan feuds refocused the Somalis' restless energies against their preferred enemies—each other.[4]

For a few years, like most of the ex-colonies, Somalia tried Western-style constitutional government. And like many of its underdeveloped neighbors, Somalian democracy experienced the usual depressing pattern: one man, one vote, one time, then the sickening slide into turmoil. The suspicious clans resorted to solving disputes in the old style, fighting it out in the streets and countryside with bullets, not ballots.

In 1969, the process of entropy reached a crisis state. March elections for the 123-seat parliament featured one thousand candidates from seventy parties, charges of massive election fraud, and widespread violence. As the bitterly split parliament assumed office, clan fighting escalated. When a jealous bodyguard killed the elected president in October, his Darood clansman, army chief Muhammed Siyad Barrah, seized power in a bloodless military coup d'etat. That would be one of the few bloodless events associated with his harsh rule.

Siyad Barrah took charge emphatically and completely, hewing to the Marxist-Leninist line then so much in vogue in the Third World. He suspended the constitution, dissolved the parliament, and restricted what rights Somalis enjoyed. To break the cycle of interclan squabbling, he determined to focus the hostile urges outward. He announced his plans to liberate Greater Somalia. The Siyad Barrah dictatorship followed the proven Stalinist model, suitably modified to include plenty of offices and graft for Darood clan cronies and a nod to Islamic beliefs.

Siyad Barrah was by no means doctrinaire in his beliefs. Indeed, he embraced scientific socialism and the USSR mainly because America backed the governments in Ethiopia, Kenya, and Djibouti, which blocked the new leader's territorial claims. The Soviets jumped at the opening, and lavished weapons and advisers on their latest client. Well armed with tanks, heavy artillery, and MiG-21 fighter jets, Somalia began threatening to seize Djibouti, northeast Kenya, and especially the Ogaden. Siyad Barrah fomented guerrilla movements in all of these regions, focusing on the weakest foe, Ethiopia. All of this kept the smoldering familial strife in Somalia aimed outward.

The Soviets backed Siyad Barrah throughout these efforts, until strongman Mengistu Haile Mariam took power in Ethiopia and declared his desire for Moscow's support in early 1977. The Russian Communists figured that they now had a lock on the two dominant states in the Horn of Africa, but the bonds of socialist revolutionary solidarity were no match for pan-Somali extremism. Siyad Barrah knew that Ethiopia was weak and he was strong and that once the Soviet arms lockers opened, this favorable condition would not last. His mentors in Moscow had taught him a few things about judging the correlation of forces, and for Siyad Barrah, it looked like now or never. Ignoring warnings from the Soviets, the dictator launched his army into Ethiopia, intent on taking over the Ogaden and its Somali nationals.

This 1977–78 Ogaden War turned out to be a disaster. The Soviets repudiated the Somali regime and, with Cuban help, assisted the Ethiopians in repulsing every Somali assault, killing thousands of Siyad Barrah's soldiers. As the Ogaden debacle unfolded, 95 percent of the people in French Djibouti voted for independence rather than unity with Siyad Barrah's faltering state, and France stationed Foreign Legion forces in the new country to ensure its defense. Finally, in 1981, to ward off more costly border fighting, an exhausted Somalia was forced to renounce its claims to Kenyan territory. Siyad Barrah's plans for a Greater Somalia were dead.

Humiliated, the self-proclaimed "Victorious Leader" determined, rather typically for such figures, that the real culprit was at home, a belief encouraged by a botched coup attempted in April of 1978.[5] To hold the line against the triumphant Ethiopians and vengeful Soviets, and buy time to clean house, Siyad Barrah turned to America for support. He counted on the Cold War idea that an enemy's enemy is a friend.

He guessed correctly. Determined to gain influence in the Horn of Africa and block Soviet pressures in Africa, the Carter and Reagan administrations both held their collective noses and backed him. Similar logic bankrolled quite a rogues' gallery over the years, including such despots as Park Chung

Hee of Korea, Anastasio Somoza of Nicaragua, Reza Shah Pahlavi of Iran, and Manuel Noreiga of Panama, to name a few notable embarrassments. Even among the worst of these, Siyad Barrah stood out for his cruelty, capriciousness, and opportunism.

World powers sometimes must deal with such devils in the pursuit of their interests. So, to keep a foothold planted in the important Horn of Africa, the United States traded arms and advice for access to ports and exercise rights. From 1983 through 1988, America funneled some $40 million a year in military assistance to the strategically located country. This included M198 155-mm howitzers, M167 towed 20-mm Vulcan air defense guns, small arms, and appropriate stocks of ammunition, all added to an already bloated arsenal procured from the Soviet Union. Somalia's stocks also included Italian-made light armored vehicles and trucks and West German weaponry for Siyad Barrah's special forces and armed police. America, Italy, and Germany would soon regret their largess.

Siyad Barrah's abysmal human rights record derailed the American gravy train in 1989, when Bush cut most ties in response to pressures from congressmen outraged by the Somali ruler's excesses. Even so, some contacts persisted. Somalis continued to attend certain U.S. military schools, and, as late as 1990, U.S. forces staged through Berbera en route to Desert Shield.[6]

Siyad Barrah's excesses finally got the better of him. After the failed Ogaden War, resistance groups began forming, naturally organized around the disgruntled leadership of other clans and even a few breakaway portions of his own Darood family. Three principal groups emerged. In the north, Abdirahman Ahmed Ali Tur headed the Somali National Movement (SNM), an Isaaq faction that drew on the same strong guerrilla traditions that once supported the Mad Mullah. In the far south, a much weaker group, the Somali Patriotic Movement (SPM), led by Colonels Omar Jess and Muhammed Said Hersi Morgan of the Darood clan, claimed to represent the interests of those Somalis "abandoned" in the Ogaden in 1978. Finally, Ali Mahdi Muhammed of the Hawiye headed the very strong United Somali Congress (USC), centered around Mogadishu. Muhammed Farah Aidid led the USC's armed component. By late 1989, all three groups, plus others, were in open revolt, armed with heavy weapons gained by defection, capture, or smuggling. A year later, they put aside their differences and formed a common front dedicated to ousting Siyad Barrah.

The struggle for Mogadishu culminated between Christmas of 1990 and February of 1991. Aidid commanded the forces that chased the hated Victorious Leader out of his battered capital, after a bruising street fight that caused forty-one thousand casualties, mostly civilians. Siyad Barrah finally turned up in Nigeria, thoroughly discredited and lucky to be alive. Behind him, he left a country in ruins.

Siyad Barrah had not only failed to build Greater Somalia, but had managed to wreck the land he had taken. The entire civil war, with its waves of reprisals and atrocities, had been exceedingly brutal, with many thousands killed and wounded between 1981 and 1991. Refugees from the years of vicious infighting numbered nearly a million, most squatting in ramshackle camps just inside bordering states. The economy, never robust, had deteriorated from merely dirt-poor to just plain dirt, bare subsistence levels.[7] The only things available in bulk appeared to be guns and bad attitudes.

With Siyad Barrah's passing, Somalian political culture degenerated into its natural state, which is to say anarchy. Predictably, the temporary front that ran out the dictator soon collapsed into internecine violence. The SNM grabbed the old British north, declaring independence within months of Siyad Barrah's fall. Colonel Jess and his SPM gunmen took the southern port of Kismayo and its environs, a stake disputed by Colonel Morgan's people. And in the center ring, Hawiye kinsmen Aidid and Ali Mahdi squared off to duel for control of Mogadishu and the rump of the Somali state.

The people of Somalia paid heavily for this continued strife. As most of the men took up arms and most of the women and children took shelter, normal agriculture and business ground to a halt. All freedom of movement hinged on the whims of the warlords and their roving "technicals," teams of Somali fighters driving small trucks and buggies armed with machine guns and rocket launchers. Named for an English-language euphemism for security guards that just happened to coincide in pronunciation with the Somali culture's term for bandit, the technicals were real-life versions of the bizarre vehicles that grace the postnuclear wastelands depicted in *Mad Max* movies. Somalia was rapidly beginning to approximate the tortured land beyond the Thunderdome.

Along with arms, bullets, and explosives, the clan chiefs began to hoard food and medical supplies. Backed by their technicals, the various faction leaders denied these basic needs to opponents and dispensed them to supporters, extremely direct means of maintaining and keeping allegiances. Deaths and miseries accumulated along a rising curve.[8]

Over the next several months, the situation careened all the way down to rock bottom, even when measured against the tragic standards of the poorest

Third World countries. A widespread drought merely served to increase already awful statistics. By the summer of 1992, about 300,000 people had starved to death since Siyad Barrah's departure, with millions on the brink—all recorded by the dispassionate video cameras of CNN and company. Wild-eyed gunmen raced here and there, spitting death from the weapons bolted onto their Toyota pickups. Most normal activity, even farming, had ceased altogether. Life in Somalia resembled the nightmare landscape conjured by Thomas Hobbes: poor, nasty, brutish, and short.[9] Even Hobbes's *Leviathan,* the unequivocal hand of iron, might not have been able to sort this one out. The UN, to include a reluctant America, tried anyway, laying down the first few bricks of good intentions on a road headed straight to OOTW hell.

Of course, hindsight is always perfect, and if we knew then what we know now, perhaps Americans and their newfound UN friends would have left bad enough alone. After all, situations in Ethiopia, Sudan, and a dozen other struggling smaller states were not much better. Why did Somalia merit special attention?

Actually, Somalia became an issue the same way all the really bad ones become an issue—incrementally. Initially, the situation was treated as pure famine relief, just another running sore in need of a Band-Aid. The usual volunteers from CARE, Save the Children, UNICEF, World Vision, Medicines sans Frontiers, and the rest had been in country since the departure of Siyad Barrah, but like the innocents they endeavored to help, they could not survive and function in the ever more violent embrace of the armed factions and ruthless technicals. In desperation, the assistance agencies hired technicals of their own, but the wily warlords quickly offered their own militiamen for these roles, and the ventures turned into mafia-style protection rackets. Aid shipments continued to go where the warlords willed. With the added pressures caused by the spreading east African drought of 1992, and predictions that up to a third of the Somali people might die due to famine, conditions were clearly spinning beyond the capacities of a few hundred unarmed humanitarian workers.

Following the breakdown of a February cease-fire negotiated by the United Nations, Secretary General Boutros Boutros-Ghali of Egypt appealed for military help from member states. He figured it would take that to get relief supplies into Somalia, in the style of Provide Comfort. With this in mind, the Security Council passed Resolution 751 on 27 April 1992. Thus began the United Nations Operation in Somalia (UNOSOM).[10]

The United States did not immediately get involved, and so the UN could only gain a minimal commitment for fifty observers, all from Pakistan. Given the scale of the troubles in Somalia, lack of American participation virtually guaranteed UNOSOM would flounder. It did. By midsummer, UNOSOM was accomplishing next to nothing. The nongovernmental aid organizations could not distribute food or provide services, and a few observers had no effect on their frustrations. Warlord militias stole the supplies they were being paid to guard, ambushed shipments bound for rival districts, and prevented aid workers from going about their business. The dying continued at an alarming rate as true starvation took hold. Things were approaching the point of no return.

The UN's little contingent in Mogadishu had just enough people to notice that everything was still getting worse, but nowhere near enough to do anything about it. In an especially graphic example of how badly the humanitarian program was going, one day in late July, two UN relief flights to Mogadishu were halted on the runway and looted from nose to tail by clan gunmen, backed by their ever-present technicals. If these adverse trends persisted, there would be a lot of Somali corpses moldering, too many courtesy of American-made arms brandished by unbridled brigands.

That was not a pleasant prospect for the Bush administration, locked in a hotly contested election. Doing nothing would have been preferred, but, well, there were those horrid images on the television every night, and everyone knew that Bush's Democratic opponent strongly supported the UN. Was Bush really a heartless Republican, a rich old white guy willing to fight for oil but not to bring food to black Africans? Already sinking in the opinion polls, the president could hardly expect reelection by feeding such cruel perceptions. Feeding some Somalians seemed like a lot better idea.

Domestic politics aside, however, U.S. entry into Somalia gave cause for much caution. Even a casual glance offered ample evidence that disarming the various factional movements was a prerequisite to any solution in the embattled country. Yet in a land where weaponry and clan struggles were part of the culture, that attempt promised a massive effort and a lot of butchery and still might well fail. Jumping with both feet into a bloody quagmire would not play any better in Peoria than doing nothing.

Perhaps a middle course was the best. Airlift looked like a good bet. After all, the U.S. had long delivered humanitarian cargo aboard its hardworking air force transport fleet, going all the way back to the Berlin Airlift of 1948. Since Desert Storm and the latest honeymoon with the ever-demanding UN, American fliers had been very busy carrying aid shipments around the globe, augmented by small joint service advisory and logistics elements emplaced at the receiving ends. Other operations under way in the summer of 1992 included Provide Hope in the Georgian Republic, Provide Promise in the former Yugoslavia, Fuertes Caminos (Strong Roads) in Latin America, Southern Watch and Intrinsic Action in Kuwait, and the continuing Provide Comfort residual effort in eastern Turkey, among many other smaller projects.[11]

These aid and nation-building projects appeared to indicate that discrete application of warpower could ameliorate Third World woes without bringing on hostilities. Of course, it was all Indian country out there, and any of these missions could have gone sour at any time. But aside from some skirmishing around the Iraqi periphery, all was quiet in the badlands in mid-1992. Apparently, American Gulf War prowess had scared most of the potential bad guys back into their holes. Any such deterrent effect, however, would have a short half-life, especially in a lawless place like Somalia.

With all of these aspects considered, Bush decided to begin a very small airlift, staging through Mombasa, Kenya. This was dubbed Operation Provide Relief, and consisted of 570 ground support and flight crew personnel, with an air strength of three C-141B Starlifters and eight to fourteen C-130Es, most from the 314th Airlift Wing. A platoon of army military police from the Berlin Brigade secured the headquarters and flight line in Mombasa. The joint forces included a few A-teams from the 5th Special Forces Group (Airborne), the sum total of actual combat troops designated for the mission. It was not much.

With this meager force available, Marine Corps Gen. Joseph P. Hoar, CINCUSCENTCOM, had to tread a fine line in getting the job done. Fortunately, he recognized the importance of the type of problem developing in Somalia and planned accordingly. Hoar drew on the experience gained by CENTCOM in Crisis Action Team Exercise 92-3, a cooperative training session with the State Department's Office for Foreign Disaster Assistance and Agency for International Development. This exercise had created and tested a Humanitarian Assessment Survey Team (HAST), an interagency group that would reconnoiter a potential relief area. It also designated I Marine Expeditionary Force (I MEF) as a standing Humanitarian-Peacekeeping JTF, configured to work in a nonpermissive environment (OOTW by yet another name), with various modular headquarters designated for action, depending on the degree of commitment required.

Thus, when orders came on 16 August to begin Provide Relief, CENTCOM was ready. A HAST launched for Somalia that afternoon. As the other selected elements organized for movement to Mombasa, Hoar appointed fellow Marine Brig. Gen. Frank Libutti as commander, JTF Provide Relief. Libutti deployed to Kenya with a tiny joint staff that same day. Hoar knew that Libutti was breaking new ground: "The operation set an important precedent for U.S. involvement in relief operations in a semipermissive environment and not pursuant to a natural disaster."[12] In plain English, this was not flood relief or reconstruction of storm damage. This was sticking Uncle Sam's uniformed representatives into a civil war. Hoar had no illusions about the dangers incumbent in this step.

As the HAST made its survey, Libutti set up shop on the ground in Mombasa. In delivering supplies to Mogadishu, the JTF commander had to juggle three competing agendas: the demands of his Kenyan hosts, the concerns of the relief agencies, and force protection, the always present guest at the OOTW decision table. Typically, those three sets of concerns did not align very well.

The Kenyans, naturally, were not exactly displeased to see their aggressive northern neighbor embroiled in internal distress, but they were less than thrilled at the prospect of many Americans on their soil solely to revive prostrate Somalia. So Kenya did not enthusiastically welcome an American JTF. Libutti and the U.S. ambassador, Smith Hempstone, convinced the Kenyans that the American force would remain small in size, limit its mission to flying in aid, and withdraw completely when its tasks were finished, in a few months at most. Libutti and the ambassador also assented to demands that the first U.S. aid flights go to Somali refugees squatting just inside the Kenyan border. Finally, the Americans agreed to pay for facilities used in Mombasa, and the Kenyans were not shy in demanding their due, plus the usual escalation factor reserved for Yankees. The port supervisors in Mombasa had been servicing the U.S. Navy for years under similar deals. The almighty dollar, as usual, worked the final dollop of magic necessary to grease the way for the American operation.[13]

Appeasing the Kenyans could be done in the time-honored ways. Satisfying the international relief people proved tougher. There was no U.S. embassy staff in Mogadishu; they had left in January 1991 in the dead of night aboard Marine helicopters, the climax of Operation Eastern Exit. Lacking diplomatic front men, Libutti had to make his own arrangements.

As in northern Iraq, there was much suspicion of the U.S. military among the dedicated pacifists who staff most of the humanitarian groups. Libutti knew that he was only in the delivery business and that the aid folks were his customers, the middlemen who would actually get the goods to the

Somalis. As much as possible, the Marine brigadier had to do things the way the relief groups favored or his airlift would accomplish nothing. The JTF commander knew that he had to give the civilians a place in the decision process. Councils of war breed timidity, as do councils of OOTW, but they can seldom be avoided in these lesser confrontations, where the team becomes diverse indeed and not often amenable to arbitrary military orders. Libutti understood that. Following ideas currently taught at JRTC and Camp Lejeune, Libutti established a coordination council to ensure that he gave the UN and private agencies airlift when, where, and how they wanted it. The big jet Starlifters had to stick to Mogadishu's long runways. Smaller C-130 turboprops could get out to damaged, hardened runways in Kismayo and Bale Dogle, plus a few forward dirt strips.

Securing the vulnerable, thin-skinned U.S. planes would be difficult. A few bursts from some technical's gun could turn a fuel-laden jet into a fireball. Libutti would have preferred to insert ground security teams ahead of his aircraft, but the International Red Cross strictly prohibited arms in and around relief cargo conveyances. The JTF commander compromised by designating an airborne Quick Reaction Force (QRF) made up of Green Berets and air force security police, which orbited overhead during deliveries, ready to land and intervene if something went wrong. The Americans on the ground were unarmed. Somalis did all the unloading and distributing.[14] It was hardly a perfect arrangement, and it appears that Libutti took the sensible precaution of putting a few of his Special Forces teams on the ground in Somalia, hoping at least to gain early warning of troubles.

Under these conditions, the first air sorties began on 28 August. Four C-130s delivered thirty-four tons of rice, beans, and cooking oil. There were no calorie-rich, pork-heavy MREs, evidence that the Americans had learned their lessons well on Provide Comfort. Flights continued on a regular basis thereafter. Somali workers off-loaded each flight, and trucks carried off the supplies.[15]

Libutti's airlift was only one aspect of the evolving U.S. and UN policy toward Somalia. In September, the amphibious readiness group organized around the helicopter carrier USS *Tarawa* and the embarked 11th MEU sailed just off the Horn of Africa in a show of force as U.S. Air Force transports landed a Pakistani light infantry battalion at the port of Mogadishu, the first five hundred men in an envisioned UN force of three thousand. The United Nations looked at this as peacekeeping under Chapter 6, but the Pakistani riflemen soon discovered that there was no peace to keep. Aidid and Ali Mahdi militias had split the city. The Pakistanis hunkered down in their dockside compound right along the base of the Green Line, named after its equally ugly cousin in Beirut.[16] With the UN troops neutered and immobilized and the Americans confining themselves to an air shuttle, the warlords went about their bloody business.

Libutti turned over JTF Provide Relief to Brig. Gen. Paul A. Fratarangelo, deputy commander of I MEF, on 11 November 1992. Libutti's people had flown in some fifty million meals and almost fifteen thousand tons of humanitarian cargo. In terms of a transportation program, Provide Relief had more than done its job. Libutti told his replacement that he expected to transfer the mission over to UN-chartered civil air carriers by January 1993.

And yet, getting the stuff there amounted to dumping goodwill on the front doorstep and then running away. Aidid and his fellow chieftans took charge of almost all of the items within hours of delivery. Hijacking convoys, looting warehouses, and harassing relief workers remained the plan of the day. Aidid's technicals even began firing on merchant ships in Mogadishu's harbor, effectively closing the port by mid-November. The UN's single small battalion of Pakistani infantry huddled in their facility, outnumbered and outgunned. By all reports, famine and mayhem in Somalia were getting worse, not better.[17] Looking at the numbers, the U.S. airlift had met all expectations, but as they say in the National Football League, statistics are for losers. Provide Relief had failed.

President George Bush had failed too. On 4 November, the American electorate repudiated him in a three-way race that gave Democrat William J. Clinton of Arkansas the victory with a 43 percent plurality. Bush, who had enjoyed almost a 90 percent approval rating in the wake of the 1991 victory in the Gulf War, garnered a miserable 38 percent of the votes.[18] By January, he would be a former president, yesterday's news.

Whatever Bush might have thought of Clinton personally, the lame-duck chief executive did not want to leave unfinished business to burden his successor. Yet the Somalis had not synchronized their collapse to match the American electoral schedule. Granting that America wanted to do something to resolve the tragedy of Somalia, that something had to be done in November of 1992. Only too conscious of history peering over his shoulder, Bush was determined not to mark time and let a million or so Somalis perish. His National Security Council (NSC) deliberated, seeking to recommend a viable U.S. policy to the chief executive.

On 20 November, during a series of four meetings at the deputy level, the second tier of political, diplomatic, intelligence, and military leadership wrestled with the mounting disaster in Somalia, trying to formulate options. Ambassador Robert B. Oakley, soon to be named special envoy for Somalia, explained why: "The inability to do anything meaningful for Muslims in Bosnia, together with a perception that we could actually help in Muslim Somalia, added to the media-driven desire for a fresh look at options."[19] This time, far more than in the Kurdish operation, CNN and the rest were driving the train.

That summarized the view of the president's men on the NSC. Of course, one could ask why America felt compelled to do anything, let alone intervene in force into the Somalian chamber of horrors. The Bush people understood no-win situations. After all, they had prudently staved off European impulses to plunge into the former Yugoslavia. Why was Somalia any more worthy of a U.S. commitment? What interests were at stake? With the pressure of media-driven policy generation during the last days of a lame-duck administration, nobody bothered to ask those hard questions. Still smarting over the electoral defeat and seemingly determined to wield power while they still held it, the Bush inner circle was looking for yet another quick win to add to the triumph over Manuel Noriega in Panama, the retaking of Kuwait, and the victorious culmination of the Cold War. Could the greatest power on earth stand by and let millions starve? For God's sake, it was almost Christmas.

As for the diplomatic view, the Department of State pressed for a larger U.S. role, consistent with the usual American predisposition for collective security. American allies pledged to join the effort as soon as Bush announced it. Saving the hungry in Somalia would require American ground combat troops—no quick cruise missile barrages or offshore shows of force would do the trick. No, State thought it would take riflemen, boots on the ground, the real instruments of American control, backed by the full destructive suite of Yankee airpower and seapower. Undersecretary of State Frank Wisner was already talking to UN Secretary General Boutros-Ghali about an expanded American role, but without promising anything. Boutros-Ghali knew, though, that Wisner would not be speaking to him unless a major escalation was in the offing.

The intelligence people really were noncommittal, although they presented a grim summary of conditions on the ground. The civil war raged on unabated. A half million Somalis were already dead and up to a million soon to expire from lack of food. Almost a million Somalis had fled to Kenya and Ethiopia, and they were in bad shape too. Food could not get inland through the warlord cordons. Despite the best efforts of the Red Cross and friends, JTF Provide Relief, and the United Nations peacekeeping contingent, the Somali famine was spreading.

The military alone, represented by vice chairman of the Joint Chiefs of Staff Adm. David Jeremiah, remained opposed to major intervention, as they had been all along. Stark images on CNN aside, there were too many questions. What would constitute success? How could America avoid becoming caught in the tentacles of a confusing, several-sided civil war? Would the American people support the effort? How many lives would it cost? How long would it last? How could the Americans be extricated? And, most important of all, so what? Even if America led a massive security and relief effort, what would prevent things in Somalia from sliding right back to business as usual a few months after America left? Those sorts of concerns had motivated the military to urge caution.

The deputies hammered out three options to present to Bush. The first, and least escalatory, increased support (verbal, financial, and a few small service support units) for the small UN peacekeeping effort. The second, more difficult to pull off, envisioned America organizing a large coalition intervention force, including U.S. air and seapower, but specifically excluding American ground combat troops. The third and strongest option involved an American-led multinational force spearheaded by U.S. Army and Marine infantry, modeled on Desert Storm and Provide Comfort. Jeremiah acknowledged that the military, especially in Hoar's CENTCOM, had done some contingency planning for these options, even the third one. But given the Joint Chiefs' strong reservations about placing infantrymen on Somali soil, the NSC deputies figured on the middle course. They scheduled another meeting the next day, a Saturday, to flesh out the details. Nobody expected anything extraordinary.

They were wrong. In Oakley's words, Jeremiah "startled the group by saying 'If you think U.S. forces are needed, we can do the job.'" Jeremiah described a major operation built around two divisions, one Marine, one army.[20] The NSC deputies were surprised and impressed. Led by its powerful chairman, Gen. Colin L. Powell, the JCS had reversed course. Obviously, they had been thinking seriously about intervention for a long time. Jeremiah's operational plan, complete in many particulars, had not been yanked out of a hat.

Why the switch? Certainly, the military understood that Bush wanted to act in Somalia. Powell and his fellow armed forces leaders had several incentives to get aboard this moving train. After the triumphs in Panama, the Gulf, Kurdistan, and in the end games of the Cold War, the senior uniformed officers knew very well how much George Bush had done for them. He had, for the most part, told the military what to do, not how to do it—no small issue for men who had lived through the micromanaging of the Vietnam War and other Cold War escapades. The armed forces could thank Bush's leadership for their recent victories, their superb public reputation, and, especially, the low casualty lists. As Bush explained a year later to a gathering of military leaders, "We did the politics and you superbly did the fighting." Now this president, on his way to retirement, was asking them for one more operation. Personal loyalties are deadly serious in the armed services. The military, especially the JCS and the upper rungs of the uniformed chain of command as they existed in late 1992, owed Bush.

One must also consider that in those heady days, America's armed forces were enjoying a peak period of success and acclaim around the world, astride the globe like a near-omnipotent colossus. With regard to going into Somalia, there was a strong feeling that, as Oakley put it, "no other country either could or would undertake it." Powell explained why this was so: "We have certain unique capabilities in the armed forces of the United States that don't exist in many other armed forces." As they used to say in the old television show, this was a job for Superman, or in this case, Superpower. The decision to enter Somalia in strength betrayed an American strain of what the Japanese after Pearl Harbor learned to rue as "victory disease."[21] Uncle Sam's armed forces were feeling their oats, probably a little too much.

Personal ties and service pride aside, Powell and his flag officers knew that Bush could order them to execute regardless of JCS opinions. As a minimum, most in uniform agreed that Somalia was better than Bosnia, another potential media-driven area for intervention at that time. By agreeing to the more manageable of the two schemes, the generals and admirals could expect the usual Bush permission to shape the effort to match military preferences.

This was exactly what happened. Two conditions were understood. The mission would be limited to securing humanitarian relief for the Somalis, and a massive effort at the outset would be used to frighten off, preempt, and, as necessary, crush resistance. The press had labeled this Powell's all-or-nothing approach because when the chairman advised committing forces, he believed in using overwhelming warpower to gain a specific end. Operations Just Cause, Desert Storm, and Provide Comfort were the models. On 21 November, preliminary warnings went out to selected headquarters throughout the U.S. armed forces: prepare for intervention in Somalia to guarantee relief deliveries.[22] When orders went out, the military would be ready.

Those orders came on 25 November. Given the consensus among the NSC membership, and Bush's expressed interest in doing something dramatic, this was to be expected. The decision briefing to the president went as expected, although Powell raised concerns about the conditions for eventual U.S. handover to the UN and withdrawal of American forces. Those issues went unresolved. Bush wanted to act, and so he did. The commander in chief authorized what became known as Operation Restore Hope.

Operation orders followed to all affected units, starting with General Hoar's CENTCOM. Bush himself went to the telephones to begin personally crafting the international coalition, reliving his presidency's greatest accomplishments—building and leading the alliance that triumphed in the Gulf. Secretary of State Lawrence Eagleburger flew to New York to tell the news to Boutros-Ghali.[23]

Emboldened by the American willingness to intervene, encouraged by Boutros-Ghali, the UN Security Council passed Resolution 794 on 3 December. With this document, the activist secretary general greatly exceeded the American desire for a narrow mandate to secure food deliveries. The humanitarian and limited security mission was in there all right, but Boutros-Ghali and the many delegations that supported him imparted their own hard spin to the large but carefully delineated American offer. As usual, most were willing to let Uncle Sam do all the heavy lifting.

Resolution 794 included the mission Bush had agreed to lead. Troops would enter Somalia "to establish as soon as possible a secure environment for humanitarian relief operations." That part looked a lot like the 1991 authorization for Operation Provide Comfort in Kurdistan and accorded with what Bush and Powell had discussed and what the Pentagon staff had started into motion. Yet Resolution 794 did not stop there. In the United Nations, the Somali operation was not being handled like Provide Comfort. For the first time, pushed by Boutros-Ghali, the world body was boldly authorizing action under Chapter 7, the use of UN force to defeat a threat to international security, "to restore peace, stability, and law and order with a view to facilitating the process of a political settlement under the auspices of the United Nations." Even the UN vote to enter the Korean conflict in 1950 had not formally invoked this chapter, and no Security Council measure had ever authorized such sweeping intrusion into a member state's internal affairs.

This was far beyond what America had agreed to do. Yet with the calendar in his office ticking off his last days, with ships and planes en route, Bush had to take what he could get. Resolution 794, though disturbingly wide in scope, would have to do. Flanked by the shades of Woodrow Wilson and Franklin D. Roosevelt, Bush announced the American-led UN intervention on 4 December.[24]

In the press to save lives in Somalia, to avoid appearing paralyzed in the postelectoral interregnum, to get it begun and done before Clinton came in, to do something, America accepted a huge dichotomy between the UN mission and what the superpower was willing to do. Clinton and American servicemen would pay for this unresolved divergence. For his part, unwilling to sanction Boutros-Ghali's line, Bush said, "This operation is not open-ended. We will not stay one day longer than is absolutely necessary. Let me be very clear: our mission is humanitarian, but we will not tolerate armed gangs ripping off their own people, condemning them to death by starvation. General Hoar and his troops have the authority to take whatever military action is necessary to safeguard the lives of our troops and the lives of the Somali people."[25]

It would be the Provide Comfort drill again—secure the area, feed the people, and get out without getting tangled up in local political squabbling. Without Iraqi tanks hanging around, with only a few of those *Mad Max* technicals to brush aside, it should have been easier than the Kurdish undertaking. Bush even speculated that he could wrap it all up before Clinton took office on 20 January 1993. Operation Provide Comfort suggested that it could go very smoothly.

Except that this time, Americans would be plunging into Somalia—a real hellhole, a graveyard for do-gooders and optimists, teeming with bad actors and stocked to the gills with weapons and ammunition. Nobody here had experienced in person the warpower of Desert Storm. In fact, most Somalis knew only three things about the American military: U.S. forces had helped the despicable Siyad Barrah for more than a decade, they had fled their embassy under cover of darkness in January of 1991, and, until now, they had not been willing to do more than deliver food—women's work. In a warrior society, such impressions did not dissipate easily.

*   *   *

At Hoar's level, there was only one mission, the president's mission. Hoar and his staff worked out this mission statement: "When directed by the National Command Authorities, CINCCENT will conduct joint and combined military operations in Somalia to secure the major air and sea ports, key installations and food distribution points, to provide open and free passage of relief supplies, to provide security for convoys and relief organization operations and assist UN/nongovernmental organizations in providing humanitarian relief under UN auspices." This was the Bush version of what to do, reduced to its military essence. And yet, invariably, as other countries joined the coalition, the UN mission would intrude on this narrow construct. The wilder elements running loose in Somalia would also have their say. No war is frictionless, even when well-meaning people try to call it a relief expedition. There would be a lot of friction before America turned out the lights on this one.

Hoar expressly avoided any ambitious plan to demilitarize the warrior groups. The CENTCOM commander in chief believed it "was not realistically achievable nor a prerequisite for the core mission of providing a secure environment for relief operations." He knew that to secure the arrival and distribution of food and aid cargoes, there would have to be some "disarming as necessary." This was the fundamental distinction between the UN and Bush missions in that Boutros-Ghali wanted the American-led troops to disarm all warring factions that resisted the UN-sponsored program of political reconciliation and unification. How to disarm and whom to disarm became raging issues as the intervention wore on.

Methods of disarmament ranged from voluntary collection to cash for weapons to forcible seizure. For those who absolutely and violently refused to hand over their shooting irons, there was always the final sanction—one between the eyes. The Americans and their allies would go in ready to try all of these techniques.

Who to disarm became intertwined with the methods chosen. Those favoring the UN intervention were more likely to deliver their arms. Those neutral or in opposition kept the arsenals that gave them power. At UN roadblocks, on patrols, on convoys, Americans and other coalition troops routinely encountered armed Somalis in civilian clothes. Then the fun began. In a country wracked by ceaseless internal violence, one could not simply take all weapons. People needed their automatic rifles to guard their families, and some of the relief agencies still depended on hired gunmen for security of local offices, living quarters, and shipments. But who were the bad guys?

American soldiers in Somalia solved it by applying what became known as the "four No's": no technicals, no visible weapons, no militia checkpoints (for tolls and other demands), and no bandits (warlord militia units). Americans had the authority to shoot first if the locals did not comply, but in practice, this was a real judgment call. Every militiaman was a potential enemy and a potential friend, and it was up to young corporals to read the moods of men whose language they did not speak. As one army commander said, disarming a bellicose populace, even partially, is an "extraordinarily

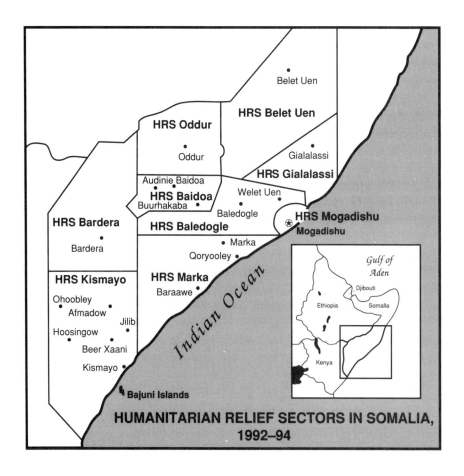

HUMANITARIAN RELIEF SECTORS IN SOMALIA, 1992–94

complex and difficult process," and one guaranteed to produce resentments, ugly little firefights, and endless, tragic mistakes.[26]

With an already tough mission to handle, Hoar restricted his operation to the nine southern districts. This left the other seven of the country's prewar areas under the sway of Tur and his Somali National Movement, who were running a separate state in what used to be British Somaliland. The north was not nearly as troubled by disorder and hunger as the ravaged south. So Hoar left that for the UN negotiators to solve and focused on the south.

There was more than enough to do down there. Almost two-thirds of the country's suffering population lived on the rolling pastures of the Haud Plateau and in the farmlands watered by the Juba and Shebeli Rivers, with a half million in Mogadishu alone. Most of the other cities claimed fifty thousand or less inhabitants, but all of them, including Mogadishu, had swelled as people wandered in, searching for food and medicine.

The ambience in all of these towns was distressingly familiar to American troops, who had seen its like in a hundred other squalid Third World locales in Africa, Asia, and Latin America. Each settlement offered the same pastiche of low, utilitarian cinder-block structures, corrugated tin roofs, animals sharing rooms with people, and a few modern buildings in disrepair, all arranged in haphazard rows along rutted dirt streets. Everything wore a coat of flourlike dust that shone like bleached bone in the dry season, an effect that gave way to gray slime and yellow-brown mud under the overcast of infrequent rains during the wet months. The few marks of modernity—the ever-present Japanese-made minipickup trucks, an occasional trademark sign blaring "Coca-Cola" or "Nike"—only served to highlight the poverty and gritty sameness of the landscape.

Hoar's forces were entering during the winter dry season, which would last until March, when the wet monsoons would blow ashore from the warm waters of the Indian Ocean. Semiarid inland, almost tropical in coastal cities like Mogadishu and Kismayo, Somalia featured temperatures ranging from 65 to 105 degrees Fahrenheit, with less humidity in the interior. Burdened by rucksacks and flak jackets, the soldiers and Marines would feel the heat, especially the light infantrymen who flew in direct from the snows of Fort Drum in northern New York.[27]

The light fighters came from Fort Drum in accord with Hoar's carefully thought-out plan, whose outline had so impressed the National Security Council deputies when explained by Admiral Jeremiah. In accord with the detailed scheme he and his staff had developed, Hoar turned to Lt. Gen.

Humanitarian Relief Sectors in Somalia

HRS	UNITAF	UNOSOM II
Baidoa	Australia	France
Bale Dogle	U.S. Army	Morocco
Bardera	U.S. Marines	Botswana
Belet Uen	Canada	Germany
Gialalassi	Italy	Italy
Kismayo	U.S. Army	Belgium
Marka	U.S. Army	Pakistan
Mogadishu	U.S. Marines	Pakistan
Oddur	France	France

Major countries providing forces are noted; other smaller national contingents were also involved in each HRS.

Sources: Maj. Gen. Steven L. Arnold, USA, and Maj. David T. Stahl, USA, "A Power Projection Army in Operations Other Than War," *Parameters* (Winter 1993–94): 6; T. Frank Crigler, "The Peace-Enforcement Dilemma," *Joint Forces Quarterly* (Autumn 1993): 66; Walter S. Clarke, "Testing the World's Resolve in Somalia," *Parameters* (Winter 1993–94): 46.

Robert B. Johnston and his I MEF to serve as the command echelon. Johnston led Joint Task Force Somalia, soon renamed Combined Joint Task Force Somalia to reflect the allied role, and finally Unified Task Force (UNITAF) to match UN desires. A veteran of Vietnam, Lebanon, and most recently the Gulf War, where he had served as chief of staff to the blistering, demanding Schwarzkopf, Johnston was well qualified for this tough job. He had been on tap for Somalia for months, and with his deputy Fratarangelo already running Provide Relief, the I MEF commander knew what to expect.[28]

He gathered a very capable U.S. force to do the job. His lead assault elements would be Col. Gregory S. Newbold's 15th Marine Expeditionary Unit (Special Operations Capable) (15th MEU), drawn from 3d Marine Division and other western Pacific Marine air and service support elements. Built around Battalion Landing Team 2/9 Marines (BLT 2/9), the 164th Medium Helicopter Squadron 164, and the 15th MEU Service Support Group, and delivered by the sailors of the three-ship USS *Tripoli* amphibious group, this force had the capability to seize and hold the Mogadishu port and international airfield. The MEU could open the operation, but with only one infantry battalion, it could not hope to do much more than the Pakistani peacekeepers unless speedily and massively reinforced. But the first step was taking the port and the runway.

Johnston fully intended to bring in the massive force envisioned by Hoar, Powell, and Bush, and that meant more than a MEU. From the 1st Marine Division at Camp Pendleton, California, most of Col. Buck Bedard's 7th Marine Regiment would fly in to marry up with equipment sets headed into theater aboard Maritime Prepositioning Force ships. These transports steamed north through the Indian Ocean, having left their anchorage at the island of Diego Garcia as soon as Hoar gave the go order. Other Marine helicopter aviation, engineer, and service support elements rounded out the six thousand or so Marines en route. Reflecting the big job of downloading the equipment transports in a bare-bones environment, more than twenty-eight hundred of the Marines worked for the 1st Force Service Support Group.[29]

The majority of the ground forces, to include most of the engineers and combat service support units, were to come from the army, with the bulk from Maj. Gen. Steve Arnold's 10th Mountain Division (Light Infantry), headquartered just south of the Canadian border at snowy Fort Drum. Arnold's soldiers had just returned from Hurricane Andrew relief work in south Florida and had learned a thing or two about humanitarian missions in a benign environment. Now the 10th Mountain, a division built around the skill and determination of selected foot infantry, lacking tanks or other heavy vehicles, was heading for Somalia. Already lean by design, the 10th only manned two of its three brigades, with proportional slices of artillery, aviation, engineers, and the like. The third brigade was supposed to be drawn from the reserve forces, but they were not activated for Somalia. Arnold's division would deploy and fight shorthanded, a circumstance that worried some, especially if the intervention did not end in a few months.

Designated Task Force Mountain, Arnold's light division became the backbone for the army commitment and acted as the overall headquarters for all U.S. soldiers. Arnold, who had also served in Desert Storm, insisted on intensified training and preparation as his force staged for deployment by air and sea. His troops became steeped in the lore of Somalia, worked on survival and acclimatization skills, and made good use of what they had learned about urban operations and winning hearts and minds in storm-torn Florida. Arnold solicited help from Lt. Col. John Abizaid, who had learned so much during Provide Comfort. When the 10th Mountain arrived in country, it would be ready to go.[30]

Airpower came courtesy of the continuing Provide Relief effort from Kenya, plus a sustained airlift by the air force's Air Mobility Command (AMC). AMC's C-141B Starlifters, KC-10A Extenders, and C-5A and C-5B Galaxies, supplemented by civil charters, ferried in twenty-four thousand U.S. troops, three thousand foreign soldiers, and nearly three thousand tons of cargo. Air Force Brig. Gen. Thomas R. Mikolajcik and two hundred airmen ran the Mogadishu terminus of this huge airflow.

The USS *Ranger* aircraft carrier battle group, including the Aegis cruiser USS *Valley Forge,* lingered just offshore, ready to strike as needed ashore. The USS *Kitty Hawk* battle group replaced the *Ranger* group after the first ten days, and a carrier remained on station from then on, until the transition to UNOSOM II in May 1993. Although many reconnaissance missions were flown, hostilities inland never required the carrier airmen or cruiser gunners to respond in anger. But they were ready and evident, a warning to those who might try something.[31]

The American forces assigned to Operation Restore Hope reached a maximum of 25,426, including those in Mombasa and offshore. About sixteen thousand were on the ground in Somalia, and of those, some ten thousand came from the U.S. Army. This was definitely an American production.

Allied contributions eventually came from twenty-one countries, and totaled thirteen thousand soldiers by mid-January of 1993. The eight most sizable contingents were the 1st Battalion of the Royal Australian Regiment, the Belgian 1st Paracommando Battalion, the Botswana Task Force, the elite 1st Canadian Airborne Battle Group, the French foreign legion's 13th Demi-Brigade, the Italian Task Force, the Royal Moroccan Task Force, and the Pakistani peacekeeper battalion already in Mogadishu. The British, heavily involved in the former Yugoslavia and a bit skeptical about trying to accomplish anything in Somalia, were conspicuous by their absence.

Other than the Botswanans, Moroccans, and Pakistanis, who were unknown but said to be decent, the other allied units were clearly first-rate. The Canadians had lengthy experience in peace operations in Cyprus and elsewhere, and the 13th Demi-Brigade came from nearby Djibouti and enjoyed the usual French Foreign Legion reputation for brooking no nonsense. The Australians and Belgians were solid, familiar American exercise partners. In all, Johnston could be satisfied with his allies. Like Shalikashvili in

Kurdistan, the Marine general mixed in national contingents down to company level as required by tasks.[32]

As he marshaled his multinational forces, Johnston knew he had to act quickly to save the starving. Johnston designed a four-phase operation, built for speed and power. First, UNITAF had to take the air and sea entry sites around Mogadishu. Next, substantial combat and support forces would flow in and expand the foothold, taking control of the food distribution sites and routes fanning out of the shattered Somali capital. With that done, Johnston would expand his efforts to Kismayo, completing the relief and security network, and thus allowing aid and food to flow. The final phase would be a handover to a beefed-up, non-American UNOSOM force, who would stay behind and keep it all working. Johnston and Hoar guessed they could have the situation in hand by 20 January 1993, when Bush left office, with U.S. withdrawal beginning shortly thereafter.[33] Get in, get it on, and get out—that was the theory. Reality, as usual, had its own say.

Everything started out exactly as forecast. The first Americans arrived in style and in power, as befits the legions of a superpower. SEALs and Marine scouts from 15th MEU paddled ashore near the port of Mogadishu in the wee hours of 9 December, to be assailed by resistance they did not expect—throngs of pushy camera crews with bright lights. As the television crews and the reconnaissance teams postured for each other, the rest of BLT 2/9 surged ashore on air-cushioned landing craft. Waves of bobbing Marine helicopters clattered overhead, Marine riflemen ran forward, and slab-sided amtracs growled and clanked as the world watched. The Marines quickly secured the airport and seaport, and the buildup began.

Other than the press, there were no impediments to progress. The clan militias and their technicals fled inland, going to ground in the face of the lead waves of Marines and the mounting arrival of follow-on forces. In this, Johnston's Marines benefited from the superb work of another veteran of Vietnam and Lebanon, albeit a foreign service veteran, Ambassador Oakley. He did more to prepare the battlefield than any SEAL team could have.

Arriving with a few Special Forces escorts two days before the landing, Oakley had boldly gone into the dangerous city. Acting in the style of some long-gone western raj, the fearless Oakley moved through the city unmolested. He met separately with Aidid and Ali Mahdi and warned them to stay clear when the Americans arrived. They agreed, and put out the word on their propaganda radio stations and by runner. The two rivals also agreed to suspend their disputes and join a follow-up meeting on 11 December with Oakley and Johnston. As Oakley put it, they would "discuss the potentially disastrous results if their followers unintentionally clashed with U.S. forces." Both warlords assented, and Johnston's men landed without any trouble from the militias.

When the session occurred, under the drone of arriving and departing transport aircraft, the normally hate-filled Somali pair were so carried away with enthusiasm that they announced a cease-fire and insisted on holding a press conference for the assembled international news media. Aidid, who held southwest Mogadishu, and Ali Mahdi, who dominated the northeast, mugged for the cameras, each trying on the mantle of "responsible leader." The chieftains vied for UNITAF anointment as the man of the hour and hoped that the increasing allied force would eliminate all rivals. On 28 December, as the press hummed along, Aidid and Ali Mahdi walked together along the Green Line, talking in generalities of some happy future day—each no doubt certain that the other would soon be at peace about six feet under, courtesy of a Marine bullet or two.[34]

While Aidid and Ali Mahdi kissed and made up, Oakley and Johnston moved quickly to get food to the hungry. On 13 December, Marines and soldiers of Lt. Col. James Sikes's 2-87th Infantry air assaulted into Bale Dogle, taking the airfield by coup de main. This set the stage for a French-Marine push to Baidoa two days later, an air and ground maneuver led by the 1st Battalion, 7th Marines. It went off without hostilities. As usual, UNITAF's secret weapon, Ambassador Oakley, preceeded the allied move and had the sense to bring a Muslim U.S. Marine with him as proof that the Americans were not coming as infidel despoilers but to help. With the hearty support of Baidoa's community leaders, relief convoys began to enter the town unmolested by warlord gunmen, the first time that had been possible in two years. Once things settled down, the Australians took over this sector.[35]

The success at Baidoa, plus the almost complete absence of any hostile response, persuaded Johnston to advance his timetable. Over the next two weeks, the controlled sectors expanded. On 19 December, 2/9 Marines and Belgian paratroopers landed at Kismayo, covered by howling jets from the *Kitty Hawk.* Soldiers from Task Force Mountain's 3-14th Infantry flew in and took over from the Marines, who returned to their amphibious shipping, poised for other assaults. The American soldiers and Belgians remained in

Kismayo, securing humanitarian supplies as they came by air, sea, and road. Warring Colonels Jess and Morgan backed off for the moment, although here, there were no media events to mark the occasion.

Johnston moved his other forces forward as they arrived. The French took Oddur and the Italians secured Gialalassi. Both operations were followed by local disarming and the immediate resumption of food and medicine distribution.

UNITAF completed its expansion on 28 December, when TF Mountain launched a brigade-scale air assault to take Belet Uen, 150 miles away from Bale Dogle. There was no discernable road to Belet Uen; the forces had to go by air. Guided in by photos from navy air reconnaissance and reports from army Special Forces, Col. Kip Ward's 2d Brigade orchestrated a major joint and combined operation. With *Kitty Hawk* aircraft orbiting overhead, army aviation, supplemented by Marine CH-53E heavy-lift helicopters and Canadian C-130s, brought in Sikes's 2-87th Infantry lightfighters and the Canadian airborne battalion. Already warned by the tireless Oakley and showered with psychological warfare leaflets explaining that UNITAF came as friends, the locals welcomed the allied forces. Arnold characterized the air assault as "executed flawlessly." With Belet Uen so neatly in hand, the Restore Hope force had staked out its nine Humanitarian Relief Sectors several weeks ahead of the most optimistic predictions.[36]

Eight Americans died in these early days. A Marine, a Green Beret, and a special operator working on Oakley's security party were victims of separate land mines, the bane of all OOTW. Two other Marines died in firefights. Traffic accidents killed two soldiers. Another drowned. They went one by one, regulars all, unremarked except as evidence of "very light" casualties. There was no outcry, but all were as dead as anyone whose name is etched on the Vietnam Memorial. It was not as if Americans did not care but more as if they did not notice what the cameras did not show. Restore Hope was making progress, and that did show up on CNN. So the country accepted the deaths as the price to be paid.

There were also plenty of nonfatal casualties, usually inflicted by the random gunshots so much a part of the Somali clan squabbling. Shootings occurred in isolated neighborhoods. The watchful American and allied professionals made short work of miscreants foolish enough to engage. The Foreign Legionnaires, as expected, opened fire with particular zeal when challenged. As one American pamphlet cautioned, "Security problems or shortfalls have contributed to the failure of force protection programs during terrorist attacks against U.S. interests in the Middle East since the 1983 Beirut bombings." Commanders at all levels took that kind of warning to heart, and ROE were quite practical, allowing UNITAF personnel to shoot first if threatened by any weapons-toting Somalis. The force ROE card ended with this pointed reminder: "Always be prepared to act in self-defense."[37] Nobody took chances, nor did they allow the humanitarian label to lull them into complacency.

Yet despite surface appearances, not all was well. The country was awash in weaponry, and the enemy was an elusive bunch to pin down. Among the Marines, officers and NCOs vacillated on the wisest policy with regard to "disarming as necessary." Some platoons confiscated all weaponry. Others tried to centralize the weapons in their areas into unofficial arms rooms, to be checked in and out by receipt. Some caches were raided and removed, others intentionally avoided. Arnold's soldiers followed their four No's, tempered by common sense, and the French and Italians aggressively disarmed the militias in their sectors. The differences were due to local situations, local interpretations, and the basic confusion between the Boutros-Ghali and U.S. ideas about disarmament. The UN secretary general wanted UNITAF to do it. Bush, Powell, Hoar, and Johnston believed, as Hoar said, that it was "a political issue, one that needs to be settled first and foremost by the Somalis."

Only Americans could have the optimism to think that men who derived their power and worth from guns would give them up in pursuit of some abstract nation-state ideal. It just was not in the cards. Gamely, Oakley tried anyway. In a series of negotiations, he talked Aidid and Ali Mahdi into placing their heavier weapons and technicals at UN-controlled cantonments, and both men made token consignments as early as 26 December. Ali Mahdi complied more fully, turning over all of his group's technical vehicles by mid-February. Aidid chose to back out and moved his heavier arms into the hinterland, to wait for the end of UNITAF.[38]

Despite the fact that people were being fed, and the warlords quieted if not defanged, the question became What next? All of the Somali leaders knew that the Americans would be leaving soon, and whatever stayed behind under the UN banner would most certainly be made of weaker stuff. As in the Kurdish case, the Americans might have declared victory and backed out. Instead, incredibly, they declared victory and then backed blithely into a buzzsaw.

*   *   *

As UNITAF units began to redeploy in the spring of 1993, they could look back on accomplishments as real as anything achieved by Shali-kashvili's people in northern Iraq. The specter of starvation had been lifted. By late February, thirty-five feeding stations in the nine UNITAF sectors were feeding a million people a week, schools had reopened, and crops were being planted. UNITAF engineers, led by the U.S. Army's 36th Engineer Group and U.S. Navy SeaBees, had resurfaced several airstrips, including those at Mogadishu and Kismayo, upgraded seven others to C-130 standards, repaired some eleven hundred miles of roads, and dug fourteen major wells—enough infrastructure improvement to permit full access by relief workers. Oakley estimated that fifty or fewer Somalis fell to UNITAF gunfire, despite hundreds of tense confrontations.[39] The Bush mission had been accomplished.

Even the Boutros-Ghali concept of nation-building seemed to be under way. Facilitated by Oakley, Aidid and Ali Mahdi, along with other clan and militia leaders, were participating in UN-sponsored discussions. In a land with no government, these jealous overlords had received their due. Of course, their agenda—who will take charge?—had been suppressed by the massive American-led intrusion. Once the Americans left, the battle for leadership seemed likely to flare anew. But America had done what could be done for nation-building, short of pumping in hundreds of thousands of riflemen to destroy the more recalcitrant chiefs.

Clinton was in the White House as the military began to disengage from Operation Restore Hope. While Powell and Bush administration Secretary of Defense Dick Cheney had seen a need to leave some U.S. technical experts, they had expected to let other countries shoulder most of the burden of what would become UNOSOM II. Cheney guessed that he could leave a MEU and its amphibious group offshore, for emergencies. "But it doesn't require continued U.S. force on the ground," he argued.[40]

And yet, as Powell had worried from the beginning, the handover to the UN was not to be tidy nor complete. The Clinton people, very much reflecting the new president's deference to Democratic icons Wilson and Roosevelt, had a predisposition for multilateral foreign policy and a warm spot for UN ventures. Preoccupied with domestic matters, Clinton simply let his instincts and his vigorous, idealistic subordinates lead him on this one.

Boutros-Ghali warned the Americans that, without the guarantee of U.S. logisticians, he would have to contract for service support, and not too many

corporations were able or willing to undertake such a complex and potentially dangerous task. America agreed to leave a logistics group under UN
authority, and to contribute expert staffers for the UNOSOM II staff and
headquarters. But there was more.

Uncertain about the fighting prowess of some of the UNOSOM II partners and concerned about the American lives at risk, Clinton's people added
a QRF to the residual package: a brigade-level headquarters, a light infantry battalion task force, an aviation battalion task force, and a tailored combat service support element. This 10th Mountain unit was supplemented, at
least in theory, by a MEU and its landing ships, which could be made available offshore from time to time. The continuing American presence com-
forted many of the countries participating in UNOSOM II. If things went
bad, the Americans would save them. In its composition, the stay-behind
contingent was not much different from what remained in the wake of Provide Comfort—except in that operation, the Americans stayed on the territory of an old, strong ally, not adrift in a land beyond the Thunderdome.

Yet Clinton's people had erected some safeguards. UNOSOM II would
be commanded by a Turkish general, with an American deputy, and a Canadian chief of staff. The QRF did not wear blue UN berets; they reported
only to the American deputy and would be used only for force protection.
If the UNOSOM II people wanted to try nation-building, they would be
doing it without American help, or at least not much. It was multilateralism
on the cheap, incremental multilateralism, another brick paving the road into
the abyss.

With a continued and subordinate U.S. role safely in his pocket, the UN
secretary general left no doubt that qualms about nation-building could be
set aside, and the business of rebuilding a viable Somalia could begin. UN
Security Council Resolution 814, encouraged by America, said as much,
ordering Turkish Lt. Gen. Cevik Bir to begin "rehabilitating political institutions and the economy and promoting political settlement and national
reconciliation." As with UNITAF, UNOSOM II operated under the tenets of
Chapter 7, endeavoring to impose peace where it did not exist.

Although only 30 percent of its UN staff was in place, and newly assigned UN units were still getting organized or en route, UNOSOM II assumed its duties, pure Boutros-Ghali nation-building, on 4 May 1993.[41] It
happened without much official notice in Washington, where the new president had other matters on his mind. Domestic issues and constituencies

came first. In this vein, motivated by preelection promises, President Clinton devoted an inordinate amount of energy to defining the role of homosexuals in the U.S. armed forces, rather than defining the role of those same armed forces in war-torn Somalia. Hard lessons lay ahead for the new commander in chief and his administration.

The shift to UNOSOM II altered the vital role of the U.S. envoy. Oakley had turned over his liaison duties to Ambassador Robert Gosende early in March. Simultaneously, UN Ambassador Ismat Kittani, an Iraqi, passed his portfolio to retired American Adm. Jonathan Howe. During the UNITAF period, Oakley had led, with Kittani in trail. Now Howe took the lead in crafting a political settlement among people who wanted each other dead. He played the same role relative to Bir that Oakley had played with Johnston, but there were no common experiences on which to draw.

Bir cooperated with Howe, but he seemed overly concerned with his rank and position. Bir was not happy that his strongest ground unit, the U.S. QRF, did not report to him. He sensed that he was attempting a mission well beyond the capacity of his polyglot mix of 28,000 UN troops, including nearly 4,000 Americans, 1,200 of them fighting men. Unlike Johnston, Bir did not try combined operations. His struggling UNOSOM II staff could not coordinate them. He simply split up the country like a pizza, sending Botswanans out to the old U.S. Marine Bardera sector and giving the by now very experienced Pakistanis responsibility for Mogadishu. Bir was not a happy commander.

Under Bir, a U.S. Army major general named Thomas M. Montgomery inherited two roles bound for contradiction. As deputy UNOSOM II commander, Montgomery answered to Bir. Wearing his U.S. hats, the commander of U.S. Forces in Somalia (USFORSOM) and commander, Army Forces, Somalia, Montgomery owned the QRF and any other combat forces that might be sent his way. Brigadier General Greg L. Gile, deputy commander of Arnold's 10th Mountain Division, acted as Montgomery's second, overseeing day-to-day operations.

Montgomery was a good man, an experienced tanker and Vietnam veteran who had held key strategy jobs on the U.S. Army and NATO staffs. But unlike the Marine generals who had gone before him in Somalia, Montgomery was not part of a fighting headquarters, coming instead from duty as the director of management, chief paper-tracker of the Army Staff. The general did not have a staff to call his own, but much like the UNOSOM II crowd, he had to build one from bits and pieces drawn mainly from the U.S. Army, plus people tasked as individuals from the other services.

Montgomery's assigned units rotated on a four- to six-month basis, as the American armed forces settled in for what looked to be a long haul. Carrier battle groups and amphibious groups would be sent only "as needed." The Mombasa airlift was over, although U.S. forces still staged through the Kenyan city. Montgomery commanded a force with very little airpower and almost no seapower. About all he owned was exactly what his enemies could field in great numbers—riflemen.

Montgomery's plight indicated that nobody took Somalia to be a war. For the American military, Somalia had become something else, another unwanted work detail, akin to chipping paint or policing up litter. Forces were allocated accordingly. Pickup teams and provisional outfits prolifer-ated, and organic units were forever either halfway there or halfway gone, tied up by the tight rotation schedules. Training and acclimating the endless dribs and drabs of new arrivals became full-time requirements, starting with the general's own staff.[42]

With this shaky command structure, the American Marines gone, and the superb Australians and Canadians soon to leave, UNOSOM II was vulner-able to a determined enemy. In Muhammed Farah Aidid, they found one.

In Somali, "aidid" means "one who tolerates no insult," and Muhammed Farah lived up to his nickname. Son of a Hawiye clan camel trader, gradu-ate of Italian and Soviet military schools, Somali army chief of staff in 1969–70, political prisoner from 1970 to 1976, field commander in the Ogaden War, and ambassador to India, Aidid had led the men who ran out Siyad Barrah. His following, called the Somali National Alliance (SNA), had grown after his open split with his former ally Ali Mahdi, also Hawiye, though of a different subclan. The SNA could call on thousands of fighters, and its fleet of technicals was supplemented by huge stockpiles of antitank rocket launchers, antiaircraft guns, mortars, light artillery pieces, and even a few tanks. Heavily armed, the SNA displayed more discipline than most of the other militias, thanks mainly to the charismatic Aidid.

More than most Somalis, Aidid understood America. Many of Aidid's fourteen children lived in America. One son, a Marine reservist, had even accompanied the UNITAF expedition into Mogadishu. Aidid had been will-ing to wait and see back in December, but when the Americans and

UNITAF left matters unresolved, he decided to make a name the same way the Mad Mullah had made his, by running out the foreigners. "I cannot accept these hundreds of UN troops," Aidid complained to reporter Rick Lyman of the *Philadelphia Inquirer.* The SNA chief blamed the UN battalions for interfering in Somali internal affairs and blocking his group's succession to power. "We intend to rule," he told Lyman.[43]

Unwavering in his goal, Aidid played along throughout the series of UN-sponsored conferences that picked up on Oakley's December initiatives. The warlord made the right gestures, up to point. Always, though, SNA jealously guarded its weapon stocks, its technicals, and its independence, as directed by the band's head man, who knew very well that UNITAF would not stay long.

Once most of the Americans departed, the SNA leader made his move. He tried a political tack first, seeking a UN imprimatur as the main figure in the contentious Somali landscape. Uncharacteristically, Aidid, who had seldom had much interest in reconciliation talks, proposed to sponsor a peace conference in late May. This conclave purportedly aimed at extending the UNOSOM II area of operations to the north, into the region past Belet Uen. It sounded too good to be true, and it was. The ploy did not fool the new UN envoy, Admiral Howe. The American knew what Aidid was trying to do.

Howe, like Oakley, had no interest in backing one local chief at the expense of others, especially the recalcitrant Aidid. Trying to keep all factions at the table, Howe himself wished to moderate the proposed warlord council, but Aidid wanted UN approval of his stewardship, not a requirement to sit as equal with lesser leaders. Aidid cranked up his anti-UN and anti-American rhetoric, talking about the evils of Western imperialists. When the UN envoy tried to calm Aidid, the warlord interpreted Howe's patience and deference as weakness. In particular, Aidid considered Howe's visit on 22 May to be almost groveling, as the courtly admiral pleaded with the Somali chief to play along. Aidid would not.

In the end, there were two conferences, one run by Howe, the other by Aidid, neither successful, and both suspended on 4 June. Each side accused the other of sabotaging the alleged reconciliation process. In Mogadishu, meanwhile, Aidid's supporters staged demonstrations, threatening to drive the UN "colonialists" into the sea. Shootings and rock-throwing confrontations increased around the capital city. General Bir had seen enough and reacted.

While other UN units, including Americans, fanned out to seize SNA weaponry, Pakistani forces marched off on 5 June. They were determined to shut down Aidid's pirate radio station, identified as the single greatest source of anti-UN agitation. But the crafty general, tipped off by sources within the UNOSOM II headquarters, was waiting for the UN personnel. His men ambushed and mowed down the careless, lightly armed Pakistani column, killing twenty-four and wounding fifty more. Americans from the QRF arrived to restore order and cover the Pakistani withdrawal and suffered three wounded in the skirmishing that followed.[44] Aidid had laid down his marker. For UNOSOM II, and indeed, for Clinton's America, the moment of crisis was at hand.

What to do? Obviously, that depended on America. Bir, Howe, and Boutros-Ghali could bluster and condemn Aidid as an outlaw and a threat to peace, but only America had the gumption to act. Would Clinton commit the QRF against Aidid and his SNA forces?

He would and did. Emboldened by a May congressional resolution backing a long-term American role in Somalia in support of the United Nations, Clinton and his people agreed with Howe and Boutros-Ghali that the ambush demanded a strong response from UNOSOM II, lest the force lose all credibility. American force protection acquired a fairly expansive definition, and the QRF joined the fight.

With U.S. approval and sponsorship, the UN Security Council authorized action against the SNA commander. Although a first draft even went so far as naming Aidid as the culprit, the final version of Security Council Resolution 837, passed promptly on 6 June, backed off a bit, requiring a full legal investigation before naming Aidid as the mastermind behind the gory act. Once the perpetrators of the ambush had been identified, UNOSOM II was empowered to arrest and detain them "for prosecution, trial, and punishment" and to use "all necessary measures" to establish UN authority "throughout Somalia."

First Aidid, then the rest—but would taking out one warlord in one city really accomplish much in a place as riven with conflict as Somalia? And what if Aidid eluded his captors? Few asked those unpleasant questions. Instead, the UN and United States fixed their attention on Aidid and his SNA, to set an example that would deter the others. Had the scheme worked, it might have had an effect beyond Mogadishu. It certainly did when it failed.

With Resolution 837 in hand, Howe promised that a "full investigation will be made into the affair and appropriate steps will be taken against those responsible." Simultaneously, and secretly, Howe called for help from the elite counterterrorists of the Delta Detachment to snatch Aidid for trial. The military recommended against that idea. The request was refused, at least for now.

Advised by Montgomery, the envoy also requested more firepower. Here he had better fortune. On 9 June, Washington dispatched four AC-130H Spectre gunships, capable of precision 105-mm, 40-mm, and 20-mm fires in the dead of night.[45] Assisted by air force special warfare experts, Montgomery and his staff began thinking about how best to use the inbound aerial reinforcements.

While Montgomery planned, the UN investigation team completed its brief work. The project amounted to a curious formality, because Admiral Howe's rhetoric left little doubt that Aidid had become UNOSOM II's public enemy number one and a target for instant apprehension. A conscious nod to police procedures, the first of many in this case, supposedly would help to strengthen Somalia's nascent UN-sponsored police and penal system, or so argued Howe, trying to paint Aidid as a common criminal. This thinking might have appeased Somali jurists, had there been any to speak of, but it smacked too much of *Dragnet* and not enough of what was really going on here—war.

Howe and others thought otherwise. As the pursuit of Aidid began, President Clinton gravely explained that "a warrant has been issued for his arrest." It is hard to imagine issuing a court order to apprehend and try Rommel or Yamamoto, but this sort of thing can happen when U.S. leaders fail to see OOTW as real war.

Aidid surely did not appreciate the American-style legal niceties. He did not retain counsel or begin polishing up depositions. Instead, tipped off by Howe's public bluster, the SNA leader vanished into the backstreets of Mogadishu. His supporters took arms, determined to inflict casualties on the UN and, especially, the Americans, and hence send them home. Some had served in advisory elements in Latin American insurgencies, and most remembered American reactions to casualties in Vietnam and Beirut. For the SNA, victory equaled holding out and killing Americans.[46]

The Americans and their UN allies went right to work, in what felt, looked, sounded, and smelled a lot like war, especially to the unlucky SNA gunmen caught in the crosshairs. Starting at 0400 on 12 June, the quartet of Spectres hosed down Aidid's radio station, while QRF AH-1F Cobra attack choppers pumped TOW missiles into four other SNA targets. American infantrymen of 1-22d Infantry seized one weapons cache and a radio substation, helped by French infantry. The Pakistanis gleefully assaulted and destroyed the radio center that had cost them so heavily a week before.

The next night, the Spectres smashed up Aidid's headquarters compound and home, followed by yet another raid in the dark hours of 14 June. That night, the targets included the home of Osman Ato, deputy head of the SNA. In a 14 June engagement, AH-1F Cobras participated. One TOW broke its wire and went wide, wounding a Somali woman. A day of large-scale anti-UN and anti-American street demonstrations followed this raid.

With Aidid's SNA damaged by the air attacks, Montgomery helped Bir prepare what the American called a "decapitating strike." Early on 17 June, the multinational effort began, aimed at the block containing the Ato and Aidid houses and wrecking the Jess compound as a side benefit.

The operation began before light, as the Spectres circled, knocking out roadblocks, dumping warning leaflets, playing searchlights, and thundering loudspeaker warnings to clear out. Under this racket and suppressive fire, Italian tanks and Royal Moroccan mechanized units moved to seal off the objective area. A tight cordon was in place by 0545, and two Pakistani infantry battalions prepared to assault the selected housing complexes, backed by a few light armored vehicles.

Colonel James Campbell, the QRF commander, flew overhead in a UH-60L Blackhawk rigged as an airborne command post. He watched the Pakistanis go in, methodically clearing each building, then setting charges to complete the demolition of these bullet-pocked structures. Campbell judged the Pakistani assault to be "clicking on all cylinders" by 0630. American liaison teams with each UN force helped them adjust Spectre and Cobra fires, eliminating pockets of snipers and machine-gun nests, one after another.

While all went well inside the objective, the Moroccans began to take fire on the outer perimeter. Worse, street demonstrators, many women and children, assembled to shield the armed militiamen. Heavy weapons started to fire from nearby roofs and doorways. Just before 1030, a recoilless rifle shell disabled the Moroccan command vehicle and killed the regimental commander. Excited by the success, Somalis surged forward, closing on the Moroccan cordon. From his perch above, Campbell thought it looked like "a real hornet's nest." The Moroccans hung on, firing and firing as the crowds milled and ducked for cover, with armed individuals working closer and closer.

French reinforcements, including tanks, arrived an hour later, and the Somalis melted away into the alleys and battered houses. It took till 1830 to finish cleaning out all of the shattered target buildings, an exhausting but seemingly productive day. Aidid had escaped, if indeed he had ever been there that day. In Washington, Clinton avowed that "the military back of Aidid has been broken." In country, Campbell agreed. "I am confident right now," said the QRF commander, "that he is in a world of hurt."[47]

It was wishful thinking. The fugitive warlord remained very much at large and in charge, a crook on the lam, a mafia don gone underground. American rhetoric sharply played on this imagery. Madeline Albright, American ambassador to the United Nations, referred to Aidid as a "thug." For his part, Howe called Aidid "a menace to public safety" and "a killer." To underscore this tough talk, Howe had UNOSOM II helicopters drop leaflets offering a $25,000 reward for the SNA chieftain's capture. The notes did not say "wanted dead or alive," but the flavor was surely there.

None of this helped anyone, except maybe Aidid. The man's SNA loyalists, and indeed other Somalis, could not help but notice who had done most of the killing to date and who owned the death-dealing Spectres and Cobras. Some local sympathies began to tilt toward Aidid, especially in Mogadishu. And like Francis Marion, George Washington, Mao Tse-tung, and Ho Chi Minh, Aidid did not need to win. Surviving promised victory. Hitting back, hurting, and killing strengthened SNA resolve.

Undaunted by American insults and threats, unbowed by the mid-June raids, and unimpressed by the 24th MEU and the USS *Wasp* amphibious group off the coast, Aidid kept up the pressure. Evidently, as he plotted, the SNA leader consulted informants inside the amateurish UN headquarters. On 2 July, Aidid's men shot up an Italian checkpoint deep in what the UN troops thought to be safe Ali Mahdi territory. Three Italians died, and twenty-four were wounded. American Spectres and Cobras retaliated on 12 July, blasting a meeting of Aidid's fellow clan elders, killing seventy-three people, some of them women and children crushed by tumbling rubble. Enraged Somalis, possibly not even SNA types, set upon four unlucky foreign journalists motoring in the area and beat them to death with blunt objects and stones.[48] Having traded this latest set of injuries, both sides backed off.

During the breather, the MEU offshore sailed away, and the AC-130Hs departed, possibly to entice Aidid to bargain. The SNA leader did not bite. He was moving in OOTW time—his time—waiting for his chance.

As July turned to August, the QRF used this period to swap out forces, bringing in Col. Michael Dallas and his 10th Aviation Brigade staff from

Fort Drum to run the contingent. This type of outfit was an unlikely choice to head a ground combat mission, although written army doctrine said it could be done. Unwritten experience warned against it, an unfair imposition on fliers already burdened with a hard enough task. One army study of this decision, admittedly made with full knowledge of what later occurred, opined, "An aviation brigade is not organized or structured as well as other types of maneuver brigades for the command and control of what is, predominantly, a ground maneuver force." Soldiers knew this. But 1st and 2d Brigades had just done their turns. So, as the books say, 10th Mountain "accepted risk" and put pilots in charge of riflemen.

The infantry were sound, led by Lt. Col. William David, a veteran of Desert Storm, a former military assistance group chief from Belize, a man who knew about OOTW. His 2-14th Infantry task force supplied the QRF's ground element. Since David had taken charge in December of 1991, his unit had secured Haitian refugees in Guantanamo Bay, Cuba, gone to south Florida to help with hurricane relief, deployed to the port of New York en route to Somalia only to be waved off at the last minute, and sent Company A to Mogadishu with 1-22d Infantry's QRF rotation, all besides standard training exercises. It was a good battalion, well-trained in the fundamentals and even schooled in the nuances of these dirty quasi-wars. Like most of 10th Mountain, however, David's men had been ridden pretty hard.

Just as he had lent units to his fellow commander in 1-22d Infantry, David's battalion included augmentees from 1-87th Infantry and other 10th Mountain units. The QRF's composite aviation task force, built around Lt. Col. Lee Gore's 2-25th Aviation, showed the same seams. It included a Blackhawk company drawn from the 101st Airborne Division's 9-101st Aviation, itself featuring some crewmen from other 101st units. Here, in the unfamiliar, stitched-together corners of these units, lay the price of stringing out the busy 10th Mountain Division. After Guantanamo, Hurricane Andrew, and UNITAF, let alone the essential training grind, the division's two brigades of active duty forces were getting pulled very thin indeed. Many soldiers were on their second stint in the Horn of Africa.

Along with the stresses imposed by the dangerous Somalia deployment, the routine changes that characterize any large organization went on, adding still more friction. Weeks after setting up his headquarters in Mogadishu, UNITAF veteran Dallas turned over command to Col. Lawrence E. Casper, a routine transfer. The army needed Dallas for other things, and his prescribed term of command was over. So he departed, in accord with normal peacetime policies. But this was not peacetime.

The QRF received a rude introduction to Somalia when an unseen Somali ambusher detonated a buried mine by remote control, blowing a Humvee and four military policemen into bloody wreckage. Three of the dead came from the 977th Military Police (MP) Company of Fort Hood, Texas. The fourth was a filler from the 300th MP Company of Fort Leonard Wood, Missouri, indicative of the reliance on add-on individuals and borrowed pieces of units that typified many of the American forces in country by this time. The explosion also reminded Montgomery's Americans, the Somali people, and the world beyond that Aidid was still at large.

A series of mortar attacks on the QRF heliport at the Mogadishu airfield highlighted Aidid's persistence. These culminated in a barrage on 22 August that wounded six and damaged some of the U.S. Army aircraft.[49] Helicopters conferred one of the only American advantages left, and now the SNA was grinding away at that edge.

Howe and Bir had seen enough. Trading bullets rifleman to rifleman gained little but losses and frustration, and a few U.S. helicopters, even if they survived the mortar rounds, could not tip the balance in Mogadishu's fruitless war of attrition. Howe was chasing Aidid with a ball-peen hammer (the small QRF really could not be called a sledge). To get around the gunmen and technicals, to leap over the mines and human shields, to penetrate into the deepest SNA warrens and excise the organization's brain, the admiral needed stainless steel forceps—select supersoldiers, the Delta professionals and their usual cast of friends. Again, Howe asked for a skilled strike team to grab Aidid. This time, Clinton said yes.

It was the mission that American special warriors had waited for since 1980, when the Iran hostage rescue mission went awry during its staging phase. In Grenada, some special operators had argued that they could have done the whole mission unassisted, but cautious admirals and generals thought otherwise and weighted the main effort with paratroopers and Marines. In Panama, certain special warriors argued for a "surgical" pickup of Noriega, but in the end, America resorted to a massive intervention by conventional forces to suppress and break Noriega's command system and defense forces. In Iraq, the CINC of USSOCOM proposed a direct-action mission to get Saddam Hussein during Desert Shield; Schwarzkopf, who had been involved in the Grenada operation, said no.

And now, in Somalia, the day of the ninja had come. Could American SOF pull off a snatch in a hostile city? Yes, if the Intelligence Support Activity (ISA) undercover advance people checked out the area thoroughly, if the 160th Special Operations Aviation Regiment pilots could insert the Delta shooters and their Ranger security teams on and around the right target, and if they got in and out before the enemy responded, it was possible. Plucking Aidid from his guards was much like rescuing a hostage. Similar missions had been done over and over in training.

Yet all did not stand convinced. General Hoar recommended against the use of Delta, reminding his superiors that special operators work in an arena of high risk. They fight outnumbered, substituting unique skills for firepower. These small, elite teams depend heavily on speed and surprise, fragile commodities in any combat environment but especially in the alleys and hovels of a guerrilla commander's home turf. Historically, at least half or more special missions fail outright, snagged by friction, aborted in the face of strong enemy reactions, or launched into dry holes based on the usual intelligence—partial, estimated, guessed, and often merely hoped. Direct action by special warriors is a crap shoot, and the dice come up snake eyes a lot, especially on rescues and prisoner retrievals aimed at small, moving targets.

Hoar could point to many examples: the superbly executed 1970 raid on the Son Tay prisoner of war camp that found an empty facility, the abort and crash at Desert One during the attempted Iranian hostage rescue in 1980, Delta's bloody repulse trying to extract political prisoners from Richmond Hill Prison in Grenada in 1983, and the several missed pickups of Noriega in the 1989 Panama operation. Son Tay and the Iran mission failed completely when the special warfare forces could not accomplish the mission; there were no fallback plans. On the other hand, despite some tough breaks on certain special missions, Grenada and Panama succeeded because the U.S. had committed sizable conventional forces too. The warpower strength that could have provided similar insurance in Somalia had left months before. Gambling on a Delta snatch meant winning big—or losing big. There would be no middle ground.

For many in the U.S. Special Operations Command, that was exactly why this mission must go, to validate the utility of these one-of-a-kind assets. As with aircraft or tanks in the early days, there seemed to be many hidebound conventional fighters unwilling to trust the "snake-eaters" on their own. Deep down inside, many special operators, perhaps even a majority, harbored a streak of Douhet-style conviction that commando units alone, properly employed, could decide a campaign like Somalia.

Those who believed so passionately conjured some favorite examples to make their case for taking on the Aidid mission. The Israelis had faced greater odds at Entebbe in 1976, gone anyway, saved the innocents, and thrilled the world. The British had "taken down" the captive Iranian embassy in London in 1980, freeing captives as the world's cameras stared in admiring wonder. And, as all counterterrorists knew, the skilled German Grenschutz Gruppe 9 had stormed a hijacked Lufthansa airliner in 1977, right at Mogadishu Airport, of all places. Delta and its American comrades could boast no such high-profile triumph, despite many less-trumpeted victories of equal difficulty. In the eyes of most Americans, Delta's best missions featured Chuck Norris and Lee Marvin and existed only in movies. That rankled the quiet, tough, smart Delta people. As the men of the British Special Air Service say, "Who Dares Wins."[50] Well, the boys in black were ready to dare great things. And now Clinton had given them their chance.

The forces assembled and designated Task Force Ranger comprised the best of the best, the very sharp tip of the spear. The Joint Special Operations Command (JSOC) deployable headquarters element, replete with the latest international communications and staffed by handpicked experts, took charge. A reinforced rifle unit, Company B from the 3d Battalion, 75th Ranger Regiment, joined with the 130 men of Squadron C of 1st Special Forces Operational Detachment–Delta to make up the fighting core—the Rangers to secure the site, Delta to do the actual grab. A mix of sixteen or so MH-60 Blackhawk troop carriers and MH-6 and AH-6J Little Bird special gunships came from the 1st Battalion, 160th Special Operations Aviation Regiment, the Night Stalkers. Flown by the best night fliers in the world, these sturdy helicopters would carry the men into battle. Finally, a small team from the ISA, already in country and tied in with the CIA network, endeavored to find Aidid and guide in the raiders.

Major General William F. Garrison, a veteran Green Beret with two Vietnam tours, had commanded Delta for four years. He knew that outfit and its partners inside and out. He had been running JSOC since the summer after the Gulf War, training his superb operators in many demanding and dangerous exercises, deeply involved in every major crisis, including Somalia. If anyone could catch Aidid, he would be the man. But to whom would he report?

Obviously, working for the Turkish General Bir was out of the question. With UNOSOM II penetrated by SNA informers and barely in control of its own constituent forces, let alone Mogadishu, that would never work. It might have made sense to put Garrison under Montgomery in his

USFORSOM role, like the QRF, but even that made the JSOC people queasy. With Aidid long aware that he was targeted and Clinton insiders whispering way too many hints to the news media about Delta on the way, Garrison had to work hard to preserve some shred of cover for his dangerous operation, which so depended on surprise. Working for Montgomery's bastard headquarters risked too many potentially lethal revelations and mistakes.

There was another alternative. Since it began in 1987, USSOCOM always had the capability to run certain select projects directly for the president, independent of the regional CINCs. Given its sensitive taskings, JSOC often works in that mode, to preserve maximum security. Well, this one demanded as much cloaking as JSOC could generate. So the direct setup was recommended.

Hoar weighed in here, much as Schwarzkopf had done during the war against Iraq. If JSOC was in his area, he wanted them under his authority. With the clock ticking and Aidid still on the loose, the special operators compromised. Garrison reported through CINC USCENTCOM and General Powell of the JCS to Clinton and Secretary of Defense Aspin, with a coordination line to the CINC at USSOCOM and Montgomery in USFORSOM. It was understood that Hoar would not interfere except in extraordinary circumstances and that Montgomery would be permitted to stop TF Ranger missions only if they endangered U.S. or UN troops. In essence, Garrison still worked in the usual special operations "stovepipe" right into the White House, as the Delta folks preferred. This satisfied JSOC.[51] Unfortunately, it also created one UN and two separate U.S. chains of command in Mogadishu, about two too many for an operation as fraught with perils as chasing Aidid.

But for now, the push was on to get the special warriors into Somalia. They were ready, fully briefed and rehearsed to their usual exacting standards. Indeed, Gen. Wayne Downing, CINCUSSOCOM, had thought that a raid back in June might have worked, and on his orders, Garrison had formed TF Ranger back then. The force drilled relentlessly all summer. On 22 August, Garrison, disguised as a replacement lieutenant colonel for the USFORSOM staff and accompanied by a small advance party, slipped into Mogadishu. His men and aircraft came in four days later, aboard six mammoth C-5B Galaxy jet transports.

Task Force Ranger went right to work. After some area orientation, Garrison checked the local intelligence trails. There were no leads. The ISA and CIA had lost track of the SNA chief, who had not been seen since July. The intelligence cells at the U.S. and UN headquarters could only offer guess-work. As mortar shells rained down on the airfield on 29 August, Garrison elected to do something, to try a raid. He sifted through the best available evidence and sent in his men.

At 0300 on 30 August, TF Ranger executed a textbook lightning strike. A dozen blacked out helicopters rose from the airfield, formed up, and then clattered over to the nearby target house, where they pulled up one by one, bobbing to hover in loose formation above and around the sleeping com-pound like a swarm of great black bumblebees. Instantly, several of the aircraft spit down black ropes, which waved lazily in the dark downwash. As soon as the lines touched dirt, soldiers followed. Dropping down the thick, springy "fast ropes" like firemen sliding down greased poles, Ranger security teams sealed off the objective as Delta "door-kickers" went in to get Aidid.

They found eight men, none of them the SNA warlord. In fact, they were United Nations Development Program contract workers, allegedly good guys. (But in Somalia, who could really be sure?) Nobody in the headquarters of Montgomery or Bir knew they lived there. The first Ranger raid had

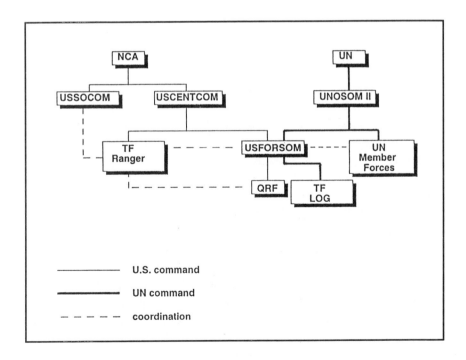

The Chain of Command in Mogadishu
3 October 1993

NCA = National Command Authorities
QRF = Quick reaction force
TF LOG = American logistics task force
UN = United Nations
UNOSOM II = United Nations Operation in Somalia II
USCENTCOM = U.S. Central Command
USFORSOM = U.S. Forces, Somalia
USSOCOM = U.S. Special Operations Command

UN Member Forces (numbers): Bangladesh (948), Belgium (952), Botswana (247), Egypt (539), France (1,118), Germany (1,727), Greece (110), India (3,606), Ireland (80), Italy (2,672), Korea (251), Kuwait (156), Malaysia (871), Morocco (1,347), Nigeria (614), Pakistan (5,003), Romania (236), Saudi Arabia (678), Sweden (148), Tunisia (142), United Arab Emirates (683), Zimbabwe (894).

USFORSOM under UN command (3,121).
USFORSOM under U.S. command (1,447).
TF Ranger: (450).

Sources: "Multinational Mission," *Washington Times,* 8 October 1993; Capt. Fred Swope, USA, *Task Force Ranger Operations in Somalia* (Fort Benning, Ga.: U.S. Army Infantry School, 23 February 1994), 3, 9.

failed. Hoar chastised Garrison, and the news media screamed out the embarrassing results.

Now all suspicions were confirmed, all rumors given concrete form. Garrison had lost strategic surprise back in June, when the UN and Howe told Aidid he was a wanted man. TF Ranger gave up operational surprise with this blown raid. Everybody knew they were in theater and in town. Only local, tactical surprise remained, tied to the idea that the Night Stalker choppers could let Garrison's men get in and out unexpectedly.

Now TF Ranger faced an odd circumstance. With no real fix on Aidid, the task force became, in essence, a souped-up QRF, waiting for word of Aidid to pounce. Garrison knew that there would be misses, as there had been tracking Noriega, but he banked on speed to get in and out so fast that the

SNA could not react. Of course, this forced TF Ranger to use a templated approach, to cut down reaction time. A standard "footprint" evolved, based on ISA recon, a quick fast-rope insertion of Rangers and Delta into the tight streets and onto sagging roofs, and a rapid extraction, with entire ground time not to exceed a half hour. Sturdy Little Bird attack helicopters held in aerial orbits, ready to deliver suppressive fires. There were variations practiced and tried: day and night attacks, ground insertions and extractions. But, basically, it would be the same thing each time, relying on skill and speed to stun those on the target.

The flaky intelligence—and who could really be surprised?—led Garrison to broaden his search to key SNA lieutenants as well as Aidid. A snatch on 14 September went well, but mistakenly netted UN ally Ahmed Jilao, the erstwhile head of the new Somali police agency. On 18 September, the Delta teams narrowly missed getting Osman Ato, SNA financier. They got him three days later, the first clear success. The next week, guided by radio intercepts, TF Ranger knocked out several SNA transmitter teams.[52] Every mission followed the rapid-fire pattern, and only one Somali had to be killed by the skilled U.S. operators, so quickly did the Deltas come and go. All of this hurt the SNA, kept them off balance, and served notice of American capabilities. But the prime target, Aidid, eluded the Americans.

He struck back as the raids continued, letting it be known that he was still in action, still defiant. His militia could not catch TF Ranger, but they could easily strike at the slow-footed UN troops, and this brought on skirmishing with Montgomery's QRF. On 5 September, SNA forces killed seven Nigerian soldiers and took one prisoner. On 9 September, QRF Cobras flew in, guns blazing, to save an embattled Pakistani outpost. Dozens of Somali women and children died in the cross fire. On 11 September, SNA-incited crowds killed four CNN employees in retaliation, a repeat of the 12 July episode. It was bad, getting out of control. Most of UNOSOM II, even those stationed well outside of Mogadishu, headed for their holes, unwilling to get in the way of all this pain.

Not so the Americans. Two days after the CNN people died, Bill David's 2-14th Infantry got in its first big firefight during a dawn cordon and search near Benadir Maternity Hospital. As the Americans cautiously worked through nearby buildings looking for heavy weapons, SNA snipers opened up from the hospital. They showed the American lightfighters that they had heavy weapons aplenty, offering deadly proof when they began firing rocket-propelled grenades on the American force's trucks. In David's words, the first reaction among his privates was disbelief and amazement that they were being shot at, with soldiers standing there "looking at RPGs scream down the street." But 2-14th was well trained and, the initial shock over, returned accurate fire. The SNA people backed off, melting into the side streets. As the Americans headed back to their nearby base at the Somali National University, the enemy firing started again. The Americans withdrew with the weapons stores they had seized, shooting all the way. Three Americans suffered wounds.[53]

So it went, Aidid probing, the UN getting shot, and the QRF reacting. On 15 September, rock throwers engaged the Pakistanis again, and snipers killed two Italians inside that contingent's fortified camp. But that was not the worst. Undeterred by TF Ranger's raids, SNA RPG men made another appearance, this time coordinated with the mortar men harassing the airfield.

Just after midnight, Colonel Dallas at QRF headquarters received reports of mortar shells bursting at the airport. He ordered a spotter aircraft aloft to direct U.S. mortar and Cobra counterfire. This had been done most nights, under a program called "Eyes Over Mogadishu." At 0130, CWO Dale Shrader and his crew took off. Typical of the mixed units in country, his five aviation crewmen hailed from three different units, though he had formed them into a solid team. Tonight, as before on similar occasions, they went hunting.

Instead, they became prey. Trolling along 130 feet up as his men looked for the hostile mortar position, the pilot heard a ripping explosion to his rear and felt his ship lurch. The craft had taken an RPG round in the cabin. A hot, smoky, white-yellow fire erupted instantly as Shrader struggled to crash-land his stricken helicopter. The Blackhawk hit hard on a dirt street, the tail boom sheared off cleanly. Onboard fuel tanks immediately burst into flames, turning a bonfire into an inferno.

Shrader and his copilot, CWO Perry Alliman, barely got clear of the blazing wreck. The three men in back were obviously charred corpses, swathed in the brilliant, roaring flames. "I told Perry we had to get out of here," recalled Shrader. He grabbed his partner and they headed around a dirty cinder-block wall, then stopped, breathing hard, waiting to face pursuing SNA men not far behind. The bad guys wanted to fight, and the two fliers had to shoot it out with pistols in the dark alley before being picked up by a patrolling armored car from the United Arab Emirates. Bill David's Company C lost three wounded, two quite seriously, pushing up contested streets to recover the burned bodies of the dead.[54]

So now Aidid had RPGs and knew how to use them. The final American advantage, the helicopter, was in serious jeopardy. Worse, the SNA had watched six Ranger raids by the end of September. "If you use a tactic twice, you should not use it a third time," said SNA Col. Ali Aden. Aden and his men knew the U.S. footprint only too well. The next time, they intended to amputate, to make the Yankees pay.

In hindsight, most of those in charge saw the bad omens. Task Force Ranger's inability to bag Aidid, coupled with the pattern of spiraling confrontations as September wore on, had already caused President Clinton, Secretary of Defense Aspin, and Secretary of State Warren Christopher to begin talking of a "two-track" solution, with greater emphasis on a political settlement with Aidid. Along these lines, Aspin casually ignored a request by Montgomery for armored forces to beef up the embattled QRF. Despite recommendations from Hoar and Powell to send tanks, Aspin tabled the request, doing so "in the context of an evolving policy" now stressing a political solution.

Some diplomats wanted to go even further. Oakley's nearly invisible successor, Ambassador Robert Gosende, urged President Clinton to give up, back off, and reopen negotiations. Others in the State Department felt the same way. The Ranger ploy had not worked, they argued, and things were only getting worse. A political adviser to Admiral Howe, John Drysdale of Great Britain, who had held clandestine meetings with the SNA leadership even as the Americans hunted them, resigned in protest over the continued pursuit and the resulting firefights. But all of this remained so much wind, tilting, and talk, not real policy. Howe stayed adamant, determined, like the proverbial Mountie, to get his man. Clinton let it all ride.

For Garrison, none of this mattered. His mission stood: get Aidid. Aware of the SNA's deadly new toys and tactics, he continued to trust in his proven professionals, in his tested template. He knew that it would not be easy. The next raid smelled like trouble. "If we go into the vicinity of the Bakara market, there's no question we'll win the gunfight," he told his officers confidently, then added, "But we might lose the war."[55] Unfortunately, that turned out to be one of the few accurate intelligence forecasts of the entire episode.

*   *   *

Task Force Ranger's last mission started exactly like the six others launched and the forty-odd others planned and canceled, with an intelligence tidbit. At about 1300 on Sunday, 3 October, a Somali agent reported that two key SNA lieutenants, Omar Salad Elmi and Muhammed Hassan Awale, planned to meet with twenty others later that afternoon at a building near the Olympic Hotel in the Bakara Market district, right in the heart of SNA territory. An egg-shaped Little Bird went aloft, and its observer watched through a telescopic lens as their contact drove in front of the suspected target house. The Somali halted his auto, got out, raised and lowered the hood, then got back in and drove off. The aerial observer marked his street map and returned to the airfield, the special operators' base.

As soon as they plotted the chosen structure, Task Force Ranger planners knew they would be trying to chew on a very tough nut. Garrison's men had never raided into this dangerous district, nicknamed "Bosnia" by the world press and jaded UN workers and referred to as "really Indian country" and "a bad place" by Montgomery. Americans knew only too well that the Bakara served as an Aidid stronghold, replete with caches of weaponry and ammunition. Trying a daylight raid into this nest of vipers accepted a lot of risk, especially in light of the QRF's recent clashes with RPG-armed Somalis. Speed would be essential. Drop the footprint, get the "precious cargo" (the SNA men), and pull out. Task Force Ranger knew the scheme by heart.

As TF Ranger's elite soldiers geared for battle, passing around target photographs and checking street maps, they had little time to dwell on the perils they might face. Garrison acknowledged the very real dangers, but as he explained, "ultimately, there are only four options: up the middle, up the left, up the right, or don't go." Well, TF Ranger was going, all right. There could be no question of that. The unit mottos told their own stories: "Rangers Lead the Way," "Night Stalkers Don't Quit." These were not just idle words but ingrained realities, ways of life and thinking. At the trigger-pulling level, the men looked at this mission as car mechanics might regard a tricky valve job, or surgeons would discuss a knotty heart bypass. It came down to a choice of techniques and instruments. "After they shot down that Blackhawk, you knew they were going to try it again," noted Pfc. Alberto Rodriguez. His personal response was typical. He tripled his ammunition load.[56]

With preliminaries completed, TF Ranger prepared for launch aboard fourteen helicopters. Insertion would be by air, down the ropes, given that the congested houses offered few landing zones big enough to put down a chopper, even a small one. Four MH-60 Blackhawks carried fifteen Rangers each, who would seal off the target block; once they dropped their troops, these aircraft would orbit nearby, ready to land as necessary to backhaul casualties. Another carried a fifteen-man Ranger reaction team, a flying reserve ready to swoop in to intervene. A sixth MH-60 acted as a flying command post, carrying Lt. Col. Lee Van Arsdale, the C Squadron commander, and Lt. Col. Thomas Matthews, the 1/160th commander. The last two Blackhawks carried twelve Deltas each, part of the actual snatch team. Four bubble-nosed MH-6 Little Birds, similar to the small chopper featured in the television show *Magnum P.I.,* lifted the rest of the element, sixteen black-uniformed shooters who rode two to a side on narrow benches attached above the skids of the small craft. Two AH-6J Little Birds, laden with machine guns and rocket pods, flew shotgun. Another two AH-6Js waited back at the airfield, on standby for this operation. Finally, Lt. Col. Danny McKnight, commander of 3/75 Rangers and the Ranger portion of Garrison's task force, led a twelve-vehicle convoy of three five-ton trucks and nine Humvees manned by over fifty Rangers, tasked to pick up and extract the raiders and detainees by ground. All stood ready by 1500, but a refinement of the exact objective—the suspect house actually lay a block to the west of the one marked—caused a thirty-seven-minute delay.

While Garrison and his officers scrambled to adjust their assault plan, Montgomery personally heard of the raid, although his USFORSOM staff and Casper's QRF had received notification at 1414. Montgomery had been out of Mogadishu, visiting U.S. and German troops in Belet Uen, at the far limit of the UN area of operations. The USFORSOM commander gave his assent and noted that QRF commander Casper had already alerted Bill David and his lead unit, Company C, 2-14th Infantry, for a potential reaction role, though only in the vaguest possible terms. Montgomery's strong right hand, Brigadier General Gile, moved to the TF Ranger command post at the airport, just in case.

Casper's QRF prepared for action. At Mogadishu Airport, Lee Gore briefed and fueled a strong attack aviation team, two OH-58 scouts and three Cobras. Like the Little Birds, the Cobras loaded 70-mm rockets, uprated versions of the 2.75-inch models of the Vietnam era. Crews remained near their aircraft, ready to scramble.

Two miles to the west of the airfield and two-plus miles south of the objective, the 10th Mountain infantrymen of 2-14th's lead company waited

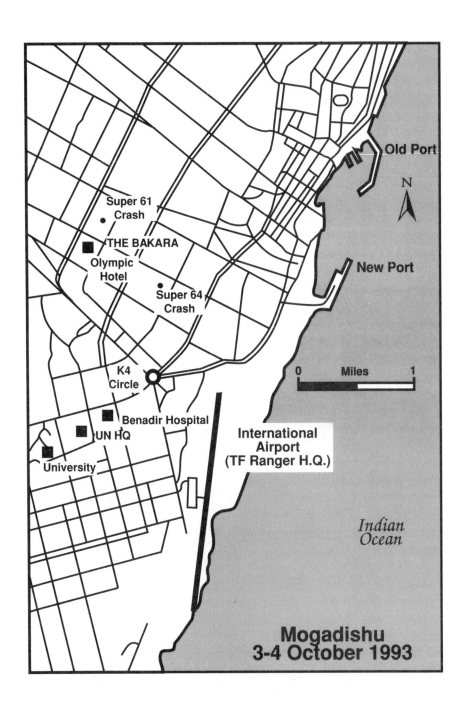

Old Port

N

Super 61
Crash

THE BAKARA

Olympic
Hotel

Super 64
Crash

New Port

K4
Circle

0   Miles   1

Benadir Hospital

UN HQ

University

International
Airport
(TF Ranger H.Q.)

Indian
Ocean

Mogadishu
3-4 October 1993

at the university, their sandbagged five-ton trucks and Humvees lined up and ready to roll. But to where, and to do what? David and his leaders did not really know. As TF Ranger officers later admitted, their planning was "not integrated with [the] 2-14 mission." If the view of Montgomery, Gile, Casper, and David could be described as dim, then the picture among the allies was nearly opaque. Nobody told Bir's leaky, creaky UNOSOM II staff or informed the other national contingents until TF Ranger actually went in. The possibility that the Americans could need help from UN troops had not been considered at all.[57]

At 1540, Task Force Ranger descended on its target, rapidly establishing the usual pattern: an outer ring of Rangers and an inner core of Deltas, with heliborne aid and McKnight's ground column nearby. One Ranger fell off the fast rope and plummetted forty feet to the hard-packed street, badly injured. He was the only casualty. Curious Somalis watched from nearby doorways and windows, and a few shots rang out. But overall, TF Ranger's arrival went smoothly. Within twenty minutes, the Deltas had secured their twenty-four prisoners, marching them out with their hands held behind their backs by plastic "flex cuffs." The Delta troop commander called the command aircraft, reporting that he had taken the SNA men as planned. "We're ready to get out of Dodge," he concluded. With that, the ground convoy headed toward the secured target. As McKnight said later, "We definitely achieved surprise. We were right on track and in good shape."[58]

This time, though, the SNA reacted a few minutes more quickly than usual. That made all the difference. As McKnight's truck element arrived on the scene and started to embark the prisoners and their guards, the Rangers on security reported a distinct increase in hostile fire. Specialist Michael Kurth thought "things were getting a little hairy." The SNA displayed awful marksmanship, but they seemed to have no shortage of bullets, and some found their marks. Ranger and Delta Kevlar body armor protected a man's torso, but not his arms and legs. The volume of enemy fire built steadily. About 1610, the Somalis started firing RPGs. Five minutes later, one hit an orbiting MH-60, callsign Super 61. It dropped like a stone, crunching in three hundred yards east of the objective building.

"At the point when the helicopter went down, the entire mission changed," said Matthews later. Now Garrison, his Delta leaders, aviator Matthews, and McKnight all had a serious problem. Though well into the withdrawal phase of the raid, they could not simply leave the downed aircraft and its seven men to their fates. The contingency had been considered, and without hesitation Garrison and his commanders acted. They ordered the insertion of the flying reaction team, the move of the assault force to the crash site, and notification of the QRF to prepare to execute a ground attack to link up with TF Ranger.

The rescue effort started with Matthews's Night Stalkers. Chief Warrant Officer Karl Maiers shoehorned his small AH-6 into the open spot near the crashed MH-60, then fired his personal weapon to cover his copilot, who dismounted to pull two survivors from the downed ship. Somali bullets punched through and ricocheted off his sturdy little helicopter as the two fliers bundled the wounded aboard. Somehow, working his controls with one hand and shooting with the other, Maiers got up and away.

As Maiers careened away, the reserve MH-60 flared to hover. Its heliborne reaction force tossed their ropes out the yawning side doors and slid down, almost atop the twisted wreckage of Super 61. When the Blackhawk wobbled, raising yellow dust, hidden SNA shooters engaged with automatic weapons and RPGs, knocking the main rotor disk askew. The helicopter dipped drunkenly, struggling to stay aloft, and almost throwing the last two men off the lines. Somehow, manhandling the uncooperative controls, the flight crew got their ship righted, put the rest of the team in, and then limped back to the airfield, trailing a dirty contrail of black smoke.

On the ground, as the aerial team inserted, Ranger Rodriguez and his comrades closed on Super 61's resting place. The Rangers quickly took up positions in some cinder-block buildings and behind cement rubble piles. They beat the SNA to the crash by less than a minute.

The opposition arrived from all sides, drawn to the spectacle, exultant in this SNA coup against Uncle Sam's high technology. Behind the cover provided by the next set of alleys and streets, hundreds of Somali gunmen milled about, intermixed with women and children. Individually and in small groups, armed men and some armed females and boys ran up out of side streets, darted out of doorways, and leaned suddenly from open windows. Staying just out of hand grenade range, the militia fighters started shooting at the Rangers. The SNA sympathizers displayed more enthusiasm than skill, and while they burned up many crates of ammunition, their aim rarely matched their determination.

Task Force Ranger, on the other hand, shot back in deadly earnest, the result of many hours spent on ranges, in shooting houses, and during realistic live-fire exercises. Rodriguez, who had brought plenty of bullets, began using them. He shot one Somali rifleman through the head, close enough to see the opponent's brain matter blow onto a nearby cinder-block wall. Next, the Ranger dropped an RPG man, and when the wounded Somali tried to slither over to his rocket launcher, Rodriguez finished him off. An AK-47 shooter hid behind two laughing women, popping out to shoot single rounds at the Rangers. "I hosed the guy and the ladies," Rodriguez said afterward. That was the way things were going, and the way they went, for the next ten hours or so.

McKnight, with the captives and the first wave of TF Ranger wounded aboard his trucks, received orders to reinforce the TF Ranger perimeter congealing around Super 61. With only a few able-bodied Rangers aboard to reply to SNA fusillades, McKnight tried to move his trucks the few blocks toward the shattered aircraft. As the trucks bounced their way to the east, every building spat tracers and RPGs. The Ranger commander was wounded, his own Humvee hit repeatedly by gunfire. One truck took an RPG round in the cab, which ripped off the driver's head and caused the big, sand-colored vehicle to slow to a halt, its diesel motor rattling like the throat of a dying man. With only a general idea of the crash site, tormented by endless gouts of wild firing, McKnight and his convoy got lost, friction taking its inevitable toll.

When the laboring string of shot-up vehicles passed the Olympic Hotel for the second time, Garrison ordered McKnight to back out, to get his precious cargo of prisoners back to TF Ranger headquarters at the airfield. Frustrated, bleeding, enraged, wanting very much to find his men out there in those wild streets, McKnight reluctantly obeyed. If the SNA leaders were not evacuated, the raid would certainly fail. Commanders must always weigh accomplishing the assigned mission against the welfare of their men—and if forced to choose, the mission must come first. Well, McKnight had been forced to choose—a horrible choice, the hardest one any officer or NCO will ever make. He stuck to the mission and pulled out.

While McKnight was going through his purgatory in the Bakara neighborhood, a second MH-60, Super 64, took an RPG through the tail while orbiting its mate's carcass. As the crew wrestled with the balky controls, heading south toward the airfield, the damaged craft fluttered lower and lower. Suddenly, the tail rotor blades split from the shaft. The Blackhawk plunged to the ground, hitting hard some two miles south of the raid objective, scattering tin roofs and flimsy wallboards as it impacted. The four men aboard, including CWO Michael Durant, were alive. But their situation looked bad. Armed Somalis poured out of the alleyways and ran from the doors of the local houses, gathering in a shouting, hooting mob just behind the cluster of shacks ringing the aircraft. Both sides began shooting.

The second downed chopper finished off TF Ranger's final fragment of flexibility. To deliver continuous supporting fires, Matthews was already rotating his AH-6Js and his remaining sound Blackhawks over the primary objective, breaking off only to refuel and rearm. Landing extraction aircraft was not an option. Gravity prevents going up a fast rope very rapidly, and pulling men out by hand-over-hand climbing would only get more Americans killed. Americans, especially the Rangers and Delta men, would never willingly abandon the bodies of the dead, including one aviator wedged into Super 61's ravaged cockpit. So TF Ranger was stuck down among the dead men, and Garrison had almost nothing left to influence the action. He told Montgomery that he needed the QRF, and fast.[59]

Lieutenant Colonel David and his men had been following the radio traffic as they waited at the university. One of his NCOs, SSgt. Richard Roberts, remembered that "things were getting more and more active. Then we found out that the Ranger task force was pinned down." They heard of Super 61's demise and, at 1629, received word to send the lead company to the airfield to prepare to reinforce TF Ranger. As their officers and sergeants shouted last-minute instructions, the men began to mount up, knowing that the Rangers' lives depended on them. "We all knew," remembered Roberts, "that American soldiers were stuck out there and needed help."

That help could not come very quickly, because David's riflemen had to swing by the airfield to get integrated into the ongoing operation. In movies, you can simply pile into your trucks and race off, but driving out with your hair on fire can send you back home in a box without helping anyone. To avoid "blue on blue" deaths, to focus combat power against the enemy, to be able to talk to each other under fire and tell friend from foe, David and his chain of command had to get oriented, to find out where to aim before they started shooting. Now the separate TF Ranger chain of command, and the desire for secrecy that spawned it, started taking its real toll, a price paid in time and blood.

The infantry's location at the university complicated the issue, especially because Aidid's SNA dominated the neighborhoods between 2-14th Infantry and the airport, not to mention that stretch between the lightfighters' base and the Bakara. The force could have been prepositioned, but then again, they had not been needed on the other six missions, and that precaution had not been taken. Given the tumult in the Aidid-held quarters of the city, the move took even longer than it might have. To avoid getting bogged down en route, on Casper's orders, David's sixteen trucks followed the long, secure route that skirted to the south, going around Mogadishu's SNA neighborhoods. They reached the airport at 1724.

On arrival, David and his key leaders met General Gile, Colonel Casper, and General Garrison in the TF Ranger command post. David's men were told to work directly for TF Ranger on this mission. Garrison wanted the lightfighters to retrieve Durant's downed aircrew. TF Ranger staffers laid out the situation. It looked grim. David immediately realized that this task, against this enemy and in this city, required more force, a lot more. He wanted to bring in the rest of his battalion. Garrison preferred not to wait, hoping that speed could substitute for lack of firepower. TF Ranger promised David attack helicopter support from the Little Birds, and Casper offered to augment that with QRF Cobras. It was all they could do. David left the command post and got ready to give it a try.

While David updated his men and prepared to move, TF Ranger did what it could to help him. A scratch outfit of TF Ranger headquarters troops, including cooks and clerks but not many heavy weapons crews, responded to a call for volunteers. The men clambered aboard six Humvees, not quite sure where they were bound, driven only by a conviction that friends needed aid. It appears that they led David's movement—Rangers Lead the Way, in spades—but they did not coordinate with the QRF. Rather, they left a few minutes early.

With nightfall approaching, at 1747 David followed the Rangers and led his first company out into the streets. The troops knew that one helicopter was down and secured, the other not. The 10th Mountain riflemen headed for Durant's crashed aircraft, into a battle they could see and hear raging to their northwest. When the trucks rolled, the horizon sparked with tracers, and dark smoke billowed in the distance.

Like McKnight's group, David's men used Humvees with Kevlar armor, as well as five-ton trucks with their beds reinforced by sandbags and their sides built up with dirt-filled ammunition boxes. All vehicles had weapons, with machine guns on the big trucks and some Humvees, mortars on a few, and Mark-19 automatic 40-mm grenade launchers on others. This sort of flying column had allowed the QRF to operate all over Mogadishu, and the 2-14th soldiers had plenty of experience using these armed trucks, including the firefights of 13 and 25 September.

At first, the twenty-two vehicles, moving in a group of six and a group of sixteen, rumbled north at thirty miles an hour. "We were taking fire almost from the time we left the gate," said Sfc. Richard Lamb, an NCO from the Ranger command post. Even so, the long convoy kept moving.

That changed north of the K-4 traffic circle, which delineated Aidid territory. At 1754, the U.S. truck convoy encountered a hail of gunfire from the east. Ahead of David, one Ranger Humvee veered out of the road, burning. Then another Ranger vehicle was hit. The whole column slowed and closed up. As they did, SNA fighters engaged from both sides of the street and in a big way. "It was a lot more than we expected," recalled Capt. Michael Whetstone, the company commander on the scene. "Tracers were flying everywhere. We were hit by probably 200 or 300 rocket propelled grenade attacks and lots and lots of small arms fire and machine gun fire."

Under heavy fire, the American infantry and the small Ranger element dismounted near a milk factory. Observers at the airfield saw black smoke boiling up from near K-4, and tracers etched the evening sky. David dropped off the QRF radio nets, an ominous development. Minutes dragged by without regaining communications. At Casper's QRF command post, the brigade commander feared the worst. Were the infantry lost, erased in some massive SNA broadside of an ambush?

No, but by any measure, the U.S. troops had their hands full. The Americans fought back, badly outnumbered. The men shot some sixty thousand rounds of ammunition, trying to drive away the growing ranks of SNA militia. Thanks to poor Somali marksmanship and vigorous return firing, the Americans took only two wounded. But the bruising gun battle ended the U.S. advance. When David resumed radio contact at 1815, he reported glumly that forward progress had been stymied.

Once again, in the standard OOTW fashion, a lieutenant colonel stood at the vortex of a desperate situation. David's options hardly seemed encouraging. If the Americans remounted and moved forward, the enemy's RPG teams would finish off the vehicles one by one with militiamen killing off those who survived. Moving on foot, fighting house to house through miles of defended slums to find and secure Durant would take hours, if it was even possible. Clearly, the initial reaction unit lacked the combat strength to get the job done. Durant and his Super 64 crew would get no help from this push. David and his men fought on until recalled at 1821 by Gile and Casper. It took almost an hour to break contact, and that only with help from 2-14th's Company A and 2-25th Aviation Cobras.[60] The QRF's first attack had failed completely.

Overhead, Matthews of the Night Stalkers waited for the QRF to reach Super 64. He heard the radio messages as the ad hoc Ranger element backed out and followed David as he too met heavy contact and stalled well to the south. Durant and his people were still in action, under heavy fire. The injured aviator had lost track of his pilot, CWO Raymond Frank, who had gotten out. The Somalis were laying back, plinking rounds into the inert, broken aircraft.

Matthews refused to let his four AH-6 crews land, fearful of losing another chopper out in these baddest of badlands. But, when he realized that the QRF would not be on site for hours, if at all, the 1/160th commander committed a MH-60, Super 62, which carried two Delta snipers, MSgt. Gary I. Gordon and Sfc. Randall D. Shugart. Super 62 overflew a sobering sight, Somalis massing, pressing toward the crash scene. There seemed to be thousands of them, most armed, and none looking friendly.

The rescue chopper touched down about a hundred yards southwest of Durant's smashed craft. "They knew they were going to have to do it on their own," said Sgt. Paul Shannon, crew chief on Super 62. Gordon and Shugart jumped out to almost certain death, two men against a mob. The MH-60 tried to fly cover for the pair, but an RPG slammed through the cockpit, knocking the copilot into unconsciousness, ripping the leg off the aircraft's door gunner, and threatening yet another helicopter smash-up. Super 62's pilot, CWO Michael A. Goffena, barely got the thing back to safety, crash landing in the dock areas when he could not reach the airfield. With Super 62 gone, Gordon and Shugart were, indeed, on their own.

Only Durant survived to provide an account of what happened next. The two Deltas reached him as hundreds of Somalis closed in, shooting single bullets and ripping bursts, throwing rocks, and shouting epithets. Shugart and Gordon pulled Durant out of his seat; the flier had broken his leg, compacted his spine, and could barely move. They laid him on the side of the hull away from the crowd, then crossed back over and began shooting. For a few minutes, the two snipers held their own, methodically firing round after round.

Shugart was killed first; Durant heard him cry out. Gordon brought Durant a loaded M16A2 rifle, then returned to battle the Somalis, now within thirty feet. Within minutes, the scale of firing rose dramatically, then petered out. A Somali head appeared above him, then another, then a ring of them. Durant lay back, his rifle across his chest, helpless. The militiamen took him prisoner, and though they roughed him up considerably, they did not kill him. The time bought by the Delta snipers enabled SNA leaders to gain control of their men before they finished off Durant. The pilot was convinced that the Delta pair's courage saved his life. Based on Durant's testimony, Shugart and Gordon were both awarded the Medal of Honor, the first such honors accorded since the Vietnam War.

Heroism can inspire and win battles, but the two Delta sergeants' unquestioned gallantry had not saved Super 64. Only Durant would survive, and that after eleven days of brutal captivity. Laughing Somali families later desecrated the bodies of the other Americans, dragging them through the dirt in gleeful celebration of their victory.[61]

As darkness came over Mogadishu on 3 October, nobody could guarantee that the ninety or so TF Ranger troops circled around the shards of Super 61 would not follow Gordon and Shugart into oblivion. Garrison had nothing else. Matthews kept his Little Bird gunships up (and, oh, how everyone missed the firepower of the AC-130 Spectres so cavalierly removed in early August). McKnight readied some fifty Rangers for another try at a ground breakthrough. But as happened in certain cases in Grenada and Panama, the special operators now had to depend on conventional troops to bail them out. Unlike those two campaigns, this time the conventional commander could not offer very much.

That night, every economy in USFORSOM came into sharp relief. Montgomery had no airpower beyond his army helicopters. While the QRF quickly tasked the TF 2-25th aircraft to help Matthews, the Cobras were not very capable at night, and the Blackhawks could not land and dared not try while enemy gunfire continued to erupt in such profusion. Army AH-64A Apaches, night-capable gunships so useful in Provide Comfort, were not in theater. Naval gunfire, carrier aircraft, air force attack jets and AC-130 Spectres—USFORSOM lacked all of these, any of which could have made short work of the massed SNA infantry.

Armored forces, with the protection to shrug off machine-gun slugs and rifle bullets, could have broken through the masses of SNA small-arms shooters surrounding TF Ranger. Thanks to Aspin's inaction on Montgomery's request, however, Bill David could not call on any U.S. tanks or armored infantry carriers. Instead, he, Casper, Gile, Montgomery, and their key staff officers found themselves in the port area as night fell, searching for help from UN allies. This contingency had never been honestly contemplated, let alone rehearsed; the commanders were well off the script by now, working by guess and by God.

Impressed by the urgency of the crisis, the UN allies with armor responded willingly. The Italians offered their tanks and carriers, but it would take hours to get them into the right part of Mogadishu, even if the hostiles did not contest the movement. In the port area, two other national contingents offered immediate help, proposals gratefully accepted by the USFORSOM leadership. The Pakistanis volunteered four U.S.-manufactured M48 tanks, and the Malaysians offered thirty-two Soviet-built BRDM wheeled armored cars, all an interesting commentary on the world arms market, if nothing else. Few of the Pakistanis or Malaysians spoke English, and there had been no previous training or development of procedures for working together. Now, under the pressure of an unforgiving clock and a ruthless foe, this polyglot ensemble would try one of the most difficult tasks in the military playbook, a night attack through a city.

Liaison teams were exchanged. The column slowly assembled and, after a fashion, exchanged information in several tongues. Four Humvees full of McKnight's Rangers tagged along. It took almost three hours simply to get this far, and the plan, to say the least, would not pass muster at Fort Polk's JRTC. David charitably called it "a mess," and a USFORSOM officer later said the operation resembled "a three-ring circus." But with TF Ranger still under heavy pressure, with most of its men on the ground now wounded, it would have to do.

At 2324, the convoy, swollen to seventy vehicles, thirty-six of them armored, headed west from the port, covered by 2-25th Aviation scout choppers and rocket-carrying Cobras. The Pakistani tanks led, taking the most direct route, through a checkpoint garrisoned by their countrymen. Lieutenant Ben Matthews, a 2-14th officer riding on the lead Pakistani tank, watched his vehicle's commander slow to a halt less than a half mile into the attack, despite only sporadic gunfire. The Pakistani refused to go through a roadblock, fearing mines. Matthews fired a magazine of 5.56-mm bullets through the tangled barrier and ordered the Pakistani to keep moving. He did.

After traveling a few more city blocks, the Pakistani company commander intervened, refusing to permit his big M48s to lead anymore. Cajoling did no good. The Malaysians were still game, so two of their BRDMs moved out, setting the pace. Unsure of the route, the crews made a wrong turn, stalled, and were set upon by SNA gunners, who raked them with machine-gun and RPG fire. The Pakistanis, unwillingly back in front, also attracted several RPGs and a spray of machine-gun slugs. The forward M48 returned fire, then halted. To its rear, the column piled up. Somehow, Ben Matthews got the tank and its fellows to advance a few more blocks, but that did it. They were close enough. About five hundred yards short of the Ranger perimeter, the American lightfighters dismounted, probing forward carefully to find the surrounded force.[62]

Sergeant Robert L. Jackson, a squad leader in Company A, had ridden north in a Malaysian BRDM. Once, he felt the thin-skinned, Russian-made armored car shake as a rocket glanced off its hull, but the vehicle gunned its engine and rolled on. When they reached the dismount point, Jackson led his men out into the night, his AN/PVS-7B goggles down in front of his eyes creating a greenish, fuzzy view, split by bright green lines of tracers and thicker streaks tailing behind RPGs.

Jackson led his soldiers forward, working around the edges of buildings to avoid the blizzard of SNA firing. As they crossed alleys and garbage-strewn streets, Jackson's troops shot back with rifles and machine guns. Each exchange of gunfire suppressed the Somali militia and allowed the Americans to leap ahead a few more houses while their unseen enemies ducked and reloaded. After moving forward slowly for several blocks, the firing died away. A private just ahead peered around a house's corner. The rifleman whispered back to him, "Sergeant Jackson, what are those blinking lights up front?"

Jackson looked, and through his goggles he saw the winking, rhythmic flashes of the Rangers' infrared strobe lights, showing the limits of the American-held position. He notified his chain of command, and the forces exchanged proper recognition signals. At 0155, the QRF linked up with TF Ranger. Company C veered south to check out Super 64's wreckage, but they found nothing but blood trails around the abandoned, battered airframe. There would be more fighting and more wounded, but the worst of the ordeal was over.

Garrison's force had gotten their quarry, all two dozen of them. In the strictest military interpretation, the raid succeeded. But the cost had been Pyrrhic: nineteen American dead and missing, seventeen from TF Ranger, and eighty-four wounded, sixty from TF Ranger. One Malaysian died, and seven fell wounded, along with two Pakistanis hurt. Materiel losses included two helicopters destroyed and four seriously damaged, along with a five-ton truck ruined. A few Humvees would need extensive repairs. The SNA later said that 312 Somalis died and 814 suffered injuries, a figure in line with U.S. and UN estimates.

It had been brutal, primal, a toe-to-toe knife fight deep in Indian country that had ripped the heart out of TF Ranger. The aftermath affected all who saw it. "They were stacking the dead here, the wounded there, and some of the guys were mauled, missing fingers, missing limbs," remembered TF Ranger's Sergeant First Class Lamb. "Others had chunks gone."[63]

That pretty much described U.S. policy in Somalia by October of 1993. The big firefight near the Olympic Hotel effectively concluded the U.S. operation in Somalia, as surely as the truck bomb chased Americans from Beirut in 1983. Horrified by the vicious battle and its sordid epilogue, Clinton gave up. On 7 October, he announced that America would bring in enough force to ensure a safe withdrawal by 31 March 1994. Not surprisingly, most of the UNOSOM II contingents followed suit.

His victory assured, with no desire to sacrifice any more supporters, Aidid declared a cease-fire on 9 October. Shortly thereafter, the SNA chieftain released Durant and the Nigerian soldier taken in early September. Muhammed Farah Aidid had confronted Uncle Sam and pulled it off, becoming the most renowned of Somalia's fifteen major warlords, with more than a little help from America's aborted pursuit. As final proof of his enhanced stature, Aidid received U.S. military transportation to a peace conference in Ethiopia in December, the work of Robert Oakley, who was back in the picture to try to retrieve something from the American operation.[64] With all the blood spilled for nothing, even Oakley could not save this one, and the ill-considered act outraged the American public, already more than ready to shut down the show.

The Aidid trip occurred as all sides made peaceful noises. Under a streamlined U.S. chain of command, tanks and helicopters, soldiers and Marines, jets and ships poured into the theater, a belated but important gesture toward force protection. That became the only U.S. mission in Somalia—surviving, hunkering down, avoiding the truck bombers, and then leaving. Violence mounted as the departure date approached, and, obviously, everything was heading back down the black hole, back to where it had been before America came in. Forty-two Americans had died, and 175 had been wounded—and for what? Among the troops, the question was asked a lot in the final days.

On the way out, in a last futile act, America left behind two C-5A loads of weapons and ammunition, five thousand rifles, five thousand pistols, and three million bullets. Supposedly, this had been sent for the use of the Somali police corps, a virtually nonexistent arm of a nonexistent central government.[65] American taxpayers, though, can rest assured. In Somalia, those guns will definitely get used.

Somalia showed American foreign policy at rock bottom, aimless and costly, worse than Beirut because it followed that tragedy, and policy makers from two administrations should have known better. The Beirut analogy holds almost to the month: a start in August, a different type of mission by December, a chance to withdraw the following May, trouble building over the summer, a shattering disaster in October, and a buildup to cover a pull-out by the next March, with nothing resolved.

As in Lebanon, many mistakes had been made, mostly rooted in overestimation of U.S. influence on internal Somalian affairs. At the strategic level, Bush had committed America to a difficult mission, one that only a superpower could do. The mission looked sure to creep, to grow beyond the narrow task of giving out food—and it did. Feeding the hungry in Somalia in the heart of a civil war required cooperation with the UN and the warlords, and it necessitated fighting. Once involved, the U.S. could not easily withdraw. Perhaps a reelected Bush might have pulled out in May 1993, leaving the African country to its fate. He says as much now, but hindsight often sharpens one's perspective.[66]

To Clinton, though, belongs the responsibility for the most fateful choices and nonchoices. Clinton let Howe chase Aidid, sent in Garrison and his special operations forces, and allowed matters to drift along, with ever-increasing fixation on events in Mogadishu rather than a holistic consideration of the entire country. American policy under Clinton finalized the breakup of Somalia and assured continued internal war, probably for the next few decades, if not forever. It seems like a steep price for some transitory security and short-lived improvements in nutrition. Like Reagan, Clinton knew that the responsibility for a failure of this magnitude rested with the commander in chief. Clinton followed Reagan's precedent and allowed no judicial action against subordinate commanders, although not sending tanks eventually played a part in Les Aspin's dismissal from his post as secretary of defense.[67]

The armor nondecision hinted at what went wrong at the operational level after the shift to UNOSOM II in May 1993. Few could argue with the resources employed under UNITAF, a good execution of a murky policy in which mass permitted much leeway in carrying out tasks without unduly risking American and UN lives. By contrast, in all respects, UNOSOM II's reach far exceeded its grasp, a clear mismatch between unlimited ends and limited means. Focusing the QRF on Aidid in June meant that the United States had gone to war with the SNA, a reality not admitted in the higher Washington policy circles, although Aidid knew it and fought back accordingly. A QRF adequate to protect American logistics troops was much too small and weak to root out an urban guerrilla movement. Nobody seemed willing to commit the warpower needed to carry out that difficult task, and like Reagan in Lebanon, nobody wanted to get out.

Instead, where Reagan and his people had simply held out, Clinton and his folks became seduced by the promise of a special warfare raid, much as President Jimmy Carter banked all on the Iranian hostage rescue raid of 1980. It seemed to promise victory without much of a commitment, a shortcut to success, an almost nonmilitary surgical strike, the mythical grail sought by many in Washington's policy elite. Much as Carter labeled the Iranian raid "humanitarian," Clinton bought into the concept of a bloodless apprehension. It turns out that, as Howe admitted, TF Ranger soldiers could have shot Aidid on several occasions. "Yes," conceded the admiral, "we've had many opportunities to eliminate him. That's not our job. We're trying to arrest him."[68] For his part, Aidid displayed no such restraint, and in the end, his interpretation triumphed over visions of a clean Delta pickup.

Clinton's exclusive trust in the special warriors, against military advice from Hoar and others, flew in the face of American warpower practice, which emphasizes mass and versatility in applying force. Relying on one tactic and one tiny force, no matter how good, leaves little tolerance for friction and a thinking enemy, both very much present in Mogadishu. This flawed operational choice negated American tactical skill, as much in evidence as it had been in other contemporary operations. However misplaced the thinking that dispatched TF Ranger and the QRF into the Bakara on 3 October, one cannot argue with the performance of the men under fire in the toughest close-quarters fighting since the Vietnam War.

The military made mistakes in country, notable the fouled chain of command, overreliance on provisional units, and a misplaced contempt for SNA capabilities, all of which contributed to the toll on 3–4 October. But none of these caused the overall campaign to fail. To their credit, American forces displayed no complacency, no sense that they were safe at home, and as a result, no debacle transpired at the hands of terrorists. In this sense, at least, all present had learned the tough lessons of Beirut.

Much as in Beirut, Americans failed in Somalia because they exceeded the limits of the warpower present. You can only do so much by force of arms, and good intentions are not a recognized force multiplier. In May of 1993, America joined a civil war on the cheap. As he weighed the sorry mess in the Horn of Africa, Clinton might well agree with a young Ranger, wounded in the Bakara: "We had a good plan for going in. But it turned out we didn't have such a good plan for getting out."[69] Like Task Force Ranger, America left anyway, carrying her precious dead, costly penance for the greatest of all sins, the sin of pride.

Notes

The epigraph is from Michael Herr, "Narration," in Francis Ford Coppola's motion picture *Apocalypse Now* (Los Angeles, Calif.: Omni Zoetrope Studio, 1979).

1. Walter S. Clarke, *Somalia: Background Information for Operation RESTORE HOPE* (Carlisle Barracks, Pa.: Strategic Studies Institute, December 1992), 1–3, 5–9.

2. Helen Chapin Mertz, ed., *Somalia: A Country Study* (Washington, D.C.: U.S. Government Printing Office, 1993), 3–9, 101–2, 143–44. The name "Mogadishu" originated during the medieval period, and means either "last northern city" or "city of the shah," depending on whether one accepts an African or Arabic derivation.

3. Mertz, *A Country Study,* 10–15; Clarke, *Somalia Background,* 17–20.

4. U.S. Department of the Army, Center for Army Lessons Learned, *Somalia* (Fort Leavenworth, Kans.: Center for Army Lessons Learned, January 1993), A-1.

5. Mertz, *A Country Study,* 176–77, 183–86, 189.

6. Ibid., 211–14.

7. Center for Army Lessons Learned, *Somalia,* A-3 to A-9; Brig. Gen. Raymond E. Bell Jr., USAR, "Somalia: Quo Vadis?" *Officer Review* (December 1993): 1–3; Rick Lyman, "Encounters with a Warlord," *Philadelphia Inquirer,* 9 October 1993; Rick Lyman, "Are the Somalis to be Blamed?" *Philadelphia Inquirer,* 11 October 1993.

8. Maj. Gen. Steven L. Arnold, USA, "Somalia: An Operation Other Than War," *Military Review* (December 1993): 31.

9. Thomas Hobbes, *Leviathan,* in *Great Books of the Western World* (Chicago: Encyclopedia Britannica, 1952), 23: 85; Lt. Col. T. A. Richards, USMC, "Marines in Somalia: 1992," *Proceedings* (May 1993): 133.

10. Gen. Joseph P. Hoar, USMC, "A CINC's Perspective," *Joint Forces Quarterly* (Autumn 1993): 57; Maj. Gen. Waldo D. Freeman, USA, Capt. Robert B. Lambert, USN, and Lt. Col. Jason D. Mims, USA, "Operation RESTORE HOPE: A USCENTCOM Perspective," *Military Review* (September 1993): 68. Freeman was USCENTCOM chief of staff; his coauthors

served on the staff. See also Walter S. Clarke, "Testing the World's Resolve in Somalia," *Parameters* (Winter 1993–94): 43; Rick Lyman, "Cracks in the Facade of Progress," *Philadelphia Inquirer,* 10 October 1993. The UN Operation in Somalia (UNOSOM 1) ran from 27 April 1992 until 4 May 1993, partly concurrent with the Unified Task Force (UNITAF) of 3 December 1992 to 4 May 1993. UNOSOM II began on 4 May 1993. Sometimes, careless editors allowed the acronym to be rendered as "UNISOM," the trade name of a popular brand of sleeping pills.

11. Gen. David M. Maddox, USA, *U.S. Army Europe: The Right Force for a Changing World* (Stuttgart, Germany: Headquarters, USAREUR, 1993), 7–8, 9, 10; John F. Morton, "The U.S. Navy in Review," *Proceedings* (May 1993): 125. A navy-Marine amphibious task force landed in Bangladesh in the spring of 1991 to assist typhoon victims as part of Operation Sea Angel.

12. Richards, "Marines in Somalia: 1992," 133; Hoar, "A CINC's Perspective," 56–57; Mertz, *A Country Study,* xxxii; Freeman, Lambert, and Mims, "Operation RESTORE HOPE," 67.

13. Hoar, "A CINC's Perspective," 57; Rick Lyman, "A Humanitarian Mission's Deadly Slide," *Philadelphia Inquirer,* 8 October 1993.

14. George J. Church, "Anatomy of a Disaster," *Time* (18 October 1993): 42; Richards, "Marines in Somalia: 1992," 133–34; Hoar, "A CINC's Perspective," 57. In Operation Eastern Exit, Marines spearheaded a very difficult, highly successful noncombatant evacuation of America's Mogadishu embassy, conducted under cover of darkness in early January 1991. See Arnold, "Operation Other Than War," 26.

15. Richards, "Marines in Somalia: 1992," 133.

16. Ibid.; Freeman, Lambert, and Mims, "Operation RESTORE HOPE," 68–69; Lyman, "Cracks in the Facade of Progress," 1.

17. Richards, "Marines in Somalia: 1992," 133.

18. U.S. Department of Commerce, *Statistical Abstract of the United States* (Washington, D.C.: U.S. Government Printing Office, 1993), 263.

19. Robert B. Oakley, "An Envoy's Perspective," *Joint Forces Quarterly* (Autumn 1993): 45.

20. Ibid.; Freeman, Lambert, and Mims, "Operation RESTORE HOPE," 68–69; Church, "Anatomy of a Disaster," 41–42.

21. Oakley, "An Envoy's Perspective," 45; Kim Masters, "Salute to the Old Chief," *Washington Post,* 21 October 1993; C. Robert Zelnick, "Clinton's Somalia Troubles Began with Bush," *Christian Science Monitor,*

29 October 1993. For a good description of the Japanese "victory disease" of 1942, see Gordon W. Prange with Donald M. Goldstein and Katherine V. Dillon, *Miracle at Midway* (New York: Penguin, 1982), 370–71.

22. Freeman, Lambert, and Mims, "Operation RESTORE HOPE," 68–69; Hoar, "A CINC's Perspective," 58; Mertz, *A Country Study*, xxxiv.

23. Oakley, "An Envoy's Perspective," 45–46.

24. United Nations, *United Nations Security Council Resolution 794* (New York: United Nations Publications, 3 December 1992); Clarke, "Testing the World's Resolve in Somalia," 44. The United Nations referred to Chapter 7 to authorize actions in Korea (1950), Rhodesia (1966), South Africa (1977), Iraq (1990), the former Yugoslavia (1991), Libya (1992), and Somalia (1992). Rhodesia, South Africa, and Libya entailed only political and economic sanctions. In the Korea and Iraq cases, the UN relied on a U.S.-led military coalition to conduct combat operations, in the former case, under the UN flag. In Yugoslavia, the UN has yet to authorize full-scale military operations against designated hostile forces; UN forces still function under Chapter 6 provisions as peacekeepers. In Somalia, however, the UN attempted to create a UN military force and conduct combat operations against Aidid's SNA factional militia.

25. Clarke, "Testing the World's Resolve in Somalia," 47; Freeman, Lambert, and Mims, "Operation RESTORE HOPE," 68.

26. Hoar, "A CINC's Perspective," 58; Arnold, "Operation Other Than War," 31; Maj. Gen. Steven L. Arnold, USA, and Maj. David T. Stahl, USA, "A Power Projection Army in Operations Other Than War," *Parameters* (Winter 1993–94): 17; Col. F. M. Lorenz, USMC, "Law and Anarchy in Somalia," *Parameters* (Winter 1993–94): 27–32. Lorenz was the staff judge advocate for Operation Restore Hope. Also useful for a unit-level view of ROE is Lt. Col. William David, USA, "Infantry Precommand Course 6-94 Videoteleconference," Fort Drum, N.Y., to Fort Benning, Ga. (Fort Benning, Ga.: U.S. Army Infantry School, 4 March 1994).

27. Center for Army Lessons Learned, *Somalia*, ii, 1–3; Arnold and Stahl, "A Power Projection Army in Operations Other Than War," 6.

28. Col. Mackubin T. Owens Jr., USMCR, "The U.S. Marine Corps in Review," *Proceedings* (May 1993): 132; Oakley, "An Envoy's Perspective," 46, 52; Clarke, "Testing the World's Resolve in Somalia," 42–43; Freeman, Lambert, and Mims, "Operation RESTORE HOPE," 67–69.

29. Richards, "Marines in Somalia: 1992," 134–35; Headquarters, 1st Force Service Support Group (Forward), "Combat Service Support

Forward," *Marine Corps Gazette* (November 1993): 79–88; Lt. Col. John M. Taylor, USMC, "Somalia: More Than Meets the Eye," *Marine Corps Gazette* (November 1993): 75–77.

30. Dennis Steele, "Army Units Deploy to Assist Starving, War-Torn Somalia," *Army* (February 1993): 25; Arnold, "Operation Other Than War," 28–30.

31. Frank Oliveri, "Force Restores Hope," *Air Force* (May 1993): 18–19; Richards, "Marines in Somalia: 1992," 134–36.

32. Steele, "Army Units Deploy," 25; Freeman, Lambert, and Mims, "Operation RESTORE HOPE," 72; Arnold and Stahl, "A Power Projection Army in Operations Other Than War," 6, 9; Clarke, "Testing the World's Resolve in Somalia," 47; Hoar, "A CINC's Perspective," 62.

33. Richards, "Marines in Somalia: 1992," 134–36.

34. Ibid.; Oakley, "An Envoy's Perspective," 46–47.

35. Richards, "Marines in Somalia: 1992," 135; Oakley, "An Envoy's Perspective," 48–50.

36. Richards, "Marines in Somalia: 1992," 135–36; Arnold, "Operation Other Than War," 30, 32.

37. Steele, "Army Units Deploy," 27, tells the story of Lawrence N. Freedman, a retired sergeant major from Fayetteville, North Carolina, killed by a mine explosion while doing advance work for Ambassador Oakley. Three others were injured. Freedman's mission fits the profile of ISA, CIA, or Delta protective work. For details on application of ROE in Somalia, see Center for Army Lessons Learned, *Somalia*, 20–21, and Lorenz, "Law and Anarchy in Somalia," 30.

38. Maj. Stephen G. LeBlanc, USMC, "Cordon and Search in Somalia," *Marine Corps Gazette* (November 1993): 91–93; Oakley, "An Envoy's Perspective," 47; Richards, "Marines in Somalia: 1992," 135.

39. Clarke, "Testing the World's Resolve in Somalia," 47–48; Lyman, "Cracks in the Facade of Progress," 1.

40. Zelnick, "Clinton's Somalia Troubles Began with Bush," 19.

41. Hoar, "A CINC's Perspective," 62–63; Church, "Anatomy of a Disaster," 43; United Nations, *United Nations Security Council Resolution 814* (New York: United Nations Publications, 26 March 1993); Freeman, Lambert, and Mims, "Operation RESTORE HOPE," 73; Arnold, "Operation Other Than War," 33; T. Frank Crigler, "The Peace-Enforcement Dilemma," *Joint Forces Quarterly* (Autumn 1993): 66. Crigler served as U.S. ambassador in Somalia from 1987 until recalled in 1990, prior to the January 1991 evacuation of the embassy.

42. Crigler, "The Peace-Enforcement Dilemma," 66; Clarke, "Testing the World's Resolve in Somalia," 50; Arnold, "Operation Other Than War," 33–35; Keith B. Richburg, "Somalia's Scapegoat," *Washington Post*, 18 October 1993; "Somalia Mission Lessons Are Detailed," *Baltimore Sun*, 19 January 1994; U.S. Department of the Army, "Resume of Service Career of Thomas M. Montgomery, Major General" (Washington, D.C.: Deptarment of the Army, 28 April 1993). Admiral Howe named the revamped U.S. effort Operation Continue Hope, though this name never came into wide use. The UN called the effort UNOSOM II. France referred to their troop deployment as Operation Oryx (a type of African antelope); Italy called it Operation Ibis (an African water bird).

43. Lyman, "Encounters with a Warlord"; Douglas Jehl, "An Elusive Clan Leader Thwarts a U.N. Mission," *New York Times*, 7 October 1993; "Son of Aideed is a U.S. Marine," *Washington Post*, 10 October 1993.

44. Clarke, "Testing the World's Resolve in Somalia," 52–53; Crigler, "The Peace-Enforcement Dilemma," 68–69; Rick Lyman, "The Day Everything Changed in Mogadishu," *Philadelphia Inquirer*, 6 October 1993; Tom Donnelly, "Upping the Ante," *Army Times*, 28 June 1993.

45. Donnelly, "Upping the Ante"; Michael Elliott, "The Making of a Fiasco," *Newsweek* (18 October 1993): 34; Church, "Anatomy of a Disaster," 43; United Nations, *United Nations Security Council Resolution 837* (New York: United Nations Publications, 6 June 1993); Lyman, "The Day Everything Changed in Mogadishu." For a digest of quotations from U.S. and UN policy makers regarding Aidid, see "What's the Policy?" *Washington Times*, 21 October 1993.

46. "What's the Policy?"; Col. A. J. Bacevich, USA (Ret.), "Learning from Aidid," *Commentary* (December 1993): 52–53.

47. Donnelly, "Upping the Ante," 12–14; "What's the Policy?"

48. Lyman, "A Humanitarian Mission's Deadly Slide"; "What's the Policy?"; John Lancaster and Keith B. Richburg, "U.N. Rejected Somali Overture," *Washington Post*, 17 October 1993; "24th MEU Stands Ready Off Somali Coast," *Marine Corps Gazette* (July 1993): 5; "24th MEU Lends a Hand in Somalia," *Marine Corps Gazette* (August 1993): 4.

49. Elliott, "The Making of a Fiasco," 34; "Somalia: Casualties of War," *Washington Times*, 8 October 1993; Sfc. Elroy Garcia, USA, "We Did Right That Night," *Soldiers* (February 1994): 17–18; U.S. Headquarters, Joint Task Force Somalia, "Issues and Lessons Learned," 1 December 1993, 11.

50. Bill Gertz, "Commander in Somalia Opposed Aidid Manhunt," *Washington Times*, 14 October 1993. For a discussion of special warfare

community beliefs about the viability of campaign-ending prisoner snatch raids in Grenada, Panama, and the Gulf War, see Douglas C. Waller, *The Commandos* (New York: Simon and Schuster, 1994), 239–42. The failure rate for special operations snatch-rescue raids is addressed in Benjamin F. Schemmer, *The Raid* (New York: Harper and Row, 1976), 41, 237–38, 266. The 1977 GSG9 rescue in Mogadishu and the British SAS are both discussed in Col. Charles A. Beckwith, USA (Ret.), with Donald Knox, *Delta Force* (New York: Harcourt Brace Jovanovich, 1983), 11–12, 116.

51. U.S. Headquarters, Task Force Ranger, "Operations in Somalia" (Washington, D.C.: Army Staff, 23 February 1994), 3, 9; Rick Atkinson, "The Raid That Went Awry," *Washington Post,* 30 January 1994; Michael R. Gordon and John H. Cushman Jr., "U.S. Supported Hunt for Aidid; Now Calls U.N. Policy Skewed," *New York Times,* 18 October 1993; U.S. Department of the Army, "Resume of Service Career of William Frederick Garrison, Major General" (Washington, D.C.: Department of the Army, 1 July 1992). For a description of the chains of command in Mogadishu, see Maj. Gen. Thomas M. Montgomery, USA, "Command in Somalia was Direct, Tight," *Army Times,* 22 November 1993. Descriptions of relationships between JSOC, Delta, the ISA, and the 160th Aviation are described in Terry Griswold and D. M. Giangreco, *Delta* (Osceola, Wis.: Motorbooks International, 1992), 50, 64, 78–87. See Waller, *Commandos,* 215–16 for remarks on the ISA and other special forces reconnaissance and 251–52 for comments on the special operations chain of command in the Gulf War.

52. Atkinson, "The Raid That Went Awry," 1; Elliott, "The Making of a Fiasco," 34; Michael R. Gordon and Thomas L. Friedman, "Disasterous U.S. Raid in Somalia Nearly Succeeded, Review Finds," *New York Times,* 25 October 1993; Task Force Ranger, "Operations in Somalia," 4, 8, 11; Mark Fineman, "Rangers' Somalia Mission Marked by Lapses, Errors," *Los Angeles Times,* 21 October 1993; Donna Peterson, "General Said to Take Blame for Failed Raid," *Army Times,* 8 November 1993.

53. Lyman, "A Humanitarian Mission's Deadly Slide"; David, "Video-teleconference"; Headquarters, 10th Mountain Division (Light Infantry), Public Affairs Officer, "Notes on Welcome Remarks for TF 2-14," 16 December 1993.

54. Lyman, "A Humanitarian Mission's Deadly Slide"; 10th Mountain Division Public Affairs Officer, "Notes on Welcome Remarks for TF 2-14"; John Lancaster, "U.S. Helicopter Force Maintains 'Eyes Over Mogadishu,'" *Washington Post,* 19 October 1993; "Downed Pilots Wage Battle for Freedom," *Fort Campbell Courier,* 21 October 1993.

55. Atkinson, "The Raid That Went Awry"; Lancaster and Richburg, "U.N. Rejected Somali Overture"; Keith B. Richburg, "U.S. Envoy to Somalia Urged Policy Shift Before 18 GIs Died," *Washington Post,* 11 November 1993; Secretary of Defense Les Aspin, "Memorandum for Correspondents No. 302-M" (Washington, D.C.: Department of Defense, 7 October 1993).

56. Atkinson, "The Raid That Went Awry"; Kirk Spitzer, "The Siege of Mogadishu," *Gannett News Service,* 26 November 1993; Malcolm McConnell, "Betrayal in Somalia," *Reader's Digest* (April 1994): 65–66. Atkinson provides excellent and detailed coverage of TF Ranger and, in his 7 October 1993 report, of the QRF. Spitzer describes the human drama experienced by the encircled TF Ranger troops and downed helicopter crews. McConnell tells the story of the pilots and the TF Ranger ground convoy. Taken together, these pieces paint a fairly complete picture of the operation.

57. McConnell, "Betrayal in Somalia," 66–67; Montgomery, "Command in Somalia was Direct, Tight"; Atkinson, "The Raid That Went Awry"; Garcia, "We Did Right That Night," 18; Task Force Ranger, "Operations in Somalia," 9; Gordon and Friedman, "Disasterous U.S. Raid in Somalia Nearly Succeeded, Review Finds"; David, "Videoteleconference"; Col. Lawrence E. Casper, USA, "Quick Reaction Force: Summary of Combat Operations on 3 October 1993" (Washington D.C.: Army Staff, October 1993) 1–2.

58. Rick Atkinson, "Night of a Thousand Casualties," *Washington Post,* 31 January 1994; Rick Atkinson, "Deliverance From Warlord's Fury," *Washington Post,* 7 October 1993; Paul Quinn-Judge, "Film of Somalia Gunfight Shows It Was Not a Rout, U.S. Says," *Boston Globe,* 3 November 1993.

59. Spitzer, "Siege of Mogadishu"; Quinn-Judge, "Film of Somalia Gunfight."

60. Garcia, "We Did Right That Night," 18–19; Casper, "Quick Reaction Force," 2–3; Atkinson, "Deliverance From Warlord's Fury"; Sean D. Naylor and Steve Vogel, "A Smooth-Starting Raid Ends in Catastrophe," *Army Times,* 18 October 1993; SSgt. Keith D. Butler, USA, "Captive in Somalia," *Soldiers* (February 1994): 22–23.

61. Tom Post et al., "Firefight From Hell," *Newsweek* (18 October 1993): 39; Atkinson, "Night of a Thousand Casualties"; Spitzer, "Siege of Mogadishu"; Butler, "Captive in Somalia," 22–23; McConnell, "Betrayal in Somalia," 67–70. Shugart's and Gordon's families accepted their posthumous Medals of Honor at the White House on 23 May 1994.

62. Casper, "Quick Reaction Force," 3–5; David, "Videoteleconference"; Naylor and Vogel, "A Smooth-Starting Raid Ends in Catastrophe"; Atkinson, "Deliverance From Warlord's Fury"; Gordon and Friedman, "Disasterous U.S. Raid in Somalia Nearly Succeeded, Review Finds."

63. Post et al., "Firefight From Hell," 39; Spitzer, "Siege of Mogadishu"; Atkinson, "Night of a Thousand Casualties"; George Boehmen, "Soldier Braves Somali Fire for 'My Guys,'" *Washington Times,* 8 October 1993.

64. For the full text of President Clinton's 7 October 1993 speech, see "I Am Committed to Getting This Job Done in Somalia," *Washington Post,* 8 October 1993; Michael R. Gordon, "Europeans Plan Early Pullout from Somalia," *New York Times,* 13 October 1993; Douglas Jehl, "U.S. Shifts Troops to Defensive Role in Somalia Mission," *New York Times,* 20 October 1993; Rowan Scarborough, "Once-Targeted Somali Warlord Gets U.S. Escort," *Washington Times,* 3 December 1993.

65. Sean D. Naylor, "Assault Rifles a Parting Gift to Somalia?" *Army Times,* 7 February 1994. Total U.S. casualties in Somalia amounted to 42 dead and 175 wounded. The 42 dead included the 8 UNITAF fatalities, the 4 killed in the mine explosion of 8 August, 3 men killed in the 25 September helicopter crash, the 19 killed (including one who died of wounds) in the 3–4 October fight, and the 8 AC-130H crewmen killed (one is still missing, but presumed lost) over water en route to Mogadishu from Kenya on 16 March 1994. For examples of soldier discontent with the results of the campaign, see Carol J. Castaneda and Bill Nichols, "Somalia Casts a Shadow Over Clinton Visit," *USA Today,* 16 March 1994.

66. Thomas L. Friedman, "A Broken Truce: Clinton vs. Bush in Global Policy," *New York Times,* 17 October 1993.

67. "Ranger General Takes Blame for 18 Deaths," *Washington Times,* 29 October 1993; Ronald A. Taylor, "President: Deaths in Somalia No One's Fault," *Washington Times,* 16 October 1993.

68. "Transcript: It Would Be a Disaster If the U.S. Pulled Out Now," *Washington Times,* 11 October 1993. For President Carter's characterization of the Iran rescue raid as "humanitarian," see President James Earl Carter, "Rescue Attempt for American Hostages in Iran, 25 April 1980" in *Public Papers of the Presidents: Jimmy Carter, 1980–81,* bk. 1 (Washington, D.C.: U.S. Government Printing Office, 1981), 772–73.

69. Atkinson, "Deliverance From Warlord's Fury."

CHAPTER 8

The House of Pain:
Intervention in the Former Yugoslavia, 1992 to 1995

In the nightmare of the dark,
all the dogs of Europe bark,
and the living nations wait,
each sequestered in its hate.
W. H. Auden

Even while things went from bad to worse in Somalia, there were many other candidates, all over the globe, waiting for the Americans to come. Along with the traditional charity cases and victims of the lesser-developed lands, the former Second World, the ruins of the Communist experiment, had its own problems—a dozen Somalias clamoring for UN and U.S. assistance. Some of these could have swallowed the entire Regular Army and Marine Corps whole, along with good slugs of airpower and seapower, and still shown little improvement. Nagorno-Karabakh, Moldavia, Ossetia, Abkhazia—the names themselves sounded threatening, like something large and oily loose in the basement, snuffling for rotting flesh.

The only post-Soviet strife that enthralled most Americans arose in Yugoslavia, a country that at least had a name that could be easily pronounced in English. It was only fair, since the place had been concocted in deference to Woodrow Wilson's insistence on national self-determination in the wake of World War I. Wilson and his colleagues had an odd definition of "nation," as they lumped together Orthodox Serbs, Catholic Croats, and Muslim Serbs, not to mention sundry Slovenes, Montenegrins, Macedonians, plus trace groups of Albanians, Bulgars, Magyars, Greeks, Italians, Romanians, Czechs, Slovaks, Turks, Ruthenians, Russians, Ukrainians, Poles, Austrians, Vlachs, and Gypsies.[1] Almost all of these ethnic groups loathed each other, or could be convinced to do so. As in Lebanon, it was only a matter of time before the violence started.

When it did, the United States, as always, got the call. But chastened by the contemporaneous frustrations in Somalia, not to mention a recollection of blood-soaked Balkan history, the Clinton administration preferred to draw a line as the fighting in Bosnia-Herzegovina intensified during 1993. America got involved, of course, but only in limited ways, always with an eye toward protecting American lives first. In this area, the ends and means lined up sensibly. It was not easy and did not salve very many consciences, especially as CNN played on and the bodies piled up. Emotion argued for doing something, but that urge peaked just as the caskets came back from downtown Mogadishu. Clinton and his people heeded the warning.

In confronting the Yugoslav challenge, America did not call in Doctor Feelgood. Rather, in accord with Bismarckian realpolitik, whether by design or by happenstance, the United States quarantined the problem and held that line, much as John Mitchell and the boys did in Korea. Essentially, American warpower dug a figurative firebreak around the Bosnian inferno, flew in a few dampening missions, treated the survivors when possible, but by and large, stood back to let this one burn itself out.[2]

Nobody in authority tried to solve eight centuries of bad blood with bombs or Marines, indicating that, if nothing else, the crew in Washington had learned something in Somalia. If Provide Comfort exemplifies OOTW done right, and UNOSOM II OOTW done wrong, then U.S. operations in and around the former Yugoslavia remind us of OOTW in its purest form— indecisive and maddening but steadily keeping the lid on, sitting on the problem, watching, waiting, and soldiering on. If done long enough and well enough, as in Korea or in the Sinai, that can metamorphose into a form of victory, the status quo maintained by the greatest status quo power of the age. When keeping watch around the house of pain, it would be nice to offer a cure, but a realist will settle for keeping the pain inside. So it went and goes, in the former Yugoslavia.

Yugoslavia is an invention, not really a country but six major ethnic groups, plus splinters of others, that flew in loose formation throughout much of the twentieth century. The Balkans, the "cockpit of Europe," came unglued during the nineteenth century, as the Ottoman Turkish Empire slowly expired, and the other major powers jumped in to stake their claims and back their favorites. Greece, Bulgaria, Romania, and Albania emerged from the wreckage of the lingering Ottoman collapse.

In the western Balkans, the mountainous terrain led to several clusters of intermixed groups, all of south Slavic heritage, but deeply divided along religious and cultural lines. Seeking influence, the various eastern powers chose and armed their protégés, much as America and the USSR did decades later in the Middle East. The Orthodox Russians supported the Orthodox Serbs (41 percent of the populace of the former Yugoslavia), Macedonians (6 percent), and Montenegrins (3 percent), while the Austrian-Hungarian amalgam and their German friends encouraged the Roman Catholic Croats (20 percent) and Slovenes (8 percent). The Muslim Slavs (9 percent), later sorely afflicted in Bosnia, could only call on the weakened Turks for help, and not much came. They took it on the chin, then and now, forever viewed as collaborators by the Serbs, Croats, and others.[3] Stirring the pot in the Balkans entertained several generations of European statesmen, but their fun ended when one stir too many brewed up World War I.

Schoolchildren know that a Serbian gunman named Gavrilo Princip shot Archduke Franz Ferdinand of Austria-Hungary while that notable was visiting Sarajevo, Bosnia, then under the control of the dual monarchy of Austria-Hungary. This act sparked the third Balkan war in three years, with Austria-Hungary assailing Serbia, Russia coming to Serbia's defense, Germany supporting Austria-Hungary, France backing Russia, and then Britain jumping in once the Germans crossed into Belgium en route to Paris. The German regiments never made it to the French capital, but the ensuing world war killed or wounded thirty-five million.[4] And it all started with mucking around in the Balkans, a lesson not lost on European leaders of today.

From 1918 until 1941, Yugoslavia existed as an entity, generally under authoritarian Serb-dominated governments. In April of 1941, the Germans invaded, smashing apart the fractious kingdom in a blitzkrieg of less than two weeks. The Germans then carved up the prostrate country among Hungary, Bulgaria, and Italy, leaving an independent Croatian puppet state. Most of Serbia and Slovenia fell under the tender mercies of Nazi occupation. It looked like another quick win for Hitler's Wehrmacht.

In fact, the opening triumph proved hollow. Communist partisans under Croat Josip Brozovich (known to followers, and soon the world, as "Tito") and Chetnik bands representing the prewar Serb establishment took turns killing each other and Axis soldiers. Predictably, the Croat rump state fielded a pro-Axis army and a ruthless militia, the dread Ustashi, and waged war against the other ethnicities. That brutality merely paid back the Serbs

The Former Yugoslavia

and others for past indignities. The Muslim Slavs, seemingly doomed to guess wrong at every turn, joined the German Waffen SS in large numbers. This was a good idea in 1942 but not so wise by 1945. It further reinforced their reputation as collaborators.[5]

When the dust settled, Tito the Communist reigned supreme, beneficiary of U.S. and British aid and a Soviet ground invasion. Until his death in 1980, Tito successfully walked the tightrope between the superpower blocs, founding the Nonaligned Movement, a collection of ostensibly neutral smaller states. In fact, Tito hewed closer to the Moscow line than the Western viewpoint, allowing the Soviet 106th Guards Air Assault Division to stage in his country during superpower shadowboxing related to the 1973 Arab-Israeli War. Such leanings aside, Tito's strange mixture of personal rule, semicapitalist economics, and Communist rhetoric sufficed to unite Yugoslavia into an approximation of a real country, home of the 1984 Sarajevo Olympics and the ugly, wretched (but cheap) Yugo subcompact car.[6] Tito's state hung together a decade after he passed on.

By 1991, as Communist-held eastern Europe decomposed into successor states, Yugoslavia too felt the pulls of rising nationalism among its ethnic constituents. On 25 June 1991, Croatia and Slovenia declared independence from the Serbian-controlled Belgrade government. When Serb troops crossed the Slovenian border two days later, it touched off civil war, with Croatia and Slovenia ranged against the residual Yugoslav state.

Fighting escalated during 1991, as the Serbs made use of irregulars to extend the war throughout Croatia. By early 1992, the European Community and the United Nations intervened to stop the fighting. Led by traditional Croat-Slovene-ally Germany, the Europeans recognized the new microstates, and on 21 February, the UN Security Council approved dispatch of a peacekeeping force. The first fourteen thousand UN peacekeepers arrived, with the goal of protecting relief deliveries in the now independent regions. Working through guerrilla fronts, Serbia retained effective control over a third of Croatia.[7]

Apparently having learned their timing from their coreligionists in Kurdistan, the Muslim Slav plurality of Bosnia-Herzegovina chose this inauspicious moment to declare independence from Belgrade. The Muslims made up 44 percent of the populace in this region, and they were city dwellers, concentrated around the major urban areas. In the countryside, the third of the new state who were Serbs quickly made common cause with their Belgrade brothers. The Croat faction, about a fifth of the total in this area, were massed in Herzegovina and wasted little time in tying into the Croat-Slovene support network. This cleared the decks for a three-way horror show.

The Serbs, as always, held the initiative, and the Belgrade government actively supported their relatives in Bosnia. Freed from additional operations on the Croatian front and now veterans of the latest version of the old Balkan game, Bosnian Serb forces fell on the hapless Bosnian Muslims with real vengeance. By 6 April, Bosnian Serbs, backed by strong Serbian assistance, invested Sarajevo, a Muslim stronghold. That siege persisted unabated for almost two years, soon to be joined by similar encirclements around Banja Luka, Bihac, Gorazde, Majlaj, Tuzla, and Zepa. In Herzegovina, local Croats, aided by their home country, laid siege to Mostar. When not busy "cleansing" Muslims in accord with gruesome Hitlerian means, the Serbs and Croats warred on each other. By mid-November, seventeen thousand were dead, and two million people, half of Bosnia-Herzegovina's population, were refugees, one step ahead of the mortar shells and cleansing squads. As winter drew on, survival seemed like a dicey proposition for the Bosnian Muslims.[8]

The United Nations, Europe (in its various European Community, Western European Union, and NATO manifestations), and America all fiddled while Bosnia burned. Unlike the bomb-dazed Iraqis or Somali warlord bands, the Bosnian Serbs were obviously a better-armed grade of opponent, consisting of both regulars and irregulars, working in familiar mountainous terrain, and armed to the teeth with relatively heavy weapons. There were at least three sides, no front lines, and no likely political solution short of outright extermination (and the locals were more than happy to try that). The greater powers acted, but they did not enter this charnel house willingly, nor in great numbers. And contrary to public perceptions, the Americans were there right from the outset.

Foreign powers entered Bosnia the way a barefoot man enters a pit of vipers—slowly and carefully, on tiptoes, with both eyes wide open. There were really three actors involved: the UN, the Europeans, and America. Each hoped that one of the others would do the job and somehow stop the slaughter. Not surprisingly, the United Nations and the amorphous blob known as Europe both looked to America to solve the problem. It was the same old tune—trying to write checks on Uncle Sam's account and hoping he would pay up. This time, Sam was not willing to pony up very much.

The United Nations took interest in several aspects of the Yugoslav war, to include investigating war crimes (a growth industry in the Balkans), sponsoring largely fruitless peace negotiations, and establishing political and economic sanctions to isolate the war zone. All of this burned up a lot of paper and debate time, but in the absence of a military outcome on the ground, accomplished very little else.

United Nations military efforts proved more effective, at least as far as isolating the problem. Sea and air exclusion zones were announced in

November 1992 and March 1993, thereby blocking some external aid to the warring parties, and thus indirectly limiting the scale of violence in country. Here, the UN deferred to the Western European Union (WEU) and NATO, including America, who patrolled the Adriatic Sea and the skies over the Balkans under UN approval, but not under the world body's baby blue ensign.

Getting Europe and America to guard the boneyard proved relatively easy. The harder mission was doing something about the war. Ending it would have been preferred but also gargantuan in scale, a job for America, and neither the Bush nor Clinton administrations were willing. So the UN settled for a more limited goal on land, guaranteeing humanitarian aid. United Nations General Assembly Resolution 46/182, passed on 19 December 1991, first spelled out this role, which authorized UN members to intervene physically to ensure relief shipments, with or without invitation. There would be more resolutions, a veritable paper blizzard, reiterating the concept.

In line with this idea, the establishment of the United Nations Protection Force (UNPROFOR) in February 1992 originally guaranteed supplies in Croatia but expanded in October of that year to provide interposition and convoy escorts in and around Muslim enclaves in Bosnia. The UNPROFOR tasks included demilitarizing UN protected zones, verifying cease-fires, overseeing disarming of combatants, supervising activities of local authorities and police, ensuring safe passage of humanitarian convoys, and monitoring evacuation of the injured. Any one of these duties could absorb several divisions of soldiers.

By early 1994, UNPROFOR directed some 28,000 troops from twenty-two countries, split into regional commands for Croatia (14,000 headquartered in Zagreb), Bosnia (13,000 led from Sarajevo), and Macedonia (1,000 controlled from Skopje). This sounds like a lot of people, until you consider that back in 1944, Nazi Germany and its wartime allies employed some 700,000 troops trying to maintain order in the region. Calling on Luftwaffe dive-bombers, tanks, and heavy artillery, and unrestricted by anything resembling humane ROE, the Germans never came close to controlling more than the dirt on which they stood.[9] Is it any wonder that a few thousand lightly armed UNPROFOR troops did less?

In league with UNPROFOR, hoping to take advantage of what security could be created, a combined military and civilian international relief effort endeavored to bring in food to the beleaguered Muslims by air and ground means, a project often interrupted by fighting. It was the Kurdistan and Somalia approach again, plagued by similar problems. UNPROFOR did what it could to assist deliveries, but the UN commanders lacked the warpower to pacify the region. Instead, they attempted to keep a peace that did not exist. Humanitarian aid flowed intermittently, and UN blood flowed regularly, to the tune of 850 casualties, 71 of them dead, by mid-January of 1994. In announcing his resignation about that time, UN Bosnia commander Lt. Gen. Francis Briquemont of Belgium complained bitterly, "There is a fantastic gap between all these Security Council resolutions and the means available to execute them."[10]

Unable to dominate Bosnia through superior warpower, if in fact such a thing could even be done, UNPROFOR resorted to the U.S. Marine approach during the Beirut expedition: try to stay neutral, avoid provocation, and hope for the best. As in Lebanon, the locals did not share the UN's wishful self-perception.

It was incredible to assume that UNPROFOR could be thought of as impartial when UN policy clearly favored protecting the embattled Muslim Slavs, and Serbia groaned under the stresses of political denunciations, economic strictures, and air and sea blockades. But the standard UN style, perfected over decades, favored good old Chapter 6–style peacekeeping and interposition, and so the UNPROFOR troops bravely tried to follow the usual rules.[11] Such restraint made sense in the MFO case, but not here. This was not the Sinai, with most of the opponents abiding by the rules. Serbs, Croats, and Muslim Slavs all shot back. And UNPROFOR paid the price.

Even within the UN fold, the Europeans took leading roles. The quarrelsome extended family of the continent, who had once entertained dreams of a United States of Europe to begin in 1992, found reality to be a lot less accommodating. Many governments made big noises about Yugoslavia being a European problem that demanded a European solution. Talk, however brave and inspiring, did not stop the war. That would necessitate armed intervention, and Europeans knew what could happen if they jumped recklessly into this mountainous meatgrinder. If the Americans would come, well, then maybe Europe would act. Otherwise, rhetoric and supporting the UN's limited efforts would have to suffice.

So, despite their fondest desires, Europeans found themselves following the same approach as the UN. The large European Community (EC) could only agree to issue strongly worded documents and sponsor Britain's David Lord Owen in his political settlement ventures with UN envoy Cyrus Vance, a veteran U.S. diplomat. The EC-UN Vance-Owen plan, revealed on 22 January 1993, carved Bosnia-Herzegovina into a patchwork of ten disjointed ethnic areas, about the best reasonable men could do. Naturally, the locals would have none of this and kept fighting. Even so, Vance-Owen remains the model for most proposed peace agreements and all subsequent negotiations. If the war ever really ends, its final outcome may look a lot like the Vance-Owen outline.[12] That was about all the EC could produce.

The more restrictive Western European Union (WEU—essentially NATO without America, Canada, Greece, or Turkey) allowed for military action not subject to the American veto. France, where anti-American posturing seems to enjoy certain domestic advantages and not part of the formal NATO military command structure anyway, liked the WEU for these reasons. Pressed by France, WEU forces enforced the sea interdiction campaign, which from the start also fell under NATO oversight. The WEU, however, featured major and predictable disagreements between the French, British, and Germans on how much warpower to apply and who should take charge. Without the United States to referee, the best the WEU could generate was the excuse for French participation in the naval "surveillance" begun on 3 July 1992.[13] Consensus never formed for air strikes or ground intervention.

It fell to NATO, the erstwhile scourge of Lenin's dead empire, to pull together the European sea and air cordons around the former Yugoslavia. Never intended to address internal disputes of members, not to mention nonmembers, NATO alone possessed the integrated command architecture to conduct an extended campaign in the Balkans. The UN, EC, and WEU could threaten all they wanted. But NATO could act, admittedly in accord with its labyrinthine, plodding ways, full of nods to the concerns of the lesser states. Encouraged by Britain, NATO almost immediately assumed control of the naval and air interdiction campaigns around the former Yugoslavia.[14] And that brought in America, NATO's really big gun, the only power that could make all of this stick.

Having to rely on the arrogant, pushy American cousins did not make any of the European leaders particularly happy. Once again, as had become habitual since 1917, Europe looked across the Atlantic for leadership. It was not lost on Britain, France, Belgium, the Netherlands, and Norway that they had fingers stuck into every pie: troops in UNPROFOR, roles in the EC debates, ships and planes responding to WEU and NATO, and their own individual relationships to the United States. These European powers would have their say and exert their influence. They, after all, were in the line of fire. They would not meekly defer unless America really wanted to take charge, to put young Americans in harm's way on the scale of Desert Storm, Provide Comfort, or Restore Hope.[15]

That America would not do. Bush agreed to a humanitarian airlift, a program extended by Clinton. Bush also joined the sea and air blockades, strengthened by Clinton. The latter eventually deployed a token ground force to Macedonia. Neither administration, though, pressed for a wider role or for boots on the bloody ground of Bosnia. Americans joined in the UN and NATO operations, eventually playing a key part in the latter. But this time, unlike in the Gulf or in Somalia, Washington did not take the lead. As a result, the Bosnian war sputtered on, contained but not quelled. Contrary to sometimes impassioned public exhortations to do more, containment was, in fact, good enough for the UN, Europe, and America.

American airlifter crews and logisticians entered the former Yugoslavia in July of 1992, about a month before similar groups went into Somalia. Operation Provide Promise initially looked a lot like Provide Relief, only smaller. The 435th Airlift Wing, at Rhein-Main Air Base in Germany, oversaw the effort. On average, three C-130E or C-130H Hercules turboprop transports, drawn from a variety of active, Air Force Reserve, and Air National Guard squadrons, flew two missions a day into the airdomes at appropriately titled Split or Zagreb, both in Croatia. About half the aircrews flew directly into encircled Sarajevo. UN and private relief groups, aided by UNPROFOR troops, unloaded up to twenty tons of food, medicine, and other humanitarian items from each flight.[16]

Provide Promise was expanded in two significant ways after its small beginnings. In November 1992—about the same time Robert Oakley, Frank Wisner, and Admiral Jeremiah labored over a plan to intervene in Somalia—the United States deployed the 212th Mobile Army Surgical Hospital (MASH) from Wiesbaden, Germany, to Camp Pleso, just outside Zagreb. This sixty-bed facility, manned with some three hundred Americans, was tasked to provide the main treatment center for all of UNPROFOR, as well as for humanitarian workers and the local people. The site was carefully chosen, picked intentionally to be well beyond the Bosnian fighting. About every six months, the personnel changed over, first to the army's 502d MASH, then to the air force 48th Air Transportable Hospital, and later to a provisional navy outfit named Fleet Hospital

Zagreb. The statistics for the 48th Air Transportable Hospital reflect a very busy medical team: 6,000 outpatients, 450 inpatients, and even children from the Zagreb area in a specially configured pediatric ward.[17] Running a hospital was not a typical American role in a UN operation, but it was effective, both absolutely and as a political symbol. Americans had a role on the ground in the former Yugoslavia, but not in the line of fire. That suited Bush, and it suited Clinton too.

As things got worse for the Muslims, Clinton stepped up the pace of airlift. On 28 February of 1993, Provide Promise received orders to begin airdrops to Bosnian Muslim villages and towns cut off by Bosnian Serb forces. Landings in Sarajevo increased to two dozen a day, half by Americans, the rest by British, Canadians, French, Germans, and Swedes. These missions often dodged antiaircraft fire on approach and departure, along with sweating out mortar, artillery, and rocket fire targeted on the runways and parking aprons. Parked planes were juicy targets, so fast turnarounds became imperative.

Air Force TSgt. Scott Womack of the 41st Airlift Squadron, flying in with his crew in February of 1993, experienced the ultimate nightmare. After unloading supplies, his pilots readied their turboprop C-130E for departure. The number 3 engine refused to turn over. Nobody relished trying to clear the mountains around Sarajevo with three engines, especially if forced into evasive maneuvers. Waiting for repairs was out of the question; the longer they sat, the more likely that gunners hidden on the looming ridges would finish off the aircraft. Womack had to solve this problem and fast.

Naturally, the spartan facilities in Sarajevo offered nothing. Womack traced the problem to a faulty igniter plug and bad lead wires. Working quickly with a few hand tools and a lot of experience, the sergeant crafted a jury rig that brought the big Allison T-56 engine coughing to life. The crew taxied out and took off, saved by an NCO's hot-wiring job. For this action and others like it, Womack received recognition as the Air Force Association's 1993 Crew Chief of the Year. As it turned out, no U.S. aircraft took crippling hits on the tarmac, though one plane took a shot through an aileron on 11 January, and the Sarajevo airport was closed several times by rocket and shell fire.[18] Even considering the risks, airlanding was preferred, because it delivered more goods right into the cities. But when things really got bad, the allies resorted strictly to night parachute drops.

The aerial resupply flights ordered by Clinton began after dark on 2 March 1993. On average, American Hercules crews flew six to twelve sorties three to four nights a week, a rate usually supplemented by the work of two French and two German airdrop crews, also flying from Rhein-Main. This rate rose during the winter months when the pallets included bulky blankets and sleeping bags.

To avoid antiaircraft fire, the C-130s dropped from ten thousand feet, more than ten times higher than they would prefer. "Because you're dropping from such a height, it doesn't always hit the right spot," explained Col. John L. Booth, one of the operations staff officers who directed the airlift. In Kurdistan, the inability to solve the accuracy problem soon resulted in the deployment of ground forces, something the Clinton administration did not intend to do in Yugoslavia. The transport jocks had to get the job done.

This time, even in the equally mountainous terrain, the air force greatly improved their effectiveness. Having studied the results of Provide Comfort, the service's airdrop experts, including engineers contracted through the RAND Corporation, produced acceptable dispersion patterns. In some cases, the fliers showered densely populated areas with individual food packets. These little food bags fluttered down relatively slowly, moving at about the speed of a hard-hit softball and would bounce off buildings and Bosnians without doing any permanent damage. The separate items also reduced the killings that resulted when hostile guerrillas ambushed villagers congregating around larger bundles.

Bulk cargo, however, typified most drops. Army riggers of the 5th Quartermaster Detachment cut down the edges on the canopies of the parachutes, permitting the deliveries to drop at higher speeds and to float more directly downward. Thanks to superb piloting and improved release techniques by the U.S. and NATO flight crews, the bulk drops placed 85 percent of the half-ton bundles within a mile of their targets, the airdrop equivalent of threading needles at 150 miles an hour.

As in northern Iraq, some people on the ground were injured as the massive pallets came swinging down at forty-five to seventy miles per hour. Others got hurt when the heavy packages tumbled down rocky slopes, pulled by wind and gravity. One pilot noted that UNPROFOR liaison officers "tell us not to worry about hitting the houses because they're all destroyed anyway." That was easy enough to say but, in truth, all Provide Promise paradrops carefully balanced the needs of crew safety and possible injuries and damage at the receiving end. In extreme cases, aircrew protection took priority, but, clearly, the fliers took pride in getting their loads through, even in the teeth of opposition.

And there was opposition, all right. Several of the unarmored, lumbering four-engine airplanes sustained damage from antiaircraft fire in December of 1993, and no fliers ever crossed Bosnia without watching for ground fire, and usually seeing some. Due to the skill and luck of the fliers, plus the increasing show of force of NATO airpower, the Serb air defenders never scored a fatal blow. No lives were lost, and, in company with the continuing airlanding flights, Provide Promise delivered forty-six thousand tons of relief goods, more than a quarter by parachute or packet scattering, in an operation that surpassed the Berlin Airlift as the longest American aerial resupply in history.[19]

Air freight is the most expensive and least efficient means of bringing in sustenance. That is well known, and the military much prefers sea and ground transport, both unreliable in violent, nearly landlocked Bosnia. The alternatives to a successful airlift involved starvation or commitment to a major ground war. By staving off those possibilities, the air bridge did its job, demonstrating once again that the unglamorous "trash haulers" are every bit as vital to the joint team as the flashiest F-15E Strike Eagles.

Provide Promise put a foot in the door. As 1992 became 1993, the rest of the American warpower triad gradually arrived and took up their respective places in the arena. Seapower came first, followed by airpower, with land force, as usual, a cautious and careful third. All but the single ground battalion fell under the time-tested NATO command structure, specifically Allied Forces South (AFSOUTH), run in 1992 through 1994 by American Adm. Jeremy M. "Mike" Boorda from his headquarters in Naples, Italy.

Boorda's marching orders incorporated the carefully circumscribed U.S. policy. Here is how Secretary of Defense William Perry explained American goals in the former Yugoslavia:

First, to stop the war from spreading beyond Bosnia and even beyond the Balkans. And the second objective there is to do what we can to limit the violence, particularly the civilian casualties, while the negotiations are going on. Our main thrust has been on diplomatic initiatives, not military initiatives. . . . It is crucially important for not only NATO, but the United Nations, and the United States, when it is making statements about what it will or will not do, not to be making empty threats. We should not be threatening an action which we do not have the ability to follow through on.[20]

America, like the UN and NATO-WEU, settled on a limited role in the conflict.

Boorda's mission, therefore, was simple: contain the fighting by enforcing the sea, air, and land cordons and render support to UNPROFOR. That last point, especially in terms of possible air strikes, formed the centerpiece of rancorous debates in the UN, the EC, the WEU, NATO, and the state assemblies of most of the participating countries. As it turned out, things never got much past the bluffing stage as far as true armed intervention to "limit the violence," presumably by killing many of the bad guys (no shortage of varieties), an unusual definition of the term limit.

Instead of getting snared in that briar patch, Boorda focused on the containment mission. The sea services began operating on 3 July 1992, to "intercept and challenge," but not board, suspect merchant vessels bound for ports in the former Yugoslavia. Operation Sharp Guard saw a U.S. aircraft carrier battle group almost continuously offshore, supplemented in late 1993 by British and French carrier forces, along with escorts from other NATO-WEU countries. The American and allied ships initially restricted their mission to monitoring shipping off the Dalmatian coast, identifying and tracking arms carriers. On 16 November 1992, this tightened to a de facto blockade, though nobody used that provocative term.[21] A blockade, after all, is an act of war.

United States Marine expeditionary units, aboard amphibious shipping, also sailed in the Adriatic Sea during Sharp Guard. In 1993, the carriers USS *Theodore Roosevelt* and *America* even embarked Marines, six hundred and two hundred respectively, to provide on-call infantry assault capability without tying down precious amphibious shipping already overworked off Somalia and elsewhere. These so-called "Adaptive Force Packages" created a few headaches: carrier attack jets bumped to assimilate Marine helicopters, not enough Marines for more than a quick raid, and no real staying power for much else. Along with tactical concerns, there were issues of service culture as the navy and Marine Corps mixed gray and green, mud and microchips at the most visceral level. But that was precisely the point—to experiment, to try a new idea. Some lessons were learned, and some icons smashed. Power projection "from the sea" means Marines and carrier planes, and under such plans, they worked together very closely. If a small incursion had been necessary, these forces could have pulled it off.

More to the point, the closely integrated navy-Marine team put iron teeth into Sharp Guard: "If ships tried to run the Sharp Guard embargo," said one

SEAL officer, "somebody has to be there to try to stop them. There is no better way than actually putting people on board and compel the captain to either stop or seize the captain and the ship." By 1 June 1993, Sharp Guard had challenged 11,700 ships, stopped and boarded 760, and diverted 165.[22] No substantial military cargo made it through to any of the belligerents. America and its friends ruled supreme in the Adriatic, proof positive of what a naval superpower can do.

American airpower, already the mainstay of Provide Promise, formed the core of the force responsible for executing Operation Deny Flight, the aerial no-fly zone imposed over Bosnia. Beginning on 12 April 1993, some seventy aircraft began patrolling the Balkan skies. Most of these NATO-WEU planes, of course, bore American markings.

Boorda commanded the air effort through the 5th Allied Tactical Air Force (5ATAF), which ran the operation from Del Molina Air Base near Vicenza, in northern Italy. U.S. Air Force Maj. Gen. James E. Chambers ran the Yugoslav campaign from Del Molina. Conveniently, and by design, he was also the joint forces air component commander (JFACC—in charge of all airpower) for the Provide Promise airlift. Thus, Del Molina deconflicted and synchronized airlift and Deny Flight air missions. Within days of the declaration of the no-fly zone, the relief flights enjoyed close and continuous fighter escort.

This was an important point, because while NATO had agreed to scour the no-fly zone for the UN, the alliance had not taken on formal requirements to direct the humanitarian air bridge, which remained under national control, a fine point of policy which did nothing to help the wary transport crews. In a similar legalistic vein, the French couched their participation in a WEU capacity, sidestepping their withdrawal from the NATO military command structure. Chambers's Del Molina headquarters sorted all of that out.[23] In practice, 5ATAF, specifically the Americans, ran the whole show— airlift, air superiority sweeps, tankers, reconnaissance, and, eventually, preparations for air strikes.

By early October of 1993, about the same time Task Force Ranger endured its trial by fire in the Bakara market, Deny Flight had expanded to over 130 combat jets, flying from Aviano Air Base near Venice, Italy. The U.S. pilots hailed from the air force, the Marines, and the carrier air wing aboard USS *America* at sea in the Adriatic. The multinational force at Aviano included dozens of French, Dutch, British, and Turkish aircraft. Every day, these squadrons overflew the mountainous Bosnian battleground, ready to gun down any interlopers. Aside from a training flight doing touch-and-go landings in July and a similar escapade in September, no Serb or Croat jets rose to challenge the Deny Flight effort.

There were, though, plenty of helicopter flights, and here, as with Schwarzkopf in Iraq, 5ATAF chose not to interfere. Blowing away a jet fighter was one thing. Dumping a utility chopper full of passengers was another. "We worried about shooting down helicopters carrying women and children," explained one NATO planner. "Or," he continued, "even if they were carrying arms, we worried that someone would stick civilian bodies in the wreckage just in time to be filmed by CNN." Unlike the Iraqis, the Serbs in Bosnia did not make concerted use of their helicopters, instead flying their Soviet-made Mi-8s and French-built Gazelles in ones and twos, mainly to resupply isolated outposts. When challenged, the rotary-wing craft had always landed. NATO observers judged that "their military value is negligible," and quit trying to force down the wandering helicopters.[24]

As with sea interdiction, enforcing the air blockade acted to confine the war to Bosnia-Herzegovina. Airpower indirectly affected the scale of violence by denying Bosnian Serbs the weight of air strikes they had previously used to strengthen their ground attacks and sharpen their siege efforts. As 1993 wore on, however, and the Serb factions continued to gain at the expense of the Muslims, many argued forcefully for air strikes by 5ATAF, or, as a minimum, arrangements for close air support to aid hard-pressed UNPROFOR troops.

With this in mind, 5ATAF began to work hard at perfecting an integrated ground attack capability tied in with UNPROFOR. Taking advantage of the allied-dominated skies, jets began cataloging potential targets, enemy flak dens, approach and exit routes, and coordinating with ground spotters. Each major UN unit was linked into 5ATAF's forward air controllers. All the headquarters, to include those sea task forces directing strike aircraft, exchanged liaison teams to assist in planning and, if necessary, execution. For hours at a time, the aviators trained over the same terrain they might one day attack, gaining priceless experience. In essence, 5ATAF launched "dry" strikes every day, perfecting procedures and creating a well-drilled outfit that overcame its heterogeneous composition.

Along with tactical air control parties on the ground with UNPROFOR, fliers also worked with U.S. 10th Special Forces teams and British special air service elements roaming through the war zones. They did not play the convoluted UNPROFOR game and therefore allowed America, Britain, or any NATO ally to hit targets without UN approval. Even better, the Green Berets and SAS men carried laser designators to guide in smart bombs to particular vital targets. If these people came into play, it would be one bomb, one kill. Or so went the concept.

Practice with both UN and special operator "eyes on the ground" continued day and night, even in foul weather. All parties resolved language, terminology, and equipment compatibility wrinkles.[25] In doing so, the constant procession of low-flying aircraft made an unmistakable statement to those fighting below—NATO owned the skies and could unleash death from above at will.

Bombing and strafing were not to be done lightly. The UNPROFOR leadership wanted the authority, and got it, to plan for and employ air strikes for self-defense. But the disparate, small UN troop detachments did not relish the aftermath of NATO air attacks. Unless 5ATAF could erase the bad guys in one massive swipe—and nobody in authority entertained that fantasy—the repercussions after initiation of bombing could get very ugly. Presuming the airpower struck on behalf of the UN and/or the Muslims, heavily armed Bosnian Serbs and Croats would hit back hard, killing, taking hostages, trading an eye for an eye on a scale that might make Mogadishu look like a church social. The routine sniping and shelling was already bad enough, but it only hurt UNPROFOR here and there, a trickle of bleeding. The peacekeepers loathed to open themselves up to massive, and terminal, hemorrhages.

For this reason, as well as the reluctance of the UN, EC, NATO, WEU, United States, and all the involved countries to get deeper into this mess, the procedures to initiate close air support were intentionally "cumbersome," to quote Secretary of Defense Perry. A UN unit, working through an air controller, would have to clear missions through the UNPROFOR headquarters in Bosnia, then the UNPROFOR commander for former Yugoslavia, and, finally, with the UN envoy for the mission, Admiral Howe's equivalent number. With this done, and positive "eyes on" target control on the ground, the strike could proceed.[26]

Needless to say, this procedure would be considerably accelerated after the first use of the capability. It would need to be. Playing "tit for tat" with numerous, fierce, and thoroughly armed foes was not a good idea. Once the first NATO munitions dropped in anger, it was back to General Powell's dictum, "all or nothing." If the allies bombed, they were in the war, not just sealing off the scene of the crime. Failing to transition to full belligerency would cost lives, perhaps a lot of lives, as in Lebanon or Somalia. Without U.S. troops in line to eat the first few rounds, the allies were not anxious to experiment. So air strikes remained mostly just air. And the blockade took priority.

The clampdown around the Yugoslav area had a single U.S. land component, an understrength infantry battalion in newly independent Macedonia, wearing blue berets and reporting to United Nations commanders. Initially drawn from the Berlin Brigade, an American unit with no mission by 1993, this border patrol force joined the so-called Nordic Battalion. This composite MFO-style unit, commanded by Brig. Gen. Finn Saemark-Thorsen of Denmark, included a mix of eight hundred Danes, Finns, Norwegians, and Swedes. Their mission was to watch the border with Serbian-controlled Kosovo province, to observe and report, and thereby discover and, hopefully, deter any Serb military attempts to cross the new boundary.

Saemark-Thorsen, initially skeptical about commanding "trigger-happy" Americans, found the men of Company C, 6-502d Infantry, to be superb peacekeepers. The little task force kept one platoon forward, strung out patrolling and manning outposts in a rugged fifteen-mile stretch of the ill-defined border. A second platoon defended the U.S. base at Petrovec airfield, a former Yugoslav Air Force facility near Skopje, the capital of the infant republic. The third platoon trained and stood by as QRF. As always in these things, a lieutenant colonel, 6-502d commander Walter Horton, held the reins. Anyone who had served in the Sinai or in the Korean DMZ would recognize the routines very well: stand-to, patrols, loaded weapons, strict ROE, and, always, vigilance—keeping eyes peeled for the death hiding out there in the Great Gulp.

Operation Able Sentry forces, as they were called, carried out their duties without incident. In January 1994, soldiers of the 3d Infantry Division's 1-6th Infantry replaced 6-502d, the first of what would no doubt be several rotations. The Americans were in country for the long haul, and the troops had no illusions about the gravity of their role. As Lt. Darren McMahon of 1-6th Infantry remarked, "Their names could be sitting on the President's desk because they made the wrong decision. They're at the front line of American foreign policy."[27] For many reasons, including fear of reprisals and bigger game to hunt near Sarajevo, the Serbs and their henchmen elected not to probe the U.S. tripwire. It was a different story in the skies over Bosnia.

*   *   *

Bombing was the great bogey, the big "if" that NATO and the UN constantly trundled out to threaten the Bosnian Serbs and their sponsors in Belgrade. Throughout 1993, President Clinton and others kept promising bombing raids, strong words that frightened the locals not a wit as the civil war ground on. To paraphrase Mark Twain's comment about the weather, everybody talked about bombing in Bosnia, but nobody really did anything about it. The Serbs and Croats kept right on shooting, cleansing, burning, and blasting their way through Muslim-held turf.

Why? The Serb and Croat aggressors in Bosnia were not bombed for two major reasons. The first, already discussed, had to do with the safety of the outmanned, outgunned UNPROFOR battalions scattered around the contested cities and towns. The second caused the first. The UNPROFOR commanders did not want to try bombing because whatever it did would not be enough. "You start backing them into a corner and start bombing them," warned Canadian Maj. Gen. Lewis MacKenzie, a former UNPROFOR commander in Bosnia, and "you've got yourself a major problem, a long term problem." Succinctly stated, that problem would be 13,000 UNPROFOR troops in Bosnia surrounded by 170,000 enraged, heavily armed Serbs and Croats.[28]

Destroying the anti-Muslim forces around Sarajevo, Tuzla, and the other encircled cities seemed very unlikely. Airpower is best employed against things that do not move: bridges, power plants, runways, factories, barracks, and rail yards. It is not easy to hit small, mobile stuff like towed howitzers, trucks, tanks, and people, especially in wooded, mountainous country. It does not help when the objects insist on hiding and firing back.

You can, in fact, bomb small army-type targets with effect, even in pretty gruesome terrain. The trick is finding the enemy. If the hostiles cooperate and line up in a predictable pattern and move in fixed paths, aircraft can do some significant damage. Unfortunately, this was not the case in Yugoslavia. The old Yugoslav People's Army had always emphasized decentralized insurgent warfare, in the tradition of Tito, the original partisan. When the state fragmented, the resultant mess defied any conventional attempts at prediction by hard-pressed intelligence sections. All the successor forces displayed their own unique ways of fighting. Bosnia featured five major contenders—the Bosnian Serb regulars (with the backing of the Belgrade Serbs), Bosnian Serb irregulars, Bosnian Croats, Bosnian Muslims, and Croat army regulars. And there were others, lots of others.

The Yugoslavs could have taught Aidid and company a few things about the guerrilla chieftain business. Independent actors, each with anywhere from a few dozen to a few hundred armed supporters, ran local operations that owed more to *The Godfather* than to any military chain of command. In the Croatian phase of the civil war, outside observers tabulated a colorful list of identified splinter elements, most of which found roles in the Bosnian campaign too. The Serbs backed the Serbian Guard, the Serbian Volunteer Guard, the Serbian Chetnik Movement, the Marticevci, the Knindze, Dusan Silni, and Beli Orli. Croatia encouraged the activities of the Croatian Defense Union, the Zebras, the Black Legion, and the Wolves of Vukovar. The Muslims had their own armed factions, including Bosnian adherents of Hezbollah and Islamic Jihad. About the only gangs not represented were the Crips and the Bloods. Given this vicious hodgepodge, God alone—or more likely Beelzebub—knew what method determined their movements and positions.[29] Targeteers stared into chaos. Attempting to find, strike, and paralyze decisive points or command-and-control networks in this violent soup seemed hopeless.

Bosnia, then, would not be a rerun of Desert Storm. In the Gulf War, 2,780 Coalition aircraft (all but a quarter American) flew more than twenty-three thousand sorties against Iraqi ground forces, a predictable enemy defending on somewhat more open terrain than Bosnia. (To be sure, the desert is not a yellow-brown billiard table. It does have vegetation and relief, and even the overmatched Iraqis hid a lot in its dusty folds.) Postwar studies credited the allied effort with killing or wounding 26,000 of 336,000 Iraqis (nearly 8 percent), and knocking out 1,100 of 2,475 pieces of artillery (just over 44 percent). Most observers agree that the Desert Storm air campaign was about as effective as it could be.

A Yugoslav equivalent, wishing away bad intelligence, rough ground, and a much more diverse, fanatic set of enemies, would be a lot less effective, at least given the forces allocated by early 1994. NATO's 5ATAF disposed about two hundred combat aircraft, a fraction of the Desert Storm air armada. Bombing at a Gulf War level of potency, these NATO strikers would cause thirteen hundred casualties and destroy 270 of the 600 heavy weapons surrounding Sarajevo. That would hurt, but it could hardly be decisive.[30] The Serb ripostes, on the other hand, might well finish off several UNPROFOR outposts, with predictable effects (the usual "we did not sign up for this" rigmarole on many shocked homefronts).

And yet, in the bitter cold of January 1994, with the Serbs in control of 70 percent of Bosnia's territory, the Croats exhausted, the Muslims desperate, and the UN, EC, NATO, and the various Western states anxious for some kind of resolution, talk turned for the umpteenth time to bombing, with special interest in doing something about the howitzers pounding Sarajevo, the focus of military, political, and media attention. By World War II standards, the shellings barely constituted nuisance firings, but the steady, slow rain of projectiles sometimes closed the airport and bashed holes in neighborhoods, slow death arriving one round at a time.

On Saturday, 5 February 1994, a single 120-mm mortar round arced into Sarajevo, one more lethal gift from the Bosnian Serb batteries dotting the hillsides above the beseiged city of 380,000 people. This piece of ordnance fell into the Markale Marketplace, crowded with Saturday shoppers. The conical shell struck a hard tabletop and detonated in a white-hot flash, spraying hundreds of jagged, razor-sharp fragments through the crowd. "Body parts flew everywhere—brains, arms, legs, eyes, everything," recalled one of the wounded. With a single shot, the Serb gunners claimed sixty-eight lives and injured nearly two hundred, more than the entire U.S. toll for the Somalia expedition, and all in an instant. A similar firing had killed ten other Sarajevans in a food line the day before. But CNN and the rest of the world media had missed that one.

They were right on top of the Saturday morning massacre, however, and soon beamed grisly full-color scenes around the world. The UNPROFOR allies, as well as those involved in Provide Promise, scrambled to assist in medical treatment and evacuation. American C-130s landed under sniper fire to take out casualties. Some eighty-six of the most seriously wounded made it to the U.S. Army hospital in Landstuhl, Germany. The news cameras showed it all, proof that though the war in Bosnia had been "contained," the violence continued.[31] Maybe it was even getting "worse," always a relative concept in a festering sump of hatred like the former Yugoslavia.

Compared to the pictures of a four-year-old girl with bloodied eye sockets or a seventy-year-old man sporting the gory stump of a hand, it was hard to listen to informed commentary suggesting, quite rightly, that the bombardment was not so bad by historical standards and that the 5 February shot was merely a fluke. No, as in other times and places, the public drumbeat began, especially in America, to do something.

Something meant air strikes. They would not and could not end the fighting. Most of the leaders in the UN and NATO agreed on that point. But if focused on the tormenting guns around Sarajevo, air attacks might at least alleviate the pain. And, after all, with a major joint campaign out of the question and only a few UNPROFOR troops on hand, airpower was the only punitive tool available for use. Everybody had talked and practiced long enough. The pilots were as ready as they could be, and the UNPROFOR people were game to try something, as long as they retained the final authority to call in the strikes.

Thus, with the blessing of President Clinton and the United Nations, NATO announced an ultimatum on 9 February: the Bosnian Serbs must cease shelling Sarajevo and withdraw all guns outside a 12.4 mile (20 kilometer) radius of the city by 0100 local time on Sunday, 20 February 1994. As Clinton said, "No one should doubt NATO's resolve. NATO is now set to act. Anyone shelling Sarajevo must recognize this fact and be prepared to deal with it."[32] The gauntlet had been thrown down.

It was not an especially big or heavy gauntlet, but it would have to do. In the Adriatic, the carriers USS *Saratoga,* HMS *Ark Royal* of Great Britain, and *Foch* of France readied to send their broods into battle. At Aviano Air Base in northern Italy, U.S. Air Force and Marine planes stood by. British Royal Air Force aircraft prepared for action at Gioia del Colle. French jets waited at Cervia and Istrana, and Dutch fighters staged at Villafranca. All forces were on hand and ready and fully conversant with the target array.[33] After all, these same two-hundred-odd crews had been flying dry missions around Sarajevo for months. They could probably do serious damage to the Serbian gun emplacements around Sarajevo. Would it be enough? Experts said no. But experts also would not be on the receiving end of the explosives.

It is, after all, easy to sit in a comfortable chair and dismiss as ineffective the munitions conveyed by a few relays of modern fighter-bombers, but the Serb gunners around Sarajevo could not afford to be so confident. If those bombs fell, somebody, some hundreds of Bosnian Serb somebodies, would die horrible deaths, eviscerated by the spinning shards of bouncing cluster bombs or erased in the blast of laser-guided 2,000-pounders. Shooting up largely defenseless Muslims was one thing. Getting arbitrarily blotted out by rampaging, unstoppable aircraft was another. Yugoslavs had still enjoyed enough peace back in 1991 to watch the tapes of the Desert Storm bombings, and those videos played on in the heads of the various regular and irregular leaders in the Serb battery positions. Airpower's influences on the mind have always been more impressive than airpower's effects on the ground. And so the Clinton-NATO ultimatum, backed by memories of what happened to the Iraqi army, began to corrode the will of the Serb siege force. Somewhere out there, the ghost of Giulio Douhet must have been smiling.

By all logic, the Serbs should not have backed down. But they did. On 20 February, as advised by the UNPROFOR commanders, UN Envoy Yasushi Akashi, announced: "I am satisfied we have achieved effective compliance with the requirement to remove or place under UNPROFOR control all heavy weapons within the 20-kilometer exclusion zone."[34] There were no air strikes. For the first time in nearly two years, no shells fell in Sarajevo. The siege had been partially lifted, although the ground cordon definitely remained in place.

In the general round of backslapping and self-congratulation, even speculation about applying a "Sarajevo solution" to other embattled cities, it was easy to overlook two important matters that had nothing to do with the air ultimatum and everything to do with the Serb response. First, along with the fear of airpower, NATO owed its success to its former foe, Russia. President Boris Yeltsin's Special Envoy Vitaly Churkin had engineered Serb compliance by offering to move a Russian airborne battalion from UN duty in Croatia into the ring around Sarajevo, a move far more shrewd than anything Tsar Nicholas II and his people tried back in 1912–14.[35] Russia simultaneously improved its own standing and guaranteed its continued support for its longtime clients. Moscow had not played any role in the NATO ultimatum. But from now on, Russia would have to be consulted, and the ramshackle superpower still wielded a UN Security Council veto, not to mention a treasure trove of armaments. Russia, friend of the Serbs, could soften, perhaps even reverse, the UN tilt toward the Muslims. The Churkin initiative promised all of that, and the Serbs were willing to give their big brothers the benefit of the doubt.

Russian help was important, because the dream of a Greater Serbia continued to burn brightly among the Bosnian Serbs. And a second consideration also mattered a lot. The Serbs had only turned in about a third or so of their weaponry, and UNPROFOR, NATO, and America knew that. Most had been pulled back to be used another day, leaving only older items in the hands of UN peacekeepers. Sarajevo had been ceded, for the moment. But Serbs still dominated more than two-thirds of Bosnia-Herzegovina. This war had been going on for hundreds of years, and a single transitory UN

Allied Combat Airpower Committed to Bosnia-Herzegovina as of 20 February 1994

NATO 5th Allied Tactical Air Force (enforce no-fly zone)

Combined Air Operations Center (Del Molina, Italy)

NATO Airborne Early-Warning Force
8 E-3A Sentry AWACs aircraft (Trapani, Italy)
1 E-3D Sentry AWACS aircraft (Aviano, Italy)

United States
12 USAF F-16C Fighting Falcon fighter-bombers (Aviano, Italy)
8 USAF F-15E Strike Eagle fighter-bombers (Aviano, Italy)
12 USAF A-10A Thunderbolt II attack aircraft (Aviano, Italy)
8 USMC F/A-18A Hornet fighter-bombers (Aviano, Italy)
5 USAF EC-130E ABCCC command post aircraft (Aviano, Italy)
10 USAF KC-135R Stratotanker tankers (Pisa, Italy)
2 USAF AC-130H Spectre gunships (Brindisi, Italy)

aboard USS *Saratoga* (Adriatic Sea):
24 USN F-14A Tomcat fighters
24 USN F/A-18A Hornet fighter-bombers
12 USN A-6A Intruder attack aircraft
5 USN EA-6B Prowler electronic warfare aircraft
5 USN E-2C Hawkeye AWACS aircraft
8 USN S-3B Viking antisubmarine aircraft
4 USN KA-6D tankers
6 USN SH-3 helicopters

Britain
8 F-3 Tornado fighter-bombers (Gioia del Colle, Italy)
12 Jaguar attack aircraft (Gioia del Colle, Italy)
2 K-1 tankers (Milan, Italy)

aboard HMS *Ark Royal* (Adriatic Sea):
6 Sea Harrier fighter-bombers

France
16 Mirage 2000-D fighters (Cervia, Italy)
5 Mirage F-1 reconnaissance aircraft (Istrana, Italy)
8 Jaguar attack aircraft (Istrana, Italy)
1 E-3F Sentry AWACS aircraft (Trapani, Italy)
1 C-135 tanker (Istres, France)

aboard *Foch* (Adriatic Sea):
6 Super Etenard attack aircraft

The Netherlands
14 F-16A Fighting Falcon fighter-bombers (Villafranca, Italy)
4 F-16A reconnaissance aircraft (Villafranca, Italy)

Joint Task Force Provide Promise (humanitarian airlift)

435th Airlift Wing (Ramstein, Germany) (tactical control of elements)
United States
12 C-130E/H Hercules transports (Ramstein, Germany)
48th Air Transportable Hospital (Zagreb, Croatia)
France
2 C-160 Transall transports (Ramstein, Germany)
Germany
2 C-130 Hercules transports (Ramstein, Germany)

ABCCC: Airborne Battlefield Command and Control Center
AWACS: Airborne Warning and Control System

Sources: "Ready to Strike," *Washington Times,* 22 February 1994; Tim Ripley, "Bosnia Mission Stretches Airborne Eyes and Ears," *International Defense Review* (January 1994): 54; "Navy to Take Over Hospital in Zagreb," *European Stars and Stripes,* 12 March 1994; Chuck Sudetic, "Pilots on the Bosnia Food Run Hope for Bad Weather," *New York Times,* 20 March 1994.

success would not change that. As if to underscore that ugly truth, eight days after peace allegedly started to break out, NATO fliers had to open fire to make things stick. As usual, the fingers on the triggers were American.

The United States has shot down forty-seven hostile aircraft since the close of the Vietnam War. Thirty-nine bore Iraqi markings, and these went down during the Gulf War and its aftermath. Four of the others were Libyans, splashed by U.S. Navy fighters in the 1981 and 1989 incidents over the Gulf of Sidra.[36] The rest fell over Yugoslavia on the last day of February 1994. For some reason, the Bosnian Serbs chose that day to challenge Operation Deny Flight.

After months of droning, uneventful patrols over Bosnia, the men of the U.S. Air Force's 86th Wing did not expect to see action. They were flying loaded as always, with some of the F-16C Fighting Falcons carrying bombs in case flak sites or even UNPROFOR-requested targets had to be hit. The NATO air umbrella had never encountered hostile fighters. But, as in so many other cases out in Indian country, from the Korean DMZ to the no-fly zones over Iraq, there is no such thing as being too careful.

At 0631, the NATO E-3A Sentry AWACS (airborne warning and control system) confirmed the unthinkable: two fighter-sized bogeys (unknown contacts) rising from Banja Luka. The radar operators categorized them as Jastreb J-1s, single-seat light attack versions of Galeb trainers designed and built in Yugoslavia in the 1970s. The AWACS alerted two American F-16s, call signs Wilbur and Zulu, circling near Mostar. The Americans headed north, scanning with their powerful Westinghouse APG-68 multimode radars. Wilbur found his quarry first, detecting a radar signature minutes after being warned by the AWACS.

The big, four-engine AWACS plane, slowly turning in wide ovals over the Adriatic Sea, watched Wilbur and Zulu close in. The senior officer aboard directed the F-16s to descend to visual range. Both Americans slid slowly downward, helmeted heads craning in their bubble cockpits. They quickly found the two Jastrebs, hurtling along above the forested mountains. Ahead of that pair, four more of the Yugoslav jets flew in loose formation. Zulu thought they were "flying low to try to avoid our NATO early warning radar and also our own radar on our aircraft." It was 0635.

The American flight lead, Wilbur, keyed his radio and attempted to warn off the six hostile craft, now positively identified as bandits, bad guys. There was no reply. Wilbur tried again two minutes later. Still, the J-1s bored on. Technically, the enemy had not yet shown "hostile intent," although, obviously, the no-fly zone had been flouted. If the Jastrebs just buzzed around, the Americans could not engage, merely intercept and report, as they had done.

As if on cue, the Jastrebs now fulfilled the ROE definition of "hostile intent." Evidently unaware of their pursuers, the lead jet broke off, climbed to ten thousand feet, and dropped a bomb on a ground target, a built-up Muslim area that was reportedly a factory. That did it.

At 0643, apprised of this activity, Maj. Gen. James Chambers back at Del Molina authorized engagement. Two minutes later, Wilbur unleashed an AIM-120A AMRAAM (advanced medium range air-to-air missile), a long stovepipe with a nosecone, triangular fins, and its own radar. The weapon hissed off the belly of Wilbur's Falcon and zipped down, spearing an unwitting Jastreb. The small plane expoded into an angry mass of flame, smoke, and debris.

With his wingman following, Wilbur roared downward. He punched off two AIM-9M Sidewinder heat-seekers, thinner, lighter items that sprang off the American fighter's wingtip rails and sped up the tailpipes of the hapless J-1s. Two more fireballs blossomed. There were no parachutes, no survivors.

The remaining trio of Serbs, by now aware that they were under attack, split up. Two headed to the west, with the third lagging a little behind. Another pair of U.S. Falcons rolled in, and the lead pilot, call sign Yogi, fired at the trail Jastreb with a Sidewinder. The small enemy jet jinked violently, and the American missile's infrared tracker lost its lock-on. Its simple electronic instincts thoroughly confused, the missile veered wide and tumbled away, useless. Yogi, however, had stayed in the fight. He lined up immediately and fired again from fairly close range, definitely less than a mile. This time, the Sidewinder stayed true and smacked home. The J-1 disintegrated in a puff of fire. Again, nobody bailed out.

The American fliers could have taken out the last two, but the fleeing light attack jet pilots dropped almost literally into the trees, throttles wide open, tearing for a safe haven in a Serb-held portion of Croatia. The NATO AWACS director and Chambers at Del Molina curbed the fighter crews. The point had been made. It was 0659, less than a half hour after the first radar sighting. It had gone down so quickly that President Clinton was not even awakened until after the fight.[37]

The one-sided engagement added to the general impression that, if nothing else, NATO and America were serious about preventing escalation. As Admiral Boorda said, "If this was a test, I think we passed the quiz." The policy goals of containing the conflict had been served.

Another NATO officer had a better summary: "We killed some people Monday morning."[38] That, in fact, was what containment, OOTW, and peacekeeping really meant. It wasn't neat or pretty. More of the same soon followed.

In a place like Bosnia, all weapons on hand get used sooner or later, so it is hardly surprising that on 10 and 11 April, not long after the J-1 shootdowns, UNPROFOR finally resorted to long-available NATO (read American) close air support. At issue was the safety of fifteen United Nations military observers and several dozen humanitarian workers trapped in encircled Gorazde, a Bosnian Muslim town of sixty-five thousand that happened to stand on one of the favored Muslim arms smuggling routes. Taking it would severely hamper the already staggering Muslim war effort, and the Serbs knew that. They invested the town in 1992 and remained entrenched in strength in the high ground all around the place. Sporadic fighting had flared off and on around the ragged perimeter, depending on the mood of local Bosnian Serb commanders and the relative progress of similar sieges across Bosnia.

As in most of the really hot spots in the country, UNPROFOR had an interest in Gorazde. Declared a United Nations safe haven, Gorazde did not yet include the usual token battalion or so of blue-helmeted peacekeepers. The UN troop units slated to occupy and enforce the protected enclave had never been able to get in. Of course, UNPROFOR lacked the warpower to force an entry.

The Bosnian Serbs made a major push to take Gorazde in late March, serving notice that the Sarajevo episode was just that, a hiccup of hesitation in the prosecution of a long, bloody war. Backed by tanks and heavy guns, Serb infantry steadily tightened the noose on Gorazde, killing some seven hundred Muslim civilians and wounding several of the UN personnel in the area. By the first week of April, the fall of Gorazde seemed imminent. So much for a UN safe haven.

Ideally, the UN would have acted firmly to reverse this situation. But the multinational, lightly armed UNPROFOR could never pull that off. Staying alive was becoming enough of a challenge. After an interminable series of specific warnings and threats by various UN political and military officials, including Boutros-Ghali on 10 April, the UNPROFOR team in Gorazde finally asked for help from the air. Menaced by Serb armor and artillery, with up to eight shells a minute plunging into the town, Lt. Gen. Sir Michael Rose, the UNPROFOR commander for Bosnia, requested a NATO air strike to hit the encroaching forces. Rose, a former SAS commander with plenty of experience in small wars, wanted to use just enough strength to get the job done. He knew that on short notice, 5ATAF could send in only a few patrolling jets and, as always, the weak UN units could not sustain the backlash that might well follow major NATO attacks. So this would not be any massive air campaign. Rather, the strike would act purely to protect the UN observers stuck in the war zone. If the NATO airmen did a good job, perhaps the implied threat of more attacks might even cause the Serbs to back off and negotiate.

Rose called for the bombing mission at 1630. By 1655, the local UN political and military hierarchy had okayed the request and passed it to NATO's Allied Forces South shortly thereafter. Admiral Leighton "Snuffy" Smith, who had replaced Boorda only days before, forwarded the request to his air commanders at 5ATAF. After more than a year of dry runs and one air fracas, at long last NATO was really going to bomb.

Two U.S. Marine F/A-18 Hornets headed toward the target area. Like the rest of the NATO airmen, they had flown many times over Bosnia and rehearsed such close air support tasks many times. Now it was real, and, predictably, friction arose. The British forward air controller with the SAS contingent in Gorazde could not establish reliable radio contact with the jets. Following about a half hour of futile swooping and monotonous exchanges of unanswered calls and countercalls on the designated frequencies, the Marine aircraft broke off, frustrated. Unimpressed by yet another NATO airshow, the Serbs kept right on firing.

A pair of U.S. Air Force F-16C Fighting Falcons rolled in next. These 86th Wing pilots had better luck talking to the British controller on the ground. The UNPROFOR man tried to align the jets to take out some Serb tanks, but the airmen could not find these targets. The weather over Gorazde was foul, intermittently rainy and foggy, with few shadows and little contrast. Ground objects like camouflage-painted tanks proved very hard to find. When the fliers sighted what the UNPROFOR later called a "command post tent complex," the British controller cleared them for attack. It was 1822.

The Falcons each loosed two Mark-82 500-pound bombs, then pitched up and sped away, unaffected by a fountain of late Serb antiaircraft firing. The four unguided projectiles hit one of the tents and also a nearby tank, pretty good bombing in nasty weather, but hardly decisive. Still, after a few more rounds for spite, the Serb gunners ceased fire for the night.[39]

The Serbs were back at it by sunup, unaffected by the loss of a tent, a tank, and a few soldiers. By noon, the UNPROFOR team in Gorazde wanted another air strike. U.S. warplanes roared low over the Serb positions, dropping flares as warnings. The Serbs kept on shooting, and many fired at the Americans as they raced overhead.

At 1407, Rose again requested a NATO air attack. Two Marine F/A-18s, already in the area, responded immediately. This time, communications went well. At 1419, one Marine Hornet broke through the scudding gray cloud deck and unleashed three bombs on a concentration of Serb combat vehicles, hitting near a tank and two armored personnel carriers. Aiming went well despite the horrid weather. Effects, however, left a lot to be desired.

For whatever reason, two of the bombs did not detonate. Waved off by the ground spotter, the second Marine jet dropped no weaponry, though it did engage with 20-mm gunfire. So that did it, one live bomb and some cannon shots into the mud. Their mission ruled complete, the two American aircraft sped off.

This paltry display, of course, only encouraged the enemy gunners. The Serbs reacted by increasing their barrage, pointedly targeting UNPROFOR headquarters in Gorazde. A large shell impacted just outside the structure a few minutes after the Marines broke off. The explosion blew out all the windows and injured several UN personnel. That was enough for Rose.

The UNPROFOR Bosnia commander made a telephone call to the local Bosnian Serb commander, Gen. Ratko Mladic, who, of course, blamed the Muslims and marauding NATO aircraft for the continuing mayhem. The UN headquarters log summarized Sir Michael's reply in cryptic militarese: "Stop tank, antiaircraft, and artillery fire into town. If not, will have no option but to attack." Mladic ceased fire for a few hours, a minor success for Rose.

During the breather, various political leaders in the UN, NATO, and America professed satisfaction at the measured use of force. Now that the Serbs had a taste of NATO fire, they would choose to talk rather than fight, wouldn't they? Western opinion leaders, including President Clinton, hoped for that. Various cease-fire plans, including one sponsored by the Serbs' Russian allies, proposed to resolve the circumstances around Goradze. It all played well on CNN—statesmen doing state business, guys in suits rationally reconciling differences, all of this serious dealing supposedly spurred on by a few well-placed bombs.

Somebody forgot to send a script to the Bosnian Serb units. The morning after the Marine air strike, Mladic's men resumed their offensive against the crumbling Muslim army. The defenders of Gorazde could not stem the tide, and the Serbs crunched into the town's shattered outskirts. NATO remained involved, in a limited, ineffectual way. A French reconnaissance aircraft was hit by an SA7 shoulder-fired surface-to-air missile on 15 April; the aviator managed to wrestle his wounded plane back to the flight deck of the carrier *Foch*. By 16 April, Serb tanks had entered the town. When UNPROFOR brought in NATO aircraft to protect a hospital serving UN wounded, the British Sea Harrier jets could not locate their targets in the low clouds and rain, and Serb gunners downed one of the planes. The Serb assault grew in strength, and Gorazde seemed doomed.[40]

The air support provided certainly did not slow the Serbs. NATO delivered seven pieces of ordnance—a Balkan drizzle, not a Desert Storm—and barely even viable close air support. In truth, the UNPROFOR team in Gorazde survived at the pleasure of Mladic's battalions. About all that can be said is that the air attacks were executed professionally, bought a few hours of safety for a handful of UN observers, and kept U.S. and NATO intervention extremely limited.

What happened at Gorazde stands as a warning that bombs do not send any message except "boom." Those seeking to employ such tit for tat measures to energize negotiations might do well to recall that the North Vietnamese never read the "signals" presented in the Flaming Dart and Rolling Thunder bombing programs, which supposedly reflected a "progressive, slow squeeze," in John McNaughton's memorable words.[41] If one picks up the big hammer of airpower, he had better be ready to swing hard, to kill and destroy, and to keep swinging until the job is done. Anything else merely hazards brave pilots for no good reason.

In the aftermath of the ineffectual raids, at least one man did not lose his faith in high-technology, high-performance aircraft and their lethal eggs, albeit in more impressive volume. As Bosnian Serbs made and broke ceasefire agreements almost as quickly as they shelled prostrate Gorazde, President Clinton resorted to the approach that had quelled the siege of Sarajevo. In company with NATO and the UN, on 22 April America promised to lead a series of powerful air attacks on the Serb assault regiments and their guns. The Western alliance gave the Serbs until 0200 on 24 April to withdraw about two miles from the city center, to permit UNPROFOR troops to enter and to cease firing. If not, the UNPROFOR commanders could bring in some two hundred NATO warbirds to destroy part of the besieging forces.

As in the Sarajevo case, the amount of airpower on hand would not be enough to do a thorough job, especially considering the usual rough terrain, awful weather, and dispersed, fleeting targets. NATO officers talked boldly about a scheme "to bomb the crap out of them," and let it be known that they would strike about two dozen targets, including Serb gun emplacements, command posts, fuel storage sites, and ammunition dumps. Perhaps this sequence of strikes might have really hurt the Serbs, but in the long run, the means available fell far short of the ends intended. The proposed air offensive could only destroy bits and pieces, and when the dust settled, the Serbs would still control the turf. And worse, they would be highly irritated.

That, as always, was the rub. Regardless of how effectively the bombardments proceeded, the isolated UN blue helmets feared overwhelming Serb reprisals. A mob of Serb women successfully interdicted a combined

French-Norwegian-Ukrainian relief column bound for Gorazde, indicative of the relative weakness of the multinational contingent. Nobody could rule out punitive assaults on the nearly defenseless U.S. hospital in Zagreb or on the handful of American infantry strung out along the Macedonian border. No, the Serbs might not have much of an air force, but thanks to their disheveled but numerous soldiery, they still held many high cards in this round. NATO was talking loudly but carrying a pretty small stick.

The bombing ploy had worked once around Sarajevo, but how long could America and its allies persist in this brand of gambling? Some Clinton administration officials began to fret that if the Serbs called NATO's air strike bluff, a lot of ground troops and other forces might be necessary—real warpower, the whole ugly show. Visions of bodies dragged through the dirt streets of Mogadishu haunted many contemplating such escalation. The clock ticked, and the Serbs postured.

Then, incredibly, and probably for their own inscrutable reasons, Mladic's Serbs knuckled under. After a fashion, that is. They pulled back their most aggressive patrols into their main body of forces, allowed some UN people to enter Gorazde, and made happy noises. As in Sarajevo, the UN accepted this half-effort and declared success. UN representative Yasushi Akashi, by this time quite the expert on proclaiming cease-fires, announced another, evidenced by a reduced volume of Serb shelling on the outskirts of Gorazde and a few less rocket strikes around the UN building there.

NATO leaders fumed, their hands tied by the UN people to whom they ceded final authority. But given the complete reluctance of all Western powers to leap headlong into the Great Gulp of the Balkan inferno, such half- and quarter-measures must be counted as positive developments. At least, they do no harm. With their Gorazde "victory" won, Clinton and his NATO colleagues prescribed the same medicine for the other embattled cities of Bosnia.[42] If not paying close attention, one would think that the Atlantic Alliance had really changed their views on ending the Yugoslav war. In fact, despite a few new instruments in the band, the song remained the same.

So did the war. Out in the hills and valleys, oblivious to all of these intrigues and high hopes, events took their own sad course. As the Serbs, Muslims, and Croats know, this has been, and will be, a long war. Two steps forward, one step back—keep shooting, keep talking, and sooner or later the outlanders will lose interest and leave locals to sort out their own messes.

The NATO strikes and bluster of April 1994 reflected another incremental addition to the war in the former Yugoslavia. Rearranging Bosnian dirt amounted to doing something, and doing it without risking a lot of U.S. infantry. There will likely be more warnings, and more use of airpower, some of it on a larger scale, as UNPROFOR persists in its thankless duties. Because the grab bag of bad guys shoot back, there will be people hurt and killed on both sides, a few here and a few there. There will be no resolution, at least not one palatable to America. The whole thing resembles squirting off an extinguisher bottle in the midst of a roaring forest fire. There is transitory, local relief. But the woods burn on.

The American intervention in the former Yugoslavia had not succeeded by 1995, and, of course, success may never come. There are, however, a few useful insights to be gained from the course of events so far. Thanks to the bloody nose in Somalia, the Clinton administration followed the Bush lead and settled for manning the fence lines, plus occasional recourse to brandishing the flail of airpower. This did not make editorial writers and television pundits happy. But it served American interests in the region, limited at best.

Yugoslavia, like the boundary of the two Koreas, Lebanon, the Sinai, Kurdistan, and Somalia, is a place where troubles and ill will come together. Pacifying Yugoslavia might never work, and to their credit, none of the governments involved have even tried. This has resulted in some exceedingly painful interludes, but better their pain than ours. That is, after all, what force protection is all about.

There is no guarantee that things will remain in the bloody stasis that developed in early 1994. They could get better, and they will, at some point, get worse. About the only thing that is certain is that America will stay in the game. By limiting involvement to match its limited ends, the United States has not created many lucrative targets. Even so, one could imagine awful consequences if a plane goes down, a ship is struck, or trouble starts in the compounds at Zagreb or Skopje.

The chance of a serious reverse would increase if more force entered the war zone. President Clinton and his people have repeatedly spoken of sending in up to twenty-five thousand American peacekeepers if a comprehensive peace settlement ever emerges in Bosnia-Herzegovina. Such a political deal would be highly suspect—these people solve their problems with guns, not documents. The best that could happen might be a fragile, half-baked bargain of convenience, and, in that case, Americans and others would land at their own peril, as in Lebanon and Somalia. In any event, in 1995 even that kind of passing agreement does not seem likely, despite occasional conciliatory noises by most of the parties involved.

There have been diplomatic moves since the Sarajevo ultimatum, the U.S. shootdowns, and the Gorazde episode that followed, including a widely celebrated pact on 18 March 1994 between Bosnia Croats and Muslims which effectively ended the isolation of Mostar. The Serbs, of course, have gone their own way, and the war drags on.[43] Nothing has really changed, and the bloody status quo persists. With their United Nations and European allies, Americans continue to keep their twilight watch, waiting for a dawn that will probably never come.

Notes

The epigraph is from W. H. Auden's 1940 poem "In Memory of W. B. Yeats." Secretary of Defense William J. Perry used this quotation in a speech in Boston, Massachusetts, on 12 February 1994, during a period of heightened crisis in Bosnia. See Meg Vaillancourt, "The Best (and Verse) Defense," *Boston Globe,* 13 February 1994.

1. Richard F. Nyrop, ed., *Yugoslavia: A Country Study* (Washington, D.C.: U.S. Government Printing Office, 1982), 61–62.

2. Brig. Gen. Mark Hamilton, USA, "Ethnicity and Contrasting Values" in *Ethnic Conflicts and Regional Instability* (Carlisle Barracks, Pa.: Strategic Studies Institute, 1994), 116–18.

3. Capt. Peter A. Hutchhausen, USN (Ret.), "Back to the Balkans," *Proceedings* (June 1993): 43.

4. R. Ernest Dupuy and Trevor N. Dupuy, *The Encyclopedia of Military History* (New York: Harper and Row, 1984), 990.

5. Richard Rustin, "Tito and his Partisan Army: Yugoslavia, 1941–1945," *Strategy and Tactics* (July/August 1980): 5–8. Lt. Col. Mark F. Cancian, USMCR, "The Wehrmacht in Yugoslavia: Lessons of the Past?" *Parameters* (Autumn 1993): 75–84.

6. Leonard J. Cohen, *Broken Bonds* (Boulder, Colo.: Westview Press, 1993), 22–26.

7. Cohen, *Broken Bonds*, 223–63.

8. "Special Report—Protecting Bosnians: Where Next?" *Washington Times,* 23 February 1994.

9. U.S. Department of Defense, *Former Yugoslavia Handbook* (Washington, D.C.: U.S. Army Intelligence and Threat Analysis Center, 22 April 1993), 2–6; John M. Collins, *Balkan Battlegrounds* (Washington, D.C.: Congressional Research Service, 1992), 12; Jeffrey I. Sands, *Blue Hulls: Multinational Naval Cooperation and the United Nations* (Alexandria, Va.: Center for Naval Analyses, 1993), 11; United Nations, *United Nations General Assembly Resolution 46/182* (New York: United Nations Publications, 19 December 1991); Cancian, "The Wehrmacht in Yugoslavia," 79, 84.

10. "Belgian Quitting as Commander of U.N. Peacekeepers in Bosnia," *Washington Post,* 5 January 1994; Carol J. Williams, "Frustrated U.N. Troops Humiliated in Bosnia," *Los Angeles Times,* 16 January 1994.

11. For an example of impartiality in action, see James L. Graff, "Another Day of Peacekeeping," *Time* (10 January 1994): 12.

12. "Special Report—Protecting Bosnians," A14; Cohen, *Broken Bonds,* 246. The European Community (EC) changed its name to the European Union (EU) in November 1993.

13. Sands, *Blue Hulls,* 20.

14. Collins, *Balkan Battlegrounds,* 15.

15. Tim Ripley, "Bosnia Mission Stretches Airborne Eyes and Ears," *International Defense Review* (January 1994): 54; Cohen, *Broken Bonds,* 241–42.

16. Rick Atkinson, "Bosnia Airlift Delivers the Goods," *Washington Post,* 17 March 1994; Vince Crawley, "Hope Held for U.S. Plan to Double Relief Air Drops," *European Stars and Stripes,* 2 December 1993.

17. "Navy to Take Over Hospital in Zagreb," *European Stars and Stripes,* 12 March 1994.

18. Atkinson, "Bosnia Airlift Delivers the Goods," 32; C. V. Glines, "Another Title for the Crew Chief," *Air Force* (February 1994): 61; Frank Oliveri, "C-130 Damaged in Provide Promise," *Air Force* (March 1994): 12; "Fighting Halts Airlift of Aid into Sarajevo," *Baltimore Sun,* 12 January 1994.

19. Atkinson, "Bosnia Airlift Delivers the Goods," 32; "More Support for Bosnia Effort," *Air Force Times,* 10 January 1994; Wayne V. Hall, "Nation Grateful, Gore Tells AF Crowd," *European Stars and Stripes,* 13 December 1993; Chuck Sudetic, "Pilots on the Bosnia Food Run Hope for Bad Weather," *New York Times,* 20 March 1994.

20. "Gambling on ex-Soviet States," *USA Today,* 15 March 1994.

21. Sands, *Blue Hulls,* 20–21; "Special Report—Protecting Bosnians," A14; Tony Capaccio, "SEALs Await Call to Spot Bosnian Targets, Board Ships," *Defense Week,* 12 October 1993. The NATO mission was called Maritime Guard. The WEU operation received the name Sharp Fence. French carrier forces conducted Operation Balbuzard. British Royal Navy carriers operated under the code name Grapple.

22. Capaccio, "SEALs Await Call," 1; Comdr. Tom Katana, USN, "SEALs to the Carriers," *Proceedings* (June 1993): 61–63; Maj. William T. DeCamp III, USMC, and Maj. Kenneth F. McKenzie Jr., "A Hollow Force?" *Proceed-*

ings (June 1993): 66–70; Comdr. Christopher Wode, USN, "USACOM Mixes New Recipe," *Defense News* (28 March–3 April 1994): 32.

23. Comdr. Massimo A. Annati, Italian Navy, "Stand By, We Are Boarding," *Proceedings* (March 1994): 55; Capaccio, "SEALs Await Call," 1; Gen. John Shalikashvili, USA, "Remarks to NATO Workshop, Budapest, Hungary, 4 June 1993," *Officer Review* (November 1993): 4; Ripley, "Bosnia Mission Stretches Airborne Eyes and Ears," 54.

24. Rick Atkinson, "NATO Vows to Patrol Bosnia Skies," *Washington Post,* 20 March 1994; Julie Bird, "After the Bosnia Shootdown: What's Next?" *Air Force Times,* 14 March 1994; Tony Capaccio, "The Fully Deployable Air Campaign," *Air Force* (January 1994): 50–51; Catherine Crier, "Interview with Secretary of Defense William J. Perry," ABC-TV *Nightline,* 28 February 1994.

25. Capaccio, "The Fully Deployable Air Campaign," 51–52; Secretary of Defense William J. Perry, "Remarks at George Washington University," 14 March 1994; "A Plan for Action," *Jane's Defence Weekly* (23 October 1993): 32. For references to special operations teams on the ground, see Sean D. Naylor, "U.S. Feeds Intel to Bosnia Peacekeepers," *Army Times,* 14 February 1994; Edward Gorman and Michael Evans, "SAS Active Behind the Front Line in Bosnia," *London Times,* 17 March 1994; and Sudetic, "Pilots on the Bosnia Food Run Hope for Bad Weather," 10.

26. Perry, "Remarks at George Washington University." A French UNPROFOR unit actually requested air support from a U.S. Air Force AC-130H Spectre gunship on 12 March 1994. See Michael R. Gordon, "Serbian Gunners Slip Away as U.S. Planes Await U.N. Approval," *New York Times,* 14 March 1994.

27. SSgt. C. E. Taylor, USA, "Mission in Macedonia," *Soldiers* (October 1993): 7–8; Vince Crawley, "Task Force in Macedonia Marks Quiet 3 Months," *European Stars and Stripes,* 2 November 1993; Michael R. Gordon, "U.S. Troops to Relieve Scandinavians for Bosnia," *New York Times,* 11 March 1994; Steve Vogel, "Training for Macedonia Duties," *Army Times,* 17 January 1994; Ron Jensen, "Serb Watch Can Spark Tension," *European Stars and Stripes,* 12 May 1994. Jensen's article describes two confrontations with armed Serbs, both resolved without shooting.

28. Collins, *Balkan Battlegrounds,* 22.

29. Ibid., 9; Nyrop, *Yugoslavia,* 242, 246–47; Cohen, *Broken Bonds,* 254.

30. U.S. Department of Defense, *The Conduct of the Persian Gulf War* (Washington, D.C.: U.S. Government Printing Office, 1992), 107; Eliot A.

Cohen, director, et al., *Gulf War Airpower Survey,* vol. 2, *Effects and Effectiveness* (Washington, D.C.: U.S. Government Printing Office, 1993), 168, 170, 211–21, 341; Ruth Marcus and Barton Gellman, "U.S. Urging Serbs Not to Redeploy," *Washington Post,* 22 February 1994; "Ready to Strike," *Washington Times,* 22 February 1994. Calculations of likely effects were made by extrapolating Persian Gulf performance using the numbers of strike aircraft available to attack Bosnia.

31. Roy Gutman, "Shelling Victims' Stories of Terror," *Long Island Newsday,* 8 February 1994; Tony Smith, "Americans Under Fire Evacuate Injured," *Washington Times,* 7 February 1994.

32. President William J. Clinton, "Statement Regarding Proposals to Deal With Situation in Bosnia," The White House Press Office, 9 February 1994.

33. "Ready to Strike," A12.

34. Robert H. Reid, "Serbs Move Most Guns, Avert Attacks," *Washington Times,* 21 February 1994; Marcus and Gelman, "U.S. Urging Serbs Not to Redeploy," 1.

35. Victoria Clark, "Diplomatic Footwork Worthy of the Bolshoi," *Washington Times,* 22 February 1994; Roger Cohen, "On a Hilltop Outside Sarajevo, A Serbian Battery Defies U.N.," *New York Times,* 22 February 1994; "Owen Says Russia Nearly Quit Talks over NATO Threat," *London Times,* 18 March 1994. The Russian battalion was drawn from the 106th Guards Air Assault Division of Tula, Russia.

36. Department of Defense, *Conduct of the Persian Gulf War,* 160; Cohen et al., *Gulf War Airpower Survey,* 111.

37. Julie Bird, "Controlling Unfriendly Skies," *Air Force Times,* 14 March 1994; Michael R. Gordon, "NATO Craft Down 4 Serb Warplanes Attacking Bosnia," *New York Times,* 1 March 1994; Jac Lewis, "Four Shot Down on 'Deny Flight,'" *Jane's Defence Weekly,* 5 March 1994. Aircraft and missile data can be found in Susan H. H. Young, "Gallery of USAF Weapons," *Air Force* (May 1993): 135, 145–46. The names of the U.S. airmen were not released to the press to preclude terrorist reprisals.

38. Gordon, "NATO Craft Down 4 Serb Warplanes Attacking Bosnia"; Atkinson, "NATO Vows to Patrol Bosnia Skies," 20.

39. Chuck Sudetic, "NATO Jets Bomb Serb Forces Assaulting Bosnian Haven," *New York Times,* 11 April 1994; Michael R. Gordon, "Air Strikes on Serbs Are a Show of Force," *New York Times,* 12 April 1994; Norman Friedman, "Getting Our Bluff Called in Bosnia," *Proceedings* (June 1994), 85–86.

40. Chuck Sudetic, "U.S. Planes Bomb Serbian Positions for a Second Day," *New York Times,* 12 April 1994; Gordon, "Air Strikes on Serbs Are a Show of Force"; Tom Squitieri, "Gorazde at Serbs' Mercy," *USA Today,* 18 April 1994; "F/A-18s Hit Serbs," *Marine Corps Gazette* (May 1994), 7. The British Sea Harrier pilot hit on 16 April successfully ejected and was recovered safely.

41. David Halberstam, *The Best and the Brightest* (Greenwich, Conn.: Fawcett Publications, 1973), 501; Lt. Col. Mark Clodfelter, USAF, *The Limits of Airpower* (New York: The Free Press, 1989), 59–60.

42. Rick Atkinson, "NATO Has Plans For Massive Airstrikes Against Bosnian Serb Forces," *Washington Post,* 25 April 1994; Roger Cohen, "Bowing to NATO, Serbs Pull Back from Muslim City," *New York Times,* 25 April 1994.

43. Peter Grier, "U.S. Official Start to Sell Public on U.S. Troops for Bosnia Peace," *Christian Science Monitor,* 15 March 1994; "Bosnia Serbs List Demands on Talks," *New York Times,* 25 March 1994. Bosnian Serbs now refer to their territory as "the Republic of Srpska."

EPILOGUE
Pax Americana

You don't get your picture on the cover of Newsweek
by killing Canadians. You've got to kill Americans.

Lewis MacKenzie
Major General, Canadian army

From the accession of Octavian as Augustus of Rome in 27 B.C. through the death of Emperor Marcus Aurelius in A.D. 180, the Mediterranean World experienced 207 years of relative tranquility, the famous Roman Peace, the Pax Romana in the language of the day. In the capital city, the gates of the Temple of Janus, opened when the Roman state made war, closed for only the third time in the turbulent history of the city, and, as Christian tradition explains, "the whole world" was at peace. Well, not quite—the evangelist Matthew recorded Jesus' warning that "there will be wars and rumors of war," and there were plenty, even then. Roman legions and Roman fleets, aided by allied cohorts and flotillas, fought the Parthians, the Germans, the Dacians, the Britons, the Picts, Jewish rebels, and, now and then, each other. But these battles and campaigns went on far from the imperial center. The metropolis of Rome did not have to face invaders, nor did most of the Empire. Commerce flourished, and the twenty million citizens and one hundred million other inhabitants of the imperial holdings went about their business without much concern for the 450,000 volunteer legionnaires, auxiliaries, and sailors holding the *limes,* the boundary forts.[1] For all but those struggling along the far frontiers, the world was at peace.

In a similar way, from the victory at Waterloo in 1815 until the outbreak of the Great War in 1914, the United Kingdom of Great Britain, Scotland, Wales, and Ireland presided over ninety-nine years of stability, the Pax Britannica, a title consciously borrowed from the Roman example. London

378

and its far-flung population of thirty-seven million prospered, reaping the benefits from the opening waves of industrialization. This transpired behind the thin screen provided by some 420,000 regular troops and Royal Navy sailors, volunteers all, who patrolled British enclaves all around the restive planet. Along with a limited contest in the Russian Crimea in the middle years of the nineteenth century, British forces fought many minor wars, in round after round of expeditions aimed at Asian and African foes: Abyssinians, Afghans, Ashanti, Boers, Chinese Boxers, Burmese, Dervishes, Kaffirs, Marathas, Pathans, Pindaris, Sikhs, Somalis, and Zulus, to name a few. If you asked any British gentleman of Queen Victoria's era, he would have considered his country to be at peace, although he might have been aware of some trouble "out there somewhere or another."[2] With a nod to Rudyard Kipling, that sort of thing belonged to Tommy Atkins and Jack Tar, who were paid to handle such matters while the better sort of people continued to enjoy the blessings of peace.

Now, it is America's turn, the full flowering of Henry Luce's "American Century," a true Pax Americana. Since 1945, the United States of America has imposed its own brand of stability on a seething globe, buttressed by the threat of nuclear weaponry and the hard work of, by 1994, 1.7 million soldiers, Marines, sailors, and airmen. The 255 million or so Americans have built the richest society in history, and they have brought almost a billion people along for this golden ride. The other 4 billion unfortunates get the crumbs and the pain, some of it inflicted by American forces in a variety of limited wars, counterinsurgencies, quarantines, punitive strikes, expeditions, interventions, and, in the current parlance, operations other than war. In Toledo and Topeka, America is at peace and has been since "the Big One" formally ended aboard the USS *Missouri* in Tokyo Bay. But it has been a flawed peace, as always in history.

Go look at the names on the polished black wall of the Vietnam Memorial and then think about the names that could be chiseled into the walls that have never been built: Korea, Lebanon (twice), the Dominican Republic, El Salvador, Grenada, Panama, the Gulf War, Somalia, and many, many others.[3] Those names represent the installment payments on what we call peace, what the Romans and British called peace, about the best that can be done in a world of imperfect humans. The trick, as always, is to keep names off future walls and to keep the peace we have built, incomplete though it may be. That is why these small wars demand study. They are what great powers must do to stay great. We will only see more of them. That said, what can we learn from our experiences since the victorious conclusion of the war against Iraq?

It would be both presumptuous and exceedingly difficult to attempt to draw definitive lessons from work very much in progress. In many respects, trying to summarize what we know about the recent American experiences in small "wars of peace" resembles the challenge of standing on a big rock promontory and trying to describe (and predict) the course and composition of a mountain stream racing downhill in full spring flood. We know in general where the water came from and where it is going. The banks can be seen, with full recognition that they may shift over time. The rate of flow can be measured, at least for now. And we cannot help but notice that the same brands of flotsam and jetsam are whizzing by, tossed by the boiling waves, certainly indicative of what the stream is doing to its surroundings. Having acknowledged the magnitude of the challenge, it is still worthwhile to give it a try, knowing full well that these preliminary observations may well suffer from the fate of any streamside surveyor—becoming partially or all wet. Anyway, here we go.

Each of the cases considered so far is unique, yet there are definite common threads. They are part of that same stream and feature some of that same bobbing debris. America's military record in operations other than war since early 1991 displays certain common characteristics, reasonably predictable by reference to previous, similar episodes in the Korean DMZ, the Sinai, and in Lebanon. These can be conveniently discussed under four headings: the nature of OOTW, strategic concerns, operational matters, and tactical issues, recognizing that this neat taxonomy collapses and fuses rather freely in the stresses of active campaigning on the far frontiers. As a basis for discussion, it serves our purposes well enough.

Operations other than war cannot be avoided or wished away. With millions of American citizens active in countries around the world and billions of U.S. dollars at work in every far corner, some idyllic retreat into Fortress America is not even worth considering. The pace and scale of OOTW commitments may ebb or flow, but they will not end. To keep the status quo that makes their country a superpower, Americans will continue to intervene in other countries. Their business is our business. The statecraft comes in figuring which countries demand attention and how much. The present global condition sometimes makes America appear to be like Doctor Ben Casey surveying the ruins of Nagasaki: capable, determined, and overwhelmed.

Triage is the name of the game. Not every case can get the same treatment. Some can be saved more easily than others. Some need an aspirin, others require brain surgery. And a few may be terminal, worthy of sympathy but not salvageable. So OOTW has many faces, ranging from a few advisers to I Marine Expeditionary Force backed by the jets of the USS *Enterprise*.

In all their guises, however, OOTW are wars—pure and simple. America has enemies everywhere, and they are never glad to see us. Long-winded, tortuous debates about peacekeeping versus peacemaking, Chapter 6 versus Chapter 7, and war versus OOTW miss the point. When Americans take up loaded firearms or attach live ordnance to the wing hardpoints, then enter somebody else's country, they are at war. Somebody will fight back, or at least pose the potential of doing so. Whether a battalion or a few air-lifters deploy in harm's way, even on something billed as humanitarian, everything we know about war, its dangers of painful death and grisly wounds, debilitating physical effects, random uncertainties and vagueries, and general reference to Murphy's Law, all come into play as surely as if we were on Little Round Top at Gettysburg in 1863. To believe otherwise is to court disaster.

Still, OOTW are wars under definite and shifting conditions, typically expressed by rules of engagement that may be more restrictive than those customarily associated with the clash of conventional forces. Carefully delineated bounds on the use of force have characterized most American military ventures since 1775.[4] The World War II model is the exception. Even there, one should never get the impression that GIs raced around Europe laying waste in the style of the proverbial Mongol hordes, or that all means were used à outrance. Interludes like the bombing of the abbey of Monte Cassino or the fire raids on Tokyo have gained notoriety because they were unusual. For the most part, the military exerted great efforts to limit collateral damage to civil populations, even at the expense of the Americans involved. The costly daylight precision bombing campaign over Germany in 1943–45 reflects this concern. Nelson Miles and Ranald MacKenzie of the frontier army, who lost bluecoats on the fringes of many Indian villages without retaliating, would have understood completely. Americans make war with regard for civilian lives and property. And OOTW, the superpower antithesis to Mao's thesis of guerrilla insurgency, is at its heart a war for control of a population, be they Kurds, Somalis, or Bosnians. Killing them all is not an approved solution.

Given the risks involved in entering hostile lands, air, and waters, the U.S.

government dare not engage in OOTW lightly. At the strategic level, the use of force demands some direction at the outset. Each deployment must be weighed, means applied versus ends desired, and adjusted as the situation develops. In short, the president describes a mission (a task and purpose—who, what, when, where, and why) and an intent (a definition of success in terms of the situation and friendly forces). Then the chain of command, working with the rest of the government, allies, and local authorities in the theater of operations carry out the mission, making changes as events dictate. That sort of process would be ideal.

Real life seldom seems so tidy. In Kurdistan, Somalia, and Bosnia, the mission and intent had to be derived from a variety of sources, and contradictions resolved or at least acknowledged. The military must puzzle out what they think they have been told to do, then feed that supposition back up the chain for approval. We often hear military leaders grouse about "lack of a clear mission and endstate," but such things can be hard to come by in OOTW. It is the military's responsibility to clarify the mission and intent and raise concerns. Do the ROE match the mission? Do we have enough to do the job? Who is really in charge? Civilian policy makers often do not think in these terms, and it is up to the military to ask, and keep asking, these tough questions. That process worked well in northern Iraq and in the former Yugoslavia. It broke down during the Somalia episode, leaving Rangers and 10th Mountain Division riflemen to sort out the confusion at bayonet point.

Missions can and will creep, and if the ends begin to exceed the means, the military professionals must sound an alert. It is not possible to define an ironclad goal and stick to it under every circumstance. As the Marines in Beirut discovered, hewing to the same old mission under changed conditions can also be deadly. So commanders at all levels will adjust their mission to match changing situations. If the ends exceed the means, America has the usual choices: reduce the ends, increase the means, or declare victory and exit. In Somalia, as in Beirut a decade before, holding a losing hand only delays the inevitable and often increases the human toll. In this regard, the last thing Americans need are well-meaning foreigners (like the UN general secretary) diddling with the goals or resource levels of ongoing operations.

This leads to the second issue of strategic concern—allies. Along with a clear mission, the military prefers U.S. command of the warpower committed. Experience to date indicates that America can take charge on request, and indeed, when the United States does not lead, not much happens, or at least not much of importance or value. About the time the Somalia operation went down the drain, the Clinton administration was drafting Presidential Decision Directive 13 (of course), concerning U.S. participation in peace operations. Early versions proposed routine U.S. service under foreign and UN command, and even spoke of some nebulous standing force of American logisticians on call for United Nations missions. The Rangers' final raid in Mogadishu, and the embarrassing rebuff of an advisory team at the dock in Port-au-Prince, Haiti, about the same time, cooled the Clinton people's ardor for such undertakings.[5] The caution is fully justified, though it should be recalled, Americans, not the UN, created most of the command mix-ups in Somalia.

In the United Nations, infused with new vitality in the aftermath of the Cold War, the reach continues to exceed the grasp. It is still Student Council Week at Global High. Ambassador Alexander Borg-Olivier of the UN Office of Humanitarian Affairs recently remarked that the United Nations had settled on "two new major issues"—"attaining global peace and stability" and "sustaining development of the human race."[6] With that sort of boundless optimism, the quest for immortality and the ability to transmute lead into gold cannot be far behind, especially if America pays the bills in money and blood.

In Somalia, the Clinton administration has already seen only too well what can happen when UN rhetoric runs ahead of practicality. The president has acted accordingly in Bosnia, largely ignoring the high-flown verbiage emanating from Turtle Bay in New York City. Whatever policy directive on peace operations eventually comes out of the White House, it will not look like a booklet of blank checks made out to UN Secretary General Boutros Boutros-Ghali.

But rest assured, there will be allies, and often under the blue flag of the UN. All three of the major operations considered here proceeded under United Nations auspices, with portions of the Somali and Yugoslav interventions featuring U.S. troops actually sporting blue berets. Regional alliances, such as NATO or the WEU, played parts in each of the three missions, but especially in the Balkans. In deference to the long-standing American bias toward collective action, we should expect these types of setups. General Shalikashvili's performance in Kurdistan offers the optimum model —be polite, be considerate of other national sentiments, and then take charge, issuing orders, not requests. In most cases, if America intervenes,

America should lead. The other countries may complain, but that is mostly out of habit. Power, especially superpower, conveys its own legitimacy in international affairs.

Although a U.S. commander may be at the pinnacle of an operation, he will rarely be in charge at all echelons, or in each aspect of warpower. Americans should not be loathe to participate under foreign command at any level, provided that command is competent and the U.S. retains the sovereign right to disengage if the allied efforts begin to outstrip American policy and force commitments. In particular, America should carefully assess the professionalism of any proposed UN or coalition command team before integrating U.S. armed contingents. It is not difficult to envision Americans working for a British, Canadian, French, German, Japanese, or Korean admiral or general, or even a Dane, Swede, Pole, or Brazilian. It is more difficult to see U.S. troops responding to the direction of a Bolivian, a Laotian, a Senegalese, or a Luxembourger, not because they are bad people or innately incompetent, but because they lack the experience of directing sophisticated modern joint military operations. There are still plenty of American officers who find this pretty challenging, so we should not be surprised that those who never do it are not too good at it. Rather than say yes or no to the difficult question of foreign command, it is best to say it depends and leave it at that.

At the operational level, where strategic ends and means must be translated into useful warpower, there is nothing to be gained by being parsimonious. A big foot stomps many ants, and operations that succeed are not shy about brandishing powerful air, sea, and land forces, the kind that make America a superpower. The team usually includes some of each, tailored to fit the precise situation encountered and designed to allow sufficient capability to destroy bad guys and control ground and peoples. Rarely, if ever, will one form of military power be adequate.

Overreliance on one aspect of military strength, whether special forces operations chasing Aidid or NATO warplanes over Bosnia, simplifies the opposition's reactions. To gain the overmatch that makes America the world's strongest country, air, sea, and land elements must all be part of the equation. As the Rangers discovered in Mogadishu, there is nothing like a carrier air strike, a Spectre gunship, or a Marine Corps tank column when you really need one. OOTW necessitates that the whole range of U.S. warpower be available, just in case. Thus, a successful American-style OOTW comes in strong and hard, not necessarily shooting, but ready to open up if the bad guys want to play games. That method definitely works. One can always ease up over time. Clamping down slowly, gradually turning up the heat, is much harder, as America found out in Vietnam.

The "big foot" pattern served America and its allies well in northern Iraq and in the opening phase of Operation Restore Hope in Somalia. As the situations developed under the influence of U.S. and allied warpower, both Shalikashvili and Johnston enjoyed sufficient surplus of forces and capabilities to overawe most opponents without resorting to fighting. "To subdue the enemy without fighting is the acme of skill," said Sun Tzu, and for the hostile folks that means using the staring eyes of CNN and company to dramatize their causes. For America and friends, though, nothing beats a very big club and the control that club can exert. This is why General Powell repeatedly advocated "all or nothing"—either go in strength, or do not go.

There are those, particularly the Canadians, British, and Scandinavians, who see the American "all or nothing" form of entry as contrary to the spirit of peacekeeping, which they have determined to imply limited use of force and strict impartiality. This line has some validity, if one sees peacekeeping as an endless roundelay of interposition between passive, clearly defined opponents willing to mind their own business.[7] In such a view, goodwill substitutes for fighting strength, and the peace troops become hostages to the whims of the belligerent parties. Certainly the American experience in the Sinai MFO mission conforms to this idea.

But the MFO situation, and those few like it, really constitute exceptional environments. There have been a few successes, in places like Cambodia and Nicaragua, where the various warring parties cooperated for their own reasons. There are failures, as in Somalia's UNOSOM II and in Haiti in 1993, where the blue berets proved unready to fight it out to a finish, or at least to a favorable stalemate. In most cases, of course, UN peacekeepers just sit there impotently as wars rage around them, with UNIFIL in Lebanon perhaps the worst case in recent memory. That may make people feel better, but its contribution to world peace and stability is probably negligible, like policemen driving by rapes and murders. Wisely, the United States has not plunged into too many of these "opportunities," and usually prefers to send money or individuals, not formed units.

Why do most UN peacekeeping missions accomplish so little? Mainly, they enjoy few real successes because they are simply present for duty, not really doing anything except surviving and usually inadequately manned to do even that very well. The happy trust in the virtues of a good example and kindness rarely impresses the hard-bitten guerrillas and terrorists who cause the mayhem that sparks UN intervention, and trusting in documents initialed by insurgents reflects gullibility worthy of Doctor Pangloss and Candide. No, you cannot keep a peace that does not exist, and why bother going if there is already peace? So much for the glories of the impartial approach.

In the real world, impartiality is damn hard to come by, especially given that enemies do wait out there in the countryside and urban warrens. Usually, at least a few factions in war-ravaged lands are not happy to see outsiders show up and make their discontent known. Even the UN cannot please everyone. Would anyone claim that those who entered northern Iraq, Somalia, or Bosnia were impartial, given that UN directives pointedly sided against Saddam Hussein's military, the Aidid militia, and the Bosnian Serbs? Impartiality is no substitute for zeroed weapons, alert troops, and a full suite of warpower. Otherwise, the hateful types will see it for what it is—weakness—and react appropriately. Not placing too much trust in local good faith goes double for Americans, already carrying significant burdens of envy and mistrust as they move among the four-fifths of the world who do not live like Yankees.

Going in like warriors works best, and that relates to tactics. The tactics of OOTW are the same tactics trained at Hohenfels, at Fallon Naval Air Station, at Nellis Air Force Base, and at Camp Lejeune—shoot, move, communicate, and sustain. The methods are modified by situational ROE but, in essence, they follow the same patterns as they might in the Gulf War. Tactics allow for friction in all its aspects.

Along with the chance of getting killed, Americans engaged in OOTW must deal with many difficult factors at the lowest levels. Sergeants and petty officers end up talking to Save the Children representatives, political commissars, State Department officials, rebel chieftains, mayors, allied battalion NCOs, and Reuters correspondents. It is wrong to think that rifle platoon sergeants will become expert negotiators and press handlers, but it is equally incorrect to think that modern overseas operations occur on some sterile battleground devoid of anyone but uniformed good guys and bad guys. Modern American training replicates this dirty, complex arena.

Because they offer one of the most direct links between trigger pullers and policy makers, journalists, particularly the seemingly omnipresent electronic news media, can play a huge role in giving tactical events operational and strategic significance. A standoff at a roadblock, a shot fired into a bunker, or a downed helicopter can take on national and international importance when powerful imagery flickers onto the television screens from Tupelo to the White House. The coverage of Kurdish suffering in the spring of 1991, the pictures of an American body being dragged through the streets of Mogadishu, the bloodbath in the Markale Marketplace in Sarajevo— these haunting films rolled on and on, and all three influenced important choices regarding operations in progress.

Pilots, ship captains, and rifle company commanders should be aware of the intrusive character of the modern press, but one cannot make too much of the latest clips on *CNN Headline News.* The media remains more of a mirror than a window, and, in the final analysis, videotapes do not make decisions. Leaders decide, from the president down to the corporal out in the DMZ, and they choose based on their sensing and professional judgment. Even so, cameramen will be looking over the shoulders of the lead flight crews and Marines, and they should be ready for that likelihood.

The tactics of OOTW have yet to reveal a silver bullet or magic jujitsu technique to cure all ills. About all we can say for certain is that some types of units have been very useful, and others less so. When going into a small war, the regional CINC will usually allocate enough joint warpower. Getting the most out of what is made available necessitates knowing about the most talented actors on the joint team, and that knowledge cannot stop at the admiral and general ranks. Five types of forces may be considered essential for OOTW: air and sealift, sustainers, air combat units, ground combat battalions, and special operations forces.

Lift, both air and sea, sets the tempo for every American peace operation. It is no coincidence that the Air Mobility Command's intercontinental transports, along with their smaller C-130 cousins, led the way into Kurdistan, Somalia, and the former Yugoslavia. Sealift brought in the heavier weapons, trucks, and supplies in Mogadishu. American forces have started to rely on prepositioned stocks, both ashore and afloat. In general, getting there always comes first. Air and sea control must be ensured for this flow to start and keep going. Thanks to the might of the U.S. Air Force and Navy, that is seldom a problem.

Sustainers, the unglamorous supply, medical, and intratheater transporters, also go in very early on these operations. Lightly armed and numbering many women among their ranks, these forces represent one of the things America can do that other countries cannot. In the transition to UNOSOM II, General Bir and his people wanted American logisticians, and the Sinai MFO depends on a U.S. service support battalion. These are not accidents.

In UN missions, foreign commanders prefer to incorporate American prowess at transnational sustainment rather than Uncle Sam's rifle companies. This may not make infantrymen or Marines happy, but it is a fact. Combat service supporters lead the way more often than Rangers.

Air combat squadrons, the killing part of airpower, offer the standard means of making up for the lack of infantry and other close-combat outfits that typifies most American interventions. Air supremacy will be achieved, and although bombing and strafing may not win the war single-handedly, raining deadly munitions furnishes a degree of physical and psychological destruction that ground units cannot generate. The initial batch of airpower usually comes aboard a carrier, but for a prolonged campaign, ground-based air should reinforce and, eventually, supplant the early-arriving navy wings. Airpower might not have salvaged U.S. policy in Somalia, but strikes could definitely have helped Task Force Ranger in its death struggle in the Bakara Market. Fighting without significant air support, relying only on a few small helicopters, reminds one of General Longstreet's comment about fighting without one of his divisions: "I never like to go into battle with one boot off."[8] Americans today do not prefer to try that any more than Longstreet did back in 1863.

Ground combat battalions, army and Marine, also have major roles in OOTW. They put the feet on the ground that exert control, and they can be most effective when backed by airpower, either ground- or sea-based. Landing troops requires airfields and ports, the routine objectives at the outset of Provide Comfort, Restore Hope, and Provide Promise. Marines often come in first, although army paratroopers and air assault battalions also can force an entry into an enemy country. The army usually stays for the extended missions, but Marines also have done that now and then. Once on the ground, all of these men physically secure what needs to be secured. They take and hold ground, as their predecessors have done since Roman times. Americans put emphasis on riflemen, but when lift constraints allow, tanks and mechanized forces can be not only useful, but vital. This is one of the reasons for prepositioning, to get more armor forward earlier on during a contingency. Even so, in an age of high technology, America relies a lot on a few riflemen far from home.

Finally, tactics allow a major place to special operations forces, who typically enter the theater of operations right along with, or even before, the first airlifters. Much ink has been spilled over their exciting direct action role, the win-big/lose-big propositions like the Task Force Ranger raids in

Mogadishu. Less thrilling to newshounds, but more important by far, are the other duties carried out by SEALs, Green Berets, and their friends: liaison with locals, reconnaissance in the hinterlands, guiding in airdrops, spotting for strikes, pyschological operations, and civic action. All of these take place out in the Great Gulp, in the realm of danger and death. If OOTW are the late-twentieth-century equivalent of expeditions into Indian country, then the special warriors serve as the Indian scouts, blazing the trail.

The nature of OOTW, strategy, operations, and tactics have an unnerving tendency to neck down to about the level of lieutenant colonels or colonels, commanders, and captains. In the three big post–Gulf War operations, time after time, the key decisions fell to men with a lot to do, men with twenty years experience or less, men without a vast staff or modern telecommunications. Presidents and CINCs propose, but those in the dirt and above it dispose. Think of Lt. Col. John Abizaid leading his paratroopers as they pried out Iraqis in front of his airborne battalion's advance into Kurdistan. Consider Col. Buck Bedard bringing his 7th Marine Regiment into the Somali town of Baidoa, working with French Foreign Legionnaires. Look at Lt. Col. Walt Horton, taking his battalion to Macedonia under a UN flag to watch the border with Serbia. Those are the people carrying the burdens of American foreign policy in their rucksacks, along with the souls of the young men they command. That is not a light load.

They are out there now, as you read these words in comfort somewhere warm and dry. In the Adriatic, in the yawning darkness, an F/A-18 Hornet is on final approach, the aviator feeling for the nearly invisible, rain-soaked deck, another patrol over Bosnia completed without incident. On Outpost 3-11, on a rocky island on the Strait of Tiran, a young private first class with heavy green binoculars scans the blue waters below, watching the small craft go by, while at his side, his partner cleans his rifle. Another C-130E Hercules takes off from Incirlik Air Base, bound for the forward strip at Silopi, Turkey, making the flight despite mountain snow squalls— medical supplies must get through. And in the Korean DMZ, in the footsteps of John Mitchell and so many others, young Americans of the JSA Battalion still walk, heads swiveling slowly from side to side, weapons loaded and ready, searching for infiltrators, for trouble, and for things that go bump in the night.

There are not many of them, not really. As of 1994, less than 1.7 million Americans serve in the armed forces, with fewer every day as the military completes a reduction to about 1.4 million. Our military is strong, but relative to our populace, not very large.

We owe a lot to our men and women in uniform, out there on the contested frontier. They guarantee our safety, our prosperity, our general welfare, and our way of life. When we get into a fracas in some godforsaken niche way out there, they will come and get us, or die trying. They hold the line for us, keeping the bad guys out there, far away. In the rain, in the dark, and often in danger, they remain on watch, enforcing our Pax Americana, walking the distant borders that define our savage peace.

Notes

The epigraph is from Storer N. Rowley, "Canadian Vet of Bosnia Warns U.S.: Keep GIs Off UN Front Lines," *Chicago Tribune,* 12 January 1994.

1. Edward M. Gibbon, *The Decline and Fall of the Roman Empire,* vol. 1, *180 A.D. to 395 A.D.* (New York: The Modern Library, 1980), 17, 37–38. The Romans maintained approximately 2 percent of their citizenry in arms. The idea of the Roman Empire as "the whole world" can be found in Luke 3:1. The phrase "wars and rumors of war" comes from Matthew 24:6.

2. The numbers on population and men under arms (army and navy) reflect the statistics for British subjects in 1890. See Paul Kennedy, *The Rise and Fall of the Great Powers* (New York: Random House, 1987), 199, 203. The British kept about 1 percent of the United Kingdom's subjects in the Queen's military service.

3. The American population in 1993–94 was reckoned at 255 million. Current numbers for men and women in all services, 1.7 million, can be found in U.S. Department of Defense, "Defense Almanac," *Defense 93* (September–October 1993): 24–27. The United States has less than .7 percent of its population on active duty in the military.

4. Maj. Mark S. Martins, USA, "Rules of Engagement for Land Forces: A Matter of Training, Not Lawyering" (thesis, University of Virginia, 1994).

5. For a description of the evolution of PDD-13 into PDD-25, a much more traditional policy, see Doyle McManus and Art Pine, "Administration Assessing Hard Lessons of Somalia," *Los Angeles Times,* 25 March 1994.

6. Ambassador Alexander Borg-Olivier, "Remarks to the Conference on Peacemaking, Peacekeeping, and Coalition Warfare: The Future Role of the United Nations," Norwich University, Northfield Vermont, 25 February 1994.

7. Julia Preston and Daniel Williams, "Report Faults U.S., U.N., Aideed," *Washington Post,* 31 March 1994. In its postmortem on the Somalia operations, UN investigators blamed Americans for conducting operations "inconsistent with basic tenets of U.N. peacekeeping."

8. Douglas Southall Freeman, *Lee's Lieutenants,* vol. 3, *Gettysburg to Appomatox* (New York: Charles Scribner's Sons, 1944). 114.

Appendix A:
American Wars and Operations Other Than War
1775–1995

Revolutionary War (1775–83)
  Shays' Rebellion (1786–87)
  Miami Indian Campaign (1790–94)
  Whiskey Rebellion (1794)
  Quasi-War with France (1799–1800)
  Tripolitan War (1800–1805)
  Pike Expedition into Spanish Colorado (1806)
  Gulf of Mexico Antipirate Operations (1806–10)
  USS *Chesapeake* Incident (1807)
  Incursions into Spanish Florida (1810–18)
  USS *President* Incident (1811)
  Shawnee Indian Campaign (1811)
War of 1812 (1812–15)
  Caribbean Antipirate Operations (1814–25)
  Algiers War (1815)
  Tripoli Show of Force (1815)
  First Seminole Indian Campaign (1817–18)
  Seizure of Oregon Territory (1818)
  Antislavery Operations off Africa (1820–23)
  Cuban Antipirate Operations (1822–25)
  Puerto Rico Antipirate Operations (1824)
  Greek Antipirate Operations (1827)
  Falklands Expedition (1831–32)
  First Sumatra Raid (1832)
  Black Hawk Indian Campaign (1832)
  First Buenos Aires Show of Force (1833)
  Peru Show of Force (1835–36)
  Second Seminole Indian Campaign (1835–42)
  Incursion into Mexican Texas (1836)
  Creek Indian Campaign (1836)
  Second Sumatra Raid (1838–39)

First Fiji Islands Expedition (1840)
Drummond Island Raid (1841)
First Samoa Raid (1841)
Incursion into Mexican California (1842)
Canton Incident (1843)
Ivory Coast Show of Force (1843)
Tourane Bombardment (1845)
Mexican War (1846–48)
First Jaffa Show of Force (1851)
Johanns Island Raid (1851)
Argentina Expedition (1852–53)
First Nicaraguan Landing (1853)
Japan Show of Force and Landings (Perry Expedition) (1853–54)
China Yangtze Patrol (1854–1941)
Second Nicaraguan Landing (1854)
Second Fiji Islands Expedition (1855)
First Uruguay Landing (1855)
Third Seminole Indian Campaign (1855–58)
First Panama Landing (1856)
Kansas Intervention (1856–61)
Third Nicaraguan Landing (1857)
Second Uruguay Landing (1858)
Third Fiji Islands Expedition (1858)
Second Jaffa Show of Force (1858–59)
Tientsin Intervention (1859)
Harper's Ferry Incident (1859)
Paraguay Show of Force (1859)
Mexican Antibandit Incursion (1859)
Angola Landing (1860)
Civil War (1861–65)
Shimonoseki Island Bombardment (1863–64)
Second Panama Landing (1865)
Mexican Show of Force and Incursion (1866)
Comanche Indian Confederation Campaign (1866–75)
Fourth Nicaraguan Landing (1867)
Japan Legation Security Landings (1868)
Third Uruguay Landing (1868)
Mexican Antipirate Incursion (1870)

First Apache Indian Campaign (1870–71)
Korean Intervention (1871)
Modoc Indian Campaign (1872–73)
Third Panama Landing (1873)
Incursions into Mexico in Pursuit of Indians (1873–96)
Second Apache Indian Campaign (1873)
First Hawaiian Landing (1874)
First Sioux-Cheyenne Indian Campaign (1876–77)
Nez Perce Indian Campaign (1877)
Bannock Indian Campaign (1878)
Second Cheyenne Indian Campaign (1878–79)
Ute Indian Confederation Campaign (1879–80)
Egypt Show of Force (1882)
Fourth Panama Landing (1885)
Third Apache Indian Campaign (1885–86)
Korean Landing (1888)
First Haiti Landing (1888)
Samoa Landing (1888–89)
Second Hawaiian Landing (1889)
Second Buenos Aires Show of Force (1890)
Second Sioux Indian Campaign (1890–91)
Second Haiti Landing (1891)
Bering Strait Antisealing Expedition (1891)
Chile Legation Security (1891)
Third Hawaiian Landing (1893)
Fifth Nicaraguan Landing (1894)
First Korean Legation Security (1894–96)
Colombia Landing (1896)
Sixth Nicaraguan Landing (1896)
Seventh Nicaraguan Landing (1898)
Spanish–American War (1898)
   Leech Lake Indian Uprising (1898)
   Eighth Nicaraguan Landing (1899)
   Samoan Crisis (1899)
   Philippine Counterinsurgency (1899–1913)
   Boxer Rebellion Intervention (1900)
   Colombia-Panama Intervention (1901–14)
   Honduras Legation Security (1903)

First Dominican Republic Landing (1903)
Beirut Landing and Show of Force (1903)
Abyssinia Legation Security (1903–4)
Morocco Show of Force (1904)
Second Dominican Republic Landing (1904)
Second Korean Legation Security (1904–5)
First Cuban Intervention (1906–9)
First Honduras Landing (1907)
Ninth Nicaraguan Landing (1910)
Honduras Intervention (1911–12)
Nicaraguan Intervention (1912–33)
First Cuban Landing (1912)
Constantinople Legation Security (1912)
Mexican Yaqui Valley Evacuation (1913)
Mexican Intervention (1914–17)
Third Haiti Landing (1914)
Third Dominican Republic Landing (1914)
Haiti Intervention (1915–34)
First Dominican Republic Intervention (1916–24)
Second Cuban Intervention (1917–22)
World War I (1917–18)
North Russian Intervention (1918–19)
Siberian Intervention (1918–20)
Mexican Antibandit Incursions (1918–19)
First Panama Intervention (1918–20)
Dalmatia Landing (1919)
Constantinople Legation Security (1919)
Second Honduras Landing (1919)
Guatemala Landing (1920)
Russian Island Security (1920–22)
Panama Show of Force (1921)
Smyrna Landing (1922)
Third Honduras Landing (1924)
Fourth Honduras Landing (1925)
Cuba Show of Force (1933)
USS *Panay* Incident (1937)
Iceland Occupation (1941)
Undeclared Atlantic Antisubmarine Campaign (1941)

World War II (1941–45)
  Trieste Intervention (1945–53)
  North China Intervention (1945–49)
  Iran Crisis (1945–46)
  French Indochina Counterinsurgency (1946–54)
  Greece Counterinsurgency (1946–49)
  First Philippines Counterinsurgency (1946–55)
  Turkey Show of Force (1947)
  Palestine Legation Security (1948)
  Berlin Blockade-Airlift (1948–49)
Korean War (1950–53)
  Korean DMZ Defense (1953–present)
  Quemoy-Matsu Incidents (1954–62)
  South Vietnam Counterinsurgency (1955–65)
  Laos Counterinsurgency (1955–65)
  Morocco Show of Force (1956)
  Suez Crisis Evacuation of Egypt (1956)
  First Lebanon Intervention (1958)
  Second Cuban Landing (1959–60)
  Dominican Republic Show of Force (1960–62)
  First Congo Airlift-Evacuation (1960–64)
  Bay of Pigs Support (1961)
  Berlin Crisis (1961)
  Cuban Missile Crisis (1962)
  Thailand Landing and Show of Force (1962)
  Haiti Evacuation (1963)
  Panama Show of Force (1964)
Vietnam War (1965–75)
  Dominican Republic Intervention (1965–66)
  Guatemala Counterinsurgency (1965–74)
  Thailand Counterinsurgency (1965–85)
  Second Korean Conflict—USS *Pueblo* Incident (1966–69)
  Second Congo Airlift (1967)
  USS *Liberty* Incident (1967)
  Jordan Show of Force (1970)
  Israel Airlift (1973)
  Cyprus Evacuation (1974)
  SS *Mayaguez* Incident (1975)

Lebanon Evacuation (1976)
Panmunjom "Axe Murder" Incident (1976)
Uganda Show of Force (1977)
Kolwezi Evacuation (1978)
Iran Evacuation (1978)
El Salvador Counterinsurgency (1979–91)
Iran Hostage Rescue Attempt (1980)
Afghanistan Proinsurgency (1980–91)
Honduras Military Assistance (1981–present)
Nicaragua Proinsurgency (1981–90)
Panmunjom Czech Defector Incident (1981)
First Libyan Aircraft Shootdown (1981)
Sinai Peacekeeping Mission (1982–present)
Falklands War Airlift (1982)
Second Lebanon Intervention (1982–84)
AWACS Deployment to Egypt-Chad; Show of Force (1983)
Grenada Intervention (1983)
Second Philippine Counterinsurgency (1984–present)
Panmunjom "Russian Defector" Incident (1984)
Angola Proinsurgency (1985–91)
SS *Achille Lauro* Incident (1985)
Counternarcotics Operations, Western Hemisphere (1986–present)
Gulf of Sidra Confrontation against Libya (1986)
Bolivian Counternarcotics Intervention (1986)
Persian Gulf Convoy Escort (1987–88)
Honduras Show of Force (1988)
Panama Show of Force (1988)
Second Libyan Aircraft Shootdown (1989)
Philippine Anti-Coup Operations (1989)
Panama Intervention (1989–90)

Gulf War (1990–91)

Liberia Evacuation (1990)
First Somalia Evacuation (1991)
Iraq Peacekeeping—Relief (1991–present)
Bangladesh Typhoon Relife (1991)
Somalia Peacekeeping (1992–94)
Former Yugoslavia Peacekeeping (1992–present)
Haiti Peacekeeping Attempt (1993)

Korean Show of Force (1994)
Rwanda Evacuation and Airlift (1994)
Haiti Peacekeeping-Relief (1994–present)
Kuwait Show of Force (1994)
Korean DMZ Helicopter Shootdown (1994)
Second Somalia Evacuation (1195)

Sources: Ellen C. Collier, *Instances of Use of United States Armed Forces Abroad, 1798–1989* (Washington, D.C.: Congressional Research Service, 1989), 2–19; John M. Collins, *America's Small Wars* (McLean, Va.: Brassey's, 1991), 14; R. Ernest Dupuy and Trevor N. Dupuy, *The Encyclopedia of Military History* (New York: Harper and Row, 1984), 725–1,464; Barry M. Blechman et al., *Force Without War* (Washington, D.C.: The Brookings Institution, 1978), 547–53; Philip D. Zelikow, "Force Without War, 1975–82," *Journal of Strategic Studies* (March 1984): 46–47.

Appendix B:
The Unified Commands, 1995

Regional Commands

U.S. Atlantic Command (USACOM)
North America, the Atlantic, and the Caribbean
Headquarters: Norfolk Naval Base, Virginia
CINC's service: usually Navy (currently a Marine)
Major forces—
   Army: I, III, XVIII Airborne Corps
   Navy: Second Fleet
   Marine Corps: I, II Marine Expeditionary Force
   Air Force: Ninth, Twelth Air Forces
   Special operations forces

U.S. Southern Command (USSOUTHCOM)
Central and South America
Headquarters: Quarry Heights, Panama (relocating to U.S. by 2000)
CINC's service: Army
Major forces—
   Army: 5th Battalion, 87th Infantry
   Navy: Special Warfare Group 8
   Marine Corps elements
   Air Force: 24th Wing
   Special operations forces

U.S. European Command (USEUCOM)
Europe, Mediterranean coast, north/west/sub-Saharan Africa
Headquarters: Brussels, Belgium
CINC's service: usually Army (one Air Force general has served)
Major forces—
   Army: V Corps
   Navy: Sixth Fleet

Marine Corps: embarked Marine Expeditionary Unit
Air Force: Third, Sixteenth, Seventeenth Air Forces
Special operations forces

U.S. Central Command (USCENTCOM)
Middle East, eastern Africa, Persian Gulf, Arabian Sea
Headquarters: MacDill Air Force Base, Florida
CINC's service: Army or Marine Corps (alternating)
Major forces—no forces permanently stationed in theater
Army elements
Navy elements
Marine Corps elements
Air Force elements
Special operations forces

U.S. Pacific Command (USPACOM)
Pacific Ocean, Indian Ocean, east Asia, Japan, Korea, Taiwan, China,
Australasia, Indonesia, the Philippines, south Asia, Southeast Asia
Headquarters: Pearl Harbor Naval Base, Hawaii
CINC's service: Navy
Major forces (less Korea)—
Army: 25th Infantry Divisions
Navy: Third and Seventh Fleets
Marine Corps: III Marine Expeditionary Force
Air Force: Fifth, Eleventh, Thirteenth Air Forces
Special operations forces

Combined Forces Command/United Nations Command/U.S. Forces Korea
Republic of Korea
Headquarters: Yongsan, Republic of Korea
CINC's service: Army
Major forces —
Army: 2d Infantry Division
Navy elements
Marine Corps elements
Air Force: Seventh Air Force
Special operations forces

Functional Commands

U.S. Strategic Command (USSTRATCOM)
nuclear deterrence
Headquarters: Offutt Air Force Base, Nebraska
CINC's service: Air Force or Navy
Major forces—
　　Army elements
　　Navy: ballistic missile submarine fleet
　　Marine Corps elements
　　Air Force: Second, Eighth, Twentieth Air Forces

U.S. Transportation Command (USTRANSCOM)
intertheater movements
Headquarters: Scott Air Force Base, Illinois
CINC's service: Air Force
Major forces—
　　Army: Military Traffic Management Command
　　Navy: Military Sealift Command
　　Marine Corps elements
　　Air Force: Air Mobility Command

U.S. Special Operations Command (USSOCOM)
train and provide special operations forces; command when directed
Headquarters: MacDill Air Force Base, Florida
CINC's service: Army
Major forces—
　　Army: Special Forces, Rangers, civil affairs, psychological warfare units
　　Navy: Special Warfare Groups
　　Marine Corps elements
　　Air Force: Special Operations Wings and elements
　　Joint Special Operations Command: counterterrorist forces

U.S. Space Command (USSPACECOM)
launch and operate military satellites and ground stations
Headquarters: Peterson Air Force Base, Colorado
CINC's service: Air Force

Major forces—
 Army elements
 Navy elements
 Marine Corps elements
 Air Force: 9th Space Division, 1st, 2d, 3d Space Wings

Sources: Adm. Paul D. Miller, USN, *Both Swords and Plowshares* (Cambridge, Mass.: Institute for Foreign Policy Analysis, 1992), 19–21; "Special Double Issue: Unified Commands," *Defense 93* (March/April 1993); "1993 Green Book," *Army* (October 1993); "Naval Review," *Proceedings* (May 1993); "1993 USAF Almanac," *Air Force* (May 1993).

Unified Command Plan

Regional Commands:
USACOM	= U.S. Atlantic Command
USPACOM	= U.S. Pacific Command
USEUCOM	= U.S. European Command
USCENTCOM	= U.S. Central Command
USSOUTHCOM	= U.S. Southern Command

Functional Commands:
USSTRATCOM	= U.S. Strategic Command
USSPACECOM	= U.S. Space Command
USSOCOM	= U.S. Special Operations Command
USTRANSCOM	= U.S. Transportation Command

Source: Adm. Paul D. Miller, USN, *Both Swords and Plowshares* (Cambridge, Mass.: Institute for Foreign Policy Analysis, 1992), 20.

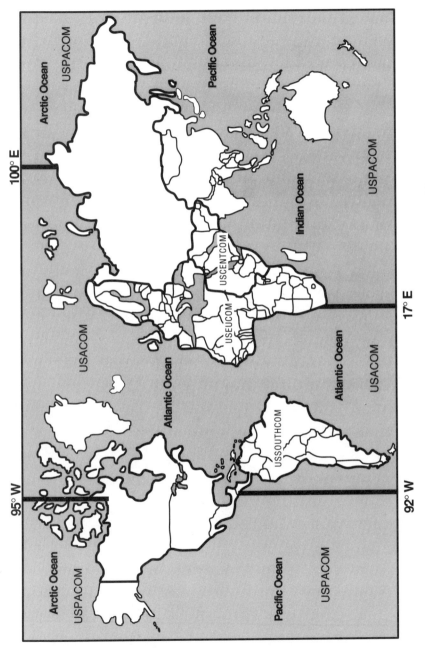

Commander's Area of Responsibility

INDEX